# The Economics of
# African Development

# The Economics of
# African Development

BY

## Andrew M. Kamarck

*Revised Edition*

FOREWORD BY
PIERRE MOUSSA

**PRAEGER PUBLISHERS**
New York · Washington · London

PRAEGER PUBLISHERS
111 Fourth Avenue, New York, N.Y. 10003, U.S.A.
5, Cromwell Place, London S.W.7, England

Published in the United States of America in 1971
by Praeger Publishers, Inc.

This is the revised edition of a book
originally published in 1967 by
Frederick A. Praeger, Inc., Publishers

© 1967 by Frederick A. Praeger, Inc.
© 1971 by Praeger Publishers, Inc.

Library of Congress Catalog Card Number: 70–126778


Printed in the United States of America

# Contents

v

# Maps

# Foreword

BY PIERRE MOUSSA

The problem of the economic development of Africa is of great importance in today's world; it is without doubt one of the tests by which our generation shall be judged.

Many books have been written in the past few years on various aspects of African economic development; there are numerous studies illuminating one aspect or another of the economic growth of particular African countries or regions or of particular sectors of the economy, either for a part or the whole of Africa. However, very few syntheses have been written on the economic development of Africa as a whole, covering all sectors; this is because it is difficult to know all fifty countries, independent or dependent, of Africa; very often comparable information is lacking from one country to another and it is therefore very difficult to make meaningful generalizations.

The great merit of Andrew Kamarck, who knows Africa very well—from north to south and from east to west—is that he did not shrink from this considerable task. I think he made a great success of it, and I am honored that he asked me to write the preface to his book. After all, to do so is for me the mark of a permanent friendship that has existed for well over ten years (beginning even before the three years when we worked together in the African Department of the World Bank), since he and I became acquainted at a colloquium on Africa in Princeton, and were happy to find that even though we came from very different backgrounds and had had very different experiences in Africa, we agreed so well on the subject.

Africa must be considered the most underdeveloped continent of the world—at least if the word "underdeveloped" is understood in its literal sense.

In current usage, the adjective "underdeveloped" has come to mean "poor." In this respect, Africa is not the most underdeveloped continent because it is not the poorest one. Although some African nations—Ethiopia, Somalia, and most of the countries situated in the interior, without any contact with the coast—have per-capita incomes comparable to those of India and China, the average African per-capita income is higher than the Asian. (On the other hand, it is lower than Latin America's.)

But if underdeveloped means—as it should, according to its literal sense—the scant development of the economic potential of a country or region, well, then, I feel sure that Africa is exceedingly underdeveloped. When Mr. Kamarck, in Chapter VIII, treats of electric power, he reminds us first that the African continent possesses two-fifths of the world's total hydro-electric potential—more than Europe and the two Americas put together—and, then, that present production is ridiculously small (all of sub-Saharan Africa, South Africa excepted, produces 20 billion kwh—that is to say, about equivalent to the consumption of a large European or American city). Such examples could be mentioned by the dozen. We can also add that African resources are not only very little exploited, but often very little known. Mineral resources have been relatively little exploited so far; research on tropical soils is at the first stages; knowledge of water resources is minimal (one might mention the case of Lake Tanganyika, the gradual rise of which in recent years engulfed, among other things, a large part of Burundi's port, nobody knowing why and nobody knowing how long the rise was likely to continue). The economist Gabriel Ardant proposed this significant expression to designate the underdeveloped world: "the fallow world." Africa is pre-eminently the fallow continent.

Africa's human resources have lain fallow quite as much as its material resources. In education, Africa lags far behind Asia and Latin America. In Africa, the percentage of school enrollment of school-age population is 40 per cent in primary school, 3 per cent in secondary, 0.2 per cent in higher education. To reach the same levels as in Latin America, these percentages should be multiplied by two in primary school, by five in secondary school, by fifteen in higher education.

This lack of education is certainly responsible, to a large extent, for the low capacity Africans have shown so far in technical and economic inventiveness. It is quite possible, of course, that the predominant races in Africa are naturally inclined more to excellence in rhetoric than to excellence in technology. In many respects, the African races seem to be "hyper-Latin" races. But one must guard against exaggerating ethnic characteristics. More important in this respect was undoubtedly Africa's isolation: for a whole range of reasons, resulting from climate, the winds, the hazards of history, the African continent (above all, Africa south of the Sahara) was cut off from the rest of the world and, in particular, was excluded from the great civilizing adventures of the Occident and Orient. Even during the nineteenth century and at the beginning of the twentieth, Africa's contact with Europe remained astonishingly superficial; the Europeans, in most of Africa, stayed near the coast. Only a few soldiers, a few administrators, and commercial representatives went into the interior (except, of course, in some privileged areas, such as Katanga and the two Rhodesias).

For all these reasons, then, Africa is now, more than any other, *the* underdeveloped continent. Its present lag behind other continents is all the more notable in that, if one considers the history of humanity, the situation was quite different in other epochs. From 7,000 to 2,000 B.C., the great center of civilization was, as everybody knows, the Near East—that is to say, the most western parts of Asia and the northeast corner of Africa. Most of the inventions that are still the basis of our life originated there: i.e., agriculture, livestock-raising, building with bricks, pottery, etc. To go back even further, during the paleolithic era, from 500,000 to 200,000 B.C., one continent was continually ahead of the others, and it was Africa. It was the center of invention, from which radiated all the great technical concepts of the era, especially all advances in stone-cutting.

Today, Africa presents not only an extreme condition of underdevelopment, but also a pure one. Elsewhere, particularly in Asia, underdevelopment is closely bound up with overpopulation (of course, the two phenomena are organically related in Asia). Africa, on the other hand, except in a few regions, is not yet overpopulated. Africa therefore poses the question of how to break the vicious circle of underdevelopment in a form uncomplicated by other essential problems that beset other continents.

To break this vicious circle, assistance from industrialized countries is essential. I, as well as Andrew Kamarck, am among those who believe that international aid to underdeveloped countries must be progressively increased. But I would like to mention here why I think that Africa has a right to very special treatment as regards aid from the West.

The first reason why Western countries cannot forsake Africa is based on the fact that Europe has a serious responsibility for the present situation in the African continent. I do not mean, as some assert in an overly tendentious way, that the colonial period was a disaster for Africa; on the contrary, I think that the colonial period, despite grave defects, brought some incontestable benefits, notably in the fields of peacekeeping and public health. In my view, the West's main fault lay in the slave trade, rather than the colonization. Mr. Kamarck is right to refer several times to the importance of this trade, although, thank God, it belongs almost completely to the past. Nobody can assess the damage that must have been done to Africa, over generations and generations, by the continuous removal of a great number of people (who of course were chosen from among the best and strongest Africans) and their transfer to another continent. Mr. Kamarck estimates that between 12 million and 15 million were transported out of Africa; in addition, as he himself points out, there should be added to these figures the great number of human beings who were killed in the slave raids or who died during the trip. This is not all: to obtain this human merchandise, the Europeans encouraged inter-tribal hostilities, and the seriousness of this error is evident when one considers that excesses of tribal feelings are to this day one of the plagues of Africa.

The second reason that I would like to advance as to why the West has a special obligation toward Africa is that Africa needs Western aid more than any other continent. In *financial* terms, Asia and Latin America need capital from the industrialized countries as much as Africa does. It is in *human* terms that the difference becomes apparent between Africa on the one hand and the rest of the *tiers monde* on the other. Asia and Latin America are better endowed than Africa with educated people and leaders. But for a long time, most African countries will be unable to function or to develop satisfactorily without large-scale technical assistance—as is the case today, since around four-fifths of the total number of technical-assistance personnel on duty all over the world are on the African continent, although in terms of population Africa represents only about one-seventh of the underdeveloped world. In the rest of the developing world, foreigners represent only 1 per cent of the high-level manpower; in Africa, four-fifths.

Not only does Africa badly need the help of the West in personnel; it must also take over from the Western countries their languages and, to a large extent, their philosophy. One can assert, without offending the respectable and humanly attractive deep-lying African traditions, that they cannot constitute for the African civilization of tomorrow a spiritual framework to be compared to what China or India can derive from their own philosophies. In other words, Africa depends much more than Asia on the West's intellectual contribution.

Without a large-scale financial and human contribution from the industrialized countries, the destiny of the African countries is scarcely in doubt: the peril that lies in wait is certainly not so much the adoption of Communist governments (at least within the meaning of the term in Europe and Asia), but rather an immense anarchy, a regression to the darkness of the Middle Ages.

# Preface to the Revised Edition

This revision is meant to reflect the changes in Africa and in my thinking about Africa since the first edition of *The Economics of African Development* was published. This year—1970—turned out to be a good year to review the progress of Africa, since for most of Africa it marked the end of the first decade of independence, and it is just before the world commits itself to the Second Development Decade (DD II). In general, much of what five years ago appeared likely to happen has in fact been accomplished. On the whole, Africa has done rather better than it seemed reasonable to expect but not so well as it could have done had there been more help from abroad and more pragmatic leadership at home in many countries. After re-surveying African problems and prospects for the rest of this century, my major conclusion is that, although Africa has many unique developmental obstacles and advantages, the final comments of the Pearson Commission are fully applicable to Africa. They stated:

> The goal of the international development effort is to put the less developed countries as soon as possible in a position where they can realize their aspirations with regard to economic progress without relying on foreign aid. This goal will not be reached at once. The illusion of 'instant development' . . . only leads to frustration and disappointment. But can the majority of the developing countries

achieve self-sustaining growth by the end of the century? For us the answer is clearly yes. In our view, the record of the past twenty years justifies that answer. We live at a time when the ability to transform the world is only limited by faintness of heart or narrowness of vision. We can now set ourselves goals that would have seemed chimerical a few decades ago and, working together, we can reach them.

The origins of this book lie in the course in African economic problems that I have given for a number of years in the African Studies Program at the School of Advanced International Studies of The Johns Hopkins University—a program under the benign leadership of Professor Vernon McKay. I have also drawn on my practical experience of two decades of economic work for the World Bank Group. The first edition of the book was mostly written at the African Studies Center of the University of California at Los Angeles during my stay there as Regents Professor in 1964–65. For this, I owe a special debt of gratitude to James S. Coleman, then Director of the Center, and other members and staff.

The opinions expressed in the book are my own and do not necessarily reflect the official views of any institution with which I may be connected. In this revision, I have benefited from and am grateful for the comments and suggestions of many people; of those whose comments have most affected the way in which I have approached the new text (even though they may disagree with the results), special recognition needs to be given to Henry J. Bitterman, Paul Clark, and E. S. Mason. Dr. Mason in particular bears a heavy burden of responsibility both for having many years ago initiated my interest in economics and, since then, for shaping the way in which I do my economic work. I also wish to acknowledge my gratitude to Mrs. Virginia Weyrich for her efficient typing of my various revisions and to Margaret Kamarck for her forbearance at losing me for so many weekends and evenings while this revision was being written.

ANDREW M. KAMARCK
September, 1970

# The Economics of
# African Development

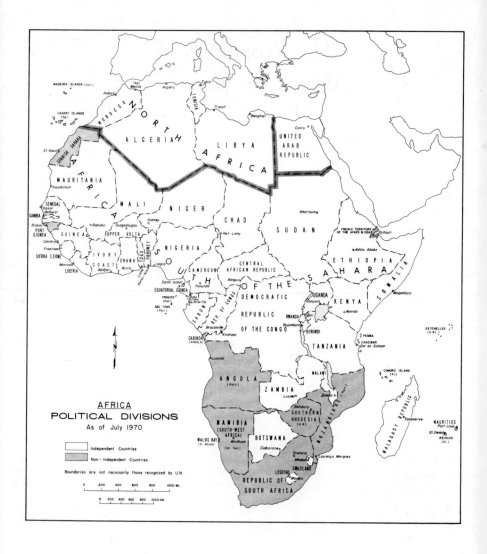

MADEIRA (ISLANDS (Port.)

CANARY ISLANDS
(Sp.)

El Aaiun
SPANISH SAHARA

SENEGAL
Dakar
GAMBIA
Bissau
PORT
GUINEA
Freetown
SIERRA LEONE
Monrovia
LIBERIA

(Sp.)
Melilla
Rabat
MOROCCO

Algiers
A L G E R I A

TUNISIA
Tunis

N O R T H

A F R I C A

MAURITANIA
Nouakchott

M A L I

Bamako
Ouagadougou
UPPER VOLTA

GUINEA

IVORY
COAST
GHANA
Accra
Abidjan
DAHOMEY
TOGO
Lagos

N I G E R
Niamey

N I G E R I A

Tripoli

Benghazi

L I B Y A

A F R I C A

C H A D

Fort-Lamy

Khartoum

S U D A N

Cairo

U N I T E D
A R A B
R E P U B L I C

FRENCH TERRITORY
OF THE AFARS & ISSAS
Djibouti

Addis Ababa

CAMEROON
Santa Isabel
EQUATORIAL GUINEA
PRINCIPE
(Port.)
SAO TOME
(Port.)

Yaounde

CENTRAL
AFRICAN REPUBLIC

Bangui

S O U T H

O F   T H E

S A H A R A

E T H I O P I A

S O M A L I A

Mogadiscio

GABON
Libreville

REP. OF CONGO

Brazzaville
Kinshasa

CABINDA
(ANGOLA)

D E M O C R A T I C

R E P U B L I C

O F   T H E   C O N G O

RWANDA
Kigali
Bujumbura
BURUNDI

UGANDA
Kampala

K E N Y A

Nairobi

PEMBA
ZANZIBAR
Dar es Salaam

SEYCHELLES
(U.K.)

Luanda

A N G O L A
( Port. )

T A N Z A N I A

MALAWI

Z A M B I A
Lusaka

Zomba

COMORO  ISLAND
(Fr.)

NAMIBIA
(SOUTH-WEST
AFRICA)
(S. Africa)

WALVIS BAY
(S. Africa)
Windhoek
(Int. Terr.)

Salisbury
SOUTHERN
RHODESIA
(U.K.)

MOZAMBIQUE (Port.)

MALAGASY REPUBLIC

Tananarive

MAURITIUS
Port Louis
St Denis
REUNION
(Fr.)

B O T S W A N A

Gaborone

Pretoria
Mbabane
SWAZILAND

Lourenço Marques

LESOTHO
Maseru

R E P U B L I C   O F
S O U T H   A F R I C A

N

AFRICA
POLITICAL  DIVISIONS
As  of  July 1970

☐  Independent Countries

▨  Non - Independent  Countries

Boundaries  are  not  necessarily  those  recognized  by  U.N.

0    200    400    600    800    1000 MI.

0   200   400  600  800  1000 KM.

# I

# African Economic Development
# in Historical Perspective

*What is past is prologue; what to come,*
*In yours and my discharge.*

WILLIAM SHAKESPEARE

It is now becoming accepted theory that the first man to appear on earth was an African; that is, that Africa was the birthplace of man himself. Darwin prophesied that the continent of Africa would prove to be the place of man's origin, and he appears to have been right. The discoveries of Dr. L. S. B. Leakey in East Africa show that not only did man begin in Africa but for some 600,000 years afterward, Africa was the spearhead of man's progress. It was in Africa that the first cutting tools from stone were made nearly two million years ago—making available to early man a whole new source of food and starting him on the road to the machine-based economy of today.

After man had spread to the rest of the world, much of Africa was cut off from the lands north and east of it by the desert that crept across the Sahara and Arabia. Isolated from the rest of the world from about 5,000 B.C., Africa began to lag behind in *material*

development. According to Arnold Toynbee, "Geography kept sub-
Saharan Africa out of the history of civilization. . . . The desert in
the north, the falls at the mouths of rivers which prevented navigation, isolated Africans and deprived them of the mingling of peoples
which produces civilization. The result is that they're 5,000 years behind and paying the price for it. I think Africans are as competent
as other people, and . . . 5,000 years is really a short time, but they
have a long way to catch up." (Toynbee, p. 1.)

The geography of Africa south of the Sahara, including its location
in the tropics, has been and still is a dominant influence in its economic development. It was responsible for the long isolation of
Africa from the rest of the world and of Africans from one another.
It is largely responsible for Africa's poverty today.

The obstacles nature placed in the way of communications and
transport south of the Sahara were so great that they could be overcome only after the rest of the world has progressed sufficiently to
have invented self-propelled machine transport (the railway and
then the automobile and the airplane) and to have a sufficient surplus of wealth to aid Africans to acquire these necessary means to
break out of their isolation.

There was a trickle of trade across the Sahara from the Mediterra-
nean from the times of ancient Egypt and Carthage. The western
Sudan (including the medieval empires of Ghana and Mali), from
about the eighth century on, is supposed to have been the chief
supplier of gold to the Western world until the discovery of America.
The Phoenicians first circumnavigated Africa as long ago as 500 B.C.
The East African coast was visited by Indian, Chinese, and Arab
traders for many centuries before the modern era. And, in modern
times, Christopher Columbus is believed to have visited West Africa
ten years before his voyage of discovery to America. The entire
African coastline became known soon thereafter, long before the
coastlines of the American or Australian continents—indeed, even
before the coastlines of Europe and Asia (in the distant north) were
fully explored. Yet, with all this, to the rest of the world Africa
remained a coastline and not a continent until about a hundred
years ago.

In addition to isolation, sub-Saharan Africa also suffered from the
fact that her tropical climate and soils made settled agriculture virtually
impossible over most of the area. (See below, chap. V.) Most Afri-

cans, therefore, were unable to get the full benefit from one of the fundamental transformations of man's life on this earth—the domestication and cultivation of plants, which elsewhere in the world made possible a settled existence and, consequently, the progress in civilization that comes from urbanization.

## The Obstacles of Geography and Climate

The geographical and climatic reasons why neither Africans nor the restless Europeans were able to bring sub-Saharan Africa into the mainstream of world commerce and life were formidable, and they are still important in holding back African economic development. Access from the sea to the land in most of Africa is not easy. Most of the African coastline below the Sahara is a forbidding one— where the desert does not come right down to the sea, the visitor sees mostly swamp or lagoon. Africa is by and large a plateau, with rivers falling over the escarpment in a series of falls or rapids near the coast. It is usually impossible in Africa to penetrate the interior by sailing up rivers, as was done, for example, in North America; the fact that beyond the falls there are navigable stretches of water was unimportant for a long time. (The Niger River is navigable, but, because of the mangrove swamps and the division of the river into many distributaries in the delta, this was not known to non-African explorers until 1830.) The very block shape of the continent is such that most of the interior is remote from the sea; of all the continents, Africa has the shortest coastline in relation to area. It is not surprising then that Africa has very few natural harbors where ships can lie safely at anchor. Before artificial harbors were built, ships had to remain at sea during the few months when it was safe to lie off shore, and their sailors were forced to depend on small boats to get through the surf for any contact with the land.

The second major set of economically significant obstacles derives from the single fact that Africa is pre-eminently *the* tropical continent. Over 9 million of Africa's 11.7 million square miles are in the tropics.

Only the North African countries and the Republic of South Africa do not predominantly have some variety of tropical climate. The equator almost neatly bisects the continent; there are 2,400 miles of land to the north of it and 2,600 miles to the south. While in the temperate zones it is now almost legitimate to ignore climate as a factor in the economy—it is rarely even mentioned in economics courses in universities—in Africa it may determine the very structure of the economy and the pace of its growth. It is still a pervasive, continuing influence on Africa's development; in earlier centuries, added to other difficult geographical features, it helped to prevent Africa's economic development from even starting. Among the most effective impediments were the many tropical diseases, such as yellow fever and malaria, that levied a heavy toll of death on all visitors to tropical Africa. The diseases carried by the tsetse fly deserve special mention. While the human sleeping sickness the tsetse fly may carry is bad enough, a critical economic factor is the animal disease it carries—trypanosomiasis, which kills horses and cattle and thus made it impossible to use animal transport to penetrate the interior from the coast. Commerce had to depend on human porters, the most costly and inefficient of all transport systems. This meant that the only trade of consequence that could take place over most of tropical Africa was in commodities of great value and little bulk—i.e., gold and ivory — or commodities that were provided with their own legs—e.g., slaves. And these were inevitably the main African exports, particularly slaves.

The tropics presented other grave difficulties (these will be considered later), but the transport obstacle alone was quite sufficient to stop any appreciable economic development for centuries.

### The Slave Trade

As far as one can ascertain, slaves were for several thousand years and until quite recently a major export of sub-Saharan Africa. The slave trade was certainly going on in the ancient world, albeit intermittently and in very small volume. The possession of the rare African slave may have been a prestige symbol compared to ownership of the run-of-the-mill European slave. After the rise and spread of Islam, the slave trade continued across the Sahara and along the east coast of Africa to Arabia until the beginning of this century. Remnants of it persist to this day. (*The New York Times*, April 7, 1967.)

The trade to the Arab countries assumed fairly large proportions quite early.* By the late ninth century, even slave merchants from Asia were established in Fezzan (present southern Libya), dealing with suppliers to the south (Fisher and Fisher, Chap. III). The slave trade from West Africa grew to a large volume in modern times when the Portuguese began to import slaves into Western Europe around 1442, and when the Spanish brought slaves to the New World after 1517. The large-scale Atlantic trade with North America, the Caribbean, and South America continued for three and a half centuries, with the last trickle not ceasing until perhaps 1880.

While a considerable number of the slaves sold abroad had been stolen by non-African slave traders—especially the Arab traders in East and Central Africa in the nineteenth century—in the main, the trade was an African economic phenomenon. That is to say, Africans sold slaves to slave traders because this was the only means available to raise the money to buy the commodities they wanted (mostly guns, powder, rum, and textiles). As an anti-slavery leader expressed it at the time:

> We attempt to put down the slave trade "by the strong hand" alone; and this is, I apprehend, the cause of our failure. . . . The African has acquired a taste for the productions of the civilized world. They have become essential to him. . . . The sale of children, subjects, and neighbors is the only means as yet afforded, by European commerce, for the supply of those wants which that commerce has created. . . . When we shall have experimentally convinced the African that it is in his power to obtain his supplies in more than their usual abundance, by honest means, then, and not until then, we may expect that he will be reconciled to the abolition of the slave trade. (Buxton, p. viii.)

Philip D. Curtin has pointed out that it was African ability to organize large-scale commerce that "made the slave trade possible. A genuinely primitive society could not possibly have reorganized itself to supply up to 100,000 captives a year." (Curtis, p. 44.)

Unfortunately, the slave trade, in addition to being an inhuman and, in a real sense, immoral activity, was a particularly destructive type

---

* By 869 A.D. there were a sufficient number of African slaves to engage in a large-scale revolt against the Arab Empire in what is now Iraq. They defeated army after army sent against them. In 871 they took the port of Basra. By 878 they were raiding within a few miles of Baghdad and dominated large areas of what is now southern Iraq and southwest Iran. They were not finally put down until the end of 883. (Lewis, pp. 103–6.)

of commerce. It drew off from the continent human beings at their most productive ages. Worse still, it encouraged tribe to fight tribe and encouraged conflict within tribes. Finally, and perhaps most important, any advantages that Africa derived from contact with the rest of the world—the learning of some skills, the introduction of new foods such as maize and manioc—were more than offset by the slave trade's plunging vast stretches of Africa into anarchy. Whatever else economic development requires, it does need a basic minimum of personal security. The fact that rulers along the West African coast were successful in building up states on the middleman traffic in slaves did not mitigate the disastrous impact of the trade on the peoples further inland. (In addition, in their desire to monopolize the slave trade, the coastal states were careful to allow no penetration of the interior by people from outside.)

There are no good estimates as to the total number of slaves exported from Africa from the beginning of the large-scale trade in modern times to its end in the last century. K. O. Dike (p. 3) proposes a figure of 5 to 6 million West Africans. To these would have to be added the slaves sold from the Congo and Angola to Brazil, from the Sahara to North Africa, and from the lands along the Indian Ocean to Arabia. Altogether, the figure must be at least 10 million and may be as high as 15 million. Countless millions in addition lost their lives in the slave raids, in the journey to the sea in the slave coffles, in waiting in the barracoons on the coast for a slave ship to appear, and, finally, during the trip on the Atlantic or Indian oceans to the slave markets of the Americas or Arabia.

The British, who had been principal participants, withdrew from the slave trade when their government prohibited it in 1807, an abolition made possible partly by the beginnings of industrialization, which enabled Liverpool merchants to shift from trading in slaves to trading in cotton for the growing textile factories. The government not only banned the trade for its own subjects but also took active steps to stamp out the traffic altogether. The Royal Navy began to stop slave ships of British and other nationalities, as treaties were made with other nations allowing such actions against the trade. But slave trading continued across the Atlantic under the protection of the American flag. Senators from slave states prevented any American cooperation with the Royal Navy's police actions. Worse still, the United States' insistence on its sovereign rights as protecting any ship flying the American flag meant that a slave merchant caught in the act by a British warship had only to hoist the Stars and Stripes to go freely about his business. It was only when the southern states had seceded during the Civil War, 1861–65, that the U.S. Navy was finally freed to cooperate effectively with the British against the slave ships. The North Atlantic slave trade then stopped.

On the East African coast, the slave trade continued in considerable volume even after the British persuaded the Sultan to close the slave market on Zanzibar in 1873. Not until the whole of the coast came under European domination—a process completed with the Anglo-Egyptian takeover of the Sudan in 1889—did the large-scale slave trade stop. The illegal trade that continued to several of the Arab countries (slavery was still legal in 1970 in the Sultanate of Muscat and Oman, for example) was of no great economic significance, although the tragedy for the people involved was no less for that.

The abolition of the slave trade initially had a most unfavorable economic impact on the African middleman communities in West Africa.

> Along the coast of West Africa, particularly in those parts where the slave trade formed the basis of the economy of the communities concerned, opposition to abolition was the rule. In the Gold Coast, where European forts and settlements were situated close to the African states, local native resentment against the Act of 1807 led to serious riots. When Parliament rebuked the Committee of the Company of Merchants for failing to convince Africans that abolition was for the good of the natives, the Committee retorted,
>
> "Can the wildest theorist expect that a mere act of the British legislature should in a moment inspire . . . natives of the vast continent of Africa and persuade them, nay more, make them practically believe and feel that it is for their interest to contribute to and even acquiesce in, the destruction of a trade . . . by which alone they have been hitherto accustomed to acquire wealth and purchase all the foreign luxuries and conveniences of life?" (Dike, p. 12.)

As the slave trade was slowly wiped out, its basic economic role had begun to lose its meaning. A substitute for human power as a means of transport in Africa had been found—the steam engine driving the new railway locomotives and river steamers. An alternative commodity to export from the west coast of Africa was also developed at this time. This was palm oil. One of the consequences of the Industrial Revolution in Europe was that Europeans began to wash themselves regularly, and, with the spread of the habit, the demand for soap could no longer be satisfied by animal fats alone. There began to be a demand for vegetable fats, especially the oil collected from wild palms in West Africa. Palm oil was also needed in the making of candles and for the lubrication of the new machinery. It consequently became possible for Africans to sell abroad something other than slaves and for some of the African traders to turn to the new trade in oil rather than slaves. Later, of course, other exportable commodities were found in or introduced into Africa.

### The Key Role of Railways

With the invention in the early nineteenth century of the "iron horse," immune to the bite of the tsetse fly, an effective means had finally been found to penetrate the African continent. Economic development, therefore, now was no longer out of the question for Africa. While Lord Lugard's famous remark, "The material development of Africa may be summed up in one word—transport," is too sweeping, adequate transport *is* a necessary condition for progress, and as long as commerce was confined by the lack of adequate transport, the Africans were bound to remain ignorant and poor, isolated from the world and from one another.

But railways have to be paid for, and unfortunately, they are a particularly capital-intensive investment. In addition, in many areas of Africa, it was necessary to construct a port first and usually a costly artificial harbor. The minimum amount of capital required for this investment was completely beyond African possibilities to procure. (This "lumpiness" of investment so often encountered in Africa seems to have been especially true in the early stages.) Africa was caught in the dilemma that for any appreciable economic development to begin, a minimum transport infrastructure was needed, but without the infrastructure it was impossible for the Africans to earn the necessary foreign exchange to get it. The dilemma could only be resolved by help from abroad. Put in another way, the "threshold" over which Africans had to pass to begin economic growth was so high that it was practically impossible for them to get over it without help from abroad. This help did not become available until Africa passed under the domination of European powers, mostly during the period 1884–95. Railway building in Africa mainly began only then.

In this as in so many other respects, South Africa was an exception. Thanks to the Cape's temperate climate and one of the few good natural harbors of Africa, the European settlers did not encounter most of the virtually insuperable obstacles of tropical Africa. But they had enough problems to keep them struggling and poor for two centuries after the first European colonists arrived. Railway building here began in 1859 and, compared to the rest of Africa, moved fairly rapidly after the discovery of diamonds at Kimberley in 1867 and the discovery of gold on the Rand at Johannesburg in 1886. In 1897, there were 5,000 miles of railway in southern Africa and 1,800 in the rest of Africa. Of total exports worth some $140 million from sub-Saharan Africa, southern Africa alone provided some $100 million.

Africa and Australia are the only continents in the world where large investments in the construction of new railways are still being made—justifiably, in those cases where they make it possible to open and exploit large new mineral resources. Otherwise, it is more economical to place greater reliance on the automobile and airplane, which are more flexible and less capital-devouring means of transport than railways. Artificial harbors and new ports are also still being built where countries did not possess them before. Since 1960, new railway lines have been constructed in Mauretania, Liberia, Nigeria, Cameroon, Swaziland, Tanzania, Congo (Brazzaville), Uganda, and the Sudan; a 1,100-mile railway is to be built to connect Zambia to Dar es Salaam in Tanzania; ports have been built in Mauretania, Liberia (a second port, Buchanan, in addition to Monrovia, constructed during World War II), Ivory Coast (San Pedro, a second port in the west to supplement Abidjan), Ghana (Tema, a second port in eastern Ghana, to supplement Takoradi, the artificial port in western Ghana built during the 1920's), Togo, Dahomey, and Somalia.

### Europe and Africa

Although by 1899 almost all of Africa had come under the rule of European nations, any contribution these governments made to the economic development of Africa was almost purely by the way.

*The Economics of African Development*

The European powers constructed the railways primarily for their own strategic or administrative reasons—in the Sudan to facilitate the reconquest of the country; in East Africa, inland from Tanga by the Germans and from Mombasa to Lake Victoria by the British, for strategic reasons and to suppress the slave trade; in West Africa, inland from Dakar, by the French for military and administrative reasons. (The record of the United States was even worse vis-à-vis Liberia, which, though not a colony, had been established by Americans and where there was at least some moral commitment by Americans to help. ) Essentially, the basis on which the metropolitan governments operated was that laid down by Adam Smith in *The Wealth of Nations* in 1776: "Little else is requisite to carry a state to the highest degree of opulence from the lowest barbarism but peace, easy taxes and a tolerable administration of justice, all the rest being brought about by the natural course of things." The European powers restricted themselves in Africa essentially to trying to establish peace and law and order, stop tribal warfare, prevent the slave trade, etc. Of course, such activities were a major contribution to economic development in that they did create the necessary preconditions for it. A railway built for strategic or administrative reasons was no less helpful to traders penetrating the interior.

In addition, the British did provide grants-in-aid, part in loans and part as gifts, to colonies that could not meet their necessary expenditures, including service on loans raised in the London capital market, from their own revenues. Beginning in 1929, gifts or loans of up to £1 million a year were made available under the Colonial Development Act of 1929—designed primarily to relieve unemployment in the U.K. By World War II, a total of around $150 million equivalent had been made available to the African colonies under these two systems. The Imperial German government contributed about $125 million equivalent to South West Africa (Namibia) and Tanganyika before World War I. The French government also pursued a somewhat more direct policy in aiding economic development than the British. It guaranteed colonial loans made in the Paris market; there were a few direct loans made by French government agencies; and, in the early 1930's, there was even an attempt, which failed because of the Great Depression, at a program for the economic development of the colonies.

While the records of the colonial administrations themselves are mixed, as far as stimulating economic development is concerned, it is fair to say that in almost every case they did make *some* contribution—small or large. They learned something about local agricultural problems, they assembled data on soils, climate, crops. Before and during the colonial period, Western countries introduced a number of new, basic food crops into Africa, mostly from the American continents—manioc, maize, beans, and peanuts (ground nuts)—and they must have made possible a considerable increase in population in some areas where the lack of adequate food supplies was the limiting factor. The colonial governments also made a start in controlling disease. Missionary efforts to create school systems were encouraged, and the colonial governments themselves began to organize and set up schools. Offices began to collect some of the basic statistics that would be needed for policy-making. In particular cases, men like Sir Gordon Guggisberg, Governor of the Gold Coast after World War I, took an active role in initiating what even today would be regarded as good development programs. Guggisberg built the first protected harbor in the Gold Coast, Takoradi, extended the railway and road system, and organized new schools. Many· district commissioners or local officers, by introducing or encouraging new crops (such as coffee to the Chagga on Mount Kilimanjaro), left enduring traces of their work.

But by and large, development was initially turned over to private companies or concessionaires given monopoly powers over large areas, much like the companies and proprietors who were given immense grants of land in the American colonies: the Virginia Company, Lord Baltimore's colony of Maryland, Oglethorpe in Georgia, Carteret in New Jersey, etc. Among these companies were the Imperial British East Africa Company, operating in what is now Kenya and Uganda; the British South Africa Company, founded in 1887 in the Rhodesias; the Royal Niger Company; the Portuguese Mozambique Company; the Compagnie de Congo pour le Commerce et l'Industrie; the Comité Speciale du Katanga (CSK); the Compagnie des Chemins de Fer du Congo Supérieur aux Grands Lacs Africains (CFL); the Comité Nationale du Kivu (CNKi); the Société du Haut-Ogooué; the Deutsche Ostafrikanische Gesellschaft; etc. Amazingly, these companies did raise the money to build railways and ports. Private investors before World War I thought Africa would be a new America, that it was needed only to open it up and wealth would pour forth. In fact, Africa was not a new America, and most of these chartered companies went bankrupt and out of existence. The few that survived, like the British South Africa Company or Tanganyika Concessions, generally did not pay any dividends for many years, most of them not until after World War II, when the majority of the original investors had long since passed from the scene.

The immediate effects of the chartered companies' early opening up of Africa were not all positive. In the attempt to make a profit or to get their capital back, some of the companies and concessionaires indulged in activities that resembled plundering of the territory under their control more than it did economic development; the forced labor exacted from the Africans to collect and transport rubber, ivory, and timber or to construct roads and railways prevented the Africans from producing for themselves and killed off large numbers from disease, overwork, and famine.

When the Italians invaded Ethiopia in the 1890's, the draft animals they brought in for their artillery may have carried rinderpest with them. In the next few years, rinderpest swept down the east coast of Africa as far as the Cape of Good Hope, killing millions of cattle. This was bad enough, but in addition, large areas returned to the bush, and the wild animals and tsetse fly moved in. Some regions, like Bunyoro in eastern Africa, have had difficulty in reintroducing cattle ever since.*

The new network of communications brought by the Europeans spread the African diseases throughout the continent while the European diseases were added to them. Together these had such an impact that, until the early 1930's, the dominant preoccupation of local governments was concern about Africa's depopulation. In the Gabon, this continued into the 1960's, when for the first time one began to see evidence that the population was no longer decreasing but beginning to increase. Only since World War II have the ad-

---

* Stanley, on his pathblazing march across the continent in 1887–88, brought with him human sleeping sickness from west to east. This, transmitted by the tsetse fly, killed about 250,000 people around the shores of Lake Victoria in 1900–1905. In order to stop the epidemic, the lake shore had to be abandoned. One area in particular, known because of its fertility as the paradise of Uganda, was abandoned to the tsetse fly and is still deserted; it has not been possible to reclaim it successfully from the fly and repopulate it.

vances in medical science applied in Africa begun to encourage a rapid growth in most African populations. (Now, of course, the problem is becoming one of too rapid population growth!)

With the eventual failure of the chartered companies, the colonial governments of African territories perforce took a more active role in economic development. In part, this was inevitable, given the prevalent theory that colonies should pay their own way. This was notably the case in the British colonies, where the Treasury was particularly determined that civil servants were to depend for their salaries on the colonial government. With the colonial treasury dependent on the resources of the territory, colonial officials were forced to find ways to increase the wealth of the population. They had to concern themselves, Adam Smith or no, with finding some way in which Africans could earn money that could then be taxed and used to pay government expenses. The pressure of the British Treasury on the Uganda government to become self-supporting, for example, explains much of the rapid spread of cotton-growing in that country. During the colonial period, agricultural and mineral products of Africa were introduced successfully into the markets of Europe and North America.

Colonial governments also began to borrow abroad in order to provide the needed transportation systems. In the British territories, such borrowing was possible because the British government, in spite of its position that it could not and should not take any financial responsibility, did pass a Colonial Stock Act before World War I which gave colonial government securities the status of trustee investments—i.e., trustees could invest in colonial government securities. This was more important than a merely permissive ruling: since trustees could not invest in securities that did not have trustee status, funds were funneled, *nolens volens*, into colonial investment whenever there were insufficient supplies of U.K. trustee securities. The Act was in fact criticized by John Maynard Keynes for this reason. While the British government maintained that the Colonial Stock Act did not imply its guarantee of any securities so issued, the actual practice tended to be that when a colony or protectorate had difficulty in maintaining the service on its securities, it was put under strong pressure to improve its finances while the British Treasury simultaneously would make grants-in-aid in order to make continued service on the debt possible.

The French government acted more directly in guaranteeing loans raised by the colonies on the Paris market. The United States also almost got into the act. After the end of World War I, the Treasury Department proposed to Congress that the United States recognize some responsibility for Liberia and make available a loan of $5 million to help in its economic development. Congress turned down this proposal, however, and the entrance of the United States into Africa's economic development had to wait another thirty years.

By 1936, something in the vicinity of $6 billion had been invested in Africa, according to S. H. Frankel's calculations—all of it provided by private European investors with the exception of about $100 million from Americans. Of this total, colonial governments borrowed about 45 per cent and used the money to build railways, ports, and other public works. The rest was borrowed or invested directly by private investors in Africa and used mostly for the development of mines. (Minerals were the major export from Africa right up until World War II, and for practically the whole of the period from 1900 on usually represented well over half the total African exports.) More than $2.5 billion equivalent was invested in the Union of South Africa, about $2 billion in the other British territories, about $700 million in the Congo, $350 million in the French territories, and about $300 million in the Portuguese territories. The distribution of this capital also provides a rough but good proportional indication of the relative progress in economic development made by the various territories of Africa at the beginning of World War II.

By World War II, therefore, a pattern had been established in Africa according to which heavy reliance was placed on the local government to start economic development. While theorizing about "African socialism" is fairly recent, the practice of governmental initiative, it is clear, was essentially pioneered by the colonial governments themselves. Direct private investment in the African countries was most frequent and most successful in mining—and this pattern, too, continues to prevail.

### New Economic Thinking

World War II represented a turning point in the development of Africa. During it, a sea change in economic thinking and policy took place that makes the pace of development in Africa in the postwar period considerably different from the prewar period. The fundamental new assumption was that government has a responsibility for running the economic system. In developed countries, this assumption underlies the now-accepted policy that government could and should maintain full employment. In underdeveloped countries, it became the universal belief, to which all governments paid at least lip service, that government had a responsibility for promoting economic development. The final implications of these new attitudes to economic policy are still not yet fully accepted—that in developed countries the government has a responsibility for bringing about an adequate rate of economic growth, and that these countries in turn have a responsibility to aid the development of underdeveloped countries.

But the impact of this change in economic thinking on African development has nevertheless been enormous. Since the war, African countries have been able to profit from the prevalence of full employment in developed countries, which has meant that there has been a continuous demand for African products. In fact, the shift from the depressed condition of the world market before the war to the high demands resulting from full employment in the industrialized world gave the African countries favorable prices for their products over most of the period since World War II. And the sense of obligation in industrialized countries to help the underdeveloped countries has resulted in a major inflow of public capital and technical assistance into Africa. Since the need for foreign capital to finance investment in Africa has continued, the inflow of capital has been crucial.

## Postwar African Growth

The years since World War II fall into two periods—1945–60, and the years since, when most of Africa had become independent. The rate of growth of real gross domestic product (GDP), as far as one can judge, was about the same in both of these periods. The available World Bank figures show a rate of growth for Africa of 4 per cent a year for the period 1950–60 and also for 1960–69. But these figures are aggregate, and the main significance of the two periods is that there was a considerable difference in the countries that were the most rapid growers in the two periods and in how investment was financed from abroad.

In the period before 1960, the countries that grew most rapidly were mainly the Rhodesias, the Belgian Congo, Gabon, Kenya, Senegal, and Algeria, north of the Sahara. The GDP of these countries grew at rates from 5 per cent to around 11 per cent a year— among the highest rates in the world at the time. These were the countries that enjoyed a large inflow not only of capital but also of key managerial, technical, and entrepreneurial personnel from Europe. In addition, they were (aside from Kenya and Senegal) mainly mineral-producing countries, where a rapid increase in production is more easily secured.

Between 1945 and 1960, another $5 billion or $6 billion of private capital flowed into Africa. A new feature was that, in addition to this, around $9 billion of capital was provided by governments outside of Africa. In all, something like $15 billion of capital from abroad came into Africa. This large inflow of capital naturally accelerated the transformation of Africa, making possible the minimum of economic infrastructure (ports, roads, schools, hospitals, administrative buildings), without which economic growth cannot go forward.

In 1960, a new period began that roughly coincides with the coming to independence of most of the former colonial territories. Since 1960, the national rates of growth have consequently changed. Most of the countries that were the most rapid growers in the previous period experienced a stoppage of the inflow of private capital, and, in fact, there has been a sizable over-all outflow. Trained personnel from abroad have also departed in some cases. In such countries (and Tunisia and Algeria also), a main problem has been to achieve a successful transition from an economy where most of the exports and the dynamic elements were concentrated in the sector owned, dominated, and run by foreigners to an economy run by the local people. Of all the African countries, Tunisia was the first to accomplish the transition by and large successfully, and she was able to embark again on a substantially rapid rate of growth. Kenya, ably led by Jomo Kenyatta, also succeeded in handling the transfer of political and economic power from Europeans to Africans without an appreciable slowdown in economic growth by the end of the 1960's; then, however, the difficulties of welding many tribes into one nation began to become dominant. In Congo (Kinshasa), the problems of transition lasted longer, and it was almost ten years after independence before the country perceptibly began to recover and to grow again. Senegal suffered in a different way; the break-up of the Federation of West Africa at independence left Dakar with its nucleus of industries and commercial headquarters a head without a body to provide it with nourishment. The Ivory Coast, Mauretania, Zambia, Angola, and Nigeria, until the outbreak of the civil war, were among the fast growers in the 1960's. The Ivory Coast and Angola pursued the old formula of the inflow of private investment and entrepreneurs, helped by the rapid growth of coffee output and, in Angola, by the development of minerals as well. Mauretania (iron ore and copper), Zambia (copper), and Nigeria (oil) also benefited primarily from the development of minerals.

In the rest of the continent, countries like Uganda, Malawi, Cameroon, Gabon, Sierra Leone, Ethiopia, and Morocco continued the moderate rate of growth as in the 1950's, while the very poor inland countries—Upper Volta, Mali, Chad, Rwanda—had difficulties in keeping output in pace with population growth. In Guinea, Algeria, and Burundi, output probably did not keep pace.

Nearly all the African countries, in common with most of the other primary-product exporters of the world, have suffered from a deterioration in their terms of trade since the early postwar period. Roughly speaking, up to the early 1950's, the products of the developing countries experienced the demand resulting from full employment in the industrialized countries before production could sufficiently expand from the effects of the depression of the 1930's. The terms of trade of the developing countries thus greatly improved over the 1930's. But during the 1950's and 1960's, the capacity for production of primary products caught up with and in some cases outran demand. Compared to 1950, therefore, the terms of trade of the African countries have deteriorated by around 10 per cent. The impact has been uneven, of course, and variable from year to year. Generally, the food and agricultural raw-materials producers have been hard hit, while the nonferrous metals, particularly copper, have fared extremely well, particularly in the late 1960's (hence Zambia's rapid growth).

Political independence has not removed the African nations' great need for help from abroad in the form of trained personnel. There are still some 35,000 Europeans and Americans working for the governments of sub-Saharan Africa. Independent African countries are, of course, pushing as rapidly as possible to replace these "expatriates" with trained people of their own nationality, but inevitably, the "expatriates" in administration left more rapidly than trained people were available to replace them. Also, even though an "expatriate" may be replaced by a man of the same ability and same standard of training, his replacement will be less experienced. The result has been that the standard of administration throughout the continent has deteriorated in greater or lesser degree. On the other hand, it should not be overlooked that the governments of the independent countries have often found it easier to mobilize the population and get more voluntary cooperation in achieving economic tasks than the colonial administrators did. While in some countries the number of expatriates is now fewer, the number in 1970 may even be greater than in 1960. Some of the departing expatriates in administration have been replaced by technical-assistance advisers, the expansion of schools has increased the number of teachers needed before the training schools in Africa have been able to turn them out, and the growth in the economies has brought in more expatriate technicians and managers working for private industry or as consultants to government.

As compared to earlier periods, the 1960's introduced several new factors that continue to exercise an important influence on African economic growth. Perhaps the most important is the dominant need to create nations out of the colonies and collections of tribes that had achieved independence. In country after country, this political factor either dominates or strongly influences the pace of development. Sometimes it takes the form of intertribal or sectional rivalries; sometimes it appears as a conflict between a Moslem north and non-Moslem south, as in the Sudan, Chad, Eritrea, and in part in Nigeria. While there is no reason to believe that this nation-building task is near to completion or that new crises will not arise, the record of the 1960's nevertheless provides an optimistic bias to the long-term future. In particular, the remarkable achievement of Congo (Kinshasa) in pulling itself together by the end of the decade from the near chaos that at times it approached augurs well for the continent.

Among the other factors to be considered in the 1970's, the entrance of Japan into the African scene as a purchaser of African products, particularly minerals, and as an investor in industry deserves special mention. By 1970, Japanese industry had already contracted to purchase all of the iron-ore exports of Swaziland and Sierra Leone and the copper exports of Uganda, and was helping to create industries in the Sudan, Ethiopia, and Nigeria. The 1960's saw the discovery of several new mineral resources in Africa, notably oil and gas. North Africa in this period became a major world exporter; Libya alone became by 1970 the biggest single provider of oil for Western Europe. The decade also showed that Nigeria possessed a major oil and gas deposit, and there were strong indications that the continental shelf lying off Nigeria, perhaps as far west as Ghana and as far south as Angola, also possessed important deposits.

While the early 1960's saw some slowdown in economic growth in most of Africa, by the end of the decade Africa had succeeded in achieving an over-all rate of growth of around 4 per cent a year in real gross domestic product—a rate about as good as that of the 1950's. Africa's relative success in the early 1960's was due both to a step-up in the amount of external public aid (net of amortization repayments), which then continued at $1.5 billion a year for all of Africa (more than $1 billion for Africa south of the Sahara), and to the great efforts Africans themselves made to master their problems. With all her inexperience, Africa's efforts to achieve economic development compare favorably with those of other major developing regions of the world.

By 1970, measured in per-capita GDP terms, Africa was still one of the two most underdeveloped regions of the world, sharing this position with South Asia. However, the average per capita GDP in Africa, over $100, was already slightly higher than that of South Asia. The Middle Eastern countries at over $300, Latin America at almost $400, and the southern European countries at around $500 were clearly in a quite different category altogether. In a study presented by the United Nations to the Economic and Social Council in May, 1970, attempting to identify the least developed of the underdeveloped countries on the basis of various indices in addition to per capita income (i.e., consumption of energy per capita; school-enrollment ratios; number of doctors per 100,000 inhabitants), of the nineteen countries classified as least developed out of a total of ninety underdeveloped countries covered by the study, sixteen were in sub-Saharan Africa. (The countries so classified were: Botswana,

Burundi, Chad, Dahomey, Ethiopia, the Gambia, Guinea, Lesotho, Malawi, Niger, Rwanda, Somalia, the Sudan, Tanzania, Uganda, and Upper Volta, in Africa, and Afghanistan, Laos, and Yemen, in Asia.)

The Republic of South Africa, which is not included in the aggregate statistics cited above, could be said to have entered the stage of an industrialized economy in the 1960's. Economic phenomena are never easy to characterize neatly, and there is still much of the South African economy that is underdeveloped. During the 1950's, however, a large part of the growth of South Africa had continued to be dependent on inflow of foreign capital. During the 1960's, the South African economy was able to grow on its own resources alone at the fast pace of around 6 per cent per year; by 1970 the average per capita GDP of the whole population was around $700, almost seven times the average for the rest of Africa.

## Selected Bibliography

Buxton, T. F. *The African Slave Trade.* London: John Murray, 1839; New York: American Anti-Slavery Society, 1840.

Curtin, Philip D. *African History.* Washington, D.C.: Service Center for Teachers, American Historical Assn.; New York: Macmillan; London: Collier-Macmillan, 1964.

Dike, K. O. *Trade and Politics in the Niger Delta, 1830–1885.* Oxford: The Clarendon Press, 1959.

Ducasse, A. *Les négriers, ou le trafic des esclaves.* Paris: Hachette, 1848.

Fisher, A. G. B., and Fisher, Humphrey J. *Slavery and Muslim Society in Africa.* London: C. Hurst, 1970.

Frankel, S. H. *Capital Investment in Africa.* London and New York: Oxford University Press, 1938.

Hailey, Lord. *An African Survey, Revised 1956.* London and New York: Oxford University Press, 1957.

Hance, W. A. *The Geography of Modern Africa.* New York and London: Columbia University Press, 1964.

Keynes, J. M. "Foreign Investment and National Advantage," in *The Nation and the Athenaeum,* August 9, 1924, pp. 985–86. Cited by S. H. Frankel, "Some Conceptual Aspects of International Economic Development of Underdeveloped Territories." ("Essays in International Finance," No. 14.) Princeton, N.J.: International Finance Section, Princeton University, May, 1952.

LEAKEY, L. S. B. *The Progress and Evolution of Man in Africa.* London and New York: Oxford University Press, 1961.

LEWIS, BERNARD. *The Arabs in History.* New York and Evanston, Ill.: Harper Torchbooks, The Academy Library, Harper & Row, 1960.

NEUMARK, S. D. *Foreign Trade and Economic Development in Africa: A Historical Perspective.* Stanford, Calif.: Food Research Institute (Stanford University), 1964.

PEDLER, F. J. *Economic Geography of West Africa.* London and New York: Longmans, Green, 1955.

SCHMIDT, DANA ADAMS. "British Group Finds Evidence of an Increase in African Slave Traffic over the Last Ten Years," *The New York Times,* April 7, 1967, p. 13.

STAMP, L. D. *Africa: A Study in Tropical Development.* London: Chapman and Hall, 1953; 2d ed.; New York: John Wiley, 1964.

THOMAS, B. E. *Transportation and Physical Geography in West Africa.* Los Angeles: University of California, 1960.

TOYNBEE, A. "Interview," *The Washington Post,* February 16, 1964, Section E, p. 1.

UNCTAD. *Identification of the Least Developed Among Developing Countries.* TD/B/269, August, 1969.

# II

# The Structure
# of the African Economies

> *Never since the beginning of Time was
> there, that we hear or read of, so in-
> tensely self-conscious a Society. Our
> whole relations to the Universe and to
> our fellow-man have become an In-
> quiry, a Doubt; nothing will go on of
> its own accord, and do its function
> quietly; but all things must be probed
> into, the whole working of man's world
> be anatomically studied.*
>
> THOMAS CARLYLE

On a quarter of the world's land surface, Africa has about 9 per cent of the world's population—perhaps 330 million people in all. Africa is the second largest continent in the world, with an area of over 30 million square kilometers. Excluding the North African countries, the remaining area of around 22 million square kilometers is more than three times the size of the United States, and has a population (270 million) about a third greater than that of the United States. Of this African population, about 5 million are of European origin and 1 million of Asian origin (both mostly in southern Africa).

24

## Population Growth

The rate of population growth is becoming a major economic problem in much of Africa. While the collection of current demographic data by governments is still highly inadequate, enough special inquiries and studies have now been conducted for some conclusions to be drawn. One is that there is a very large range among the different areas in Africa in average birth rate (from 30 to 60 per 1,000) and in the average total number of children (3.5 to more than 8) born in the lifetime of a woman. There is a ridge of high fertility from the southeastern Sudan through parts of Uganda and Kenya, through Rwanda and Burundi and parts of Tanganyika, and through the southern and eastern provinces of the Congo into Zambia, Southern Rhodesia, and the southern province of Mozambique. Another ridge is along the coast of West Africa from coastal Nigeria to the Ivory Coast, with a branch extending up through western Liberia into parts of Niger and Upper Volta. The lowest fertility is in the region extending from the west coast of Gabon through the north-central and northwestern provinces of the Congo into the southwestern region of the Sudan. (Brass, Coale, *et al.*, pp. 166–67.) These regional variations notwithstanding, the average fertility in Africa is very high. The average birth rate in Africa as a whole is about 49 per 1,000, and the average total fertility of women is around 6½ children.

In any case, it is safe to assume that the rate of population growth in Africa has accelerated since World War II, though probably not so much as the available figures indicate. It will almost certainly accelerate more within the next decade, since the present (still high) death rates are likely to be reduced more rapidly than the birth rate. A rate of population growth of 2 or 3 per cent yearly is a datum that most African governments will have to accept as a planning parameter for some years to come.

In relating the present size of population to the area of Africa—which results in a density figure of twenty to twenty-five persons per square mile (nine or ten persons per square kilometer), or about one third that of the United States—the temptation is great to conclude that Africa is underpopulated. But "underpopulation" or "overpopulation" depends not only on the relationship of population to physical resources but on the level of technical and economic development that the people have attained, since this is what determines the numbers the economy can support at any particular point in time. For instance, in Zambia and Rhodesia, with a population living in the traditional way on the basis of shifting cultivation, ash planting, and cultivation with hoes, the land could carry in perpetuity from about six to ten or twelve people per square mile, depending upon how much wood was available to burn for ash. (Gluckman, p. 647.) With the growth of industry—the opening up of the copper mines— the numbers that can be carried have risen considerably. With traditional methods of culture, Rhodesia could have supported perhaps 1.5 million people, but today she is not overpopulated with 4.5 million. In the case of Zambia, the size of the population today is still quite close to the number that could live on the land on the basis of subsistence agriculture.

Aside from parts of eastern and northern Nigeria, Rwanda, Burundi, Kigezi in Uganda, southern Malawi, Lesotho, and the "reserves" in South Africa, there does not in general appear to be that pressure of population on *present methods* of exploitation of resources which would lead one to say that Africa is overpopulated. On the other hand, there is certainly no evidence that an absolute lack of adequate manpower is holding up development.* Yet, while there is little population pressure in Africa as a whole, the present distribution—decided by historical events (the slave trade, tribal wars, etc.) as well as by the agricultural technology of 60 to 100 years ago —is not ideal. Crowded areas often lie next door to underutilized land, with movement between them restricted by tribal considerations. Still, the absence of severe population pressure at a time when economic development has hardly begun can be seen as an important economic asset. It gives Africa a better starting point than India or Pakistan, for example, where, with about the same level of

---

* From time to time, complaint is made of the scarcity of labor for a particular activity—e.g., in Liberia in the early 1960's in the rubber plantations. But the difficulty is likely to be due not so much to an absolute scarcity of labor as to a scarcity of labor at the low wage being offered. When a low wage ceiling is imposed, as in Liberia, it is to be expected that some enterprises will have difficulty in recruiting labor. The very fact that it was felt necessary to establish a maximum wage indicates that demand was raising wages: at a higher wage, more labor might be available, on the one hand, and, on the other, some of the demand for it would disappear; if wages were to be prevented from going up, some enterprises would have to be short of labor at the legal wage.

per-capita income, there are already severe pressures on the available resources.

But a good starting point is not enough. What will count now is the rate of population growth, the rate of growth of gross national products, and the interrelations between these. In this regard, the acceleration in the rate of population growth that is now unquestionably occurring over most of Africa is a strong negative factor.

Generally, what is happening is that fertility remains high—with birth rates of 40 or 45 per 1,000 or higher—while infant mortality rates drop. The number of children rapidly increases, and the proportion of the population who are adults and economically productive drops. Typically, in a country in this stage of development and population growth, 40–45 per cent of the population is under the age of 15; most developed countries have a maximum of 25 to 35 per cent in this age group. This means that a larger proportion of the national income in an African country has to be devoted to the feeding, clothing, and housing of nonproducers than in a developed country. As between two countries, then, with the same size labor force and same national income, the one with the lower rate of population growth will have a higher per-capita income. And the difficulty the country with the higher rate of growth faces in saving a portion of its income for investment (to make possible higher incomes in the future) becomes greater just because of the high rate of population increase.

All of these difficulties occur when a country has had a high rate of population growth for many years. But they are aggravated when the rate of population growth is *rapidly* accelerating; during this period, the number of children may double or triple while the number of adults still does not increase (or increases only slightly, owing to improvements in adult medicine). In this way, the proportion of children in the population may shoot up beyond 40 to 45 per cent.

A second factor that comes into play as a result of the higher rate of population growth is this: a much higher proportion of the investment an African country is able to make must go to schools, housing, and other not *directly* productive sectors than is true in developed countries. As between two countries where all else is equal, the country with the lower rate of population growth can not only invest more in total amount but can invest a higher proportion in factories, farms, and other immediately productive enterprises than

can the one where the population growth rate is accelerating.
Of course, this is cumulative: a greater productive investment this
year results in a higher output next year, which makes possible still
greater investment.*

A special study made in 1965 for the government of Kenya concluded that the annual rate of natural increase of population was 3
per cent a year. The government demographer made a projection of
Kenya's population to the year 2000 on the assumption of a continued increase in life expectancy in conjunction with a continuation
of fertility at its current level. On this basis, the population of
Kenya would increase from around 9 million in 1965 to over 30
million in the year 2000 (*Family Planning in Kenya*, p. 4). If conceivably this rate of growth were continued, a century from now, in
2070, the Kenya population would be 480 million. This set of projections is horrifying enough, but in early 1970, the Kenya govern-

---

* A simple population model that may fairly be applied to African countries
is as follows:

Total savings and investment, 12 per cent of gross national product (GNP);
investment in the social sector—defined simply as the investment necessary to
take care of the growth in population, i.e., schools, housing, hospitals, etc.—
3 per cent of GNP for every 1 per cent in the rate of population growth; an
average and incremental capital/output ratio of 3 in the non-social sector alone,
assuming that the social-sector investment does not have any immediate effects
on output. Then, comparing two countries, both with a per-capita GNP of $100,
and assuming that Country A has and maintains an annual rate of population
increase of 1 per cent while Country B's rate increases from 1 per cent to 3 per
cent within ten years, the following table shows the results in economic growth:

| At the end of | Per-capita GNP (in dollars) Country A | Country B |
|---|---|---|
| 5 years | 116 | 113 |
| 10 | 134 | 123 |
| 15 | 156 | 129 |
| 20 | 181 | 136 |
| 30 | 243 | 150 |
| 40 | 326 | 165 |

At the end of five years, the two countries are still quite close together. But,
after twenty years, not only has Country A pulled well ahead but its GNP rate
of growth is *accelerating*. On the other hand, Country B's economic progress is
slowing down to a crawl. At the end of forty years, Country A has about
double the per-capita income of Country B and is well on its way to rapid
economic growth. (A more complex model, closer to reality, would show that
Country A can do even better than these figures indicate, since, with the higher
per-capita income, it could increase its rate of investment quite early on and its
rate of economic growth still more.)

ment discovered from the early results of its census that the population was 1 million greater than had been estimated and that the current rate of growth of population had climbed to around 3.3 per cent a year, or a rate 10 per cent higher than the one projected five years earlier.

Data such as these and reflection on what they mean are beginning to convince African governments that the policies they adopt on family planning may be the most important decisions they can make in determining their countries' economic future. The African Conference on Population, organized by the Economic Commission for Africa (ECA) in 1971, should be a big step toward the economic development of the continent.

Africa is a poor continent. The total gross national product (excluding the $15 billion GNP of the Mediterranean countries) is estimated at about $40 billion equivalent (at current exchange rates) for 1970. This is nominally less than 5 per cent of the American GNP in money terms. It is roughly equivalent to the total income of the present American black population, which numbers less than one tenth the population of Africa. It is, in fact, well below the annual increase in the American GNP in 1968 or 1969. More than one third of the total African GNP is produced in South Africa, which, with 20 million people, has less than 10 per cent of Africa's total population. South Africa's proportion in the African total has, however, dropped during the last seventy years. Few estimates have been made of national accounts of African countries before World War II, but a fair indication can be derived from export figures: in 1900, South Africa provided more than two thirds of the total exports of sub-Saharan Africa; just before World War II, the figure had dropped to just over half; in 1970, it was around one third.

## The Internal Economic Structure

Data on African economies are not sufficiently reliable or abundant to permit the application of very sophisticated analytical refinements. It is possible, however, to make a fairly rough analysis that illuminates how the African economies work.

The propulsive and dominant sectors in the African money economies are external: exports, foreign investment, and other expenditures financed from abroad. (See below, chaps. IV and XII.) These essentially still determine the size and growth pace of African economies.

An increase in money incomes results almost immediately in an increase in demand for imports—and in upward pressure on prices to the extent that imports are not immediately available. In other words, the marginal propensity to import is very high, for a number of important reasons: the "modern" sector of an African economy is relatively small and inflexible, particularly that part of it producing goods for the home market. The propensity in the private sector to save is also very small. Consequently, an increase in money incomes (whether from an increase in export earnings, from an inflow of foreign investments or foreign expenditures, or from central-bank creation of money to finance a government deficit or private activity) is offset in only small part by an increase in private savings. It results instead in increased imports. Because of the inflexibility of local production, the increase in national output is relatively small (the national income multiplier is fairly weak, probably under 2) and the rise in the demand for imports is quite rapid.

What this means for the African nation is that an increase in the price of exports, resulting in greater export earnings, will soon be reflected in greater imports (of consumer goods, if action is not taken to divert or induce the extra funds into investment). An attempt to finance investment or increased government spending by central-bank creation of money soon results in a foreign-exchange crisis.

(An International Monetary Fund study of monetary expansion in Sierra Leone in the years 1962–65 found that every increase of 100 in credit and use of non-bank reserves resulted in a foreign exchange loss of 64. That is, almost two thirds of an increase in local money supply was immediately used for foreign purchases. [Bhatia *et al.*, p. 522.])

In contrast to industrialized societies, where individuals are highly interdependent in their economic activity but socially have few close ties to other people, in Africa the individual produces mainly for his own or his family's consumption. The various attempts that have been made to produce input-output tables for African economies— tables that show how various productive sectors are related to one another—all merely demonstrate the relative unimportance of flows *within* the economy. Whereas in an industrialized economy the output of a sector typically is used largely as inputs for other sectors, in an African country outputs flow mostly directly to consumption or export or to investment. As the African economies develop, the interdependence of industries and sectors within the country will grow; now, the activities in the money part of the economy are more likely to have ties with the outside world than with other parts of their own economy.

Africa is still predominantly a rural continent. According to U.N. estimates, about a fifth of the population is urban—roughly the same proportion as in South Asia, and less than half that in Latin America. The comparative figures are as follows:

PERCENTAGE OF URBAN DWELLERS IN TOTAL POPULATION

|               | 1940 | 1960 | 1980 (Projected) |
|---------------|------|------|------------------|
| Africa        | 11   | 18   | 28               |
| South Asia    | 12   | 18   | 25               |
| East Asia     | 13   | 23   | 31               |
| Latin America | 31   | 49   | 60               |
| Europe        | 53   | 58   | 65               |
| North America | 59   | 70   | 81               |

SOURCE: U.N. *Housing, Building and Planning in the Second Development Decade*, Doc. E/C 6/90, 1969.

NATIONAL ACCOUNTS

Most of the industrialized countries began calculating their national accounts regularly only after World War II. In Africa too, the preparation of national accounts began after World War II. For most African countries, dependable benchmark yearly estimates of agricultural and industrial production are not yet available. In addition, most types of economic statistics are still rudimentary, and the number of personnel that can handle them is limited. Consequently, even though formally comprehensive and detailed national accounts have been prepared for many African countries and partial accounts for the rest, their accuracy is not great.

Aside from their incompleteness and lack of accuracy, many of the national accounts now prepared in Africa differ from those of industrialized countries in significance as well. National accounts describe best a monetary economy (although pitfalls are present even there). In a country with a large subsistence sector, as is true everywhere in Africa, the validity of the accounts is considerably attenuated. The problem is that it is impossible to ignore the subsistence activities but almost equally impossible to bring them into the accounts in a meaningful way. In fact, the process of putting a price tag on subsistence output is difficult to justify logically: how do you value something in money terms when its essence is that it is nonmonetary? As Phyllis Deane, pioneer in this work, has said: "Where the bulk of goods in a given category are traded, it does not greatly strain the conceptual framework to impute a value to the remainder. Where the bulk are *not* traded, it is obviously a highly artificial process which bears no direct relation to the physical facts of the case. The figure for subsistence output can never be more than a token figure." (Deane, p. 226.)

Besides the valuation, one must decide what part of subsistence activity can be considered economic at all. At present, economists are not agreed on which aspects of subsistence activity should be regarded as economic and, therefore, valued and included in the national accounts. For example, the first estimates made of the Nigerian national income for 1950–51 included £4 million as the value of services rendered by women in the household, this figure being based on the bride-payment made by husbands to secure their wives. (Prest and Stewart, pp. 10, 47.) The national-income estimates made since then have excluded this item, and the figure for Nigeria's income is thereby considerably reduced. A meeting of a working party of the Economic Commission for Africa in 1960 agreed that all countries should include in their national income estimated figures for subsistence activities in agriculture, forestry, fishing, building, construction, and land works by households. But it was left up to the individual countries to decide whether they wished to include processing, storage, transport, and distribution of a household's own primary output; home processing of goods purchased; and other services such as collecting firewood and fetching water.

The general practice today is to include a figure for subsistence in the national accounts, but it is quite clearly not of the same validity as the rest of the figures. With time, of course, the increased monetization of activities in Africa will give more meaning to the prices used to evaluate subsistence output. In the meantime, we have to use more than usual caution in dealing with aggregate figures in Africa.

Another problem in the meaning of the national accounts prepared for African countries arises from the economic importance in
all these countries of foreigners ("expatriates") and foreign investment. There are two usual ways of presenting material affected by
this consideration in the national accounts. One is to compute them
on a territorial basis, including whatever happens within the territorial boundaries of a country and paying no attention to national
ownership of assets or nationality of the income-receiver. In this way,
one secures what is called gross geographical product (or gross
domestic product, which is the same thing with some minor differences). The second is to attempt to identify the product resulting
from factors of production supplied by *normal* residents of the
country (gross national product). But even GNP, in countries
that have a large enclave of foreigners who are *normally* resident
in the country, exaggerates the real income and well-being of the
permanent indigenous residents. Yet if the foreign enclaves were
completely excluded, the economic position of the country would be
understated, since, after all, the country does derive some permanent benefit from the expatriates who are present and from the
enclave investments. If in Kenya, for example, where Africans took
over most of the farms, the accounts had in the past excluded the
important European farming community, the "enclave" would be
introduced into the accounts for the first time and the Kenya national income would show a misleading big jump.

A similar problem arises in handling the investments of those
Asians in East Africa who chose British citizenship rather than local
citizenship at the time of independence. Most of the money invested in fact was saved from incomes in East Africa, and many of
the people concerned had lived there for several generations.

## Sector Distribution of Activities

The typical African lives by farming. Considerably more than half
of the active population is on the land. Because agricultural work is
not so productive (in money terms) as work in mining, manufacturing, or elsewhere in the money economy; because subsistence production, as mentioned above, tends to be undervalued; and because
manufacturing products are priced relatively higher, owing to protective tariffs on domestic production and import duties on im-

ported goods—the contribution of agriculture to the gross domestic product is considerably less than the proportion of the population engaged in it. According to the ECA Secretariat, the composition of African GDP in 1960 and 1966 was as follows:*

DISTRIBUTION OF GDP IN DEVELOPING AFRICA (EXCLUDING SOUTH AFRICA)
(at factor costs)

| Sector | Per cent of Total 1960 | 1966 |
|---|---|---|
| Agriculture | 40 | 36 |
| Mining | 4 | 8 |
| Manufacturing | 11 | 12 |
| Construction | 4 | 4 |
| Commerce | 13 | 12 |
| Transport | 6 | 6 |
| Other services | 14 | 13 |
| Public administration | 8 | 9 |
| Total | 100 | 100 |

SOURCE: U.N. ECA Secretariat, Addis Ababa, May, 1968.
* See also Table 1 in Technical Appendix, pp. 56–57, for national figures.

As this table indicates, the major change in the African economy during the 1960's was the rapid growth of mining and the relative decline of agriculture. But, of course, every African economy differs in some respect from this over-all pattern. The relative contribution of agriculture exceeds 60 per cent in such countries as Rwanda, Burundi, and Ethiopia, and 50 per cent in Chad, Ghana, the Sudan, Tanzania, and Uganda. The proportion of the population in agriculture varies from a low of around 75 per cent in Kenya to 90 per cent or more in Liberia, Uganda, and Ethiopia. The subsistence element in the GDP in some cases (Niger, Chad, Upper Volta) may run as high as two thirds of the total agricultural contribution but has already dipped below one half in such countries as Ghana and Uganda.

In a few countries (South Africa, Zambia, Congo [Kinshasa], Algeria, Libya, Tunisia, and probably now Mauretania), the contribution of mining and manufacturing to GDP surpasses that of agriculture. Aside from South Africa (where manufacturing contributes 25 per cent of total GDP), only in Central African Republic, Cameroon, Congo (Kinshasa), Ghana, Ivory Coast, Senegal, Southern Rhodesia, and Tunisia does manufacturing contribute more than 12 per cent of GDP.

## THE SUBSISTENCE ECONOMY AND THE MONEY ECONOMY

In terms of the activity of the average African man or woman, the subsistence element in most African economies is probably still dominant. That is to say, the amount of time the average African spends on activities that merely keep him alive and functioning is greater than the amount of time he spends working for or spending money; the average African is more in than out of the subsistence tribal economy. For the average African, the goods and services produced within his household or by the families of his kin are still more important and include more of the necessities of life than the goods he buys or sells.

It is also probably true, however, though here again there are few data to substantiate it, that few Africans now are completely outside the influence of the money economy. Further, the money economy is becoming a dominant influence for Africans. Certainly this is already true for the majority of the population in Senegal, Sierra Leone, Ivory Coast, Ghana, Togo, Kenya, Malawi, Zambia, Southern Rhodesia, South Africa, Nigeria, Uganda, and North Africa. Whereas twenty years ago, say, the importance of subsistence activities was greater in Africa than in any other region of the world, it is now probably no more important there than in South Asia.

The permeation of the money economy throughout Africa not only has considerable importance in its own right but will influence the whole pace of economic development in the future. It is almost impossible for anyone who has not lived in a subsistence economy to appreciate how profoundly it affects one's activities and outlook. To live in a subsistence economy means to live a hand-to-mouth existence in a world of great risk and uncertainty. Without the techniques or facilities for storage of food over any appreciable period, the African depended on the yearly crop or his luck in hunting or fishing. It was impossible to provide a margin of security. He might be able to gorge himself one week and have to go hungry the next. Nearly every people had a "hungry season" when the last season's crop had been eaten and the new crops had not yet come in. And the risk and uncertainty affecting a whole village, bad as it was, was accentuated for any one individual if he tried to stand alone, since any one farmer's crops could be wiped out by a herd of elephants, a flood, or a swarm of insects or birds, and he could then survive only if the rest of the community helped him through to the next harvest.

Many writers have pointed out the profound psychological effects of this situation. In the first place, it inclines to a fatalist philosophy, interpreted often by Europeans as fecklessness or laziness. If the future is both uncertain and uncontrollable, it is better not to think about it—it might be intolerably painful and daunting to do so. It is well enough known in Western societies that there is a certain threshold of security above which forethought and effort are possible and below which resignation and fecklessness set in. (Hunter, p. 14.)

With the spread of the money economy, it is possible for individuals both to create a margin of security for themselves by setting aside a permanent store of value in the form of money and to survive apart from the community. It becomes possible for them to pass above the threshold of security; to plan ahead and to work for goals beyond bare survival from day to day. This now is happening all over Africa. The widespread thirst for education, and the willingness of parents to make great financial sacrifices to procure schooling for their children, is another indication that Africans are passing over this threshold and are losing the passive fatalism of the past.

## Uses of Resources

The average pattern of use of the goods and services available to Africans is indicated in the following approximate figures:

|  | Per cent of GDP | |
|---|---|---|
| Total gross domestic product | 100 | |
| Imports of goods and services | 28 | |
| Total resources available | | 128 |
| *Uses* | | |
| Private consumption | 71 | |
| Government consumption | 15 | |
| Gross domestic capital formation | 16 | |
| Exports | 26 | |
| | | 128 |

One important point to be noted is the size of the investment effort (gross domestic capital formation), which averages around 16 per cent. As Kuznets (International Differences, pp. 60-64) has found, most of the industrialized countries invested at a rate well below this during most of the nineteenth century. Several African countries have gone beyond this to levels higher than 20 per cent, comparable to the industrialized countries' rates since World War II. This has been true, for at least some years, of Botswana, Ivory Coast, Gabon, and Zambia as well as of Libya, Tunisia, and South Africa (which is now itself an industrialized country). (See Table 2, Technical Appendix.)

## THE PUBLIC SECTOR

From a comparatively early point in the development of Africa, the governmental role in the economy was a major one. (See above, chap. I.) Except in the Rhodesias, the Belgian Congo, and the Portuguese territories, in all of which private investment in mines and railways was more important, it was the government that constructed railways and encouraged and stimulated production. The corollary of this is the continuing importance of the government as employer and of the publicly owned sector generally in the national accounts.

In most African nations, current government expenditures usually run around 15 per cent of gross national expenditures. (In the former French colonies, this proportion has been calculated at 14 per cent, but the range is from 9 per cent in Togo to 30 per cent in Mauretania. [Bérard, p. 22.]) If one adds the operations of the (usually publicly owned) railways, electricity authorities, ports, etc., and the investment in the whole public sector, the total approaches one-third of gross national expenditure. The public sector and the export sector, which typically produces around one-quarter of the gross national product, together are therefore the dominant economic influence in the money economy of Africa.

The government and public sector is generally also the largest single, if not the major, employer of wage earners. It is true that in most African countries the proportion of the labor force in paid employment is still small, usually from 5 to 10 per cent. But, of this group, one is quite likely to find a third to a half or more working for the government or government-owned entities. In the typical French-speaking African country, total wages and salaries paid by the public administrations surpass the total paid in the private sector by around 10 per cent. (Bérard, p. 7.) Many African workers or employees, therefore, naturally expect the state or a public agency to be their employer. Among other consequences, this has the effect of reinforcing one of the worst heritages of colonialism— the Africans' acceptance of the idea that the best job to have is a government post. (See below, chap. III, p. 60.) The ablest people, as a result, think in terms of preparing themselves to fit into the public service. The 1960's have also shown, however, that in countries where other opportunities do open up, Africans freely leave the government service to take advantage of them. Another, perhaps in the long run even more significant, result is that worker and employee organizations concentrate on improving their lot through pressure on the state. African trade unions, even aside from their alliance with nationalist movements in the pre-independence period, are thus almost inevitably drawn to the political arena to gain their economic objectives.

## THE NON-AFRICAN ELEMENT

A non-indigenous or non-African element is significant in the economies of all African countries, but its importance varies from South Africa (where the economy created by European settlers during the last century is *the* economy, and only comparatively unimportant African subsistence activities are not dominated by it) through nations like Southern Rhodesia, Zambia, Ivory Coast, Gabon, and Senegal (where the position can best be analyzed in terms of a dual economy—part European-dominated and part African), to the remaining lands where the bulk of the economy is African but non-Africans play a significant role as owners and managers of large manufacturing, finance, and import-export enterprises.

Indeed, the relative economic importance of non-Africans in any African country is generally indicated by how many there are in the country. The largest number is in South Africa, where there are 3.6 million people of European origin. There are 250,000 Europeans in Angola, 200,000 in Southern Rhodesia, 100,000 each in East Africa (mostly in Kenya), Mozambique, and West Africa (mostly in Dakar), 80,000 in Zambia, 50,000 in the Malagasy Republic, and perhaps another 100,000 scattered over the rest of sub-Saharan Africa. Of the continent's more than 1 million Asians, the majority, or 600,000, are again in South Africa; another 500,000 are found in the eastern African countries.

De Kiewiet has made the point that "The development of Africa in modern times can be more easily understood if it is seen as the result of two movements of migration. The first is the migration of European traders, officials and settlers into Africa together with their skills, investments, equipment and governmental organization. The second is the migration of the African tribesmen into the new world created by European enterprise." (De Kiewiet, p. 35.) Now, with independence, a substantial outflow of Europeans has occurred, their places in the public sector taken over by Africans. But even in governmental positions, European officials will still be needed in most African countries for most of the next decade. And, in the private sector, if the economy is growing vigorously, there is often a continued need for Europeans as businessmen, managers, and technicians, even though the African-owned part of the economy may be growing most rapidly and even though foreign-owned firms may have been nationalized, as in Tanzania and Zambia.

PER-CAPITA INCOME

In most of the continent between North and South Africa, the typical per-capita GNP was around $100 equivalent by 1970. South Africa's per-capita GNP had reached $700, and the explosive development of oil in Libya had brought her to well over $1,000. Besides these two countries, which now essentially are among the higher-income countries of the world, there are three small areas that could be classed as middle-income, with per-capita GNP's in the $500 to $600 equivalent range; these were the French overseas territory of Afars and Issas (formerly French Somaliland), the French Department of Réunion, and the Republic of Gabon. By 1970, Zambia had a per-capita GNP of around $400 and a number of countries had succeeded in attaining $200 or more GNP per capita. This was true of the three Maghreb countries (Algeria, Tunisia, and Morocco), several countries in West Africa (Ivory Coast, Ghana, Equatorial Guinea), and the southern African countries of Angola, Zambia, Southern Rhodesia, Swaziland, and Mauritius. At the other extreme, per-capita GNP's in the general vicinity of $50 characterized the land-locked agricultural countries of Upper Volta, Niger, Chad, Rwanda, Burundi, Malawi, Lesotho, Ethiopia, and Somalia.

Compared to other underdeveloped areas of the world, insofar as the figures can be taken as indicative, Africa's per-capita GNP, even excluding South Africa, is on the average a little higher than that of the South Asian countries but below that of the East Asian countries excluding Japan. (No Latin American nation except Haiti and Bolivia is in the same per-capita GNP bracket as the African countries; the Latin American countries usually show a figure several times higher.) While the figure for African per-capita GNP is comparable to those of these other regions, it should be noted that Africa does not suffer from the widespread misery that is characteristic of some countries in these other areas. Also, although Africa is still very underdeveloped, the fact that it is no longer behind South Asia economically is already a remarkable fact, in the light of Africa's very late start.

The extremely low figures shown for per-capita GNP in some African countries mean that the population is living very close to the margin of existence, but they do not mean that the population is below that margin. As M. P. Miracle has pointed out, "The minimum level of consumption necessary to maintain life is much lower than most people realize." In August, 1944, the minimum yearly food budget was only $59.88 in parts of the United States, according to Stigler's calculations. "In much of the tropics the minimum physiologic level of living is probably much lower than in the temperate zone because less food is required to provide bodily warmth and because little or no clothing and shelter are required to maintain life." (Miracle, p. 295.)

Of course, the relative position of countries as shown by their per-capita GNP's must be interpreted with care. It is extremely doubtful that a country with a GNP of $200 equivalent per capita is really twice as well off as a country with a per-capita GNP of $100, but it can be taken that the former country is considerably better off than the latter.

We also know that the relative distance between the per-capita incomes of the African countries and the industrialized countries exaggerates the real differences. As countries develop, the prices of services and of local foods in particular go up without a comparable increase in the satisfaction provided. (For example, a haircut that costs $2.50 in the United States is not likely to provide ten times the satisfaction of a haircut that costs $0.25 in an African country.) A study carried out in India indicated that whereas in 1959 U.S. per-capita product was in money terms 30 times greater than that of India, a calculation of what the money would buy showed that the purchasing-power parity equivalent was more like 12½ to 1. The U.S. per-capita GNP of over $4,000 is not really worth 40 times the representative African per-capita GNP of around $100, but it is probably worth 10 to 15 times the African GNP. The relative ranking remains and the differences are still enormous; this is why the figures remain useful.

In terms of other indicators, the African countries (outside of South Africa) consume 80 kilowatt hours (Kwh) of power per capita a year; South Asia consumes 70; East Asia (outside of Japan) 110; Latin America 440. The average literacy rate in Africa is 20 per cent; South Asia 27 per cent; East Asia (excluding Japan) 58 per cent; Latin America 68 per cent.

### The Financial System*

Public finance in most of the African countries has been handled well—remarkably well, in fact, even in comparison with countries with much higher income levels. The systems of fiscal administration and taxes introduced by the British and French have deteriorated only moderately during their quite rapid Africanization in some of the newly independent nations. Tax rates and total revenue receipts have generally risen considerably after independence, and fiscal systems have successfully coped with these problems.

In terms of tax and revenue structures, African countries are fairly typical of developing nations in general: two-thirds to three-fourths of the revenue comes from indirect taxes, mostly customs, export and excise, or turnover taxes. Kenya, Rhodesia, and South Africa are exceptions, the latter two with a tax structure more typical of developed countries—i.e., with a much greater reliance on direct taxes.

* Africa's money and banking systems, because they are so closely linked to external financial arrangements, are covered below, in chap. IV.

Since exports are a major constituent of African GNPs and the principal means by which most Africans come into the money economy, export taxation is a logical type to apply. It does, of course, penalize a type of production that deserves, rather, encouragement; and, by taxing people engaged in export production and exempting people engaged in production for the home economy, it can be inequitable. But in the African context, where there is little specialization in production, what actually happens in most cases is not so much that "A," who is an exporter, is taxed, leaving "B," who is a producer for the home market, free, but rather that both "A" and "B" are taxed in their activity as producers of exports and exempted as producers for the home market.

In addition to export taxes, Ghana, Nigeria, and Uganda have also derived revenues through marketing boards that buy produce from farmers at one price and sell it abroad at a higher price. At least part of the difference is made available to the government, usually to finance development.

The African countries have pioneered in a form of personal direct tax well suited to countries where incomes are too low for the usual type of income tax. This locally assessed tax evolved out of the poll tax, and it is graduated in accordance with a few simple indicators of income or income-producing assets—number of coffee trees owned, number of cattle, wages received, etc.

African governments are rather more successful than governments in other developing countries, even at higher levels of income, in raising tax revenues. Total tax revenue (including marketing-board off-take) in relation to GNP in the last few years was, at the median, 15 per cent, the range from 7 per cent (Rwanda) to 24 per cent (Congo [Brazzaville]). Some years ago, the French-speaking countries did less well, with some figures as low as 5 per cent, but in the 1960's, in order to eliminate the need for budgetary support from France, they have carried out intensive drives to raise taxes and increase revenues, and their record now is as good as that of the English-speaking countries.

Success in raising government tax revenues, as evidenced by a high proportion of revenues to GDP, is not a desirable goal in and of itself. It is desirable only if the uses to which these revenues are put are socially and economically more desirable than the uses to which the taxpayers themselves would have put the money. On the whole, the uses African governments make of their revenues are satisfactory, since the expenditures, in the main, are for apparently quite reasonable activities directed toward the welfare of the people and growth of the economy. (In some African countries, one can come to the same conclusion on the ground that a decision by the legislature, which imposed the taxes, represents at least roughly the collective will of the people. But this is not the case in all African countries.) There are, however, at least two, rather general, exceptions. First, in quite a number of African countries, the governments have included housing schemes at noneconomic rents, subsidized airlines, subsidized luxury hotels, etc., in their budgets and development programs. Now, since the bulk of government revenue comes from indirect taxes, whose burden falls mainly on the poor, these schemes are in essence a scarcely justifiable subsidization of higher-income groups by the poor.

The second exception concerns government salary levels, which are, relatively, exceptionally high practically all over Africa. Originally, these were set on the basis of European salary levels plus an "inducement element," to get the French or British to come to Africa. When the Africans took over the jobs, they took over these salary levels and perquisites. The typical governmental wage and salary structure, even for unskilled workers, shows a large disparity between the wages offered and the average income outside, especially startling for positions that were usually filled by "expatriates" in the past. So far, with only some minor adjustments here and there, this gap between the average income level and income levels of the government elite has remained, and the drain on government finances with it.

### Intra-African Relations

There is probably a greater sense among educated Africans of belonging to a single entity than there is among people in the other major underdeveloped regions. Millions of Africans disregard national boundaries in gaining their livelihood. This is true of the nomads—the Toureg, who move as freely in the Sahara, across half a dozen national territories, as sailors on the sea; the Fulani, who herd their cattle in the savannah areas of West Africa from Guinea to Nigeria; the different groups of Somali who use the grazing grounds of southeastern Ethiopia; the Masai herdsmen of Tanzania and Kenya, etc. It is also true of the African migrant wage workers: one quarter of the men of Upper Volta are usually away, working in Ghana or the Ivory Coast, and, inversely, one quarter of the Ivory Coast's total population of almost 4 million has come from other African countries, mainly Upper Volta, Mali, and Guinea; the men of Malawi and Lesotho get the bulk of their paid employment in Southern Rhodesia and South Africa, respectively; 100,000 "Westerners" from northern Nigeria and Chad are the backbone of the labor force on the cotton farms of the Gezira Scheme in the Sudan; men and women from Rwanda and Burundi work on the coffee farms of Uganda and make up a large proportion of the miners in Katanga.

The major movement of trade of the African countries is with countries outside of Africa. Only around 10 per cent of their total trade is with other African countries. This is a very rough figure. Official trade statistics overstate the case, on the one hand, by often including the substantial trade in goods originally imported from outside Africa. On the other hand, there is trade in locally produced goods that is not recorded at all. Local produce moves quite freely across many national frontiers; customs duties on such goods are either not levied at all or not collected. Since most countries are largely self-sufficient and their habits are to consume local foods, the commodity that such trade affects most is cattle. In West Africa, there is a large cattle trade south from the tsetse-free savannah of Upper Volta, Mali, Niger, and Chad to the meat consumers of the coastal countries. The second type of fairly large-scale trade is smuggling of overseas imports and commodities produced for export overseas across national frontiers. Because of the different tariff systems, levels of prices, and export tax arrangements, such smuggling becomes quite profitable for some commodities. If, for example, the cocoa purchase price is set higher in Ghana than the Ivory Coast, farmers try to sell their cocoa in Ghana. Senegal complains periodically to Gambia about overseas goods imported into the Gambia at low tariff rates and then smuggled into Senegal, avoiding the higher tariffs there. This type of entrepôt trade is also important for Togo's economy. Congo (Brazzaville) during the 1960's was a substantial diamond exporter although there are no diamond mines there.

But aside from the cattle and frontier food trade and the smuggling entrepôt trade, trade among the African countries is significant mainly among the East African countries and the southern African countries.*

With the necessary concentration of the African governments on constructing national identities, it is not surprising that little has been accomplished in creating intra-African economic and financial links. It is logical that the national boundaries established by the colonial power—as illogical as these boundaries often are—have been fiercely maintained while the colonial interterritorial links have largely disappeared. The West African currency shared by Nigeria, Ghana, Sierra Leone, and Gambia has been replaced by individual currencies, and the East African shilling by Kenyan, Tanzanian, and Ugandan currencies. The West African airways and the palm oil, cocoa, and rice agricultural-research institutes these countries shared have also been divided up. (An attempt is now being made to re-create a West Africa Rice Development Association.) Various attempts made by Ghana to create governmental, economic, or customs ties with Guinea, Mali, and Upper Volta, on the other hand, have come to naught, as did the federation of Senegal and Mali. The former economic and financial ties among Rwanda, Burundi, and the Congo (Kinshasa), in the form of a common currency and customs union, have gone.

The economic union of Rhodesia and Nyasaland disappeared, of course, with the breakup of the Federation on December 31, 1963. An agreement between Rhodesia and Malawi to continue the free entry of Rhodesian products into Malawi against payment of monetary compensation for the customs duties foregone by Malawi pre-

---

* Almost 10 per cent of South Africa's exports in 1965 were to Southern Rhodesia, where they represented about one third of the total imports. Rhodesian exports to South Africa amounted to about 28 per cent of its total exports and 2 or 3 per cent of South Africa's imports. The breakup of the Federation of Rhodesia and Nyasaland in 1964 resulted in a drop in trade between its successor states, Zambia and Malawi, and South Africa, but trade between Rhodesia and Zambia and Malawi was quite high (Zambia bought 40 per cent of its total imports from Rhodesia) until Rhodesia's unilateral declaration of independence in November, 1965. Rhodesian trade with South Africa, on the other hand, increased in 1965, facilitated by the broadening of the trade preferences that each country gave to the other. A special trade relationship between Rhodesia and South Africa dates back many years, in fact, to the free-trade area that existed in practice between them until Rhodesia began her industrialization in the 1950's.

served part of the earlier economic entity, however. But the economic unity resulting from several political unions persists: Eritrea with Ethiopia, British and Italian Somaliland into Somalia, British Togoland with Ghana, and British Cameroons in a federation with Cameroon. The union of Tanganyika and Zanzibar into what is now called the United Republic of Tanzania was added to this list in 1964.

In the French-speaking areas, the previously existing federations of French West Africa and French Equatorial Africa were dissolved when these territories became independent. Several new economic and financial links have been established, however, and some of the pre-independence economic groupings have been preserved. The United Nations established an Economic Commission for Africa in 1958. In its first meeting, in January, 1959, there were only nine independent African states represented; the rest of the members were the colonial powers. Since then, ECA has become solidly African in membership, and from 1963 on, the Organization of African Unity (OAU), the African states' political organization, has virtually regarded ECA as its economic arm. The ECA has shown itself to be a useful center for initiating and coordinating economic and financial policy, as well as for improving economic data and policy.

## The African Development Bank

The ECA took the lead in preparing the charter and organization of the African Development Bank (ADB), which came into legal existence in August, 1964, and opened its doors for business in Abidjan, Ivory Coast, on July 1, 1966. The ADB's authorized capital is $250 million, of which half, or $125 million, was to be paid in by March, 1969, the remainder to be subject to call if needed to meet obligations. The ADB unfortunately started life with enormous handicaps. Membership was restricted to the independent African states, with the exception of South Africa, so that, unlike the other regional banks, the Inter-American and Asian, the ADB did not include any capital-exporting states (unless Libya eventually becomes such). To make matters worse, almost all countries have been in arrears on their capital subscriptions. These two considerations were bound to affect any attempt by the ADB to borrow in the capital markets of the world, and so far it has not done so. The membership provision also meant that recruitment of competent staff was hampered, since permanent staff from outside the region would always be vulnerable to pressure for replacement by personnel from within the region. And, unfortunately, there is a shortage of exactly the type of qualified staff the ADB needs in Africa, and few African governments would be willing to release the people they have. Consequently, by the end of the fourth year of ADB's existence it had not yet lent a total of $50 million, and there was serious need for reconsideration of the basis for the organization of the bank.* Early in 1970, meanwhile, the ADB had succeeded in interesting sufficient private banking and industrial interests in the developed countries as well as the International Finance Corporation of the World Bank Group to lay the basis for the creation of a multinational African Finance Corporation to help finance private investments in Africa.

Aside from the continental organizations just discussed, there are several regional economic organizations of importance in Africa.

### THE EQUATORIAL CUSTOMS AND ECONOMIC UNION

The equatorial African states—Gabon, Central African Republic, Congo (Brazzaville), and Chad—and Cameroon are united in a customs and economic union, the Union Douanière et Économique de l'Afrique Centrale (UDEAC). The objectives are not only to establish a common external tariff but to work out common internal economic policies in a number of important fields. The customs union came into effect among the equatorial states in 1959 and was extended to Cameroon in 1962; in December, 1964, the Treaty of Brazzaville set up an economic union to come into existence on January 1, 1966. Three organs were established: a council of chiefs of state to make policy, a *comité de direction* to work out the details of policy, and a secretariat to implement it.

On the customs side, the UDEAC system has as its main elements:

1. A common external tariff levied on all goods entering member states of the UDEAC except those from other members, from the

* In contrast, the Asian Bank lent in 1969, its second year of existence, $98 million. The Inter-American Development Bank in 1969 lent $631 million; it received $400 million to use for "soft" loans through its Fund for Special Operations, and it borrowed $177 million in the international capital markets in Germany, Italy, Austria, Sweden, Japan, and the United Kingdom, and from Latin American member nations.

European Economic Community, and from the African Associated states of the EEC. (See below, chap. IV.)

2. "Fiscal duties" (*droits d'entrée*) and turnover taxes levied on all goods coming into UDEAC nations except those from member states.

3. Exemption from import duty of goods circulating within UDEAC.

4. Common customs offices for all the countries and regular sharing of customs duties.

5. Creation of a Solidarity Fund excluding Cameroon. The Fund receives 20 per cent of all the common import duties levied by the common customs service. This does not apply to Gabon, which runs its own customs offices, except for goods to Gabon entering other territories. The bulk of the Fund is paid to Chad and the Central African Republic.

UDEAC will harmonize other tax, wage, and social policies and investment codes. The member states also agree to coordinate development programs and to secure an equitable distribution of industrial projects within the union. In this connection, there is to be an ingenious tax, paid by producing factories, with the proceeds to go to the countries where their goods are consumed. This will, among other things, compensate member states for any revenue loss from consuming goods originating within UDEAC rather than imports.

The UDEAC has already agreed on the location at Port Gentil, in Gabon, of an oil refinery to serve the area (its first), thus sensibly avoiding "oil-refinery inflation," which has strewn a score of oil refineries around the coasts of Africa, a good number of them of uneconomic size. It was also agreed that Cameroon should have the only match factory (but Congo [Brazzaville] has also built one financed by North Korea) and that Gabon should produce electric batteries for the whole area. The UDEAC enjoys several other common services, but these largely date from pre-independence: post and telecommunications, a savings-bank system, the Agence Transequatoriale des Communications (ATEC); * the customs service,

---

* ATEC operates the ports of Pointe Noire and Brazzaville in Congo (Brazzaville) and Bangui in Central African Republic; it operates the railway between Pointe Noire and Brazzaville and maintains the waterways from Brazzaville to Bangui and the highways connecting Chad and Gabon to the network.

export-quality-control services, etc. UDEAC members are also served by a common central bank and use a common currency.

The substantial step forward in economic cooperation represented by UDEAC began to be threatened by the end of the 1960's. In 1968, Chad and the Central African Republic announced their intention to withdraw; the latter returned, but Chad did drop out. In 1969, Congo (Brazzaville) announced that it was nationalizing all the assets in its territory of the common-service ATEC; the Central African Republic announced in response that it was nationalizing its port of Bangui and the Compagnie Générale des Transports en Afrique Equatoriale (CGTAE), which virtually monopolizes the river fleet. In spite of these actions, by early 1970 there had been no major disruption in the transport system.

If UDEAC continues, with the low level of development of its members' economies and the greater opportunities for producing for export to the rest of the world, it is likely that intra-UDEAC trade will grow fairly slowly. So far it has grown from around 6 per cent in 1958 to around 10 per cent in recent years.

THE CONSEIL DE L'ENTENTE

The Conseil de l'Entente, consisting of the Ivory Coast, Upper Volta, Niger, Togo, and Dahomey, is essentially political but has some economic significance in that it created a mutual-aid and loan-guarantee fund in 1966 to finance and guarantee foreign loans for investment projects. The total fund amounts to around $2.5 million a year, to which the Ivory Coast contributes $2 million; the remaining $500,000 is contributed by the others. The Conseil members also agreed to pool their credit and jointly guarantee international loans raised by any of its members to a total of $25 million equivalent a year. The Ivory Coast has agreed to seek no guarantees from the Fund before July, 1971. The members have equal voting rights despite their different subscriptions, and the Fund grants or withholds its support on the recommendation of a management committee composed of two representatives of each country. In 1970, the Entente states undertook to facilitate meat and livestock exports from the interior to the coastal states by improving cattle trails, setting common standards, giving uniform tax treatment, etc.

## THE EAST AFRICAN ECONOMIC COMMUNITY

The only other regional economic organization of major importance to its members is the East African Economic Community, consisting of Kenya, Tanzania, and Uganda. (Zambia, Ethiopia, Somalia, and Burundi have applied for membership, and discussions have been held. It is likely, however, that it will take many years before these countries become full-fledged members of the community.) On independence, the three countries of East Africa continued the substantial economic and financial cooperation that they had enjoyed as dependent territories. But this began to come apart in the mid-1960's. The existing community is based on a treaty signed in 1967 to preserve and to re-establish a large part of the cooperative relationship that was disappearing.

The treaty establishes an East African Community and a common market among the members. The common market, consisting of a common external tariff and internal freedom of movement of goods, is to be re-created over a period of eight to fifteen years. For the first fifteen years, each country is allowed to impose transfer taxes on goods produced in the other countries at rates below the common external tariff where this is necessary to protect existing or planned industries. A new East African Development Bank was set up in addition to the existing common-service corporations owned by the three states (which are listed below). In the interests of balanced industrial development in the three states, it was agreed to use fiscal incentives, the transfer tax, and the East African Development Bank, which is to divide its loans as follows: 38¾ per cent each to Tanzania and Uganda, 22½ per cent to Kenya, which is already more industrialized.

The community organization consists of the following:

The East African Authority—the three heads of states assisted by three ministers and a secretariat;

Five ministerial councils—Common Market Council, Communications Council, Economic Consultative and Planning Council, Finance Council, and Research and Social Council;

The East African Legislative Assembly, made up of legislators from the three countries;

The Common Market Tribunal;

The Court of Appeal;

Four Corporations—East African Railways, East African Harbors,

East African Airways, East African Posts and Telecommunications; The East African Development Bank.

Unlike the earlier arrangements, under which nearly everything was centered in Nairobi, Kenya, the headquarters for the various organizations have been distributed among the three countries: in Arusha, Dar-es-Salaam, and Mwanga, Tanzania; Kampala, Uganda; and Nairobi.

During the period of disintegration in East Africa, the earlier monetary union had been broken apart by the organization of separate central banks for each of the countries. The three countries have accordingly had to agree to harmonize their monetary policies as a part of setting up the community.

Unlike most of the rest of Africa, East Africa has long had economic ties, and these have contributed to a substantial trade among the countries. In 1965–67, 33 per cent of Kenya's exports, 6 per cent of Tanzania's, and 14 per cent of Uganda's went to the other East African countries. Total intratrade amounted to 18 per cent of the total exports of the three countries (somewhat below the comparable 21 per cent of the Central American Common Market). The individual-country figures, particularly the comparison between the low Tanzanian exports and the high Kenya exports, make clear where the tensions in maintaining the market lie.

AIR AFRIQUE

One of the most interesting examples of economic cooperation among the African states is in air services. In 1961, Air Afrique was formed by a treaty signed by eleven states: Cameroon, Central African Republic, Congo (Brazzaville), Ivory Coast, Dahomey, Gabon, Upper Volta, Mauretania, Niger, Senegal, and Chad. Each of these states has 6 per cent of the company's capital, and a private firm, SODETRAF, holds 34 per cent. SODETRAF (Societé pour le Développement du Transport Aerien en Afrique) is owned 75 per cent by Union Aero-Maritime des Transports (UTA) and 25 per cent by the French government's Caisse des Depots et Consignations. The eleven participating states, pooling their international rights, operate the interstate services in common. They also operate the Air Africa Services under an agreement signed in 1963 in cooperation with UTA. Some of these states operate national lines internally.

Shares in each of these are held 66 per cent by the state and 34 per cent by SODETRAF. There is in addition an organization called Agence de Securité de la Navigation (ASECNA), which runs the airports, supervises the construction of runways and hangars, includes telecommunications, and even runs airport restaurants. It is now financed fifty-fifty by France and the African states, including Mali as well as the member states of Air Afrique.

## THE ORGANIZATION OF SENEGAL RIVER STATES

The Organisation des États Riverains du Senegal (OERS) is composed of the West African states in the Senegal River basin—Guinea, Mali, Mauretania, and Senegal. It was founded in March, 1968, as an outgrowth of the Senegal River Committee, which began in 1963. Originally it was devoted to discussion of plans for the improvement of the Senegal River as a waterway and as a source of power and water for irrigation. The U.N. Development Program (UNDP) has helped to finance studies on these subjects—proposals for dams to improve navigation and to produce power, etc. With the passage of time and the ability of OERS to survive various political disagreements among the states, OERS has begun to discuss coordination of industrialization plans, scientific research, education, etc. In brief, OERS by 1970 was beginning to show promise of becoming a useful organ for the development of the whole Senegal River basin.

## OTHER INITIATIVES

There have been a large number of other attempts to create various economic and financial groupings. There are, for example, two multi-national central banks (see below, chap. IV). The French-speaking West African states, excepting Guinea, formed a new customs union after independence. The monetary union, consisting of a common central bank and currency, which existed under the French, still exists except for Mali and Guinea; the customs union largely broke down. In 1966, it was revived by the seven states of the customs union UDEAO (Union Douanière des États de l'Afrique de l'Ouest), consisting of Dahomey, Ivory Coast, Mali, Mauretania, Niger, Senegal, and Upper Volta. It provides for a common external tariff. Intraregional trade is subject to a duty equivalent to 50 per cent of the duties and taxes on imports from third countries. This can be increased to 70 per cent on commodities produced by existing industries for protective purposes. In May, 1970, the heads of state agreed to broaden the objectives to include economic and industrial as well as customs cooperation. A new organization, called the West African Economic Community, was to be created for this purpose by the seven states and any other states that wished to join them. This presumably is to supersede the existing agreement on a West African Economic Community that was initiated in 1966.

In November, 1966, twelve West African states (both French- and English-speaking, excluding only Guinea and Gambia) held an initial meeting to set up a West African Economic Community. In November, 1967, a meeting was held of an interim council of ministers. Articles of association have been signed expressing the desire of the twelve West African countries (Dahomey, Ghana, Ivory Coast, Liberia, Mali, Mauretania, Niger, Nigeria, Senegal, Sierra Leone, Togo, and Upper Volta) to establish a West African Economic Community. But so far, aside from intention, there have been no concrete steps taken to establish a functioning community.

On the other hand, there has been considerable progress by the African countries in establishing various informal associations that have substantial economic or financial impact. The ministers of finance of the former French colonies meet with the French Minister of Finance to discuss common problems and to prepare for international financial meetings. The English-speaking finance ministers do the same with their colleagues in the sterling area. The Central Bank governors of the African countries meet regularly. The groundwork laid in these meetings is probably an important reason why the African caucus of their representatives to the boards of governors meetings of the World Bank Group and the International Monetary Fund has had substantial impact on the policies of these institutions (e.g., in the new emphasis the World Bank Group has been giving to investment in agriculture and education, and in considering loans to government-owned industrial finance companies).

## Selected Bibliography

ABDEL-RAHMAN, A. "The Revenue Structure of the CFA Countries," *IMF Staff Papers* (International Monetary Fund), XII, No. 1 (March, 1965), 73–118.

AROWOLO, E. A. "The Taxation of Low Incomes in African Countries," *IMF Staff Papers*, XV, No. 2 (July, 1968), 322–42.

BARBER, W. J. *The Economy of British Central Africa*. London and New York: Oxford University Press, 1963.

BÉRARD, J-P. "Une république africaine moyenne." (Chapter xiii of Vol. I, *Planification en Afrique*.) Paris: Ministère de la Coopération, October, 1962.

BHATIA, R. J.; SZAPARY, GYORGY; and QUINN, BRIAN. "Stabilization Program in Sierra Leone," *IMF Staff Papers*, XVI, No. 3 (November, 1969), 504–22.

BRASS, WILLIAM; COALE, A. J.; DEMENY, PAUL; HEISEL, D. F.; LORIMER, FRANK; ROMANIUK, ANATOLE; and VAN DE WALLE, ETIENNE. *The Demography of Tropical Africa*. Princeton, N.J.: Princeton University Press, 1968.

COALE, A. J. "Population and Economic Development," in P. M. HAUSER (ed.), *The Population Dilemma*. Englewood Cliffs, N.J.: Prentice-Hall, for The American Assembly, 1963, pp. 46–69.

DEANE, P. M. *Colonial Social Accounting*. Cambridge and New York: Cambridge University Press, 1953.

DUE, J. F. *Taxation and Economic Development in Tropical Africa*. Cambridge, Mass.: M.I.T. Press, 1963.

FALLERS, L. A. "Social Stratification and Economic Processes," in M. J. HERSKOVITS and M. HARWITZ (eds.), *Economic Transition in Africa*. Evanston, Ill.: Northwestern University Press, 1964.

GLUCKMAN, M. "Social Anthropology in Central Africa," *Journal of the Royal Society of Arts* (London), CIII (August 5, 1955), 645–65.

HAZLEWOOD, ARTHUR (ed.). *African Integration and Disintegration*. Oxford Institute of Economics and Statistics and Royal Institute of International Affairs. London and New York: Oxford University Press, 1967.

HUNTER, G. *The New Societies of Tropical Africa*. London and New York: Oxford University Press, 1962.

Kenya Minister of Economic Planning and Development. *Family Planning in Kenya*. Report submitted by advisory mission of the Population Council of the U.S.A. Nairobi: The Ministry of Economic Planning and Development, 1968.

KIEWIET, C. W. de. *The Anatomy of African Misery*. London: Oxford University Press, 1956.

KUZNETS, SIMON, "International Differences in Capital Formation and Financing," *Capital Formation and Economic Growth*, National Bureau Committee for Economic Research, Princeton, N. J.: Princeton University Press, 1955, pp. 19–111.

MIRACLE, MARVIN P. " 'Subsistence Agriculture': Analytical Problems and Alternative Concepts," *American Journal of Agricultural Economics*, L, No. 2 (May, 1968), 292–310.

PLASSCHAERT, S. "Institutional Framework of Public Expenditure and Revenues in the Newly Independent Countries of French Africa South of the Sahara." Unpublished paper, International Bank for Reconstruction and Development, February, 1962.

PREST, A. R. *Public Finance in Underdeveloped Countries.* London: Weidenfeld & Nicolson, 1962; New York: Frederick A. Praeger, 1963.

———, and STEWART, I. G. *The National Income of Nigeria, 1950–51.* ("Colonial Research Studies, No. 11.") London: H. M. Stationery Office, 1953.

ROBSON, PETER. *Economic Integration in Africa.* London: George Allen and Unwin, 1968.

SAMUELS, L. H. (ed.). *African Studies in Income and Wealth.* Chicago: Quadrangle Books, for the International Association for Research in Income and Wealth, 1963.

SAXE, J. "Capital and Trade Flows in Newly Independent Countries: West Africa." Unpublished paper presented at Northwestern University Conference on Indigenous and Induced Elements in the Economics of Sub-Saharan Africa, Evanston, Ill., November 16–18, 1961.

SEERS, D. "The Role of National Income Estimates in the Statistical Policy of an Underdeveloped Area," *Review of Economic Studies,* XX, No. 53 (1952–53), 159–68.

U.N. ECONOMIC COMMISSION FOR AFRICA. "National Accounting in Africa," *Statistical Newsletter* (Addis Ababa), No. 18 (August, 1965), pp. 8–12.

———. "Public Finance in African Countries," *Economic Bulletin for Africa* (Addis Ababa), Vol. VII, No. 2 (June, 1961), chap. I.

# Technical Appendix

TABLE 1

Population (Mid-1967), GNP Per Capita (1967), and
Average Annual Growth Rates (1961–67)

| No. | Country | Population (1,000) | GNP Per Capita (US $) | Growth Rates Population (per cent) | Growth Rates GNP Per Capita (per cent) |
|---|---|---|---|---|---|
| 1 | Nigeria | 61,450 | 80 | 2.4 | 1.1 |
| 2 | United Arab Republic | 30,907 | 160 | 2.6 | 2.7 |
| 3 | Ethiopia | 23,667 | 60 | 1.9 | 2.7 |
| 4 | South Africa | 19,327 | 590 | 2.3 | 3.9 |
| 5 | Congo (Kinshasa) | 16,354 | 90 | 2.1 | —0.5 |
| 6 | Sudan | 14,355 | 90 | 2.9 | 0.2 |
| 7 | Morocco | 14,140 | 190 | 2.8 | 0.3 |
| 8 | Algeria | 12,540 | 250 | 2.2 | —3.5 |
| 9 | Tanzania | 12,181 | 80 | 2.5 | 1.9 |
| 10 | Kenya | 9,928 | 120 | 2.9 | 1.1 |
| 11 | Ghana | 8,139 | 200 | 2.7 | —0.1 |
| 12 | Uganda | 7,934 | 100 | 2.5 | 1.2 |
| 13 | Mozambique | 7,124 | 180 | 1.2 | 3.3 |
| 14 | Malagasy Republic | 6,350 | 100 | 2.4 | —0.5 |
| 15 | Cameroon | 5,470 | 130 | 2.2 | 0.6 |
| 16 | Angola | 5,293 | 190 | 1.4 | 2.1 |
| 17 | Upper Volta | 5,054 | 50 | 2.2 | —0.6 |
| 18 | Mali | 4,697 | 80 | 2.1 | 0.7 |
| 19 | Tunisia | 4,560 | 210 | 2.3 | 1.4 |
| 20 | Southern Rhodesia | 4,530 | 230 | 3.2 | 0.2 |
| 21 | Malawi | 4,130 | 60 | 2.4 | 3.2 |
| 22 | Ivory Coast | 4,010 | 230 | 2.8 | 5.4 |
| 23 | Zambia | 3,945 | 180 | 3.0 | 1.6 |
| 24 | Guinea | 3,702 | 90 | 2.7 | 2.5 |
| 25 | Senegal | 3,670 | 190 | 2.4 | —0.1 |
| 26 | Niger | 3,546 | 70 | 3.0 | 0.1 |
| 27 | Chad | 3,410 | 70 | 1.5 | —0.6 |
| 28 | Burundi | 3,340 | 50 | 2.0 | —0.1 |
| 29 | Rwanda * | 3,306 | 60 | 3.1 | 1.7 |
| 30 | Somalia * | 2,660 | 50 | 4.1 | —1.6 |
| 31 | Dahomey | 2,505 | 80 | 2.9 | 0.2 |
| 32 | Sierra Leone | 2,439 | 140 | 1.3 | 1.3 |
| 33 | Libya | 1,738 | 720 | 3.7 | 21.4 |
| 34 | Togo | 1,724 | 100 | 2.6 | 0.5 |
| 35 | Central African Rep. | 1,459 | 120 | 2.5 | —1.0 |
| 36 | Liberia | 1,110 | 190 | 1.7 | 1.5 |
| 37 | Mauretania | 1,110 | 130 | 1.9 | 6.9 |

TABLE 1 (Cont.)

| No. | Country | Population (1,000) | GNP Per Capita (US $) | Growth Rates Population (per cent) | Growth Rates GNP Per Capita (per cent) |
|-----|---------|-------------------|----------------------|-----------------------------------|----------------------------------------|
| 38 | Lesotho * | 885 | 60 | 2.9 | 1.2 |
| 39 | Congo (Brazzaville) | 860 | 190 | 1.5 | 1.7 |
| 40 | Mauritius * | 774 | 220 | 2.6 | —2.0 |
| 41 | Botswana * | 593 | 90 | 3.0 | 0.7 |
| 42 | Portuguese Guinea | 528 | 210 | 0.2 | 4.4 |
| 43 | Gabon | 473 | 410 | 0.8 | 3.5 |
| 44 | Réunion | 414 | 560 | 2.9 | 4.5 |
| 45 | Swaziland * | 385 | 280 | 2.9 | 15.4 |
| 46 | Gambia * | 343 | 90 | 2.0 | 2.3 |
| 47 | Equatorial Guinea | 277 | 240 | 1.8 | 4.7 |
| 48 | Comoro Islands | 250 | 110 | 3.6 | 4.5 |
| 49 | Cape Verde Islands | 236 | 110 | 2.4 | —1.9 |
| 50 | Ceuta and Melilla * | 161 | 280 | 0.9 | 3.4 |
| 51 | French Territory of Afars & the Issas | 83 | 580 | 1.5 | 7.4 |
| 52 | São Tomé and Príncipe | 63 | 280 | —0.2 | —0.3 |
| 53 | Ifni * | 54 | 150 | 1.4 | 3.2 |
| 54 | Seychelles Islands * | 49 | 60 | 2.2 | —0.6 |
| 55 | Spanish Sahara * | 48 | 210 | 2.3 | 3.9 |

* Estimates of GNP per capita and its growth rate are tentative.

TABLE 2
SECTOR DISTRIBUTION OF GROSS DOMESTIC PRODUCT
IN MAIN AFRICAN REGIONS, 1967

In Per Cent of Total GDP

| Sector | Maghreb * | Middle Africa * | South Africa |
|--------|-----------|-----------------|--------------|
| Agriculture | 18.8 | 43.2 | 11.6 |
| Mining | 10.8 | 5.8 | 12.2 |
| Manufacturing | 14.1 | 9.0 | 20.9 |
| Construction | 7.3 | 4.4 | 3.9 |
| Commerce | 16.3 | 12.2 | 13.3 |
| Transport | 5.8 | 5.5 | 9.6 |
| Other services | 13.4 | 9.4 | 18.9 |
| Public administration | 13.5 | 10.3 | 9.6 |
| Total | 100.0 | 100.0 | 100.0 |

* Maghreb = Algeria, Morocco, Tunisia. Middle Africa = rest of Africa, excluding Libya, United Arab Republic, and South Africa.
Figures are based on unweighted arithmetic means at factor costs of country national accounts in order to present an approximate representative pattern.

TABLE 3
ORIGIN AND USES OF RESOURCES IN AFRICAN REGIONS, 1967,
AS PER CENT OF TOTAL RESOURCES

|  | Maghreb | Middle Africa * | South Africa † |
|---|---|---|---|
| *Resources* |  |  |  |
| GDP | 97.5 | 98.0 | 102.0 |
| Net Imports | 2.5 | 2.0 | —2.0 |
| Total | 100.0 | 100.0 | 100.0 |
| *Use of Resources* |  |  |  |
| Private consumption | 67.4 | 70.4 | 62.9 |
| General govt. consumption | 16.9 | 14.0 | 12.4 |
| Gross domestic investment | 15.7 | 15.6 | 24.7 |
| Total | 100.0 | 100.0 | 100.0 |

* Excludes Botswana, Lesotho, and Swaziland.

† Includes Botswana, Lesotho, and Swaziland. Figures are for 1966, since 1967 was not a typical year. Because no separate balance-of-payments figures are available, in this table South African figures cover Botswana, Lesotho, and Swaziland.

Figures are unweighted arithmetic means in order to present an approximate representative pattern.

# III

# The African Heritage and Economic Growth

*In comparing African intellectuals with those from South Asia, particularly those from India, one sometimes gets the impression that the former, because they do not carry the same pretensions of ancient history, religion and philosophy, more easily accept the experimental and practical approach to life, and that they resemble ordinary farm boys who have made good in America or Sweden.*

GUNNAR MYRDAL

The African cultural and social background relevant to economic development is very different from that of any other developing region of the world. Because of Africa's geography, great size, and climate, it was only after 1900 that the influence of the rest of the world began to reach most of Africa south of the Sahara. Aside from South Africa, the Portuguese colonies, and a handful of African families in Dakar, Sierra Leone, and Ghana, the modernizing leaders or élite in every African country have come up in this historically brief period. In Latin America, most countries are either populated by people of European descent or derive their dominant group

59

wholly or partly from Europe. In Indonesia, the Dutch had 300 years, and in India, the British had 150 years to transmit a modernizing influence. In Africa, not only was the period much shorter but the contrast between twentieth-century technology and culture and traditional African culture was much sharper.

There are many universal problems faced by all nonindustrial economies, whether in Africa, Asia, or Latin America. Most of the following description of sixteenth- and seventeenth-century England could easily apply to the African economies of today!

> [The] . . . economy . . . was one in which the methods of production were simple and the units of production were small; in which middlemen . . . were both hated and indispensable; in which agricultural progress was seriously impeded by the perpetuation of communal rights over land. The chronic underemployment of labor was one of its basic problems and, despite moral exhortations, among the mass of people the propensity to save was low. . . . It was an economy heavily dependent on foreign sources for improved industrial and agricultural methods, and to some extent for capital, but in which foreign labor and businessmen were met with bitter hostility. In it ambitious young men often preferred careers in the professions and government service. . . . Men increasingly pinned their hopes on industrialization and economic nationalism to absorb its growing population; but industrialization was slow to come, and the blessings of economic nationalism proved to be mixed. (Fisher, pp. 17–18.)

But in some respects, at the time of independence, in 1960, the African economies were still not so far advanced as England was in the seventeenth century. In an English population of 5½ million in 1688, Gregory King listed 400,000 middle-class persons (doctors, lawyers, civil servants, officers, and merchants), 225,000 shopkeepers, and 240,000 artisans. Even as early as 1450, the diversification of occupation and craft technology was probably greater in England than in most of sub-Saharan Africa today. (Hunter, p. 7.)

Economic development cannot be separated from social and political transformation. The speed and the ease of economic development depend greatly on the character of the societies concerned. There are elements in African society that facilitate development and some that impede it. It is certainly worthwhile to try to identify those elements in the African cultural heritage and social structure that can positively help to shape Africa's economic future.

This does not mean that Africans should necessarily take another economic system or society—Western (or Communist)—as a model and assume that it is the ideal toward which Africa should move. It is far from sure that existing Western economic institutions or cultures secure the most rapid rate of economic growth or well-being. But, as they have so far been most successful in providing a reasonably rapid economic growth and a reasonably widespread diffusion of economic benefits, they do merit weighty consideration.

## The African Heritage

### OPENNESS TO INNOVATION

Zinkin has identified some ways of looking at life that are probably a precondition of economic growth. The most important of these are: "a widespread intellectual curiosity about material things" and "a willingness to accept change (not merely a willingness to innovate, but also a willingness to re-examine any tradition, custom, or belief which can be shown to stand in the way of growth)." (Zinkin, p. 2.) In general, the Africans rank fairly high on these measures. The African environment has been so difficult that in order to survive the Africans had to be much more flexible and open to new ideas than the traditional societies of Asia. As a leading anthropologist has pointed out:

> Rather than thinking of Africans as tradition-directed people perpetuating an ancient and stagnant culture, we might more accurately regard them as pragmatic frontiersmen with a persistent history of migration, settlement and resettlement of new lands, and of responding to the challenge of intertribal wars and the slave trade. In this historical perspective, Africans were experienced in adapting to and taking advantage of change, instability and movement, so that they were more prepared to adopt new paths of advancement offered by European institutions than were the populations of some of the more stable non-Western societies. (LaVine, p. 3.)

In most areas, Africans show exceptional willingness to adapt or change their institutions to the requirements of economic development. Indeed, the African openness to innovation is comparable to, or even perhaps greater than, that of the Japanese and American in the past:

Africans in general are the most present-minded people on earth.
. . . Without significant exceptions, all African leaders . . . share
the passionate desire to acquire all the good things which Western
civilization has produced in the two millennia of its history. They want
especially to get the technological blessings of American civilization,
and to do so as quickly as possible. The lack of historical conscious-
ness of their people gives the African leaders a great advantage in moving
rapidly toward this goal of modernization. They are not encum-
bered by written traditions, or by the visible and tangible physical
presence of the ruins of their own "civilized" past—as most Asians
have been. Therefore, they do not have to reconcile every innovation
with the different practices of their past. (Spiro, pp. 5–6.)

Unlike some other developing areas which depended or depend
on a socially or ethnically marginal group for innovation, the African
"elite" itself, like the American and Japanese, is open to innovation.
In those countries where a marginal non-African group exists, of
Europeans or Asians, let us say, those groups can function as a transmission belt bringing in new ideas and techniques from abroad,
rather than as the sole and alien embodiment of innovation. The
very fact that the African countries are conscious of being "new
nations" is in itself of great value, as it emphasizes to the African
people the value of "newness"—in ideas as well as things. Similarly,
the openness of Americans to technical innovation was and is probably related to the American feeling that the United States, although
possessing the oldest government on earth, is still a young country.

African willingness to learn has shown itself from the continent's
very first contacts with the rest of the world. For example, cassava
and maize spread rapidly through much of Africa as basic food crops
after they were introduced by early slave traders to some of the
coastal tribes, and this at a time when contact was limited and travel
difficult. Many other basic African foods (yams, bananas, plantains,
domestic forest goats and fowl) are also not indigenous but were
acquired in the course of limited contacts with South Asia.

This openness to change has been strengthened by the fact that
the African leaders have found in most cases little in the old African
traditions that they can use to help them and their people in the
twentieth century. Few of the old institutions have so far proved
usable for this purpose—the chiefs have been largely destroyed or

made powerless; even the local languages are irrelevant. In the past, some of the African social structures demonstrated an initially high resistance to innovation from outside: in the Akan system in Ghana, for example, there was a built-in system of checks and balances so that "decisions could not be effectively enforced from the top of the hierarchy without the concurrence of the lower levels of the political structure. . . ." In Buganda (Uganda), on the other hand, authority was concentrated at the top and flowed directly from top to bottom. Consequently, once the Kabaka decided to move, "Christianity and Western education made more progress within a quarter of a century in Buganda than they had in virtually 300 years of European contact with the coastal Akan." (Foster, pp. 25–26.)

Emphasis on the importance of economic development not only is not in conflict with the traditional African view of the world, but coincides with the African *Weltanschauung*. There has never developed in Africa, apparently, any religious scorn for the world's goods or any feeling that the body is an impediment to reaching perfection of the soul. Quite the contrary, "there is a certain tendency for traditional African religions to make the health, fertility, and prosperity of the living individual and living community matters of central importance. A great deal of the ritual communication which takes place between living persons and spirit world has as its object the maintenance or re-establishment of individual or group well being in a quite material, biological sense." (Fallers, p. 115.)

If the religious belief is assumed to be true, much of the traditional religious practices made good economic sense: If the only assurance of a good harvest or good health is the intervention of a supernatural power, expending resources on religious rites is merely investing wisely.

Traditionally, therefore, the African, like the modern American, is very much a hedonist, putting a high value on what he regards as the material comforts of this world. This does not mean that the traditional African has the same almost unlimited desire for material goods that the modern American has: his desires may be quite limited. But the important point is that there is nothing in the traditional African outlook that in and of itself tries to place a permanent ceiling on the dimensions of an African's wants or to discourage him from having any material wants at all.

## THE EXTENDED FAMILY

Perhaps even more important than religious outlook—both positively and negatively—is the influence of the continuing strength of the tribal ties to which nearly all Africans are subject. To begin with, one must consider the "lineage system," or "extended family"— under which an individual has deep ties with and feels obligation to a large number of people beyond the nuclear family of father, mother, and children. Good fortune is shared with many others, and in a crisis, one individual can call on help from many others. For survival value in a difficult environment, it would be hard to conceive of a better arrangement.

Unfortunately, in terms of potential economic development, the extended-family system has many drawbacks: it tends to discourage individual enterprise and initiative, as the burden of family obligations rises with the degree of an individual's success. A big man in the family is expected to be generous in helping others with school fees, doctors' bills, "bride-price," financing weddings and funerals, and hospitality to all relatives. Consciously or unconsciously, the knowledge that a greater income will mean correspondingly greater burdens must inhibit the efforts an individual puts forth.

There are other drawbacks: family crises tend to prevent accumulation of capital, or to drain away capital that may have been accumulated. Not only are savings in general held down, but the proliferation of small entrepreneurs is prevented. Because people with small incomes find it hard to comprehend the greater costs of living of individuals with higher incomes, a successful civil servant or company employee may be unable to withstand the pressure on him to contribute to other members of the family and still live in the style that he and his family believe is socially necessary. Hence, the temptation to accept bribes or to "borrow" from public or company funds may become great. As the expatriate manager of a bank operating in West Africa remarked to me—unconsciously revealing his own cultural biases as well as illuminating African ones—"It is very difficult for the African to learn to put his duty to his employer above his duty to his family."

One of the problems of small business everywhere is the difficulty the small businessman has in comprehending the difference between "income," on the one hand, and amortization and replenishment of capital, on the other. If he is under pressure to give help to meet some family crisis, convincing other members of the family that the cash he has in the till is not "income" may be almost impossible. This is, in fact, one of the main causes of the failure of some of the programs to provide loans to small businesses in Africa.

A book by Romain Gary takes as its central theme a remark by a Russian poet, Sacha Tsipotchkine: "Man—certainly. We are in perfect agreement—one day Man will appear. A little patience is still needed, a little perseverance; he cannot be more than 10,000 years away in the future. At the moment, there are only a few traces, a few presentiments, a few dreams. At this instant, the being who exists is only a pioneer of Man himself." In Africa, human beings may have evolved somewhat farther along the road to becoming "man" in relation to their extended family ties than is economically desirable at this time.

Emphasis on accumulating money as against meeting social obligations worried many people in the United States and Europe in the early years of industrialization. John D. Rockefeller was highly unpopular most of his life; English literature is replete with hostile references to the "New Men," such as in Dickens' *Hard Times.* But it can be argued that in this instance it was necessary to fall one step back in order to move farther forward.

When the first John D. Rockefeller was asked the secret of business success, he replied, "Never let your wife know how much money you are making." And, as a matter of fact, his wife was still doing her own laundry when he was already a millionaire many times over. In Africa, the secret of individual business success and of national economic development may turn out to be, "Never let your relatives know that you are making any money." This is not just a theoretical possibility but occurs in fact: "A small but apparently growing number of Digo and Duruma entrepreneurs are learning how to manipulate this system of sharing so that they obtain more aid and support than they give and are able to become successful businessmen in the developing market-exchange economy of the Kenya and Tanganyika coast. Certainly, one thing a coastal African should do to protect his assets and his reputation is to appear poor, hungry and needy." (Gerlach, p. 421.)

There are, of course, offsetting economic advantages of the extended-family system. The sixpences and shillings of many individuals can be pooled to finance the education of a bright child. In Nigeria, Ibo wage and salaried workers away from home band together for mutual aid and become channels for communicating ideas for development of the rural areas from which they come—and tax themselves to provide the necessary funds. (Katzin, p. 186.) Also in Nigeria, it was found that the extended family helped in the apprentice training of prospective entrepreneurs and in financing the establishment of new firms. (Nafziger, pp. 25–33.) In Nairobi, some of the workers from rural areas club together to finance small development projects; in Cameroon, the family is used as a surety for small loans to farmers; in Tanganyika, the family, using the cooperative system in some instances, pools funds to build maize mills and set up shops, and pools its credit to borrow from government agencies to help individual farmers.

In some cases, "the very desire to withhold extra earnings from one's family may deflect the more enterprising members of the family from a bureaucratic career (where earnings are fixed and a matter of public knowledge) into a business career (where earnings are uncertain and can be concealed). . . . Hence, even if the sharing implicit in the extended-family system is resented, the obligation to share may act like those taxes that stimulate individuals to greater effort at securing non-taxable gains (and at tax evasion)." (Hirschman, p. 387.)

On balance, the extended-family system in Africa so far has probably inhibited economic development more than it has helped, but it has a considerable potential for good—for example, if the extended family were guided more in the direction of acting as a kind of mutual-investment fund or trust, as in the Tanganyikan and other examples just cited, rather than of being a kind of social-service or welfare pool. If the family system became an effective way to collect small savings and use them to finance the enterprises of its most capable business members, it could become one of the most potent engines of economic development in Africa.

## Egalitarian African Society

An aspect of traditional Africa that is unqualifiedly favorable to development is the egalitarian nature of her society. There is no cultural or social differentiation as in India or even in Europe. In Africa, a man who has attained wealth or prestige is accepted as such; there is no "color bar" of "bluebloodedness" such as has plagued and to some extent still plagues Europe and, to a much lesser degree, the United States. The rewards of material success in Africa are, therefore, more satisfying, unspoiled by snubs from an earlier privileged class.

An even greater advantage of this egalitarianism is that talent can be recruited from the entire population. There are no class or caste barriers that an able African youngster must surmount like those that discourage members of certain castes in India or the sons of workers or peasants in Italy, Spain, or France. Most of Africa begins, therefore, at a stage that other societies reach only after long struggle—in which economic relations are regulated on the basis of achievement rather than by reason of traditional social rank or status.* (Hoselitz, p. 35.) African society, while still underdeveloped, already possesses the mobility among both classes and localities that Hoselitz regards as a necessary characteristic of an economically highly developed society. (Hoselitz, pp. 59–60.)

Again, because in Africa there were not the great differences in the distribution of material wealth that one finds in other underdeveloped regions, there is not a tradition of maintaining the status requirements of an upper class demanding large numbers of servants. This kind of waste is largely absent in Africa. But this is offset by the love of ostentation (when not sufficiently suppressed by the need to hide one's wealth from relatives) that to a large extent developed from the traditional African society. Showy possessions have replaced valor in war or skill in hunting as a criterion of being a "big man." "The retinue of a politician or district head must resemble that of an oriental potentate; . . . a graduate on his first job must possess a motor car that his counterpart in Britain might aspire to on retirement; . . . the laborer must possess a wrist watch and a fountain pen. . . ." (Wraith and Simpkins, p. 41.)

In a few areas of Africa, there has been a strong prejudice against certain kinds of work, and this prejudice may hinder the

---

* Ethiopia, the Sudan, Sierra Leone, and Liberia are partial exceptions to this generalization.

economy.* In the Sudan and Ethiopia, there is a bias against manual labor, on the grounds that it is fit only for slaves or serfs to do. In Ethiopia, there has been a prejudice against engaging in commerce. In Liberia and Sierra Leone, descendants of the settlers tend to regard only the government and the professions as proper occupations.

In no area of Africa, apparently, can one find a traditional attitude that there is a *positive* value in work as such, without regard to the material results. In the subsistence economy of tribal Africa, one did not find "inner-directed" individuals—driven to work hard, powered by inner guilt feelings. Nor is there evidence of the kind of personality found in and shaped by modern technological societies, to whom work is not just an economic imperative but a deeply felt habit or inner need. In traditional African society, the individual was "tradition-directed"; as in all traditional societies, time was regarded as the servant rather than as master. "Rationalism" or "efficiency" in effort or work had little priority; the important thing was the social enjoyment derived from performing a task rather than the rapidity or economy of effort. The acquisition of new attitudes toward work represents an important part of the effort toward economic development.

> The cultural situation of the educated African today may well favor a type of personality more suited, not to the enterprising Europe of the nineteenth century, but to the organized Europe of planning and giant companies and social conformity in the twentieth. Such a personality may lack the compulsive initiative and perseverance which still persists in the West as a relict of the first industrial revolution.
>
> It is remarkable how well such a view chimes with the present philosophy of African socialism. Perhaps instinctively African leaders incline toward the state-run economy as against competitive free enterprise, knowing that their peoples have neither the taste nor the capacity for this extreme of individualism and personal dedication to an economic aim. (Hunter, p. 325.)

---

* The bias toward the political sphere, reinforced under colonialism but stemming from good African roots, is, as mentioned in chap. I, above, detrimental to economic development. In traditional Africa, "whereas full-time specialization in craft production or trade is relatively rare, the specialist in government is quite common. . . . It is perhaps not going too far to assert that the *emphasis* in African systems of stratification is primarily political." (Fallers, p. 119.)

## THE POSITION OF WOMEN

The position of women in African society is another important influence on economic development. In the farming tribes, women are by custom the cultivators of the food crops grown for home consumption. However, when cash crops are added, the men assume the main responsibility. As these are frequently new crops, grown in a new way, by men who have no long tradition of husbandry to fall back on, it is not at all surprising that the men are more receptive to advice and, consequently, that these cash crops are more efficiently grown. (See below, chap. V.) (This factor may also explain why in the cattle-raising tribes, where the men traditionally looked after the herds, progress in moving into a money economy, by upgrading and selling cattle, is so much slower than in the agricultural tribes.)

As in practically all underdeveloped areas (it was true in the early years of the United States), the position of women is such that when school space is available but limited, boys get priority. (The Chagga in Tanganyika and, according to Dr. Hilda Kuper, some tribes in South Africa are exceptions.) And in general the women keep in closer contact with the countryside and the slower, rural way of life. Women either spend more time in the country on visits or may actually be left there to cultivate the farm while the husbands work in the city. They are more apt, therefore, to preserve traditional customs and remain conservative. Even in West Africa where women are active in trade and may frequently travel, their lack of education and their conservatism prevents the economy from getting the kind of impulse to growth that similar activity performed by men would impart. Félix Houphouet-Boigny, President of the Ivory Coast, is reported to have said, most perceptively, that the time necessary for Africa to catch up with the West is "three generations of mothers."

The African tradition that as a man succeeds he takes on additional wives becomes a detriment in urban life; it is perhaps the most important cause of failure of shopkeepers in Tanganyika. The wives of a shopkeeper compete to see who can get the most goods and money out of the shop for her own use. Unfortunately, only in rare cases will a wife in East Africa be educated enough to be able to run the shop on her own—though there are cases of a man with several wives using them to run a chain of shops. (Mhina, p. 9.)

ECONOMIC RATIONALITY

It was a cardinal tenet of some European "old hands" in Africa that Africans do not behave in an economically rational fashion. Of course, there are very few persons anywhere in the world who behave as a completely rational "economic man," and those who do are often insufferable; the question is really whether Africans are sufficiently motivated by economic considerations to make economic policy meaningful. The answer by economists has been unanimously "Yes." Whenever African economic behavior has seemed irrational to the outside observer, it has seemed so because of an insufficient understanding of the major forces in the African environment influencing that behavior. As a matter of fact, agricultural schemes and industrial incentives in industry that have failed in Africa often did so because the African farmers or workers figured out what would pay them best more accurately than the people who set up the schemes.*

The accusation of economic irrationality is usually couched in the terms that giving the African higher prices for produce or higher pay for work does not result in greater effort or more regular work—that better prices or wages may, in fact, result in lower output since the African will get the sum of money he wants more quickly. In actual fact, this phenomenon of the "target" worker (the worker who works to acquire a given sum of money to buy a given set of goods and is not interested in earning more) is not new. It was first identified in Western Europe when the European countries were beginning their industrialization. Max Weber described it as follows:

> A peculiar difficulty has been met with surprising frequency: raising the piece-rates has often had the result that not more but less has been accomplished in the same time, because the worker reacted to the increase not by increasing but by decreasing the amount of his

---

* One of the cultural curiosities of the behavior of economists over the last twenty years is the need that we have felt to investigate whether people in underdeveloped economies behave in economically rational ways. After considerable research, the answer, whether for India, Africa, or Latin America, is always found—though sometimes reported in a tone of surprise—to be positive. Actually, anthropologists half a century ago had already established that even very primitive peoples act completely rationally in areas where experience has taught them that they can control events by their own actions and resort to magic only where this is not true.

work. . . . [The worker] did not ask: how much can I earn in a day if I do as much work as possible? but: how much must I work in order to earn the wage, 2½ marks, which I earned before and which takes care of my traditional needs? (*The Protestant Ethic and the Spirit of Capitalism.*)

In economic terms, this phenomenon is a backward-bending supply curve for labor—i.e., the supply of labor called forth by a higher wage at a certain point bends backward and decreases instead of increasing with an increase in wages. But such behavior is completely rational. When what an individual wants to purchase with money is limited, when he has satisfied all these wants, and when the need to save money for unknown needs in the future either is not yet felt or is satisfied, it is quite understandable (and economically sensible) to stop work sooner and enjoy more leisure when the pay rate goes up. And, in fact, this happens quite frequently in highly developed societies when people's incomes for some reason shoot up more rapidly than their wants grow.

When Africa was being opened up to the outside world, the need for laborers to build railways or ports often grew more rapidly than the Africans' desires for goods bought with money. Consequently, until World War I, the governments in most parts of Africa tried to make Africans work through direct compulsion or by imposing a head tax paid in money (which forced the Africans to go out to earn the money). Indeed, such measures were quite prevalent up to World War II—the Congo-Ocean railway in Equatorial Africa was built in this way—and in Portuguese territories until very recently. Where governments were unwilling to engage in such practices or felt that they would not be effective enough, laborers were recruited outside of Africa—such as the Indians who were brought in to build the Kenya-Uganda railway and to work on sugar estates in Natal, or the Chinese who were recruited for the gold mines on the Rand in South Africa.

The backward-bending supply curve for labor is no longer a major problem in Africa, however, as far as the over-all supply of labor is concerned. (In those areas where shortage of labor is still experienced, as in parts of Liberia or the Portuguese territories, it is more probably due to wages being kept too low to attract a sufficient supply of labor than to wages being too high.) There are several forces operating: the level of income an African earns when remaining on the land, the level of wages necessary to induce him to leave the land, the amount of money that is his target income, and the number of individuals affected by these forces. As far as the individual African worker is concerned, the amount of wage labor he is willing to do tends to be inversely related to changes in village income and to changes in wage rates in the exchange sector. In the early years, once a worker got the sum of money he wanted, he quit. Now, a target income becomes more and more remote as an individual's wants increase in number and variety; it is of little significance to the "committed" workers in urban areas, who no longer move back and forth between the land and wage employment.*

In short, the shape of the aggregate labor supply curve—giving the total labor supply at each wage level—depends on the net outcome of two contrary changes accompanying each wage rise: changes in the number of people induced into wage employment; and changes in the average time each man spends at work. In the early days, the curve probably tended quite soon to turn backward: an increased wage induced only a few new laborers into employment and encouraged many already there to cut short their stay. In present-day Africa, this is no longer true: an increased rate stimulates more men to emigrate to paid jobs and leads far fewer to reduce their time in paid employment. When one remembers the great extent to which Africans move from country to country to get work, it is most unlikely that for any given country for any long length of time the aggregate labor supply would decrease when wages are raised. (Berg, pp. 468–92.)

In general, these remarks apply to African farmers too: if income rises more rapidly (due to rising prices or extraordinarily good crops) than the farmer acquires new wants, his labor supply curve will bend backward at some point. Normally, with the passage of time and the spread of education, formal and informal, however, this point

* An important factor in increasing the supply of labor in many areas has been the "push" from the rural areas resulting from the increased difficulty of attaining a desirable livelihood on the land. This may be due to the growing pressure of population on the land, given present levels of agricultural techniques and organization, accentuated in some parts of southern and eastern Africa by the forcible restriction of agriculture to confined areas in the "reserves." The pressure is also increased by the persistence in parts of Africa of "cattle culture," which leads to overgrazing and spreading poverty.

becomes less and less relevant. But in many areas in agriculture, unlike wage labor, the backward-bending supply curve may still be relevant to economic policy. If a worker quits, it is possible to find another worker; but if a farmer does not want to pick the last 10 per cent of his cotton crop, the crop is that much smaller. And it will still be true in most areas that not knowing just where the bending point is will be a handicap in forming agricultural policy.

### The Colonial Inheritance

The existing economic structures of the African states were influenced, shaped, and sometimes created by colonial regimes and their relationships to the metropolitan powers. The export trade and production, the systems of transport, the commercial, financial, monetary, tax, fiscal, and administrative structures—all were created during Africa's colonial period and have not been greatly modified since. It would be easy to criticize much of what was done or undone in the colonial period from the purely ideal standpoint of what the governing powers *should* have accomplished, especially if one applies present-day criteria. But, on the same basis, the policies applied to the European populations by their pre-war governments were scarcely better. There is no country in Africa, moreover, that suffered as severely from a laissez-faire colonial power as Ireland did, for example. In the main, it is practically indisputable that most of the lands of Africa that were formerly colonies are considerably richer materially as a result of their colonial heritage.

### THE CIVIL SERVICES

On the plus side, a number of nonmaterial assets were acquired that give most African countries some advantages over other underdeveloped countries elsewhere in the world—good systems of justice, good civil services, and a good tradition of civil-service behavior. Independent African countries have, with two notable exceptions, preserved independent judiciaries that administer the laws in an impersonal and reasonably equitable manner—certainly a necessary and favorable condition for economic progress. In all the African countries, quite obviously much more could have been done, if men had been wiser and more farsighted, to train Africans to take over the civil service. Nevertheless, the tradition of honesty and (relative) efficiency in government service is a valuable economic asset. The high prestige of the civil service in itself is also helpful, although this has its drawbacks, of course, in attracting too many of the able young Africans into the government and away from the rest of the economy.

This latter tendency is also reinforced by a most unfortunate legacy of colonialism—the very high salaries of ministers and top civil servants.

> It was inevitable that as local persons invaded the senior ranks of the service their emoluments should bear a close relation to those of their expatriate colleagues in the same or similar posts. This has had a distorting effect on the whole of the salary structure. Even where an expatriation or inducement element was introduced, the gap between the lowest paid and the senior service officers of local origin was very wide indeed and still remains unhealthily wide. (Adu, p. 21.)

The result is that, whereas in the United States, for example, top civil-servant salaries are at the maximum only four or five times the average wages of an unskilled laborer, in Africa the ratio will be more like 30–50 to 1.*

This "neo-colonialism" in top government salaries and prerequisites (houses, cars, travel allowances) swallows up an enormous share of government receipts (in the francophone African countries, two thirds of current government expenditures), thus reducing the amounts available for public investment or economic services connected with development. It also has an unfortunate impact on the economy generally. To begin with, it sets too high a standard of consumption and reduces savings available for investment. It also stimulates political unrest—always unfavorable for economic growth. High living standards of "expatriates" in the colonial period were in a way more tolerable, since the mass of people did not feel they

* The United States, in its first years, suffered from a similar carryover of a colonial pattern of privilege. Thomas Jefferson, upon taking office, gave up his coach-and-four and other colonialist luxuries. Julius Nyerere's attempt to impose austerity in Tanzania on the "Ba-Benz"—the "tribe" of government officials who drive Mercedes-Benz cars—by cutting salaries and eliminating colonialist prerequisites is so far the most notable Jeffersonian example in Africa.

could aspire to them; in the end, these unattainable standards and privileges were a factor in the demand for independence. But, when it is *Africans* themselves who are driving around in limousines, the mass of people more readily feel that they too should receive immediate and tangible benefits from their nation's independence and, when they do not, think of overthrowing the government. Such feelings were openly expressed in the Congo (Brazzaville) revolution in 1964, for example. Ready-made leaders for rebellion are already at hand in the "second generation"—the new university graduates who find that all of the "plums" have gone to men just a few years older than themselves, who are often less well qualified and who will not be retiring to make way for them for many years.

THE SCHOOL-LEAVER PROBLEM

The wage and salary structure left behind by the colonial powers is in large part responsible for a growing problem in modern Africa: the so-called school leavers, usually young men who have had a certain minimum education (elementary or junior secondary) but who are unable to find employment with position and income to match their training.* The problem is essentially that the wage and salary structure was set when the number of educated or partly educated people was very small, and the jobs that required trained personnel consequently paid well in comparison to what the mass of people earned in unskilled agricultural labor. (The salaries included a substantial element of quasi-rent, in other words.) With the rapid expansion in education, the number of people qualified for these few jobs has become a flood, but the wage and salary structure has not adjusted to the change, nor has the economy grown sufficiently or in such a way to absorb these people.

What happens, then, is that a youth who has gone to school with the expectation of getting a clerical position may prefer to remain unemployed for months or years, waiting for an opening to turn up, rather than go back to farm work and miss the glittering prize of work in a white collar. Moreover, his family, who have made many

---

* Foster has shown that the unemployed school leaver first appeared as a problem in the early 1840's in the Gold Coast and remained "a chronic feature during colonial times." Since independence, the problem has become much more prominent and is increasing.

sacrifices to send him to school, will regard him as a failure if, after all that education, he becomes a farmer like his uneducated brothers.

This is not the first time this kind of unemployment has been a major problem in Africa. The so-called poor-white problem in South Africa in the 1920's and 1930's was similar. During this period, as many as 220,000 "poor whites," one ninth of the European population, migrated from the rural areas to the towns. The difficulty was that the salary and wage structure for whites was much higher than for the other races in the Union of South Africa, and the jobs at the "white" level were considerably fewer than the number of "poor whites" demanding them. The government eventually took action to support the "poor whites" at the higher standard of living they demanded, and, after a generation of rapid economic growth, the South African economy grew sufficiently to absorb and afford the "poor whites" at the higher income level. Certainly, by the middle 1950's, the "poor white" problem had vanished.

Nor is this phenomenon unique to Africa: Italy experienced similar "sociological unemployment" during the postwar period, as peasants, principally from the south, moved from the country to the cities at a rate faster than regular jobs could be provided for them. Somewhat as in Africa, the city earnings were kept up above the real market price by trade-union and government action.

At present, in Africa, the number of men who can live in a town without regular work is in part determined by the number of opportunities there are for picking up odd bits of work or money, as was the case in Italy. In Africa, another, perhaps more important, factor is also at work: the responsibility the African feels for his brother, in the widest sense of the word. A man in the city, earning what is regarded as a good income by his relatives in the country, often finds himself having to support his unemployed relatives, who come and live off him. He may continue to acquire dependents until his (and his immediate family's) average standard of living sinks to something like the average enjoyed by his rural relatives, or until he or his wife rebels.

Some measures are now being taken to narrow the great discrepancy in income between skilled urban and unskilled rural labor—from both sides of the gap. On the one hand, attempts are being made to improve agricultural productivity and raise agricultural incomes. On the other, governments are trying to be careful not to raise urban incomes still further where there is an oversupply of applicants. In Rwanda, Tanzania, Nigeria, and Dahomey, steps have been taken to reduce the incomes of certain urban groups. To some extent, the inflation that occurred in Ghana, Mali, and the Congo (Kinshasa) served a similar purpose: the rise in prices helped to bring the real urban wage and salary structure into line with agricultural income, in a new relationship more appropriate for the new conditions of the economy.

## EXCESSIVE EXPECTATIONS FOR PUBLIC SERVICES

The paternalistic attitude of the colonial administrations, particularly after World War II, also left behind the habit of expecting considerable benefit from free public services—free schools, free medical services, free roads, free water, free sewerage, free or subsidized electricity, and subsidized housing.

The colonial governments provided most of these for Africa's cities —usually at the expense of the agricultural population. But with the growth of the cities, and the quite legitimate political demand for the expansion and extension of these services throughout the land, it becomes financially impossible to maintain them on the uneconomic basis of the past. It is also economic nonsense to consume resources in subsidies rather than use them for economic development.

Throughout the world, pressure for such services is present. The way it is kept in line with what is economically feasible is either to charge the economic price (as is the case in most places for electricity, water, and sewerage) or to hand over responsibility for the services to the *local* government concerned—in which case the citizens can make a direct choice between paying higher taxes (to get better education for their children, for instance) or using their money for other purposes. But, with the usual African centralization of responsibility for these services in the national government, this economic calculus does not occur so immediately and directly. Pressure for the services thus tends to lead the African governments constantly to increase their expenditures for them and to give lower priority to other investments that might in fact result in faster growth of the national income.

TECHNOCRATS AND MICRO-STATES

Two other legacies of colonialism also deserve mention, although extended discussion of them would lead us far afield from the central subject of this book. The first of these is the colonial regimes' over-emphasis on technocratic considerations.

"A colonial regime is essentially one of bureaucratic authoritarian-ism. . . . . The public does not participate in the political process; it is 'administered' by a bureaucratic elite, which by the system's definition knows what is best." (Coleman, pp. 46–47.) Aside from the political implications of this state of affairs, there are impor-tant economic and financial implications. The colonial bureaucrats in the technical services were often themselves technicians—doctors in charge of health services, engineers in charge of public works, etc. When they were not, the "lay" administrators of such services in-evitably tended to be overinfluenced by their views on appropriate standards and quality of services—to avoid losing the battle for control to them, or to mitigate their power. The result was that in much of colonial Africa, standards were set uneconomically high; too much money was spent on high-priced, well-equipped, expensive central hospitals, while rural dispensaries were starved for funds. Effective use of educational funds in many instances also suffered from the same attitude of "the best is none too good." African coun-tries have as a consequence been saddled with high maintenance costs and overly high construction standards that they find hard to change.

In the French territories and to some extent in the British terri-tories, civil-servant rule meant a lack of coordination among the services—each department jealously maintaining its prerogatives and rivalries. "The nomination of ministers to posts previously run by chiefs of service and directors has only reinforced these inconven-iences. There is an urgent necessity, for reasons of effectiveness and of economy, to regroup the ministries in relation to the development objectives; for example, a single ministry of rural development re-placing advantageously the distinct ministries of livestock and agri-culture." (Bérard, p. 40.)

Finally, there is what Léopold Senghor, President of Senegal, has called the "micro-state." Of the forty-three independent nations in the whole of Africa in 1970, twenty-eight had populations of less

than 5 million. The cost of maintaining a full-fledged governmental apparatus—with a full set of ministers, foreign representation,
etc.—is, viewed objectively, an absurd waste of funds for these
micro-nations. As for creating new industries, the size of the state
should not in theory be a handicap. By organizing a multi-state
customs union or free-market area, it should be possible to build
up markets of sufficient size to justify many new industries. In
practice, however, the play of political forces makes the establishment of such larger multi-national markets almost impossible. And,
where politics does not stand in the way, working out the details of,
negotiating, and maintaining such arrangements entail an immense
use of scarce economic, financial, and diplomatic talent—far better
used for negotiations to secure aid, commodity-support agreements,
etc. In reality, therefore, the political boundaries of the micro-states
that break up Africa into many small market units are real barriers
to the possibilities of economic development in Africa.

## Selected Bibliography

ADU, A. L. *The Civil Service in New African States*. London: Allen &
Unwin, 1965.

BÉRARD, J-P. *Planification en Afrique*. Paris: Ministère de la Coopération,
October, 1962.

BERG, E. J. "Backward-Sloping Labor Supply Function in Dual Economies—The Africa Case," *Quarterly Journal of Economics* (Cambridge, Mass.), LXXV, No. 3 (August, 1961), 468–92.

BIESHEUVEL, S. *Race, Culture, and Personality*. Johannesberg: South
African Institute of Race Relations, 1959.

CALLAWAY, A. "School Leavers and the Developing Economy of Nigeria," in R. O. TILMAN and T. COLE (eds.), *The Nigerian Political
Scene*. Durham, N.C.: Duke University Press, 1962, pp. 220–40.

COLEMAN, J. S. "The Character and Viability of African Political Systems," in W. GOLDSCHMIDT (ed.), *The United States and Africa*.
Rev. ed. New York: Frederick A. Praeger, for The American Assembly,
1963, pp. 39–73.

FALLERS, L. A. "Social Stratification and Economic Processes," in M. J.
HERSKOVITS and M. HARWITZ (eds.), *Economic Transition in Africa*.
Evanston, Ill.: Northwestern University Press, 1964, pp. 113–30.

FISHER, F. J. "The Sixteenth and Seventeenth Centuries: The Dark Ages
in English Economic History?," *Economica* (London School of Economics), new series, XXIV, No. 93 (February, 1957), 1–19.

FORDE, D. "The Cultural Map of West Africa: Successive Adaptations

to Tropical Forests and Grasslands," in SIMON and PHOEBE OTTEN-
BERG (eds.), *Cultures and Societies of Africa*. New York: Random
House, 1960, pp. 116–38.

FOSTER, PHILIP. *Education and Social Change in Ghana*. London:
Routledge & Kegan Paul, 1965.

GERLACH, L. P. "Socio-Cultural Factors Affecting the Diet of the Northeast Coastal Bantu," *Journal of the American Dietetic Association*,
XLV, No. 5 (November, 1964), 420–24.

HIRSCHMAN, A. O. "Obstacles to Development: A Classification and a
Quasi-Vanishing Act," *Economic Development and Cultural Change*
(University of Chicago), XIII, No. 4, Part 1 (July, 1965), 385–93.

HOSELITZ, B. F. *Sociological Aspects of Economic Growth*. Chicago:
Free Press, 1960.

HUNTER, G. *The Best of Both Worlds*. London, New York, and Toronto: Oxford University Press for the Institute of Race Relations,
1967.

————. *The New Societies of Tropical Africa*. London and New York:
Oxford University Press, 1962.

JONES, W. O. "Economic Man in Africa," *Food Research Institute
Studies* (Stanford University), I, No. 2 (May, 1960), 107–34.

KATZIN, M. "The Role of the Small Entrepreneur," in HERSKOVITS and
HARWITZ (eds.), *op. cit.*, pp. 179–98.

LEBEUF, J. B. *L'habitation des Fali (Cameroun)*. Paris: Hachette, 1962.

LEVINE, R. *Dreams and Deeds*. Chicago: University of Chicago Press,
1966.

LEWIS, W. A. "Aspects of Economic Development." Paper presented at
1965 Council on World Tensions, African Conference on Progress
Through Cooperation.

LYSTAD, R. A. "Basic African Values," in W. A. LEWIS (ed.), *New
Forces in Africa*. Washington, D.C.: Public Affairs Press, 1962, pp.
10–24.

MHINA, J. E. F. "African Traditions Which Affect Economic Development." Unpublished paper, 1965.

McCALL, D. F. "Dynamics of Urbanization in Africa," in Ottenberg
(eds.), *op. cit.*, pp. 522–35.

NAFZIGER, E. W. "The Effect of the Nigerian Extended Family on
Entrepreneurial Activity," *Economic Development and Cultural
Change*, University of Chicago, XVIII, No. 7, Part I (October, 1969),
25–33.

ROBERTSON, H. M. *South Africa*. Durham, N.C.: Duke University Press,
1957.

ROBINSON, E. A. G. (ed.). *Economic Consequences of the Size of Nations*. (Proceedings of a Conference of the International Economic
Association.) London: Macmillan, New York: St. Martin's Press, 1960.

SPIRO, H. J. *Politics in Africa*. Englewood Cliffs, N.J.: Prentice-Hall,
1962.

WRAITH, R., and SIMPKINS, E., *Corruption in Developing Countries.* London: George Allen & Unwin, 1963.

ZINKIN, MAURICE. "Cultural Change and Economic Development." Paper presented at S.I.D. Eleventh World Conference, New Delhi, November, 1969.

# IV

# Africa's Economic and Financial Position in the World Scene

*The colonial powers in fact abandoned their empires in Black Africa with remarkable alacrity. Without wishing to pretend to psychoanalyze this operation, one might well ask about the motives: why was this disengagement so easily accepted by the Belgians, the Britons, and the French? . . . If the European nations had considered Africa of vital importance, the transfer of power would not have been so easy.*

RENÉ SERVOISE

The modern part of Africa is in many basic ways a part of the Western world and is particularly close to Western Europe. While Africa is an important element in the origins of many Americans and Brazilians and among many of the Caribbean nationalities, and while Africa is an important influence in the cultures of these countries, Africa's main economic, cultural, and educational ties today are with Western Europe. English and French are Africa's primary official and modern languages. African educational systems grew from a European base, and European teachers are still an important, if not majority, element; 50,000 African students and trainees are studying in Western Europe (10,000 in the United States and 8,000 in the nations of Eastern Europe, the Soviet Union, and China).

Still, while these relations with the rest of the world, notably Western Europe, are vital to Africa's well-being and development, to the rest of the world, economic relations with Africa, while valuable, are of comparatively little importance. Africa is of scarcely more than marginal economic significance for the United States, whose stake in Cuba or Central America, for example, has been a good deal larger. And, in today's world, with the enormous flexibility arising from the development, or possibility, of new techniques and synthetics, and with the prevalence of full employment and rapid economic growth in industrialized countries, it is hard to maintain that loss of contact with any one underdeveloped region would be disastrous for any industrialized country. The underdeveloped regions, indeed, have lost in relative importance in world trade during recent years, their share going from one third of the total in 1950 to around one sixth in 1970. Trade with Africa amounts to less than 5 per cent of total world trade; West European trade with Africa is less than 10 per cent of total West European trade.

There is no doubt that loss of African supplies and markets would perceptibly affect the West European economy, but, on the whole, it could be taken in stride. No European country has the stake in sub-Saharan Africa that the Dutch had in Indonesia, for instance, nor has any European nation suffered in Africa that almost complete loss of assets and trade which the Dutch suffered in Indonesia; yet the Netherlands was never so prosperous as she has been since the "loss" of her empire there. There is no reason to believe that the loss of trade with or investments in Africa would cause greater damage to a European country than the loss of Indonesian trade and investments did to the Dutch.

As a matter of fact, it can be argued that, whatever the reasons for the extension of European domination over Africa during the nineteenth century, the economic history of the years since World War II has demonstrated that there were no *economic* reasons for the continuation of European colonial empires. The Marxist-Leninist idea that underdeveloped countries, including those of Africa, were vital to imperial powers as an outlet for investment no longer has any real basis, even in theory. (See also below, chap. IX.) As John

Strachey has pointed out, Lenin's theory of imperialism was destroyed by historical fact:

> There is not the slightest doubt that Lenin regarded the inevitability of a falling standard of life for the wage-earners and farmers within the highly-developed capitalisms as the thing which made the whole imperialist process inevitable. . . .
> He expressly states, although purely for the sake of argument, that *if* the standard of life of the wage-earners and agriculturalists could be raised at home, then the whole imperialist drive would no longer be inevitable. This neglected passage occurs at the beginning of his Chapter IV [of *Imperialism*]. . . .
> This passage is in some ways the most important in Lenin's book. For a steady increase in the standard of life of the masses and a rapid development of agriculture are precisely what *has* happened in, for example, both Britain and America. (Strachey, pp. 110–11.)

In short, the economic importance of Africa for the rest of the world depends on its value as a trade partner, and, at present, this value is not very great. This somewhat chastening fact is mitigated, however, by several factors. The first is that Africa has a valuable mineral and energy potential that may become of considerable interest to the rest of the world. (See below, chap. VI.) Secondly, the African countries should become more valuable partners as time goes on and their economic development continues—in absolute terms, even if not relatively. Finally, bilateral relationships in any case are not so important as they were prior to World War II. (See below, chap. XI.) Since World War II, international economic and financial developments are more and more influenced by policy decisions taken in multilateral economic and financial organizations. African countries have made it a point to join the United Nations and the U.N. specialized agencies, where most of these decisions are taken. There, they have the opportunity to participate in decisions affecting the world economy and, in turn, deeply affecting them. The changed arrangements for association of the eighteen African countries with the European Economic Community—from the original plan, where Africans were not represented in the decision-making organs, to the present one, where the associated African members have a full voice —is another example of how Africans can influence the international community and affect the impact the outside world has on their dependent economies.

In the main, on independence the new governments inherited "colonial economies." Before World War II, and in the extreme case even in 1960, these were still largely "enclave" economies. That is to say, there were small enclaves of production of tropical agricultural products or minerals for export abroad with very little contact with the rest of the subsistence nonmonetary economy. As John Stuart Mill pointed out, these enclaves were areas "where England (or France AMK) finds it convenient to carry on the production . . . of a few tropical commodities. . . . They were not countries with a productive capital of their own." In the extreme case, even when the export was produced by small farmers, foreign capital and management controlled the collection and marketing of the crop.

In some countries by 1960 and in nearly all countries by 1970, this simple pattern no longer existed. Public authorities or cooperatives now control or manage the marketing of the principal export crops. In a series of nationalizations at the end of the 1960's, the governments also acquired a voice in the export mineral industries. (See below, chap. VI.) Some beginnings have also been made at creating a national economy (by the building of roads, encouragement of production for the home market, etc.) that integrates the rest of the country into the same money economy as the export enclave. In some cases, as in Ghana, the export "enclave," in fact, has grown to affect so much of the economy that it can scarcely be called an enclave any more. However, largely because of the still low level of economic development, the growth rate of African economies is still largely determined by the amount of capital and trained personnel they secure from abroad and by the fortunes of their primary product exports.

## Aid and Trade

### Dependence on Non-African Capital and Personnel

Except for South Africa, Libya, Algeria, and possibly Nigeria within the decade of the 1970's, which are now able to finance economic growth without major help from abroad, Africa still depends on a flow of capital from the industrialized countries to help in economic development. (See also below, chap. IX.) Funds from non-African sources have financed a very high proportion of capital formation in Africa—over-all, according to the Economic Commission for Africa, half of Africa's total capital formation in 1950–57. In 1970, the proportion is more like one fifth, but in some countries, such as Upper Volta or Niger, it is nearer 100 per cent. In nine of the ex-French territories, French aid was also needed to balance the recurrent budget at the time when independence was won (1960), but by 1970 most of them no longer need this. In many African countries, at least half and sometimes all of the investment in the *public* sector is normally expected to be financed from abroad. But this is not unusual for small countries in the development phase. In Sweden from 1860 to 1890, more than half of domestic net capital investment came from abroad; Canada had the same degree of dependence in the early years of this century. (Kuznets, p. 38.)

A thorough and careful study made of the gross fixed investment financed by public funds in the French-associated states (Mauretania, Senegal, Mali, Upper Volta, Dahomey, Niger, Ivory Coast, Guinea, Togo, Cameroon, Gabon, Congo [Brazzaville], Chad, Central African Republic, Madagascar) for the period 1946–60 showed the following over-all results: local funds financed $1.2 billion equivalent (304 billion C.F.A. constant francs of 1960) of gross fixed investments— about 31 per cent of the total—with the remainder, or $2.575 billion equivalent (644 billion C.F.A. constant francs of 1960), financed by *external* public funds (mostly from France). The local funds included municipal budgets; special funds like road funds; port and rail authorities; and territorial and federal budgets when the old federations of West and Equatorial Africa existed. During this period, only $25 million was disbursed on aid received from the World Bank or the European Common Market Development Fund.

The proportion of investment financed by African countries out of their own savings went up considerably during the 1960's. In the 1950's, a few countries (Ghana, Nigeria, the Sudan, Uganda, and Zambia) were able largely to finance their own development by taking advantage of favorable prices for their major export commodities. In the early 1960's, these countries stepped up their development and other expenditures and became much more dependent on foreign sources. By the end of the decade, owing to the lack of growth in external help, a greater tax and savings effort by many of the countries, and an increase in foreign-exchange earnings in minerals and in a few agricultural products (cocoa and coffee), the African countries were financing a much higher proportion of their investment effort. In 1970, while the African countries' reliance on foreign help to achieve faster economic growth was still higher than that of other major developing regions of the world, the proportion of African investment actually financed from abroad no longer put them clearly in a different category.

Africa is unique in the amount of foreign assistance provided in the form of trained personnel. Around three quarters of the world's technical assistance is in the African countries. There are about 80,000 "experts" and volunteers on duty in Africa, around half in the sub-Saharan countries. The largest group consists of teachers and educational personnel—a total of 31,000, of which 13,000 are south of the Sahara. The biggest single component (45 per cent of the total) in the French aid program is this technical assistance, on which France spent around $330 million equivalent in 1967. The English-speaking West African countries, the Sudan, Uganda, Mali, and Guinea, while they still need technicians, teachers, etc., now no longer depend on administrators from abroad. Other African nations will probably need help for a few more years. Technicians and teachers will be needed for perhaps another ten to twenty years in most countries.

## BALANCE OF PAYMENTS

Detailed summary balance-of-payments estimates on the African countries are presented in the Technical Appendix to this chapter. While it is highly probable that the available figures, which are based on the official balance-of-payments data of the governments, do not present the complete picture, they are quite suggestive in a number of respects. In 1967, for example, for Middle Africa (that is, Africa between North and South Africa), the net inflow of real resources shown ("current account balance" or "net capital account") amounted to $560 million. (This compares to a figure of around $1 billion equivalent of net official flow of funds in economic and technical assistance according to the aid agencies. While a substantial part of the difference must be due to a large volume of the technical-assistance expenditures not entering balance-of-payments statistics, there is probably considerable understatement in the capital account.) The surprising figure is that net private direct investment is at around $200 million a year, or about half the figure shown for government capital receipts. The size of the remittances of investment income abroad—almost $400 million a year—is also striking.

In the North African figures, the rapid increase in exports and in investment income paid abroad is due largely to the rapid increase in Libyan oil exports.

### *Money and Banking*

With a few exceptions, all African countries are members of European currency areas. Liberia, with its internal use of the U.S. dollar, is in a currency union with the United States. Ethiopia and the French Territory of Afars and the Issas (largely because of close trade ties with Ethiopia) may be considered as in the dollar area, although not formally. Guinea left the franc area when she became independent in 1958 and has not yet made any new extra-African arrangements. The Sudan, which used the Egyptian pound prior to independence in 1956, now has her own currency; although she is not formally a member of the sterling area, she holds her reserves mostly in sterling, and her exchange rates with other currencies are related to the exchange rate with the pound sterling. Somalia is not formally a part of the lira area but has mutual trade and payments preferences with Italy. Participation of the Congo (Kinshasa), Rwanda, and Burundi in the Belgian franc area ceased when these former Belgian territories gained their independence, but a close relationship with Belgium's central bank and financial institutions may well be re-established. The Portuguese territories are part of the peseta area, although Angola and Mozambique have their own banks of issue (Banco de Angola and Banco Ultramarino).

South West Africa, Swaziland, Botswana, and Lesotho are in the monetary area of South Africa, which issues the currency for the whole area and administers payment and exchange controls. South Africa herself has had special and tenuous relations with the sterling area since World War II: she holds most of her reserves in gold and imposes controls over capital transfers to other parts of the area. She is associated with the London capital and money markets and cooperates closely with London in international financial matters.

The other independent countries of Africa are members of either the French franc or sterling areas. Every African country holds its foreign-exchange reserves principally in the European reserve currency of its area, carries out most of its foreign-exchange transactions through Paris or London, relates the value of its currency to the franc or pound, and usually allows current and capital transfers to take place more freely to the other members of its currency area. The ties are particularly close in the French franc area.

There has been a progressive loosening of ties in the sterling area. In November, 1968, when the United Kingdom devalued its pound in relation to the dollar, only Sierra Leone, Gambia, and Malawi followed suit. The other countries maintained the value of their currency vis-à-vis the dollar and appreciated it against the pound sterling. Since then, the United Kingdom has negotiated agreements with the various countries whereby, in exchange for their agreeing to keep their reserves in sterling, the United Kingdom guarantees their value in terms of dollars.

An important part of Africa's connection with the European currency areas is the continuation of most of the banking connections established in pre-independence days. Aside from a few locally owned banks in Nigeria, South Africa, and the Sudan and state-owned commercial banks in Ghana, Guinea, Mali, Ethiopia, Tanzania, Malawi, and Uganda, commercial banks in Africa were all owned by European banks, European investors, or, in a few cases, American or Indian banks. In recent years, the banks have been nationalized in Somalia, the Sudan, Tanzania, and Uganda. In other countries, some of the European banks have been converted into locally incorporated banks, or a new locally incorporated bank has been founded in the attempt to secure participation by local people. These new banks often represent a pooling of European and American banking interests with some local participation. In general, the degree of local participation, depending as it does on the number of Africans with money to invest or capabilities to contribute, is usually considerably below what the European or American banks would ideally wish.

No capital or money markets exist in Africa except for a rudimentary market in Lagos and Nairobi, a moderately developed one in Salisbury, and a more developed one in Johannesburg. In the main, Africa still depends on the money and capital markets of Europe.

## CENTRAL BANKS

All the new nations of Africa, with the exception of Gambia and East Africa, soon after gaining independence set up their own central banks. (East Africa was more of a nominal than a real exception, since after the East African Currency Board moved from London to Nairobi, it assumed more and more of the functions of a central bank and in most of its activity was practically indistinguishable from most other central banks.) Tanzania broke away from the Currency Board in 1965, and its own central bank began operations in June, 1966. Both Kenya and Uganda consequently also decided to have their own central banks. The Central Bank of Rhodesia and Nyasaland, created in the 1950's, was divided into three separate banks with the break-up of the Federation.

The former French territories preserved more of a monetary link among themselves than did the former British or Belgian areas. They share combined central banks, as follows: the Banque Centrale des États de l'Afrique de l'Ouest for Dahomey, Ivory Coast, Mauretania, Niger, Senegal, Togo, and Upper Volta; the Banque Centrale des États de l'Afrique Équatoriale et du Cameroun for the UDEAC states (see chap. II)—Cameroon, Central African Republic, Chad, Congo (Brazzaville), and Gabon; the Institut d'Émission Malgache for the Malagasy Republic. Mali in 1970 was in the process of re-establishing her ties with the central bank in West Africa preparatory to rejoining this monetary union. The currency of the first two central banks is called the franc CFA (Communauté Financière Africaine) and has the same value as the franc Malgache (i.e., fifty francs CFA equal one French franc).

Each of these central banks has an Operations Account with the French Treasury through which all its payments and receipts in foreign currency are settled. It can draw on this account as necessary (at penalty rates) to balance its international payments position at any time through an automatic, unlimited overdraft facility extended it by the French Treasury. There is French representation on the boards of the banks, which presumably should help to prevent any possible abuse of this privilege.

Guinea's central bank does not have these close ties with the French Treasury. And, during 1960–70, it did not receive the volume of effective aid that the other ex-French West African countries benefited from. Guinea, in fact, received as much (or even more) assistance from other sources, mostly nations of the Soviet bloc and China, as the other countries received from France. Unfortunately, this assistance was not accompanied by effective technical advice or applied to well-planned economic projects. The result, in spite of a large investment running well over 20 per cent of GNP, was a drop in per-capita national income. The central bank of Guinea also did not pursue the same moderate financial policies as in the other countries. During the 1960's, consequently, it suffered from inflation, loss of external values of its currency, and the necessity to adopt a full paraphernalia of external foreign-exchange and trade controls. Ghana, for somewhat similar reasons, was in the same kind of trouble before the overthrow of Nkrumah.

The fact is that central banks in Africa face a completely different environment and a completely different set of problems from those faced by central banks in developed countries. An African central bank can contribute to economic development by creating and nourishing the financial institutions needed for growth, by centralizing and managing the country's foreign-exchange reserves (both to economize on the need to hold reserves and to mitigate somewhat the fluctuations in export earnings), and by creating an objective, informal center for economic and financial research and advice for a government. In Africa today, it can do very little in the way of pursuing an independent monetary policy or controlling the supply or price or availability of credit. The economic and financial dependence of the African economies on the rest of the world is so great that they would have to possess relatively enormous foreign-exchange reserves to gain much latitude in pursuing an independent monetary and credit policy. No African country possesses such reserves, and, consequently, if any tried to expand credit more rapidly than the rest of its monetary area, for example, it would soon find its foreign-exchange reserves exhausted and would be confronted with the need to backtrack directly or indirectly through foreign-exchange controls and even devaluation. The central bank is all-important as manager of foreign exchange and as adviser to the government. As far as the management of money and credit is concerned, overambition is most dangerous.

In no country can one manage money while disregarding the outside world and the balance of payments. In Africa, this means that one has only a very narrow margin to operate in. The problem is that for a number of reasons monetary expansion in an underdeveloped country, particularly in Africa, results in a balance-of-payments problem with frightening rapidity. First, the internal flexibility in production that is present in a developed country is lacking. While there may be a surplus of unskilled labor at times, there is a shortage of complementary factors. In a developed country, if there is unemployment and demand is raised, the unemployed can be put to work with existing unused machines, or new machines may be produced—if the machines are imported and the country does not have the foreign exchange to buy them, it can make them at home; they may be less good or more expensive, but one can still go ahead. In an underdeveloped country, if the machine cannot be bought from abroad, the men cannot be put to work.

This is true not only of capital goods but also of consumer goods. If demand is increased through monetary expansion, the immediate effect is to increase demand for imported goods, the marginal propensity to import being very high. For in Africa, the people in the money economy are most interested in imported manufactured consumer goods. Domestic production of such goods is small or nonexistent, and output in absolute terms can increase only very slowly. (On the other hand, the African goods exported, with a few exceptions, are not goods that are consumed in Africa, so that an increase in money demand does not directly reduce the volume of exports).

The United States of America did not create a permanent central bank until 130 years after the American Revolution. The African nations are now all equipped with central banks. These banks can contribute to economic development; they can also, if the temptation to create money out of thin air is not resisted, become a means to hold back or destroy the prospects of development. In only three cases so far—Guinea, Mali, and the Congo (Kinshasa)—has central bank policy had severe detrimental effects. And in no case has bad policy lasted more than a few years. The record is good.

In order to help one another to cope with future problems and facilitate cooperation, the African central banks agreed in February, 1966, to organize an Association of African Central Banks, made up of the governors of the central banks and representatives of similar monetary institutions, such as a currency board where a central bank does not yet exist. Organizations with similar purposes in other parts of the world have been helpful in easing the way to solutions of international payments and problems and in encouraging central banks more effectively to promote good economic and financial policies. The creation of this organization at so early a stage in Africa's independent financial life is therefore a good augury.

## Foreign Trade

Economic dependence on the export of a few primary commodities is typical of underdeveloped countries anywhere in the world. But Africa is more involved in foreign trade than most other underdeveloped areas. Africa's money economy grew and still largely depends on output for export; it is therefore the progressive, growing part of her economy that relies on the rest of the world; the subsistence economy by definition has no concern with the outside world. The whole structure of modern African economies is shaped by their orientation toward foreign trade—the railways, the roads, the ports, the growth of the principal cities have been shaped above all by the foreign-trade flows or by the needs of production for export.

Over all of sub-Saharan Africa, exports average $20 per capita, considerably more than in underdeveloped areas elsewhere. The higher-income African countries tend to have higher dependence on exports: Ghana and the Ivory Coast, for example, have per-capita export levels of around $50.

Sub-Saharan Africa exports about a quarter of its total GNP. Generally, the poorer or slower-growing nations fall below this proportion, while the richer or faster-growing are above. In recent years, South Africa has run over 30 per cent; Ivory Coast, 33 per cent; Zambia, 40 per cent; Liberia, almost 50 per cent. On the other hand, Dahomey and Upper Volta run around 8 per cent, Ethiopia and Chad, 10 per cent; Malagasy Republic and Niger, around 15 per cent; Senegal, Cameroon, Uganda, around 25 per cent.

The direction of trade to and from Africa has not radically shifted since the independence movement swept over the continent. French-speaking African countries still trade mostly with France, although Guinea and, to a lesser extent, Mali diverted trade to the Soviet bloc for a few years. The former British territories still find the United Kingdom their best trading partner, but they have diversified markets and suppliers considerably since independence. Liberia still deals mostly with the U.S. South Africa, Ethiopia, and the Congo (Kinshasa) continue to have a variety of markets and sources of goods, mostly in Western Europe and North America. Imports into the Portuguese territories continue to be dominated by Portugal, but their exports go to a number of countries in North America and Western Europe. (See Technical Appendix.)

Trade with Western Europe is consequently still the most important for Africa. Of Africa's total trade excluding South Africa (amounting in 1969 to around $10 billion exports f.o.b. [including gold] and $8.5 billion imports c.i.f.), two thirds is with Western Europe, 12 per cent with the U.S., 10 per cent with other African countries, and 10 per cent with Eastern Europe. No other primary producing area in the world is so heavily dependent on trade with Western Europe. Only about 40 per cent of the trade of all primary producing countries is with Western Europe.

By World War II, Africa had already become an important world producer of a number of commodities, and she continues to maintain or improve her position. Although her world position is strongest in minerals, she is principally an agricultural producer. Africa continues to produce around 90 per cent of the world's output of diamonds, two thirds of the palm oil, sisal, and cocoa; around half the manganese and chrome ore; one third of the antimony and phosphate; and one tenth of the wool. In copper, her output has climbed to over one fourth of the world's total. According to figures cited by Sir Ronald Prain, Chairman of the Roan Selection Trust of Zambia, Africa's large copper producer, Africa's known reserves are estimated at about 60 million tons of copper content, or just under one third of world holdings outside the Soviet Union. African gold output, mostly in South Africa, has risen from 40 per cent of the world's pre-war output to about 90 per cent now; in coffee, her share in the world market has tripled and is now 30 per cent of the total.

The strongest incentive to development in Africa has been provided by the demand for her mineral deposits. Diamonds and gold sparked and made possible the modern development of the Republic of South Africa; gold and copper initiated growth in Southern Rhodesia and Zambia, and Katanga copper in the Congo (Kinshasa). African mines attracted, and continue to attract, more outside capital than any other activity. It is largely to the exploitation of her mineral resources that southern and central Africa owes her new ports, railways, and towns. For the immediate future, the resources that are of particular interest to American and European capital are, in addition to water power, mostly minerals: bauxite, oil, uranium, manganese, and iron. Whereas in the past mineral development occurred primarily in southern and central Africa, new resources have been located in West Africa, particularly in the former French colonies. This opens up for the first time the possibility of their more rapid development, financed to a greater extent from their own resources. (See below, chap. VI.)

## The "Commodity Problem"

Africa's exports, as illustrated by the foregoing description, are primary products—foods, agricultural raw materials, and minerals. The size of African economies or even of the total of the African economies is so small that if economic growth is to take place, exports must be one of the principal propulsive forces. But primary products have certain drawbacks that complicate and make economic growth more difficult; essentially these are fluctuations in price and in total receipts, and the fact that demand for most of these products grows more slowly than incomes in the industrialized countries.

As mentioned above, the modern economy of the African countries is built around the export sector. Government revenues and the revenues from transport, power, and other utilities depend on the incomes of the export sector. The African economies are therefore peculiarly sensitive to changes in export incomes. Prices of primary commodities are subject to wide swings, and consequently large fluctuations occur in income and activity throughout the economy. In some cases, fluctuations in price are offset by the quantities, but in most of the African commodities there are large fluctuations in the total receipts from year to year—in the case of sisal, averaging over 26 per cent in the period 1950–65. (See Table 2 in the Technical Appendix.) This, of course, may understate the problem; a sudden drop of, say, 50 per cent in earnings in one year could be fatal to a government even though averaged with stable prices over ten years this would appear as only a 5-per-cent fluctuation.

The problem of fluctuations is bad enough, but the low income elasticity of the demand for most of the primary products produced by Africa is perhaps even worse. Roughly, as income goes up by 1 per cent in the industrialized countries, the demand for food, beverages, and tobacco goes up by 0.6 per cent and the demand for crude materials, oils, and fats by 0.5 per cent. All other things being equal, if the GNP of the industrialized countries goes up by 5 per cent a year (roughly about what it did in the 1960's) the demand for most African exports will go up by 2½–3 per cent a year. Since economic growth in the African countries depends in large part on export growth, other things being equal, the rate of growth of GNP would be at this level. With population growth also at this figure, per-capita GNP would remain where it now is. This presentation, while highly simplified, does bring out the basic problem confronting the African countries.

There are several ways around this morass:

(1) External economic aid can supplement export earnings and contribute to a longer-run diversification of the African economies.

(2) Export production can be shifted to higher-income elastic products. The demand for fuels and manufactures, for example, have income elasticities considerably higher than 1; consequently, export demand for oil and manufactured products can grow more rapidly than incomes in the developed countries. But not all countries have oil, and the African countries are not yet able to produce manufactures for export).

(3) The country's share of the market for a commodity can be increased at the expense of other countries. To a considerable extent, the Africans have done this in the past—in coffee, by cutting into Latin American shares of the market; in tea, by moving into Indian and Ceylonese markets; in edible oils and rubber, by taking over part of the former Indonesian market, etc.

(4) In suitable cases, the country can participate with other producers, in a commodity agreement that will iron out fluctuations in price and/or provide a higher average price than would result from uncontrolled market forces. This is discussed below.

(5) A preferential place can be secured in a growing market. The Association Agreements with the European Economic Community (EEC), which are discussed below, essentially have this as one of their principal objectives.

(6) "Compensatory" or "supplementary" finance can be obtained to offset fluctuations or unforeseen short-falls from export earning expectations.

COMMODITY AGREEMENTS

The most important single export commodity for the African countries is coffee. Twenty-one African countries * are coffee exporters, and the total value of their coffee exports has been around $600–700 million a year, or one sixth of the total exports from Middle Africa. All the African countries are now members of the International Coffee Agreement established in 1962 and renewed in 1968 for five years. Membership covers practically the whole of world production and the bulk of the consuming countries. The agreement establishes market shares for each exporting country; African quotas total about one third of the world figure. Quotas can be adjusted each year and varied during the year by the International Coffee Organization (ICO), whose headquarters are in London, as necessary to try to hold the prices of the principal types of coffee within agreed price ranges. When the agreement was established, the world supply of coffee in annual production and stocks was considerably in excess of consumption. The agreement, by keeping the stocks out of the market, unquestionably kept the price at a higher level than would otherwise have prevailed. While an estimate of the resulting gain to the coffee producers can only be very rough, it is likely that the African producers' export earnings have been perhaps $150–$200 million more a year than they would have been otherwise.

The coffee agreement also worked in the direction of adjusting world production to demand at the price levels agreed upon. In 1969, frost damage to Brazilian coffee trees was extensive enough to make it clear that the remainder of Brazilian stocks were likely to be

---

* Ivory Coast, Angola, Uganda, Ethiopia, Cameroon, Congo (Kinshasa), Malagasy Republic, Kenya, Tanzania, Burundi, Guinea, Rwanda, Togo, Dahomey, Sierra Leone, Liberia, Ghana, Nigeria, Gabon, Central African Republic, Congo (Brazzaville).

used up in the next couple of years. The resulting pressure to build up stocks in the consuming countries sent coffee prices considerably above the price ranges the ICO was trying to maintain, in spite of substantial increases in coffee quotas. On the average, coffee prices were about 25 per cent higher in early 1970 than the ICO wished to see. While this meant an increase of around $150 million in African coffee earnings, it also represented a threat to the continued existence of the ICO, since it could mean the withdrawal of consuming countries from the agreement—and their cooperation is essential to the maintenance of the agreement. If the agreement collapses and countries respond to the higher prices by large plantings of new coffee trees, within three or four years, as the trees come into bearing, coffee prices again will be under great downward pressure, and the boom will again become a bust.

Two other commodity agreements that existed in 1970 had some relevance for the African countries but much less than did the coffee agreement. An International Tin Agreement, of which Nigeria and Congo (Kinshasa) are members, has been in existence over most of the post-World War II period and is due for renewal in 1971. The International Tin Council under this agreement tries to maintain prices between a floor and a ceiling by using a buffer stock to buy or sell tin as the price nears either limit, and reinforcing this by export quotas. It has had a reasonable degree of success but far from a perfect record in attaining its objectives.

The other commodity agreement of interest to some of Africa is the International Sugar Agreement. Almost two thirds of world trade in sugar moves in several different preferential trade arrangements that are outside the agreement. In addition, sugar is a commodity that can be produced fairly widely in both developed and developing countries, so that many of the African countries are increasing their sugar output substantially under protection to replace their former imports. The most important for the African exporters of Mauritius, Swaziland, and Uganda is the Commonwealth Sugar Agreement, which guarantees imports of specified quantities of sugar by the United Kingdom at negotiated prices to Commonwealth producers. The U.S. quota arrangements also provide reserved quotas for about 30 countries at a high price compared to world market prices. Of the African exporting countries, South Africa was originally covered by the Commonwealth Sugar Agreement but her participation was phased out at the end of 1964. She has, however, since received a quota of 46,000 tons under the U.S. sugar arrangements. Mauritius, Malagasy Republic, and Swaziland have also quotas, as had Southern Rhodesia, whose quota has been suspended.

The International Sugar Agreement attempts to regulate only the remaining free sector of international trade in sugar left after the arrangements mentioned above as well as a number of others (i.e., U.S.S.R., Cuba, EEC countries, etc.). The latest agreement came into existence at the beginning of 1969 as an attempt to bring some price stability into the residual market. As is clear from the above description, it can have only a relatively modest impact on the total world sugar market. Membership includes all the African net exporters except Southern Rhodesia (that is, Congo [Brazzaville], Mauritius, Malagasy Republic, South Africa, Swaziland, and Uganda).

Cocoa is a commodity that the African producers (Ghana, Cameroon, Ivory Coast, Nigeria, Togo), who produce the major part of the world's supply, have an interest in attempting to stabilize. An agreement was substantially negotiated among the principal producing and consuming countries by 1967. However, agreement has not been reached on the price range to be maintained. At first, this was because the consuming countries regarded the range (20–29 cents a pound) as too high—it was above the actual market price at the time. From 1967 at least through the first half of 1970, market prices were well above the range, and the producing countries did not feel any great need to press for an agreement.

PREFERENCES

Another way of mitigating the "commodity problem" for a country is to secure preferential treatment for its goods in its major markets. During the colonial period, the French had a system of price supports, stabilization funds, and preferential quotas for the major exports from their African colonies. This provided not only a sure market but often higher-than-world prices for the African export products concerned. In return, the African colonies' markets were largely reserved for French goods. During the 1960's, this system was dismantled. In its place a free-trade zone has been created between the six European Economic Community countries (France, West

Germany, Italy, Belgium, Netherlands, and Luxembourg) and former French, Belgian, and Italian territories in Africa (see below). The Portuguese territories in Africa juridically are provinces of Portugal. Here the system appears to work somewhat differently. Preference is given to products from the African territories in Portugal: while they may be imported free of restriction, competitive products, such as cotton and some oilseed products, are subject to quantitative restriction if imported from other areas. However, since Portugal is a comparatively small market, this preferential treatment is not so great an advantage as preferred access to the French market was for the former French colonies. In Mozambique, Angola (including the enclave of Cabinda), Portuguese Guinea, the Cape Verde Islands, and the islands of São Tomé and Príncipe in the Gulf of Guinea, preference is given to Portuguese products through a high tariff and quotas imposed on most competitive imports from other countries. Although Portugal is a member of the European Free Trade Area (EFTA), which also includes the United Kingdom, the four Scandinavian countries, Austria, Switzerland, and Finland, Portuguese territories in Africa were not included in EFTA and do not benefit from the lower tariffs placed on industrial products from other EFTA members.

Great Britain, under her Commonwealth preferences policy, allows most primary products from African Commonwealth members to enter duty-free. Ghana, Nigeria, and the East African countries do not grant Commonwealth preferences in return; a few preferences have been granted by Gambia and Sierra Leone. The Federation of Rhodesia and Nyasaland did pursue a policy of granting substantial preferential treatment to British and other Commonwealth goods, and Southern Rhodesia continued this policy until the Smith government unilaterally declared its independence in 1965. South Africa, since it left the Commonwealth in 1961, negotiated agreements with the United Kingdom to maintain part of its existing system of Commonwealth preferences, but these have mostly disappeared. South Africa's sugar quota of 150,000 long tons in the U.K. market, established under the Commonwealth Sugar Agreement, which was to have run to 1967, was terminated at the end of 1964.

EEC—ASSOCIATION

The most important preferential relationship between African countries and their principal markets is the Yaoundé Convention of Association between the European Economic Community (EEC) and eighteen African states.* The present convention was signed in Yaoundé in July, 1969, and is to run to January 31, 1975. It is largely a continuation of the first Yaoundé Convention that came into effect in June, 1964, which, in its turn, extended and developed arrangements that had been made in 1957 to cover the then-dependent overseas territories of the members of the EEC, when this came into being. Unlike the earlier arrangement, however, the present system was freely negotiated between the African states on one side and the European Economic Community on the other.

The convention provides for a preferential trade zone between the EEC and the associated African states. Since the convention was fully implemented (by 1969), there are no customs tariff or quota restrictions on trade among the African associates and EEC members. Provision is made, however, for the African states to be able to institute protection of infant industries by either tariffs or quotas, after consultation, as well as to establish customs unions and free-trade areas among themselves or with other states if such arrangements are in harmony with the association.

As soon as the first convention went into force, the associated states acquired duty-free entry into the EEC for most of their agricultural exports—coffee, cocoa, tea, pepper, vanilla, cloves, nutmeg, pineapples, coconuts. The EEC members' imports of these commodities, except for vanilla and cloves, are greater than the output of the associated African states, giving the latter a duty-free market for all of these products; and in this duty-free market, these products are protected against competition by tariffs levied on goods from other producers. While these tariffs have been successively lowered, they are still substantial.

| Commodity | Percentage of Tariff | Commodity | Percentage of Tariff |
|---|---|---|---|
| Coffee | 7 | Vanilla | 11.5 |
| Cocoa | 4 | Coconuts | 4 |
| Pineapples | 9 | Pepper | 17 |
| Cloves, nutmeg | 15 | Palm oil | 6 |

* The former French territories (except Guinea)—Cameroon, Central African Republic, Chad, Congo (Brazzaville), Dahomey, Gabon, Ivory Coast, Malagasy Republic, Mali, Mauretania, Niger, Senegal, Togo, and Upper Volta; the former Belgian territories—Congo (Kinshasa), Burundi, and Rwanda; and the former Italian territory of Somalia, now merged with former British Somaliland.

Duties on tea and tropical woods are suspended "temporarily" for all suppliers.

While the associated states were given duty-free entry for the bulk of their agricultural products that are noncompetitive with EEC products, they were subject to import levies applied to agricultural commodities that *are* competitive. As of June 1, 1970, the EEC, however, agreed to suppress the levies on imports from the associated states on beef, seed-oils (except olive oil), certain canned fruits and vegetables (notably pineapples), and such products as chocolate and tapioca. The levies normally imposed on sugar-content products and cereals were totally or partially eliminated. The levy on rice, for instance, exported by Madagascar in competition with Italian and French producers, was reduced by 45 per cent.

For the former French territories, the creation of a preferential trade area with the EEC involved an expansion of the existing preferential trade treatment with France to include the other EEC members. At the same time, the preferential marketing arrangements they enjoyed in France for some of their products were given up—in return, they get duty-free access to the entire Common Market area and, for many of their products, protection against competition from other producers in Africa, Latin America, or Asia.*

This preferential treatment that the ex-French territories lost had been of substantial advantage to them. Peanuts and sugar had been guaranteed a good minimum price in French markets; palm oil and pepper were given preferential tariff rates; coffee and other products benefited from quotas that limited imports from other markets to maintain a price that was often well above world market levels; cotton and other commodities received direct production subsidies. In addition, stabilization funds (*caisses de stabilisation des prix*) in the African countries concerned were able to borrow from a central French fund (*Fonds Nationale de Regularisation des Cours des Produits d'Outre-Mer*) whenever market prices fell below the prices set by it.

The additional foreign exchange secured as a result of this preferential structure amounted to as much as $60 million or $70 million annually—a substantial sum, especially for countries like Senegal,

---

* Under the association convention, the Congo (Kinshasa) had to give up the open-door commercial policy she followed under the Congo Basin treaties that originally created the Congo as a unit.

whose principal export crop, peanuts, was sold at some 75 per cent above world market prices in 1961.

Under the convention, these higher prices secured in France were eliminated, except for bananas. (French and Italian marketing organizations were permitted to remain.) In the 1964 convention, $230 million of aid was earmarked by the EEC for production and diversification, to offset the abolition of the preferential system. In spite of this aid, during the 1964–69 period, the Fund for Economic Development (FED) found it necessary to make $15 million available to the African countries in the form of advances to price-stabilization funds or as emergency assistance to offset drops in commodity prices. The bulk of this sum—$8.7 million—was given to Senegal, to offset the drop in groundnut prices.

In the most recent convention, there is no provision for direct intervention for price stabilization. However, it sets up a reserve fund out of the money provided to FED for grants (see below) to meet exceptional problems resulting either from a fall in world prices or such calamities as famine or floods. A maximum of $80 million is available for these purposes, of which up to $50 million can be spent on interest-free advances for price stabilization.

Under the first arrangement, 1957–64, a total of $497 million in grants was made available by FED to the African Associate Members. The first convention, 1964–69, increased aid to $730 million, and the second convention, 1969–75, increased it again to a total of $918 million. The relative figures are as follows:

| | 1957–64 | 1964–69 | 1969–75 |
|---|---|---|---|
| | *(in millions of dollars equivalent)* | | |
| Grants | 497 | 620 | 748 |
| Loans on special easy terms | — | 46 | 80 |
| Loans from European Investment Bank (conventional terms) | — | 64 | 90 |
| Total | 497 | 730 | 918 |

The European Investment Bank is an entity of the EEC which was authorized to make loans in Africa only at the time of the first convention. (It should be noted that there is also provision in the FED for aid to the existing overseas dependent territories, countries, and overseas departments related to the EEC countries. Of the thirteen concerned, only the French Territory of Afars and the Issas, the Comoro Islands archipelago, and the French overseas department of Réunion are in Africa. These, plus eight other French areas in other continents, are to share $41 million in aid in 1969–75, compared to $35 million in 1964–69.)

The increase in financial aid provided through FED, with the concomitant decrease in flow of U.S. economic aid to Africa, should result in the 1969–75 period in FED's not only beating the United States for the third position (after France and the United Kingdom) as a provider of aid to Africa but in its becoming twice as important. (See below, chap. IX.)

Of particular importance to the relationship of the Common Market with the associated African states is the Caisse Centrale pour la Coopération Économique (Central Fund for Economic Cooperation), an autonomous French government agency. The Caisse Centrale is a key organization in the administration of French aid in the former French territories: it handles the financial operations of direct government aid; acts as a development bank in helping to finance large industrial and mining ventures (Comilog, Miferma, Fria, etc.); and sets up and helps to finance and manage local development banks making smaller loans and investments. It also administered the French government–financed central commodity stabilization funds and, finally, in the countries where it operates, the financial operations of the Common Market's FED.

Another important aspect of the conventions is the emphasis given to technical assistance. Since, in Africa, development aid in the form of trained personnel is as vital as aid in the form of capital, this activity is particularly noteworthy.

One of the new provisions in the 1969–75 convention is a 15-percent preference for local suppliers or suppliers from another African associate member given in competitive bidding for procurement financed by FED for its projects. This is designed to encourage and provide some help to African suppliers in bidding for FED contracts. On the European side, there is a provision that companies from at least two EEC countries must participate in any projects costing more than $5 million. This is designed to insure that the bulk of the FED-financed business does not continue to flow to French companies that have maintained their predominant position in the former French colonies.

A new protocol was added to the 1969 Yaoundé Convention to meet the situation if a general preferential system for developing countries is established (see below). According to this protocol, it is agreed that the association should not obstruct participation in a world system of preferences. In 1970, the EEC countries declared that they would be willing to give up their preferences in the African associate-member country markets in order to facilitate agreement to set up a world-wide system of preferences for the developing countries. In this way, the EEC tried to meet one of the main conditions the United States laid down for its agreement to a general system of preferences.

The convention is not least important for the institutions it established for cooperation among the associated states and the Common Market. The convention established a Council of Association at the ministerial level, reporting each year on its activity to a parliamentary conference, to lay down the general pattern for financial and technical assistance among the countries concerned. Day-to-day administration is handled by a Committee of Association, consisting of one representative from each country; in formal votes, the eighteen Africans together have one vote, and the EEC members together one vote.

In short, the convention gives its associated African states preferential treatment for their exports to one of the fastest growing markets in the world; it provides them with a substantial volume of economic and technical assistance; and it attracts and concentrates the attention of Europe's rich, developed countries on this particular part of the developing world. There is little doubt but that it is of immeasurable economic benefit to the associate members.

African states outside the Association have so far suffered little direct damage from the preferential treatment given the associated states. But there is potential damage: the EEC-associated states have an inducement to expand production of protected goods more rapidly and so to exclude the products of other African states or force them to accept lower returns than their own producers can get, by having to sell either at lower returns within the EEC or outside in the world market. Even more important, perhaps, is the possibility that the Common Market will draw its associates' interest away from the rest of Africa.

In any event, some of the other African states, while not wishing to tie themselves closely to the Common Market, concluded that some form of association would be desirable and opened negotiations to that end. Among these countries are Nigeria, Uganda, Kenya, Tanzania, and, north of the Sahara, Algeria, Tunisia, and Morocco. The first to be successful was Nigeria, after almost two years of negotiations. In May, 1966, she completed negotiations to become an associate member of the EEC, but on a different footing from the other African associate members.

This agreement, coming into force in 1966, was to expire on May 31, 1969, at the same time as the Convention of Association that links the other African associate members to the EEC. It provided that most Nigerian exports would enter the Common Market on the same unrestricted basis as the exports of the other eighteen associate African states. Four of Nigeria's main agricultural exports—cocoa, peanuts, plywood, and palm products—were to be subject to quotas based on the average of the last three years and enlarged by 3 per cent yearly. In return, Nigeria was to grant a tariff preference of 2 per cent to a list of twenty-six European products—including wine, agricultural machinery, radios, and household goods. An alternative arrangement was open to the Nigerian government, under which plywood would enjoy unrestricted entry into the Common Market countries and the import quotas for the other three Nigerian products would be raised by 6 per cent a year, in return for a preferential tariff of 5 per cent on the twenty-six listed products.

The agreement also provided that Nigeria would not discriminate in respect of the rights of EEC countries to establish private enterprises in Nigeria and similar matters. Current payments on goods and services would be authorized by both parties to the agreement, but restrictions on capital movements between the two areas would be maintained. Because of Nigeria's wish to avoid any political association with the Community, the institutions to implement the agreement were to amount to no more than one meeting of a Ministerial Council each year.

Following on the Nigerian agreement, the three East African countries, Kenya, Tanzania and Uganda, signed a similar agreement in July, 1968. Under its terms, EEC agreed to suspend customs duties on most East African products and to apply annual duty-free quotas to East African exports of coffee (56,000 tons), canned pineapples (860 tons), and cloves (100 tons). In return, the three East African countries were to grant the EEC countries tariff preferences on about fifty products.

Neither the Nigerian nor the East African agreement came into operation before they expired on May 31, 1969, because the EEC countries did not complete the process of ratification. The East African countries signed a new agreement in September, 1969, essentially the same as the old agreement but extending to January 31, 1975 (that is, the same date as the Yaoundé Convention). Nigeria, preoccupied with her civil war and reconstruction, showed no interest in reviving her agreement.

The EEC staff has recommended that after the United Kingdom joins the EEC, the enlarged community should negotiate a new over-all agreement to include both the present associated countries and the former British territories in Africa and the Caribbean. The negotiations should aim for agreement by January, 1975, when the present association agreements expire.

Meanwhile, the two North African states, Tunisia and Morocco, signed agreements of association with the EEC in March, 1969, for a period of five years. The agreements provide that industrial products originating in the two countries will be granted full intra-EEC treatment—that is, may be imported free of duty and quantitative restriction. Agricultural products receive some benefits subject to controls to avoid adversely affecting the EEC's agricultural policy. Tunisia, for her part, grants the EEC countries tariff reduction on a number of products (representing 40 per cent of the volume of imports from the EEC), corresponding to 70 per cent of the preference that France enjoys. Morocco grants a 25-per-cent tariff reduction on a small number of products (7 per cent of imports from the EEC) and liberalizes her quotas on others.

Algeria benefits from a special regime. At the time of her independence in 1962, Algeria (as a part of France) had received the benefit of the tariff reductions granted the EEC members to one another. This treatment has continued, so that while she did not receive the benefit of the later complete dismantling of intra-EEC tariffs, she does have preferential treatment compared to other developing countries.

GENERAL TARIFF PREFERENCES

In the United Nations Conference on Trade and Development (UNCTAD) conference at New Delhi in 1968, agreement was reached on a proposal that the developed countries should reduce or eliminate their tariffs on imports of manufactured products from the developing countries while maintaining the existing rates on imports from other developed countries. As far as the "commodity problem" of the African countries is concerned, of course, this proposal would have no direct impact since it would not apply to the commodities the Middle African countries now export. The North African countries, through their association with EEC, already have this benefit in their largest potential market. In the longer run, it would help by providing some encouragement to industrialization and thus to diversification of the African exports. Possibly it might also help Africa by helping Latin American countries to expand their non-primary-product exports and so make it easier for African countries to take over a greater share of world markets. But all this is very long-term. Consequently, while the African countries have an interest in seeing the UNCTAD proposal implemented, they also have an interest in pointing out that, as the least industrialized countries, they will get the least benefit and that, consequently, some other special help should be tailored to their needs.

## COMPENSATORY AND SUPPLEMENTARY FINANCE

As mentioned earlier in this chapter, another line of action in dealing with fluctuations in export earnings is to have special arrangements to provide assistance to offset drops in earnings, like the assistance available for individuals through insurance or social security. The International Monetary Fund (IMF) has as one of its principal functions the provision of short-term credit (up to five years) to countries in temporary balance-of-payments difficulties. This by itself is a help. Beginning in 1963 and liberalized in 1966, the IMF created a special facility, over and beyond a country's general access to the IMF's resources, to provide more automatic access to credit for developing countries to help them meet foreign-exchange deficits due to reductions in export proceeds below the medium-term trend and beyond the control of the country. Under this arrangement, the country can draw amounts up to the equivalent of 50 per cent of its quota, although the second 25-per-cent *tranche* is available only if the IMF is satisfied that the country is trying to find an appropriate solution to its payments problems.

As a result of a study made jointly by the World Bank and the

IMF on the initiative of France and twelve French-speaking African countries, the IMF set up a new facility in June, 1969, concerned with the financing of international commodity buffer-stocks. A country may draw from the IMF for the purpose of buffer-stock financing up to amounts equivalent to 50 per cent of its quota. "However, drawings outstanding for the purpose of buffer-stock financing and for compensatory financing of export fluctuations together may at no time exceed a common upper limit of 75 per cent of quota." (IMF, *1968/69 Annual Report*, p. 39.)

The International Monetary Fund arrangements are based on the assumption that the fluctuations in export earnings will be relatively brief and that any use of credit to offset shortfalls can be soon repaid. There can also be shortfalls in expected earnings that can have longer-term effects or that the country cannot soon offset from its own earnings. The first UNCTAD conference in 1964 asked the World Bank to work out a scheme to help developing countries to maintain internationally agreed-upon development programs in the event of unexpected shortfalls in export earnings due to factors beyond the control of the country and beyond its ability to finance from its own reserves or short-term credit. The World Bank's scheme worked out in response to this request was studied carefully by an intergovernmental committee for several years. In 1969, the scheme was sent back to the Bank by the committee with the request that the Bank try to secure international agreement to set it up. The World Bank Group discovered in 1970 that the developed countries were not willing as a group to provide extra resources to launch the scheme. At the same time, because of the rather high levels of demand for primary products in the developed countries, resulting in part from the worldwide inflationary pressure in 1969 and 1970, the developing countries suffered less from the commodity problem. The result was that in 1970 the problem was at least temporarily lacking in urgency, and ways of mitigating it were low on the agendas of governments.

## Selected Bibliography

*La convention de Yaoundé.* Brussels: European Economic Commission, 1965.

European Economic Commission. *Information Memo P-33.* Brussels: EEC, July 11, 1969.

INTERNATIONAL MONETARY FUND, AFRICAN DEPARTMENT STUDY GROUP. "Financial Arrangements of Countries Using the CFA Franc," *IMF Staff Papers*, XVI, No. 2 (July, 1969), 289–389.

"Les investissements publics nationaux et extèrieurs dans les pays francophones d'Afrique tropicale 1946–1960." 2 vols. Paris: University of Paris, Institut d'Étude de Développement Économique et Social (IEDES), 1964. Mimeo.

JUCKER-FLEETWOOD, E. E. *Money and Finance in Africa*. New York: Frederick A. Praeger, 1964.

KUZNETS, S. "International Differences in Capital Formation and Financing," in M. ABRAMOVITZ (ed.), *Capital Formation and Economic Growth*. Princeton, N.J.: Princeton University Press, 1956.

LANGER, W. L. "Farewell to Empire," *Foreign Affairs*, XLI, No. 1 (October, 1962), 115–30.

LEDUC, M. *Les institutions monetaires africaines: Pays francophones*. Paris: Editions A. Pedone, 1965.

MLADEK, J. V. "Evolution of African Currencies," *Finance and Development, The Fund and Bank Review*, Vol. I, Nos. 2 and 3 (September and December, 1964).

"La Nouvelle convention d'association entre Le Marché Commun et les états africains," *Revue du Marché Commun*, No. 54 (January, 1963), pp. 22–35.

PEARSON, S. R. and SCHMIDT, W. E. "Alms for AAMS: A Larger Flow?," *Journal of Common Market Studies*, III, No. 1 (October, 1964), 74–82.

RIPOCHE, P. "Les Fonds européen de développement," *Les banques de développement dans le monde* (extract). Paris: Dunod, 1964, pp. 243–85.

———. "Le deuxième fonds européen de développement," *Les banques de développement dans le monde* (extract). Paris: Dunod, 1965, pp. 375–91.

SEN, S. N. *Central Banking in Undeveloped Money Markets*. 3d ed.; Calcutta: Bookland Private, 1961.

SERVOISE, R. "L'Avenir économique des pays tropicaux." (SEDEIS Supplementary Bulletin No. 828.) Reproduced in *Problèmes économiques, la documentation française* (Paris: Institut National de la Statistique), No. 780 (December 11, 1962), pp. 6–15.

STRACHEY, J. *The End of Empire*. London: Gollancz, 1959; New York: Random House, 1960.

# Technical Appendix

TABLE 1
IMPORTS FROM MAIN SUPPLIER AS PERCENTAGE OF TOTAL IMPORTS

|  | 1938 | 1960 | 1965 |
|---|---|---|---|
| *France—Supplier* | | | |
| Cameroon | 27 | 59 | 58 |
| Equatorial Africa | 34 | 62 | 57 |
| West Africa | 59 | 68 | 57 |
| Madagascar | 76 | 70 | 63 |
| Tunisia | 62 | 59 | 39 |
| *U.K.—Supplier* | | | |
| Ghana | 55 | 37 | 26 |
| Kenya | 45 | 32 | 25 |
| Uganda | | 23 | 27 |
| Nigeria | 55 | 39 | 28 |
| Sierra Leone | 67 | 42 | 33 |
| Sudan | 26 | 27 | 23 |
| Tanganyika | 29 | 27 | 24 |
| *U.S.—Supplier* | | | |
| Liberia | n.a. | 54 | 47 |

SOURCE: Extracted from Percy Selwyn, *Captive Markets in the 1960's*, Communications Series No. 36. Institute of Development Studies, University of Sussex, Stanmer, Brighton, 1969. Tables I, II, III.

TABLE 2
TOTAL EXPORTS OF INDIVIDUAL COMMODITIES
FROM DEVELOPING COUNTRIES: FLUCTUATION INDICES, 1950–65 *

| Commodity | Prices | Quantities | Earnings |
|---|---|---|---|
| *Minerals* | | | |
| Copper | 13.0 | 4.1 | 12.4 |
| Iron ore | 12.2 | 10.9 | 21.9 |
| Tin | 12.0 | 7.6 | 15.5 |
| Bauxite | 9.1 | 10.6 | 18.8 |
| Phosphate | 4.2 | 4.7 | 5.4 |
| Manganese ore | 14.4 | 13.2 | 19.9 |
| *Agricultural Raw Materials* | | | |
| Rubber | 13.1 | 5.1 | 16.0 |
| Cotton | 7.0 | 7.7 | 8.7 |
| Timber | 10.7 | 5.1 | 11.9 |
| Hides and skins | 11.4 | 8.0 | 15.5 |
| Sisal | 27.1 | 5.8 | 25.6 |
| *Foods* | | | |
| Coffee | 14.0 | 5.8 | 9.5 |
| Tea | 8.6 | 3.8 | 8.4 |
| Cocoa | 17.1 | 8.1 | 10.4 |
| Bananas | 5.7 | 3.2 | 5.7 |
| Sugar | 11.1 | 6.2 | 8.3 |
| *Oils and Oilseeds* | | | |
| Groundnuts | 7.6 | 10.7 | 8.8 |
| Palm oil | 9.3 | 4.9 | 8.4 |

SOURCE: International Bank for Reconstruction and Development, International Monetary Fund, *The Problem of Stabilization of Prices of Primary Products*, Pt. I, Washington, D.C., 1969, p. 56.

* The fluctuation index is the average over the period of annual percentage differences between observations and the calculated trend, disregarding signs of the differences and expressing them as percentages of the trends. The trends for a given commodity are estimated by fitting a linear relation between time and the logarithms of the annual observations.

TABLE 3
MAJOR EXPORTS OF AFRICAN COUNTRIES IN 1967

| Country | Total Exports * (Million U.S.$) | Three Leading Exports Expressed as a Percentage ( ) of Total Exports | | |
|---|---|---|---|---|
| *North Africa* | | | | |
| Algeria | 724 | Crude petroleum & products (73) | Wine (8) | Liquefied natural gas (4) |
| Libya | 1,178 | Crude petroleum (99.8) | Groundnuts (0.1) | Citrus fruit (..) |

TABLE 3 *(Cont.)*

| Country | Total Exports * (Million U.S.$) | Three Leading Exports Expressed as a Percentage ( ) of Total Exports | | |
|---|---|---|---|---|
| Morocco | 424 | Phosphates (25) | Citrus fruit (18) | Fresh vegetables (15) |
| Tunisia | 149 | Phosphates (30) | Crude petroleum & products (15) | Fruit & vegetables (11) |
| *Middle Africa* | | | | |
| Angola | 238 | Coffee (52) | Diamonds (18) | Sisal (3) |
| Burundi | 16 | Coffee (83) | Cotton (9) | |
| Cameroon | 158 | Cocoa beans & products (28) | Coffee (28) | Aluminum (13) |
| Cen. Afr. Rep. | 29 | Industrial diamonds (47) | Cotton (23) | Coffee (20) |
| Chad | 27 | Cotton (83) | Bovine cattle (6) | Meat (4) |
| Congo (Brazza.) | 48 | Saw & veneer logs, non-construction (35) | Diamonds (34) | Sugar & products (13) |
| Congo (Kinshasa) | 435 | Copper (60) | Coffee (6) | Diamonds (5) |
| Dahomey | 15 | Palm-kernel oil (21) | Cotton (9) | Fodder (8) |
| Ethiopia | 101 | Coffee (56) | Hides & skins (12) | Linseed & sesame (9) |
| Gabon | 120 | Crude petroleum (30) | Manganese (27) | Saw & veneer logs, non construction (25) |
| Gambia | 14 | Groundnuts (43) | Groundnut oil (43) | Fodder (14) |
| Ghana | 278 | Cocoa beans (58) | Cocoa butter & paste (11) | Logs & lumber (10) |
| Guinea [1] | 50 | Alumina (63) | Coffee (10) | Bananas (8) |
| Ivory Coast | 325 | Coffee (32) | Logs & lumber, non-con. (26) | Cocoa beans (17) |
| Kenya | 166 | Coffee (30) | Tea (14) | Petroleum products (14) |
| Liberia | 159 | Iron ore & concentrates (75) | Natural rubber (17) | Diamonds (4) |
| Malagasy Rep. | 104 | Coffee (32) | Spices (11) | Sugar & products (8) |
| Malawi | 57 | Tea (27) | Tobacco (26) | Groundnuts (21) |
| Mali | 17 | Cotton (30) | Live animals (25) | Fish (14) |

TABLE 3 (Cont.)

| Country | Total Exports * (Million U.S.$) | Three Leading Exports Expressed as a Percentage ( ) of Total Exports | | |
|---|---|---|---|---|
| Mauretania [2] | 70 | Iron ore (92) | Fish (4) | Resins, natural gums (1) |
| Mauritius | 64 | Sugar (94) | Molasses (3) | Tea (3) |
| Mozambique | 122 | Cotton (18) | Cashew nuts (15) | Sugar (9) |
| Niger | 33 | Groundnuts (69) | Live animals (10) | Groundnut oil (7) |
| Nigeria | 680 | Crude petroleum (30) | Cocoa beans (23) | Groundnuts & oil (18) |
| Réunion | 36 | Sugar (81) | Essential oils (11) | Rum (4) |
| Rhodesia, S. | 264 | Tobacco (20) | Asbestos (5) | Copper (3) |
| Rwanda | 14 | Coffee (55) | Tin (30) | Tungsten (7) |
| Senegal | 137 | Groundnut oil (43) | Groundnuts (23) | Oilseed cake & meal (12) |
| Sierra Leone | 70 | Diamonds (65) | Iron ore (20) | Cocoa (3) |
| Somalia | 28 | Hides & skins (42) | Bananas (34) | Live animals includes camels) (11) |
| Sudan | 215 | Cotton (55) | Gum arabic (11) | Sesame (9); Groundnuts (9) |
| Tanzania | 222 | Cotton (16) | Coffee (15) | Diamonds (14) |
| Togo | 32 | Phosphates (38) | Cocoa (30) | Coffee (11) |
| Uganda | 184 | Coffee (54) | Cotton (24) | Copper (9) |
| Upper Volta | 18 | Live animals (51) | Cotton (19) | Oilseeds (13) |
| Zambia | 658 | Copper (93) | Maize (2) | Zinc (2) |
| South Africa | 3,235 | Gold (35) | Diamonds (5) | Copper (4) |
| Total Above | 10,918 | | | |
| Other | 156 | | | |
| Total Africa | 11,074 | | | |

* Includes re-exports.
[1] Per cent of gross exports in 1965.
[2] Per cent of exports in 1966.

SOURCES: International Monetary Fund, *International Financial Statistics*, March, 1970.
United Nations, *Monthly Bulletin of Statistics*, February, 1970.
United Nations, *Yearbook of International Trade Statistics*, 1967.
Export Projections & Trade Division, Economics Dept. World Bank Group.

## TABLE 4
### AFRICA—EXPORTS BY COUNTRY, SELECTED YEARS
#### Including Gold Exports
#### (in millions of U.S. dollars)

| Country | 1938 | 1950 | 1960 | 1967 | 1968 |
|---|---|---|---|---|---|
| *Total* | 1,285 | 3,603 | 6,580 | 10,896 | 12,297 |
| Algeria | 162 | 333 | 394 | 724 | 759 |
| Angola | 15 | 75 | 124 | 238 | 276 |
| Cameroon | 7 | 47 | 97 | 158 | 189 |
| Congo (Kinshasa) | 64 | 273 | 501 | 446 | 516 |
| Central African Rep. | | | 14 | 28 | 36 |
| Chad | 8 | 45 | 13 | 27 | 28 |
| Congo (Brazzaville) | | | 18 | 47 | 49 |
| Gabon | | | 48 | 121 | 125 |
| Dahomey | 3 | 13 | 18 | 15 | 22 |
| Ivory Coast | 11 | 79 | 151 | 325 | 425 |
| Senegal | 22 | 72 | 113 | 139 | 151 |
| Niger | 1 | 3 | 13 | 33 | 38 |
| Ghana | 76 | 216 | 325 | 308 | 336 |
| Kenya | 44 | 58 | 113 | 167 | 176 |
| Uganda | 1 | 81 | 120 | 184 | 186 |
| Tanganyika | 18 | 68 | 158 | 223 | 227 |
| Liberia | 2 | 28 | 83 | 159 | 169 |
| Malagasy Rep. | 24 | 69 | 75 | 104 | 116 |
| Mauritius | 14 | 32 | 39 | 64 | 67 |
| Morocco | 43 | 190 | 354 | 424 | 450 |
| Mozambique | 9 | 37 | 78 | 133 | 154 |
| Nigeria | 47 | 253 | 475 | 680 | 587 |
| Réunion | 6 | 19 | 37 | 38 | 46 |
| Zambia | 49 | 140 | 362 | 658 | 759 |
| Malawi | n.a. | 21 | 24 [2] | 57 | 58 |
| Southern Rhodesia | 52 | 135 | 193 | 281 | 275e |
| Sierra Leone | 12 | 22 | 83 | 70 | 96 |
| South Africa | 496 | 946 | 2,018 | 3,026 | 3,235 |
| Tunisia | 39 | 114 | 120 | 149 | 158 |
| Gambia | 2 | 6 | 8 | 16 | 15 |
| Zanzibar & Pemba | 4 | 14 | 16 | 16 | 14 |
| Togo | 2 | 9 | 15 | 32 | 39 |
| Upper Volta | 3 | 3 | 4 | 18 | 21 |
| Guinea | 3 | 11 | 55 | 54 | 55 |
| Cape Verde Islands | 5 | n.a. | 11 | 13 | 16 |
| Ethiopia | n.a. | 28 | 77 | 101 | 106 |
| Libya | 6 | 10 | 11 | 1,178 [4] | 1,876 [4] |

TABLE 4 (Cont.)

| Country | 1938 | 1950 | 1960 | 1967 | 1968 |
|---------|------|------|------|------|------|
| Sudan | 30 | 95 | 182 | 214 | 245 |
| São Tomé | 2 | n.a. | 7 | 8 | 9 |
| All other | 9 | 61 | 33 | 220 | 192 |

Note 1: Conversions each year made at current exchange rate in that year.
Note 2: 1968—Gold included only in Congo (Kinshasa), Gabon, Ghana, Tanganyika, Rhodesia, and South Africa.
Note 3: Above figures are trade plus gold exports from Table 3.

[1] Included with Kenya.
[2] Derived from total given by International Financial Statistics for three countries, less U. N. figures for Zambia and Rhodesia.
[3] Included with Ivory Coast.
[4] Of which 1967 oil exports = $1165 million, 1968 oil exports = $1860 million.
n.a.   Not available.
   e   Estimate.

SOURCE: International Monetary Fund, International Financial Statistics.
United Nations, Yearbook of International Trade Statistics.

TABLE 5
AFRICA—IMPORTS BY COUNTRY, SELECTED YEARS
Excluding Gold Imports
(c.i.f., in millions of U.S. dollars)

| Country | 1938 | 1950 | 1960 | 1967 | 1968 |
|---------|------|------|------|------|------|
| Total | 1,393 | 3,752 | 7,430 | 10,298 | 10,801 |
| Algeria | 143 | 434 | 1,265 | 639 | 788 |
| Angola | 10 | 58 | 128 | 275 | 308 |
| Cameroon | 6 | 60 | 83 | 188 | 188 |
| Congo (Kinshasa) | 35 | 188 | 186 | 265 | 316e |
| Central African Rep. |  |  | 20 | 44 | 40 |
| Chad | 8 | 77 | 25 | 40 | 38 |
| Congo (Brazzaville) |  |  | 70 | 96 | 97 |
| Gabon |  |  | 32 | 67 | 65 |
| Dahomey | 3 | 12 | 31 | 48 | 49 |
| Ivory Coast | 9 | 61 | 120 | 264 | 314 |
| Senegal | 29 | 140 | 172 | 157 | 181 |
| Niger | 1 | 4 | 14 | 46 | 41 |

TABLE 5 (*Cont.*)

| Country | 1938 | 1950 | 1960 | 1967 | 1968 |
|---|---|---|---|---|---|
| Ghana | 50 | 135 | 363 | 319 | 307 |
| Kenya | 47 | 89 | 196 | 298 | 321 |
| Uganda | [1] | 43 | 73 | 116 | 123 |
| Tanganyika | 17 | 67 | 106 | 221 | 215p |
| Liberia | 2 | 11 | 69 | 126 | 118 |
| Malagasy Rep. | 17 | 85 | 112 | 145 | 170 |
| Mauritius | 12 | 37 | 70 | 76 | 76 |
| Morocco | 62 | 330 | 413 | 517 | 551 |
| Mozambique | 22 | 58 | 127 | 199 | 234 |
| Nigeria | 42 | 173 | 603 | 626 | 541 |
| Réunion | 8 | 26 | 52 | 116 | 126 |
| Zambia | 25 | 84 ⎫ | | ⎛ 483 | 515 |
| Malawi | n.a. | 21 ⎬ | 495 | ⎨ 80 | 79 |
| Rhodesia | 41 | 184 ⎭ | | ⎝ 295 | 327 |
| Sierra Leone | 7 | 19 | 74 | 90 | 91 |
| South Africa | 516 | 936 | 1,711 | 2,948 | 2,891 |
| Tunisia | 45 | 147 | 191 | 261 | 218 |
| Gambia | 2 | 8 | 9 | 20 | 20 |
| Zanzibar | 5 | 10 | 15 | 8 | 9 |
| Togo | 2 | 9 | 26 | 45 | 47 |
| Upper Volta | [2] | [2] | 8 | 41 | 42p |
| Guinea | 5 | 24 | 50 | 70 | 70 |
| Cape Verde Islands | 5 | n.a. | 12 | 9 | 10 |
| Ethiopia | n.a. | 30 | 88 | 143 | 173 |
| Libya | 47 | 19 | 169 | 476 | 645 |
| Sudan | 32 | 78 | 183 | 233 | 258 |
| São Tomé & Príncipe | 1 | n.a. | 5 | 5 | 6 |
| All other | 137 | 100 | 64 | 203 | 193 |

*Note:* Conversions each year made at current exchange rate in that year.

[1] Included with Kenya.
[2] Included with Ivory Coast.
n.a.   Not available.
  e   Estimate.

SOURCES: International Monetary Fund, *International Financial Statistics.*
United Nations, *Yearbook of International Trade Statistics.*

TABLE 6
AFRICA—EXPORTS OF GOLD, SELECTED YEARS
(f.o.b., in millions of U.S. dollars)

| Country | 1938 | 1950 | 1960 | 1697 | 1968 |
|---|---|---|---|---|---|
| Total [1] | 435.5 | 381.3 | 820.9 | 1,141.9 | 1,129.2 |
| Algeria | 9.3 | — | 0.1 | — | — |
| Cameroon | 0.4 | 0.3 | [2] | [2] | — |
| Congo (Kinshasa) | 14.4 | 11.9 | 10.8 | 5.3 | — |
| Central African Rep. | 1.0 | 1.8 | 0.1 | — | 5.7 |
| Congo (Brazzaville) | | | 0.1 | — | — |
| Gabon | | | 0.6 | 0.7 | — |
| Senegal | 3.4 | 0.8 | — | — | n.a. |
| Ghana | 23.6 | 24.4 | 31.1 | 24.5 | 28.2 |
| Kenya | 3.3 | 1.0 | 0.3 | 0.9 | 0.9 |
| Uganda | | | | — | — |
| Tanganyika | 2.9 | 2.3 | 3.4 | 0.6 | n.a. |
| Liberia | 0.1 | — | — | — | — |
| Malagasy Rep. | — | 0.1 | — | — | — |
| Morocco | — | 0.1 | 0.1 | — | — |
| Mozambique | 0.5 | — | 4.7 | 10.5 | n.a. |
| Nigeria | 0.9 | — | — | — | — |
| Rhodesia | 28.0 | 18.2 | 19.5 | 17.5 | 17.5 e |
| Sierra Leone | 1.0 | 0.1 | — | — | — |
| South Africa | 355.2 [4] | 319.8 | 750.0 | 1,082.0 | 1,077.0 |
| Sudan | 0.5 | — | 0.1 | — | — |
| Ethiopia | — | 0.5 | — | — | — |

Note 1: Conversions in each year were made at the current exchange rate in that year.
Note 2: For comparison purposes, the following table is shown:

| | Congo (Kinshasa) | Ghana | South Africa | Rhodesia * |
|---|---|---|---|---|
| Exports of gold 1946–68 | 234.7 | 615.3 | 15,838.6 | 426.0 |
| Production of gold 1946–68 | 232.5 | 605.4 | 15,437.4 | 429.0 |

* Partial estimate.

[1] Total of countries shown.   [2] Less than $50,000.   [3] French Equatorial Africa.
[4] U.S. Department of Commerce, U.S. Treasury, and S.A. Reserve Bank Bulletin.

n.a.  Not available.     e  Estimated.

SOURCES: United Nations, Yearbook of International Trade Statistics.
U.S. Department of Interior, Minerals Yearbook and Preprint, Gold, 1968.
International Monetary Fund, Balance of Payments Yearbook.

TABLE 7

AFRICA—GOLD PRODUCTION, SELECTED YEARS

(in millions of U. S. dollars at 35 dollars per fine ounce)

| Country | 1938 | 1950 | 1960 | 1967 | 1968 |
|---|---|---|---|---|---|
| Total | 514.4 | 437.7 | 817.3 | 1,122.4 | 1,141.3 |
| Congo (Kinshasa) | 15.9 | 11.9 | 11.1 | 5.4 | 5.9 |
| Ghana | 23.6 | 24.1 | 30.8 | 26.7 | 25.4 |
| Rhodesia | 28.5 | 17.9 | 19.7 | 17.5 | 17.5 e |
| South Africa | 425.7 | 408.2 | 748.4 | 1,068.7 | 1,088.3 |
| Tanganyika | 2.9 | 2.3 | 3.7 | 0.6 | 0.6 |
| All other | 18.3 | 9.3 | 3.6 | 3.5 | 3.6 |

e Estimated.

SOURCES: International Monetary Fund, *International Financial Statistics.*
U.S. Department of Interior, *Mineral Yearbook* and *Preprint, Gold,* 1968.

TABLE 8

IMPORTANCE OF AFRICA IN THE WORLD MARKET
FOR ITS MAJOR EXPORTS IN 1967
(based on quantity)

| Commodity | Percentage of world market supplied by African countries | African countries supplying more than 5 per cent of the market |
|---|---|---|
| *Foods and Beverages* | | |
| Coffee | 29 | Angola (6), Uganda (5), Ivory Coast (5) |
| Cocoa beans | 77 | Ghana (30), Nigeria (23), Ivory Coast (10), Cameroon (7) |
| Groundnuts | 85 | Nigeria (37), Senegal (12), Niger (11), Sudan (7), South Africa (6) |
| Groundnut oil | 66 | Senegal (38), Nigeria (17), Gambia (5) |
| Palm oil | 43 | Nigeria (21), Congo (Kinshasa) (17) |
| Palm kernels | 83 | Nigeria (45), Sierra Leone (6), Cameroon (5), Angola (5) |

TABLE 8   (Cont.)

| Commodity | Percentage of world market supplied by African countries | African countries supplying more than 5 per cent of the market |
|---|---|---|
| Foods and Beverages (Cont.) | | |
| Palm kernel oil | 80 | Congo (Kinshasa) (34), Nigeria (31), Dahomey (14) |
| Tea | 12 | |
| Wine | 31 | Algeria (21), Morocco (5) |
| Agricultural Raw Materials | | |
| Cotton | 13 | Sudan (5) |
| Sisal | 60 | Tanganyika (37), Angola (9), Kenya (8) |
| Rubber | 5 | |
| Tobacco | 11 | Southern Rhodesia (9) |
| Timber | | |
| Broadleaved logs | 22 | Ivory Coast (9), Gabon (5) |
| Sawn hardwood | 12 | |
| Minerals | | |
| Manganese ore | 26 [1] | South Africa (9), Congo (Kinshasa) (7) |
| Copper | 44 [2] | Zambia (25), Congo (Kinshasa) (13) |
| Iron ore | 13 | Liberia (9) |
| Diamonds [3] | | |
| Gem | 83 | South Africa (32), Congo (Kinshasa) (16), Angola (10), Tanzania (9), Sierra Leone (6) |
| Industrial | 82 | Congo (Kinshasa) (41), Congo (Brazzaville) (16), South Africa (12), Ghana (7) |
| Gold | 90 | South Africa (87) |
| Bauxite | 9 | |
| Phosphates | 9 | |
| Uranium [4] | 21 | South Africa (18) |
| Chrome | 37 | South Africa (19), Rhodesia (18) |
| Asbestos | 20 | South Africa (12), Rhodesia (8) |

[1] World production 1966.
[2] Exportable surplus 1966.
[3] Production.
[4] World ex bloc production.

SOURCES: FAO: Trade Yearbook, 1968; Yearbook of Forest Products, 1968. U.N. Commodity Survey, 1968. U.S. Department of Interior, Bureau of Mines, Minerals Yearbook Preprints, 1968. Statistical Summary of the Mineral Industry, 1962–67.

TABLE 9
MIDDLE AFRICA BALANCE OF PAYMENTS
(in millions of U.S. dollars)

| | Average 1963–64 | Average 1965–66 | 1967 |
|---|---|---|---|
| *Current Account* | | | |
| Exports of goods including non-monetary gold | 2,477 | 3,544 | 3,712 |
| Imports including non-monetary gold | —2,273 | —3,198 | —3,230 |
| Net trade including non-monetary gold | 204 | 346 | 482 |
| Net freight including insurance and other transportation | — 202 | — 305 | — 295 |
| Net travel | — 75 | — 82 | — 84 |
| Net direct investment income and other | — 214 | — 393 | — 364 |
| Net government, n.i.e. | 2 | — 58 | — 133 |
| Net non-merchandise insurance, other services | — 112 | — 177 | — 223 |
| Net private unrequited transfers | — 105 | — 120 | — 133 |
| Net central government unrequited transfers | 153 | 225 | 190 |
| Net Current Account Balance | — 348 | — 564 | — 560 |
| *Capital Account* | | | |
| Net direct investment | 194 | 233 | 172 |
| Net long-term capital other than direct investment; central government drawings on loans; net other than loans; local government net | 283 | 362 | 403 |
| Central government repayments on loans | — 86 | — 104 | — 88 |
| Private short-term capital, net | — 4 | 26 | — 9 |
| Private monetary institutions, assets and liabilities, net | 20 | — 12 | 0 |
| Central monetary institutions, assets and liabilities, net | 61 | 11 | 114 |
| Central monetary investment, monetary gold, net | 0 | — 4 | — 1 |
| Net errors and omissions | — 119 | 53 | — 31 |
| Net Capital Account | + 348 | + 564 | + 560 |

*Note:* Middle Africa includes all Africa *except* the following: South Africa, Morocco, Tunisia, Libya, and Algeria.

SOURCE: International Monetary Fund, *World Summary of Reported Balance of Payments Statistics, 1962–67*, DM/69/53, August 14, 1969.

TABLE 10
NORTH AFRICA (MOROCCO, TUNISIA, AND LIBYA)* BALANCE OF PAYMENTS
(in millions of U. S. dollars)

| | Average 1963–64 | Average 1965–66 | 1967 |
|---|---|---|---|
| *Current Account* | | | |
| Exports of goods including non-monetary gold | 1,017 | 1,460 | 1,747 |
| Imports including non-monetary gold | — 917 | —1,005 | —1,179 |
| Net trade including non-monetary gold | 100 | 455 | 568 |
| Net freight including insurance and other transportation | — 66 | — 84 | — 95 |
| Net travel | 9 | 44 | 35 |
| Net direct investment income and other | — 123 | — 254 | — 328 |
| Net government, n.i.e. | 37 | 11 | — 28 |
| Net non-merchandise insurance, other services | — 132 | — 223 | — 224 |
| Net private unrequited transfers | — 50 | — 49 | — 9 |
| Net central government unrequited transfers | 75 | 40 | — 45 |
| Net Current Account Balance | — 150 | — 60 | — 126 |
| *Capital Account* | | | |
| Net direct investment | 56 | 29 | 50 |
| Net long-term capital other than direct investment; central government drawings on loans; net other than loans; local government net | 112 | 171 | 180 |
| Central government repayments on loans | — 14 | — 39 | — 35 |
| Private short-term capital, net | 5 | 5 | — 24 |
| Private monetary institutions, assets and liabilities, net | 5 | 4 | 3 |
| Central monetary institutions, assets and liabilities, net | 37 | — 78 | — 18 |
| Central monetary investment, monetary gold, net | — 10 | — 19 | 0 |
| Net errors and omissions | — 41 | — 14 | — 31 |
| Net Capital Account | + 150 | + 59 | + 126 |

* Figures for Algeria not available.

SOURCE: International Monetary Fund, *World Summary of Reported Balance of Payments Statistics, 1962–67,* DM/69/53, August 14, 1969.

TABLE 11
TOTAL AFRICA (EXCLUDING SOUTH AFRICA) BALANCE OF PAYMENTS
(in millions of U. S. dollars)

| | Average 1963–64 | Average 1965–66 | 1967 |
|---|---|---|---|
| *Current Account* | | | |
| Exports of goods including non-monetary gold | 3,494 | 5,004 | 5,459 |
| Imports including non-monetary gold | —3,190 | —4,202 | —4,410 |
| Net trade including non-monetary gold | 304 | 802 | 1,049 |
| Net freight including insurance and other transportation | — 268 | — 389 | — 390 |
| Net travel | — 66 | — 39 | — 49 |
| Net direct investment income and other | — 336 | — 647 | — 691 |
| Net government, n.i.e. | 39 | — 47 | — 161 |
| Net non-merchandise insurance, other services | — 244 | — 400 | — 447 |
| Net private unrequited transfers | — 155 | — 169 | — 142 |
| Net central government unrequited transfers | 228 | 265 | 145 |
| Net Current Account Balance | — 498 | — 624 | — 686 |
| *Capital Account* | | | |
| Net direct investment | 250 | 262 | 222 |
| Net long-term capital other than direct investment; central government drawings on loans; net other than loans; local government net | 395 | 533 | 583 |
| Central government repayments on loans | — 100 | — 143 | — 123 |
| Private short-term capital, net | 1 | 31 | — 33 |
| Private monetary institutions, assets and liabilities, net | 25 | — 8 | 3 |
| Central monetary institutions, assets and liabilities, net | 98 | — 67 | 96 |
| Central monetary investment, monetary gold, net | — 10 | — 23 | — 1 |
| Net errors and omissions | — 160 | 39 | — 62 |
| Net Capital Account | + 498 | + 624 | + 686 |

*Note:* Lesotho is included with South Africa and therefore excluded from "Total Africa" in this table.

SOURCE: International Monetary Fund, *World Summary of Reported Balance of Payments Statistics, 1962–67,* DM/69/53, August 14, 1969.

TABLE 12
SOUTH AFRICA BALANCE OF PAYMENTS
(in millions of U. S. dollars)

|  | Average 1963–64 | Average 1965–66 | 1967 |
|---|---|---|---|
| *Current Account* | | | |
| Exports of goods including non-monetary gold | 2,467 | 2,664 | 2,899 |
| Imports including non-monetary gold | —2,028 | —2,451 | —2,764 |
| Net trade including non-monetary gold | 439 | 213 | 135 |
| Net freight including insurance and other transportation | — 118 | — 144 | — 94 |
| Net travel | — 16 | — 20 | — 20 |
| Net direct investment income and other | — 226 | — 267 | — 300 |
| Net government, n.i.e. | — 3 | — 1 | 0 |
| Net non-merchandise insurance, other services | — 50 | — 66 | — 84 |
| Net private unrequited transfers | 6 | 20 | 28 |
| Net central government unrequited transfers | 32 | 50 | 73 |
| Net Current Account Balance | + 64 | — 215 | — 262 |
| *Capital Account* | | | |
| Net direct investment | 11 | 110 | 102 |
| Net long-term capital other than direct investment; central government drawings on loans; net other than loans; local government net | — 81 | 94 | 139 |
| Central government repayments on loans | — 27 | — 36 | — 25 |
| Private short-term capital, net | — 7 | 27 | — 42 |
| Private monetary institutions, assets and liabilities, net | 44 | 12 | — 17 |
| Central monetary institutions, assets and liabilities, net | 6 | — 4 | — 43 |
| Central monetary investment, monetary gold, net | — 38 | — 32 | 55 |
| Net errors and omissions | 27 | 44 | 92 |
| Net Capital Account | — 64 | + 215 | + 262 |

SOURCE: International Monetary Fund, *World Summary of Reported Balance of Payments Statistics, 1962–67,* DM/69/53, August 14, 1969.

# V

# African Agriculture:
# Problems and Solutions

*. . . It is not loneliness that oppresses the equatorial traveller; it is too much company; it is the uneasy feeling that he is an alien in the midst of an innumerable throng of hostile beings. To us who live beneath a temperate sky and in the age of Henry Ford, the worship of Nature comes almost naturally. It is easy to love a feeble and already conquered enemy. But an enemy with whom one is still at war, an unconquered, unconquerable, ceaselessly active enemy—no; one does not, one should not, love him. . . . At latitude zero . . . the obvious is not the same as with us. Rivers imply wading, swimming, alligators. Plains mean swamps, forests, fevers. Mountains are either dangerous or impassable. To travel is to hack one's way laboriously through a tangled, prickly, and venomous darkness. "God made the country," said Cowper, in his rather too blank verse. In [the tropics] he would have had his doubts. . . .*

**ALDOUS HUXLEY**

The typical African is still a farmer or cattle herder. Ninety per cent of the African people live on farms. Almost two-thirds of Africa's exports are agricultural products, and these are the principal source of foreign-exchange earnings for all African countries except South Africa, Zambia, the Congo (Kinshasa), Central African Republic, Liberia, Sierra Leone, and Mauretania. These main exports are comparatively few in number, however—cocoa, coffee, peanut products, cotton, lumber, palm products, tobacco, sugar, rubber, sisal, tea, bananas, and hides and skins.

The key sector for economic development in most of Africa is still, therefore, agriculture. So far, only a few African countries have found and developed mineral resources, the only alternative way, at this stage, of earning foreign exchange. For most African countries, then, it is agriculture that must be depended on: to raise the standard of living of the people initially, to provide the minimum market necessary for manufactures to get a foothold, to earn the necessary foreign exchange to pay for imports, and to provide the revenues to finance needed government services. The improvement of agriculture must be the central part of any development program. How, then, can this task be accomplished?

No simple answer to this question can be found in Africa. Although husbandry is one of the first skills acquired by man, to practice it well is still among the most difficult of achievements. Unlike manufacturing, the conditions of agricultural production—climate, soil, pests, diseases, the genetic qualities of plants and animals—are not easily controlled by man. (On the other hand, agriculture usually makes only minimal demands on such critically scarce resources as investible funds, foreign exchange, and high-caliber entrepreneurial talent, all of which are needed for industrial development.) Again, more depends on raising the level of productivity of the individual in agriculture, or his attitude toward work, or his power to make intelligent decisions than is true of the workers engaged in manufacturing. In agriculture, management has to be highly decentralized. All day long, the individual farmer or the worker in the fields must make managerial decisions—Should I plant this field this morning or weed that one? should I repair this fence or clean out that drainage ditch?

Rapid progress in agriculture can be achieved only by moving ahead on many fronts. If research has discovered the best fertilizer to use for a particular plant on a particular soil, it may be necessary also to develop the varieties that will respond best to it; to work out what changes in cultivation practices are necessary—such as planting more or less densely; to develop, perhaps, a different kind of weeding tool; and to change the times and methods of planting, weeding, and harvesting.

The problems facing the African countries in this respect, while difficult, are in fact similar to those confronted and solved by many presently developed countries. Industrialization in the United Kingdom, the United States, Australia, and Japan, for instance, was preceded in every case by the development of agriculture; it depended on and was able to build on agricultural incomes as a base. To achieve the necessary increase in agricultural incomes in Africa, changes have to be made in the kind of farming practiced over the centuries. Africans and African governments have already modified the old systems of farming or experimented with them in a number of ways, attempting to improve the standard of living and to develop the economy.

## Nature

### CLIMATE

Although Africa's chief livelihood depends on the land, she is singularly ill favored by nature. "About 92 per cent of the continent may be said to suffer from one or another climatic disability—surely one of the most important facts concerning Africa. . . . [Africa] presents a picture, as far as water is concerned, of plenty where it cannot be used and of paucity where it is most needed." (Hance, p. 15.) Forty per cent of the continent is arid or desert; another 20 per cent is semi-arid. In about three quarters of sub-Saharan Africa, rainfall is scanty. Only 6 per cent of South Africa, for example, has sufficient rainfall to be fit for plowing. Around 20 per cent of the continent enjoys a savannah climate, with a long rainy and a short dry season; 8 per cent has a tropical rainy season of 10 to 12 months. Rainfall fluctuates greatly within the year and from year to year; "average annual rainfall" means little when one year may receive three times as much rain as the next, or when it does not come evenly throughout a given season of the year but falls in torrents. The degree of variation even in a large river basin such as the Volta, which drains 40,000–50,000 square miles, is very great: at

Akosombo, the flow at the peak is 125,000–350,000 cubic feet per second and only about 1,000 at the low.

But, while the African climate tends to be violent, and the sun is as often an enemy as a friend, the African heat and the absence of frost or winter over most of the continent favor the reproduction and growth of most species of life—whether animal, plant, or virus. As man learns to master the problems of the tropics, this can be turned to enormous advantage. On the present scale of research effort, however, it is unlikely that this potentiality will be fully realized in this century—but it is nevertheless there.

The forests of Africa are mostly restricted to woodland parts of the savannah—which have little in the way of commercially usable trees—and to the tropical rain forests, which do have major economic significance. What remains of the tropical rain forest begins in Liberia, stretches across to southwest Ghana, begins again in Nigeria, continues across Cameroon, Gabon, and the two Congoes to the plateau near the great lakes. There are also some remnants in the eastern part of the Malagasy Republic. It is primarily these tropical forest areas that produce four of Africa's most important exports: cocoa, palm products, timber, and rubber.

## Soil

Little is known about how best to exploit and improve tropical soils. In general, these soils tend to be poor, owing principally to the poor rock from which they were formed, because they contain little organic material. Except for the volcanic soils, African soils are generally derived from old acid parent rock which is poor in calcium and plant nutrients. The usefulness of the soils can also be easily destroyed. It may be true, however, that once the technique of the proper care has been found and applied, the soils will prove to be easily regenerated. There are already hints that this is so in a few experiments in restoring soil damaged by heavy erosion.

It took some time to learn that tropical soils are poor, for the evidence that springs to one's eyes seems to show that the soils must be very rich. Everyone who has traveled in Africa has seen fence posts that have taken root and started to grow, telephone poles that have put out branches. But nevertheless, tropical soils, even in the dense virgin forests, are usually thin and poor in fertility. In the forests, the plants and trees constantly return to the supporting soil in the form of dead leaves, branches, and trunks—the elements they borrowed from it so that equilibrium is maintained. But it is a precarious equilibrium, with very small reserves. If the tree or plant cover is removed, the thin layer of humus is soon exhausted or washed away with the first heavy rains.

Good soil is much like a complex living organism: its skeleton is made up of numerous tiny mineral soil particles aggregated into a firm and flexible structure. Intermingled with this skeleton are the organic substances, the "humus," which is the product of bacteria action on plant litter: in one pound of fertile soil, there may be 500 million fungi, 500 million protozoa, 10 billion bacteria, 400 billion algae. (Aside from their general function of creating humus, these organisms often have specific and essential functions. The successful establishment of the rapidly growing *pinus radiata* [Monterey pine] in forestry plantations in eastern Africa depended on bringing along with the seed from North America the particular fungus with which the tree roots have a close cooperative relationship.)

But for all these organisms to exist, the soil structure must be such that it can contain freely circulating air and water. In the tropics, it has to be protected against the heat of the sun, which would burn away the organic matter and kill the micro-organisms; and it has to be protected from the direct blows of the torrential rains, which would crush the structure of the soil, seal off the underlying soil from the air, and leach out the minerals or carry them so far into the earth that the plant roots cannot reach them. When the soil is laid bare and exposed to the elements, its temperature rises and the sun hastens the oxidation and disappearance of the humus; the big swings in temperature that occur in the tropics between day and night accelerate the mechanical disintegration of the soil; and the rains and the wind erode it. (Schroo, pp. 40–44.)

Tropical soils must, therefore, be protected against the sun and rain—by the existing natural vegetation, by cover crops, or by a thick mulch. Taught by centuries of experience, African farmers in some areas often plant in the same field three or four crops which mature at different times and so maintain a green canopy over the ground until the last is harvested. (This also provides a measure of security in the event one crop is lost.) Care has to be taken when introducing mechanical equipment to avoid plowing too deeply and burying the thin layer of fertile soil.

A peculiar transformation of the soil takes place in many areas of the tropics. When the forest cover is removed, silicate minerals are decomposed and leached out so that the proportion of iron and aluminum hydroxides is increased; the resulting red or yellow soil is called laterite. In some areas, the percentage of aluminum hydroxide is high enough to lead to the formation of bauxite deposits, the raw material for aluminum, as in West Africa and Brazil, and even of iron-ore deposits, as those of Bukwe in Rhodesia, or Thabazimbi in South Africa. This helps to explain why bauxite and iron are such an important factor in Africa's economic potential (although most of the iron deposits in Africa did not originate in this way). But if drainage is impeded because the soil is crushed, the oxides may become iron-hard, and the passage of tractors or other heavy implements will leave behind unworkable soil. John Phillips cites an instance in which turning 80 acres of lateritic soil in central Tanzania wore 6 inches off the diameter of the 36-inch steel discs on heavy harrows.

There are important exceptions to the poverty of soils in tropical Africa. The first is the clay soil found in the alluvial plains—along the coast, in the center of wide valleys, and, in particular, south of Lakes Albert and Kyoga in Uganda, which is one of the few large areas of fertile soil in Africa. A second main exception is the usually fertile volcanic soil found in Rwanda, Burundi, western Cameroon, Ethiopia, central Kenya from Mt. Meru extending through to Mt. Kilimanjaro in Tanzania, the Poroto Mountains at the head of Lake Nyasa, and Mt. Elgon and the Ruwenzori Mountains in Uganda. Finally, the forest soils of tropical mountains that are high enough to escape the great heat found at lower altitudes tend to be rich in humus and fertile. All in all, the African soils vary greatly in quality. Variations from place to place are much greater than in temperate-zone countries, where, moreover, over the centuries, ploughing, manuring, fertilizing, and liming have built up the quality of the soils.

One further comment must be made on Africa's soils: their chemical make-up tends to perpetuate the shortage of proteins in the African diet—a shortage that naturally has an impact on work efficiency:

As might be expected, tropical plants tend to be poor in nitrogenous constituents which must be manufactured from the precarious supplies in the soil. On the other hand they are relatively rich in carbohydrate which can be synthesized by the plant from carbon dioxide in the air and the abundant water. Sugar, manioc, rice, corn, and sweet potatoes are familiar examples of tropical foodstuffs rich in carbohydrate but relatively poor in protein. (Lee, p. 33.)

Much has been learned through intensive research efforts on how to handle the soils for tree crops in order to improve output, but for the annual crops this is not yet true. Since World War II, the experiments with fertilizer on tree crops have produced remarkably good results—in considerable gains in productivity and improved plants—but similar experiments on annual crops have so far had little success except in a few cotton-growing areas. Fertilizers are expensive, and little is known about what specific deficiencies need to be made good in tropical soils and how they can be made good. It took some twenty years to discover what trace elements (tiny percentages of minerals such as copper, cobalt, etc.) were needed in the Kenya soils to make it possible to raise non-African breeds of livestock successfully. Then, too, in areas subject to hard tropical rains, the fertilizer a farmer puts on the soil may go down the river with the next downpour, if the application is not done correctly. (See below, pp. 151–54.)

## COMPETITION FOR SURVIVAL

While the soils of tropical Africa may be poor, the climate, as noted, favors reproduction and growth. The result is that life in Africa takes on an almost infinite multiplicity of species and sub-species, but with only a relatively few individuals of any one kind in any one place. Only a mixed animal population with varying demands can survive where the heat favors food growth but the supply of any one required food is limited. As a result, the competition for survival among the species is fierce and the evolutionary cycle most rapid. (It is not surprising that the human population in Africa was also sparse and widely scattered. For man to have survived in Africa, he had to beat off assaults from every quarter. The poet for the tropics is Henley and, above all, never Wordsworth.)

These central facts of the tropics—fierce competition for survival, and the dependence on dispersion for survival—have large economic implications. Tropical lumbering, for example, is a quite different operation from temperate-zone lumbering. In the tropics, there may be only one or two trees of a particular kind—mahogany, for instance —per acre; the lumberer is engaged in an activity that is more like hunting than mass production, and costs go up. Another, even more important, effect is that it is extremely difficult to grow a concentration of any particular plant or animal. There is a good chance that among the surrounding multiplicity of species there is at least one present or potential enemy of the crop or animal. The enemy may be a microbe, a virus, an insect, an animal, a bird, or even a plant. Defense against it is an essential part of any major innovation in agriculture in the tropics. For once that enemy discovers the new growth, it will flourish at the expense of its food, until there are only a few individuals of either kind, living in precarious coexistence. (Similar problems, but on a lesser scale, confront agriculture in the temperate zones also. In Great Britain, for example, potatoes can be grown on the same land only one year in seven; in Utah, sugar beets require a four- or five-year rotation; tomatoes should not be planted in the same place two years in succession—all this to avoid the concentration and build-up of disease organisms.)

Africa is littered with the ruins of projects that neglected this factor. The British Colonial Development Corporation's million-dollar chicken-raising scheme in Gambia was completely wrecked by disease killing off the chickens by hundreds of thousands. The Richard Toll rice-growing scheme in Senegal has not yet coped successfully with the hundreds of thousands of weaverbirds (Quelea) that descend on the paddies each year when the rice is ripe. Sorghum, a basic cereal over much of Africa, is also attacked both by weaverbirds and by the purple-flowered witchweed, which feeds on its roots. (This weed has now found its way into the southern United States.) The number of weaverbirds is so great that in Bornu Province, in northern Nigeria, their nesting places are destroyed with gasoline and bombs. The resultant hot blast kills the birds but leaves them intact otherwise. They are then collected, cooked, and eaten. About 50 million birds are killed this way a year, providing about 1,400 tons of animal protein for food.

The need for constant research and defense measures is well illustrated by the history of wheat-growing in Kenya. Lord Delamere, who introduced wheat into Kenya before World War I, spent almost ten years trying to grow wheat successfully—his first crops were destroyed by wheat rust—and finally succeeded in finding a rust-resistant wheat. During the 1950's, however, a super-virulent black stem rust succeeded in breaking through again and scientists had to develop a new kind of wheat to resist it. (McKelvey, p. 329.)

The enormous variety of species in Africa also includes bearers of animal and human diseases. There is no question but that disease in Africa is a major factor holding up development. The diseases that affect animals (in particular, the trypanosomiases carried by the tsetse fly, but also the tick-carried East Coast fever, rinderpest, etc.) prevent Africa from utilizing its vast stretches of savannah for a major meat-producing industry. An example of the difference the presence or absence the tsetse fly can make is the experience of Buruli County, in Uganda: in 1945, when the tsetse fly was present, there were 144 cattle in the county; in 1961, after the fly had been eradicated, the county was raising 46,000. (Masefield, p. 96.)

## Traditional African Farming

### SHIFTING CULTIVATION AND SUBSISTENCE FARMING

Over the centuries, the inhabitants of most of sub-Saharan Africa established a method of cultivation to meet the conditions confronting them—"shifting," or "semi-nomadic," cultivation, the same solution that peoples in other tropical countries have found.

The most important factor determining the choice of a particular system of cultivation is the character of the soil, which establishes the ratio between the length of time the soil can be cultivated with satisfactory results and the length of time it must be left alone to enable fertility to be restored. On the best soils, and where the climate is also favorable, it is possible to have almost continuous cultivation, or at least a fallow of only one year or two after three or four years of cultivation. The closest approach to continuous use of land in Africa is on the volcanic soils of Mts. Kilimanjaro and Elgon and the rich soils of Buganda, where plantains and bananas are permanent crops.

At the other extreme, there are weak, leached soils which "may require twenty-five years or even more to regain a brief fertility after two or three years of cultivation. Between these extremes there is an almost complete range of gradations, so that it is very difficult to say where shifting cultivation begins and ends." (Allan, p. 6.)

The cycle of shifting cultivation is roughly as follows: the men of the village, clan, or family clear the land; trees or bushes are cut down, branches are cut off, and the trees and branches are burned on the soil to be cultivated. The land, thus enriched by the ashes, is then cultivated by the women. (In some cases, in Zambia and the southern Congo, wood is collected and burned primarily to have the wood ash enrich the soil, not incidentally, as in other areas, where the main purpose is to clear the land.)

> The spectacle is very typical: a few tall trees, either protected by taboo or considered too difficult to fell, are still standing, witnesses to the former forest splendor and also precious seed-bearers for future vegetable recolonization; everywhere the stumps are standing, and between them the soft iron hoes of the women scratch the ground to make it produce a few crops of bananas, manioc, or sweet potatoes. Here and there, dotting these primitive fields, the untidiest in the world, are the blackened trunks that have not been properly burned. . . . Two or three years, sometimes four, of this exposure of the soil to the sun's rays and to the rains, are enough to deprive it of its fertility, and then the village waits for the signal from its old men and its witch doctors to depart to a new site suitable for temporary occupation. The abandoned clearing is then reconquered more or less rapidly by the forest, and this recolonization, depending upon the nature of the sub-soil, the degree of deterioration, and the extent of the clearing, is more or less complete, or, in other words, the secondary growth forms an assemblage perhaps as rich as the forest previously cleared by the cultivators.
>
> When sufficient land is available, the semi-nomadic group, under the leadership of its chiefs, makes ten to fifteen shifts before returning to a spot formerly occupied by it. This forest land, left uncultivated for thirty to fifty years, usually has its soil restored sufficiently to allow it to withstand a fresh cultural occupation under conditions not more harmful to it than those obtaining before; that is to say, if allowed the same period of rest, it is capable of a fresh regeneration sufficient to allow still another revolution of the cycle. (De la Rue *et al.*, pp. 171–72.)

The chosen farming areas of course become smaller and smaller in relation to increasing populations. Consequently, the periods of "bush fallow" must get shorter and shorter and the productivity of the soil declines. This problem has already begun to arise in eastern Nigeria, where, for tribal or other reasons, the people cannot easily move into new areas.

Even if enough land is available, major improvements in the farmers' standard of living are practically impossible in this type of farming—it is superb for survival but only at a bare existence level. Shifting cultivation has also meant, in many parts of Africa, but not all, that one of the main advantages of an agricultural over a nomadic life—the growth of a settled community—is not attained. (In Rwanda, people live in one place and cultivate the surrounding plots in rotation. But this is possible because the volcanic soil is sufficiently rich; it is more impracticable elsewhere.) However, in a few instances, the people had no choice but to remain permanently in one place even though the soil did not encourage permanent cultivation. This was the case, for example, of the Kara, on Ukara Island in Lake Victoria, and of the Hill Pagans in northern Cameroon, who were kept out of the lowlands by their enemies. In these instances, the people had to invent a method of permanent agriculture to survive, and they did. The Hill Pagans terraced the hillsides with stone walls, rotated their crops, kept cattle for manure, collected weeds to make compost, and used these, wood ash, and night soil to maintain the fertility of their fields. All this was much more laborious than shifting their location, but there was no choice.

Most farming in Africa is still subsistence farming—that is, the farmer produces mainly to feed himself and his family. More than half the agricultural output in Africa south of the Sahara is consumed on the farm. Now an agricultural economy consisting of subsistence producers is bound to be poor and nonprogressive: the producers are isolated from other economic influences; the mechanism through which small producers cooperate with the rest of the economy—that is, the market—is missing, and the inflow of innovations and ideas accordingly limited; specialization, an important means of growth in productivity, is absent, since it can develop only to the extent that exchange takes place.

It is possible that the transition from subsistence to market agriculture is the single most important economic change taking place in Africa today. Four main stages of this change-over can be differentiated. Examples of the first stage—completely self-contained subsist-

ence production—are already very rare; perhaps they exist only in the
Kalahari and Sahara deserts. There are still many communities in
the second stage, where the opportunity to sell a small surplus above
immediate subsistence requirements occurs largely unintentionally.
The production of a small surplus is, in fact, a normal result of subsistence agriculture in an average year. Since the farmers' lives depend on the food they produce, they must plant, if possible, an
area large enough to ensure sufficient food even if the season proves
to be a poor one—otherwise they are faced with starvation. In a
normal year, therefore, this insurance will result in a small surplus,
which, if a market is available, will be marketed. In this way,
subsistence agriculture slips easily with time into the next stage.

In the next stage, a marketable crop is deliberately introduced,
but the main emphasis is still on subsistence production. Most
African farmers in south, central, and eastern Africa and in the
savannah regions of West Africa are in these middle two categories.
In the fourth stage, production for the market predominates. The
cocoa farmers in Ghana and in the Western Region of Nigeria, and
the coffee producers of Buganda, have by and large reached this last
stage.

The foregoing to some extent oversimplifies the agricultural evolution of Africa. Most of the important cash crops are commodities
that are not produced for food in Africa but were added on to the
subsistence food production for sale for eventual export. Economic
growth in most of the African agricultural economies over the last
seventy years has come from farmers bringing new land into use
(supplementing that cultivated for subsistence crops), by men who
gave up some of their "leisure" to produce the cocoa, coffee, groundnut, or cotton crops for which there was an export market. An important part in this process was played by the various traders and
trading firms who brought in new consumer products for which the
money incomes were desired and by the governments' building of
railways and roads that made possible the movement of goods within
the country. The cash or export crops, in short, except in a very few
places, did not supplant but supplemented the subsistence food
crops. As they were produced by using resources that before had been
idle, they were a net addition to the incomes of the producers.

The subsistence food crops have entered very little into the market.
With the growth of cities in Africa, however, food crops for sale for

African consumption are becoming more important. The evidence suggests that there is still considerable unused potential to increase food production as demand for it grows, even with present techniques and present plant varieties. This may entail improving roads so that a sufficient producing area can have access to the city and improving the distribution system. Beyond this, as is discussed below, there should be a very large possibility of improving the yields and quality of the food produced through research.

With the growth of cities, there has also been in some countries a considerable increase in food imports. The reasons for this do not contradict the point just made, that African farmers can greatly increase the supply of food to the cities. The increase in food imports is due in part to demand on the part of expatriates and Africans who have acquired European tastes for some food commodities not produced in their country, such as wines, bread made from wheat, and meats. In some cases, it is also due to the fact that insufficient attention has been paid to teaching farmers to grow the fruits and vegetables demanded and to improving the transport system so that domestic produce can reach the city in good condition and can compete with frozen foods or foods flown in from Europe.

In brief, the food-supply position in Africa is not similar to that of India, for instance. In Africa, an increase in urban demand for foodstuffs usually calls forth an increase in supply from the countryside; but in India, an increase in demand for food in the cities often results not only in a rise in prices but in a drop in supply. This kind of backward-bending supply curve, which occurs rarely in Africa in this particular way, is due to the farmer-supplier's using part of his increased income from the raised prices in the form of increased consumption of his own food crops and so putting less on the market. The absence of this phenomenon in Africa not only testifies to the great elasticity of supply of African foods, but—which is the same thing in another form—also shows that Africans by and large get enough to eat. (However, in large areas of Africa where the tsetse fly prohibits cattle raising, Africans may not get enough *protein* foods to eat.)

AGRICULTURAL WORK PATTERNS

Like all peoples, African farmers do not fit into a single mold.

However, as is true of most national and cultural groups, it is possible to ascertain some dominant behavior and attitude characteristics.

First of all, the African farmer is not a "peasant" and does not behave like one, being much more open and receptive to change. While he is interested in economic and social security and, therefore, in land as a means to achieve that security, he does not have the deep emotional ties a peasant has to a particular piece of land or to agriculture as a way of life. The African farmer has readily moved from one area of land to another and is still ready to move at any time. He is also generally ready to go off and become a wage-earner if this will pay better.

The absence of a peasant mentality in African farmers is not wholly a benefit. Going along with the "business approach" that regards land as something to be exploited is the desire for a quick return. With insufficient heed to the long-term results of such exploitation, the land is "mined" rather than cultivated. The lack of a peasant commitment to the land also means that the farmer mixes farming with other occupations—being a school teacher, a trader, or an artisan. The full productivity of a farm may never be attained, even though the individual may maximize his income in the short run by engaging in this wide spectrum of activities.

Most African farmers also still place a high priority on "leisure," and this continues to inhibit the growth of their money income. It is true that "leisure" is rather a misnomer, since what they desire is rather time to engage in a wide range of traditional tribal activities—the administration of tribal justice, initiation ceremonies, discussions of tribal affairs. This priority has some economic basis in the traditional economy: the necessary food crops could be grown by the women alone; there was no particular gain in growing a surplus since it could not be sold nor could much of it be stored. It made sense, therefore, for the men, like the ancient Athenians, to devote much of their time to public affairs. (It is the same pattern, in fact, that leads the middle-class American woman, who now increasingly finds herself free from the necessities of work at home, to devote herself to civic causes and politics.)

In present-day Africa, this pattern often results in a decision not to put in more labor when that labor gives more income but at a sharply diminishing rate of return. This accounts for the widespread practice in many cotton-growing areas of Uganda, Kenya, and Tanzania of leaving the last 10 to 20 per cent of the cotton unpicked. Also, as his income rises, the farmer will often spend part of the increase to hire labor to do work that he and his family are well able to do.

The African farmer is interested not only in the level of his return but, and especially, in the security of the return. With his and his family's lives at stake, he will depart from tried and true practice only when he is convinced that the new practice is absolutely safe. It may be possible to show that if he plants his crop each year at a certain time he will get better average returns, but if this includes the risk of crop failure in *one* year, he will prefer to adjust to the variable rainfall in Africa, minimize his risk, and plant the crop over a number of days.

In the same way, the cattle herder may find that he maximizes security and income by building up his herd as much as he can during the good years and selling off or losing cattle in the bad years (getting some benefit from the hides and meat). He may find this more sensible than restricting the number of cattle to the average or minimum he can carry in good years and bad. There is evident here, in addition, a conflict between what is most sensible for the individual to do and what is most sensible for the group as a whole to do. If there is a large number of competitors for scarce grass, and the individual herder cannot rely on the others to behave "sensibly" and so restrict the total number of cattle to the optimum carrying capacity, then he, like the others, will try to increase his own herd as much as possible, even though this will mean that the land is overgrazed.

Another adverse impact of the high priority placed on security is the slow development of trade in food in the rural areas. Every farm tries to grow its own basic food supply. Over much of Africa, this quite natural tendency was reinforced by requirements laid down by the colonial regimes: that every farmer grow a famine reserve—usually in the form of manioc, which can be kept by leaving it in the ground; that every district try to be self-sufficient in food supplies at all costs (e.g., the policy followed in Uganda). This second policy is still regarded as unquestionably desirable by most independent governments in Africa. Many development plans take it for granted that if a district or a region is a "food-deficit" area, action must be taken to encourage more food production there.

This desire for security, in addition to the government policies that reinforce it, has several adverse results. First, it tends to ensure that crops grown for market sale are and will remain grafted to subsistence production, slowing down the transition to a market economy. Second, cash crops tend to remain, as they began, mainly for export, since the development of a local market for food crops is discouraged, restricted to the still very small urban centers (and even here, people try to and are encouraged to grow their own food).

In short, this means that specialization in both cash export and local food crops is prevented or hindered—hence, productivity all around is held down. Not only is the farmer held back from specializing, but the best use cannot be made of the different special ecological potentials. Take two areas, for example, one especially suited to grow coffee, and the other to grow maize. If maize is grown in the coffee area, the coffee output will suffer, since the cost of growing maize in an unsuitable area may be very high. As for the other area, it may not even be able to grow coffee at all. Its inhabitants are condemned to a low standard of living—growing maize only for their own consumption and with no cash crop to enable them to buy other commodities.

Development of trade among farmers should also promote the diversification and improvement of quality in the African diet. This may not happen automatically, however. Research in western Nigeria has shown that "Nigerian parents were wealthier in villages that specialized in cocoa production but their children suffered a greater incidence of nutritional disorders than those in villages where corn, plantains, cassava, and yams formed part of the agricultural system." (McKelvey, p. 326.) The need to *purchase* food to diversify a diet in such circumstances apparently has still to be learned.

The traditional African division of labor between the sexes is often another decisive economic factor. Where the tradition is still strong, the family is virtually split into two separate enterprises, and its labor force is not considered as a single one.

There are a number of adverse consequences from this situation: the woman—who is responsible for providing the family's food by her agricultural labors, regardless of her husband's income, but who is permitted to keep any money earned by selling food not needed for the family—will resist switching land to cash crops if she will receive no benefit from the cash income. (The husband is responsible for and collects the income from cash crops grown for the market.) And she will be reluctant to contribute her labor to his crop, and he to hers. At crucial periods, therefore, the best use of labor may not be made. Since handling cattle is man's work, the use of ox-drawn plows in food production by women, even where it is feasible, is held up. One difficulty that threatened the viability of the small-holder tea-growing scheme in Kenya was that wives of the farmers in the scheme found it profitable to pick tea leaves, sun-dry them, and sell them for cash themselves, thus reducing the amount of good tea properly plucked and sent through the regular organization to the factory for processing. When the tea was properly plucked and processed, proceeds were higher, but the husbands got them.

In some of the matriarchal African societies—e.g., most of Malawi —men

> have been discouraged from looking at the farm as a source of income because, for the most part, they have had little or no control over the land. To obtain the use of land a man must not only marry, as it is the women who have the rights to the land, but he must also move to his wife's village to obtain it. If a man divorces his wife, as frequently happens, then he must relinquish that piece of land and he will not get another until he marries again. . . . A man has little influence over his successor to the land and the land has no market value (though this is changing), so the investment of time and money in it is not attractive. Such interplot mobility and the insecurity of the whole system have meant that the typical male has little interest in developing the land he was using. (McLoughlin, unpublished ms.)

The relationship between the sexes is gradually changing in Africa. With time, these problems will no longer recur. In some areas, a great desire to educate the children (school fees may absorb as much as 50 per cent or more of a family's cash income) has been one of the most effective forces bringing husband and wife to work together to earn money from cash crops.

It is probably the absence of ambiguity about the role of husband or wife on the farm that explains the otherwise curious fact that certain farms run by women are "progressive" showplaces of the agricultural-extension officers. In these cases, the woman running the farm is a widow or a wife whose husband is away for long periods; she is therefore getting the full benefit of the returns and tries to maximize them by seeking and following the extension officer's advice. There is, in short, no problem of different elements of labor and income, and the farm is operated as a single management unit. Indeed, there is an increasing number of "progressive farmers" in Africa—in most countries and most communities. More and more African farmers are receptive to new ideas and willing to experiment with them. The outstanding characteristic of these farmers is that they have had the kind of experience which broadened their horizons and increased their knowledge or skills—outside the tribal environment, whether in a clerical government job or a paid job in private or public enterprise. Even serving as a soldier, a policeman, or prison guard helps to instill a disposition to listen to the agricultural officers and to create better work habits. In Kenya and Zambia, working on a non-African farm or alongside a non-African farmer provided useful lessons. Work as a trader or artisan also seems to give not only a broader horizon but useful managerial experience, especially in handling money. Formal education too, whether or not it includes training in agriculture, seems to result in this receptivity to change.

Work experience outside the traditional environment also very often serves as a means to accumulate capital to invest in farming by the purchase of better farm tools and equipment. (This, incidentally, is a highly important kind of investment that often escapes inclusion in the national accounts' estimates.) As a matter of fact, one of the first ways in which Africans tried to raise their incomes was to combine part-time wage-labor with existing farming procedures. This is the basis of the prevalent "migratory labor" system in Africa, which also derives from what I would call "sociological underemployment" arising from the division of labor between the sexes on the farm. If men, for example, regard clearing new land for cultivation as man's work and the actual work of cultivation as women's work, then the men may be underemployed in the periods when no new land has to be cleared. A man can maximize his income by then going to work in industry or mines, returning home to clear new land when this is necessary. Of course, there may not be sufficient jobs to absorb all of the men who would periodically want them, and sociological underemployment may continue to persist for this reason. The costs and time involved for the men in getting from their farms to the job opportunities in industry or mining may also be considerable; or the men may not know of jobs available hundreds of miles away, and this may inhibit movement and prevent this cure to underemployment. But, except early in this century, when industry and mining were first beginning in Africa, and except in very special circumstances today, the latter factor does not appear of great importance; on the contrary, it is remarkable the obstacles and the distance the average African man will overcome to get to an available job.

The extent of this migratory labor in Africa is quite startling for those accustomed to labor patterns in other continents. The economies of Upper Volta, Mali, Niger, Malawi, Lesotho, the gold mines of South Africa, much of the industry in south-central and eastern Africa, the sisal plantations of Tanganyika, the large coffee farms of Uganda, the Gezira scheme in the Sudan, the cocoa farmers of Ghana and of western Nigeria, the peanut farmers of Senegal, and the cocoa and coffee farmers of the Ivory Coast—all participate in this migrant labor system. According to an Ivory Coast census, in 1965 one quarter of the population, or one million people, were of foreign origin (350,000 of them from Upper Volta and 250,000 from Mali). In Malawi, at the other end of Africa, 40 to 50 per cent of the men are away at any one time working in Southern Rhodesia or South Africa.

While migrant labor was probably necessary at one stage of African development, with time it has become clear that the gains have been exhausted and that further progress depends on a different kind of development. With the migrant moving back and forth between the money economy and the farm, he is unable to increase his productivity as an industrial worker or as a farmer but becomes stuck on a plateau of relative inefficiency in each case. And the costs in terms of time and energy wasted in shuttling back and forth are very high. But, on the other hand, as I have said, the migrant worker does acquire the potentialities and the capital required to become a "progressive farmer," if the farming structure to which he returns permits it (i.e., if there is the possibility of becoming a permanent settled farmer).

## Land Tenure

Wherever it is possible to establish permanent farms with a settled farming population, the traditional land-tenure systems may become an obstacle to economic progress. All of Africa's local variations on the communal or tribal land-tenure system are based on the assumptions that land has no scarcity value and that the right to use it depends on membership in or consent of the community as a whole. As long as population was relatively scarce and the primitive method of shifting cultivation prevailed, there was no cause to change this system; in fact, any attempt at fundamental change would have been futile and rather silly. But when permanent farms become possible and are economic, a change does become necessary to give the farmer permanent rights to the land he is cultivating.

To increase a permanent farm's output, it is necessary for the farmer to invest labor and capital—to build up the quality of the soil, to improve the drainage by digging ditches or leveling or changing the slope of the land, to protect the crops and stop wind erosion by planting trees as windbreaks, building fences, etc. For the farmer and his family to undertake all this, they must feel that they have security of tenure for themselves and for future generations. In addition, the farmer needs capital for implements and for seasonal requirements of seed, fertilizer, insecticides, etc. Economically, it makes sense to borrow, if necessary, for such short-term productive purposes as well as for capital improvement. But to borrow, the farmer needs good credit; the best collateral is the pledge of land; so, for this too, individual ownership of land is essential. The individual farmer and his family must also have every incentive to work hard, both to increase current output and to improve the farm for future output— and this is provided by farm ownership (which is why most schemes of collective farming fail, whether the Pilgrims' in the Plymouth colony or the Russians' on the steppes).

(It is possible that with highly advanced agricultural development, such as in the United States, where the soil is known thoroughly, and the application of fertilizer can control fertility, the supply of water from rainfall or irrigation is reliable, the characteristics of plants are well known, and techniques of mechanization have been perfected, farming can be handled like factory production. In such conditions, professional managers and a wage-labor force or even well-organized collective farmers might be as efficient as single-family farming. These conditions certainly are not applicable to Africa today or for the next generation.)

In recent years, the spread of cash crops and the growth of population are giving an economic value to rights in land, whether the traditional system is ready to recognize it or not. As the East African Royal Commission put it in a 1955 report:

> Increased African production requires a new conception of land rights and tenure. For, as land becomes one of the factors of production for the market, with the consequent division of labor and specialization of production which its use as a factor of production in the market economy entails, two fundamental changes occur: (*a*) the land becomes valuable as a specialized factor of production, and (*b*) an increasing proportion of the population becomes less directly dependent upon the land and is able to find new income-earning opportunities in other directions, opportunities greater than those which occupation of the land itself can offer them. Indeed, a rise in income per head in the community as a whole presupposes such a diversification of economic activities, either by increased diversification on the land itself, or by increased specialization in occupations divorced from it. A tribal community which is economically isolated from the market cannot introduce these changes. (East Africa Royal Commission, pp. 48–49.)

A member of the Commission went so far as to say:

> It is clear that the root cause of the economic backwardness of various African territories, as well as of the native areas in the Union [of South Africa], lies in the failure to modify customary control of land occupation and tenure, which has prevented the emergence of land use and ownership compatible with modern forms of commercialized production in a money economy. The failure to make of the land a viable economic factor of production has condemned the peoples on it to eke out a precarious subsistence. (Frankel, p. 7.)

While individual ownership of land is often an economic step forward, it must be recognized that so fundamental a change as a shift to individual land tenure can and should be made only when conditions are ripe for it. The World Bank's Economic Survey Mission to Uganda identified the following major necessary preconditions: a relatively high density of population; use of land to grow

cash crops, thus the imputation of money value to land; and a growing rate of litigation over land rights, showing that these are acquiring growing value. In addition, it is important that the program
not be imposed against the wishes of the population affected.
So far in Africa, the greatest progress in this direction has been
made in Kenya. (See below, p. 148 ) But conditions were quite favorable there to begin with: by the early 1950's, virtually all the land
of the Kipsigis tribe had been enclosed into individual holdings—a
movement started by the younger men in defiance of the elders. To
carry out programs for individual ownership in the African areas,
existing customary rights were surveyed and adjudicated, farms were
laid out on the new basis, and new freehold titles issued. In resettlement areas where Africans were acquiring former European farms,
the new settlers obtained freehold title from the very beginning.

In Uganda, the *mailo* land in Buganda (arising out of the Uganda
agreement of 1900, which allocated land to the leading Buganda in
square-mile blocks, hence *mailo*), while held by individuals, has certain limitations on it: it cannot be sold to non-Africans, which has
hampered its use as credit collateral; and, perhaps even more important, its full economic exploitation has been restricted by the
existence of squatters with certain customary rights. But, even with
these handicaps, the *mailo* land has aided a more rapid economic
growth in Buganda than has occurred elsewhere in Uganda without
it.

In Ghana and southern Nigeria, the increase in cash crops and
the growing scarcity of good land for such crops has led to the
evolution of *de facto* individual ownership in the cash-crop areas. As
this is an unplanned evolution, it has involved a great deal of litigation over the various rights to use of the land, as well as to the
appropriation by chiefs of formerly communal land. In brief, individual ownership of farms is occurring essentially through the rather
costly process of adjudication by courts on individual cases.

In the lands of the former French empire in Africa, the French
government had recognized two kinds of property rights: customary
rights under tribal law; and freehold title acquired by registration of
land granted, conceded, or purchased. In 1955, a law was passed
under which the customary rights were confirmed, and the machinery for transforming these rights into individual property on
request was simplified. The same arrangement was carried on in the

independent French-speaking states. Essentially, therefore, there was no legal obstacle to Africans' shifting to freehold tenure whenever the land began to acquire sufficient economic value to justify going through the whole procedure of survey and registration. This process has evidently not gone very far, however, except in the most economically advanced nations—that is, in the Ivory Coast and Senegal—and in some of the *paysannat* schemes set up before independence. René Dumont has, on the other hand, pointed out that under this law the chiefs have been able to cede exploitation rights to other people—expatriates or African strangers—who have set up plantations manned by migrant workers in areas like the Ivory Coast or eastern Cameroon while the local people have drawn incomes from this without work and without inducement to work. (Dumont, *False Start in Africa.*)

*Permanent Farms and Cash Crops*

TREE CROPS

One important way in which African farmers could settle permanently on a farm was in large part pioneered by the farmers themselves—by developing tree crops, where conditions were suitable. The main crops involved are cocoa and the oil palm in West Africa; coffee in many countries, but particularly Uganda and the Ivory Coast; and, in the last few years, tea, mostly in East Africa. Tea (in Malawi and Uganda), bananas (in Somalia, Cameroon, in the Ivory Coast), oil palm (in the Congo [Kinshasa]), and rubber (in Liberia and the Congo [Kinshasa]) are also grown on plantations. The cultivation of these tree crops largely bypasses many of the problems of arable agriculture mentioned earlier. The plants in such cases, shading and protecting the soil (although sometimes additional shade cover is still necessary), come close to achieving equilibrium with the soil and climate of the original forest. The farmer is able to have a settled farm on which he can apply the results of research and improve his methods, and so increase his productivity and income. In tropical Africa, the tree-crop farmers have been most successful in improving their lot; the other farmers sometimes have at best merely held their own.

OTHER SCHEMES

The most ambitious schemes to reorganize farming on the basis of permanently settled farmers were in Kenya and in the land-husbandry program of Rhodesia. In both of these countries, large tracts of land—because of altitude, rainfall, and soils—are suitable for permanent mixed farms—that is, farms using a rotation of crops and the manure from the livestock to help to maintain and restore fertility. In both countries, also, European farmers and governments over some fifty years came to learn how temperate-zone farming techniques had to be modified to be successful under local conditions. In both countries, trained agricultural officers or experienced farmers were available to help African farmers with new methods. Many African farmers took advantage of their work experience on European farms or of living next to European farms to acquire new techniques.

Under the Swynnerton scheme in Kenya, begun in 1954, about 2.5 million acres (around 300,000 farms) in the Central, Rift Valley, and Nyanza provinces were laid out in permanent individual farms and farmed on the basis of plans and other advice from the agricultural extension services. (This area comprises about one quarter of the high- and medium-potential agricultural land held by Africans in Kenya at the time.) This program was extended to other parts of Kenya, where conditions were favorable—that is, where the soil and climate permit such farming, where there was local demand for it, and where land settlement officers were available. From 1961 to 1970, however, the main emphasis in Kenya was on several settlement schemes, totaling around 1.25 million acres, on farms formerly owned by Europeans. These schemes have progressed on the whole quite successfully with the help of the former owners.

The land-husbandry program in Rhodesia, begun in 1951, has been less successful than the schemes in Kenya. It undertook to reorganize all of the land set aside in the African reserves into individual farms. While well worked out in concept, the program cannot be considered an economic success—partly because it was restricted to the less desirable land (it did not include land reserved to Europeans), and partly because in many tribal areas the available land was insufficient to create economically viable farms and the farmers were not granted full freehold title to the land. Moreover, the African political leaders did not accept the program, and the cooperation of the African farmers themselves was thus reduced. Furthermore, the industrial economy of Rhodesia, largely owing to political developments after 1962, did not grow fast enough to absorb the farmers who were theoretically to leave the land and become industrial workers, thus permitting the remaining farmers to acquire economically sized farms. As a result, the program virtually stopped by the end of 1962, by which time the grant of the rights to farms had covered less than 50 per cent of the arable and 40 per cent of the grazing lands.

In countries where the natural conditions do not appear suitable for mixed farming, several other promising experiments have been tried—in the Congo, a particularly promising one called the *paysannat*. The *paysannat* was a system of farming under which farmers were settled along a road on plots laid out adjacent to one another in strips perpendicular to the road. These strips were subdivided into fifteen or twenty sections. The farmers were to practice a kind of rolling rotation, moving down the strips with particular crops section by section, from year to year, leaving the sections behind in bush fallow. Since various sections would be growing identical crops at the same time, it would be possible to experiment with mechanical cultivation or harvesting going across the strips at right angles. Some 200,000 families had been settled on such schemes by 1960 when the schemes collapsed in the wake of the chaos that accompanied independence in 1960. (The extension workers who were needed to keep the scheme going then departed.)

In other parts of French-speaking equatorial Africa, other attempts were made during the 1950's to establish settled farms, similarly called *paysannats*. After a number of failures, a certain degree of success—as in the Niari Valley in the Congo—was achieved by carefully selecting sites with the best possible soil and communications, and by investing considerable amounts in roads, housing, schools, and dispensaries. Among the most successful schemes are those based on tree-crop plantations.

In Zambia, a system of rotating areas within a single farm has been tried, with considerable success, on what amounts to a pilot-project basis. There are some areas in Zambia where mixed farming on the Kenyan or Rhodesian model might be successful.

In Malawi, the main development effort of the 1950's was an attempt to reorganize agriculture somewhat along the pattern of the Swynnerton scheme in Kenya. Over the period, thirty village-reorganization schemes were carried out, covering 200,000 acres. Under these an area was first laid out on sound conservation lines (drainage, contour bunds, terraces, etc.), with the land to be used for each type of exploitation (arable, grazing, forest) clearly demarcated; individual farms with a farm plan were laid out and assigned. By the mid-1960's, the schemes had collapsed and practically vanished. There were a number of reasons for the failure. One was the particular relationship of men to land rights that was mentioned above (the agricultural-extension officers had trouble talking agriculture to the women, whose consent was crucial but who often, apparently, were not even consulted). The main reason for the failure was the fact that the schemes were pushed through before there had been sufficient experience with a pilot project to discover what would and would not work. Unlike Kenya, Malawi had no new cash crop to be grown, and there was no obvious financial reason for people to go through all the inconvenience of the reorganization.

## Government Programs

Aside from the question of whether such basic transformations as the change to permanent farming and the shift from communal to individual land tenure are carried out or not, there is much that can be done to increase output. In general, government programs to increase agricultural output in the existing agricultural structure can be subdivided into two main categories: those which alter the infrastructure and environment in which the farmer operates; and those which require changes in the way the farmer himself operates. The permanent-farm schemes of course involve both types, but in areas where natural conditions or the farmers are not ready for these, much potential growth can be realized from programs of the first type. Building roads to open up new areas, providing better water supplies, spraying crops, controlling locust-breeding places and locust swarms, providing selected seed or seedlings—all are examples of exogenous programs to improve agricultural productivity.

The output of a crop often hinges on the labor supply at a crucial time—at planting, weeding, or harvesting. But the labor available at these stages may be reduced by unavoidable calls on the time of the farming population; in particular, having to go long distances for water, for the household or livestock, or for fuel wood. New wells or boreholes and new roads, by reducing the time that must be taken away from work in the fields, can thus lead to an increase in output even with no change in traditional farming methods.

The U.N. Development Program's International Anti-Locust Organization since 1959 has systematically tracked down and destroyed, in their breeding places and in flight, locust swarms that would otherwise have destroyed the crops upon which millions of Africans depend. And for most cash crops, it has become established practice for public organizations to provide selected seed or seedlings, thus making it possible, with an adequate organization for agricultural research, to upgrade the quality or yield.

All these programs can be carried out by government or other organizations without necessarily calling on the farmer to improve his own management techniques. So far, they have been more manageable and successful than programs to improve actual agricultural skills. But it is on the latter type of program that the continued rise in African income ultimately depends.

What is the most effective way of inducing a change in agricultural techniques and having it spread through a group? The most effective way known so far is to pick out the individual farmers ("master" or "progressive" farmers) who have shown or appear to have the potential to be innovators and to give them special help in both knowledge and techniques, credit facilities, and other services to enable them to forge ahead. (See *The Economic Development of Uganda*, pp. 125–202.)

RESEARCH

The crops and techniques used by farmers in Africa are those that have been evolved over centuries of selection to meet the conditions under which Africans have farmed. The varieties of crops that are grown are those that have the demonstrated ability to produce dependable although low yields under adverse circumstances of low soil fertility, ravages of insects and diseases, and the minimum amount of cultivation that dependence on human muscle for power entails. These crops are efficient at extracting the maximum amount of nutrients from impoverished soils. If fertilizer is applied to the soil, they may use it for excessive growth in the unusable parts of the plant or may grow so tall as to topple over rather than produce more usable yield.

Over the last seventy years, a combination of techniques has been developed to improve agricultural productivity in the temperate climates. In brief, biological engineering has learned how to create new varieties of plants tailored to meet a planned set of needed characteristics. These plants are designed to be capable of converting large amounts of fertilizer into usable product rather than to excessive foliage. High response to intensive management can also be built into the new varieties. Whereas the low yields from the old varieties made the use of protectants against pests and insects often uneconomic, using these protectants on high-yield varieties may pay handsomely. Resistance to pests and to diseases may also be bred into the plants. Specially designed farm machinery for a particular crop may become economic.

This package of techniques has evolved slowly in the industrialized countries, and until recently it was not applied to the tropical countries. The experience of the Rockefeller Foundation in developing the high-yielding Mexican dwarf wheat and of the International Rice Research Institute in the Philippines in developing high-yielding rice has shown that the "package of technology" approach to tropical agricultural problems can work and that yields in the tropics can be at least as high as those in temperate climates. A rapid increase in the average yield of a commodity can be achieved through application of a complete package of "high-yielding varieties, plus appropriate fertilizer use techniques, plus adequate means of control of diseases and insect pests, plus necessary planting, cultivation, and irrigation techniques. . . . Or, in the case of animals, [through] proper strain, nutrition, and management—all at once, with nothing important left out." (Wortman, p. 24.)

However, the technology of agriculture must be specifically tailored to the conditions of each farming area. A rice variety developed for an Asian country is not likely to be best for an African country. While some of the technology is transferable, the final stages of research have to be carried out in the region for which it is designed. In Africa, most of the agricultural research in the past was done on export crops and essentially started on any appreciable scale only after World War II. Independence in English-speaking Africa resulted in a substantial drop in research, while France continued her sizable program of financing research institutes. There is still too little contact and interchange of knowledge on research programs and findings among the various research institutes across the language line and insufficient application of the "package of technology" approach. Research on the basic food crops of Africa and fruits and vegetables—some of which are potential exports—has continued to be neglected. This will be changed as the new International Institute of Tropical Agriculture being created at Ibadan, Nigeria, begins to function, during the 1970's. There is much to be done.

Not enough is yet known about the conditions facing the African farmer. There are very few areas, for example, where all the main soil types and how they respond to varying treatments are known. Still less is known about different micro-climates; what may be the best plant variety and best system of cultivation in one area may be completely wrong for a village ten miles away.

In addition to technical ignorance, there is an even greater lack of knowledge of the economics of the African farm. The agricultural extension services have been and are primarily concerned with technical problems, and have concentrated on the yield to be gotten out of a piece of land. The African, on the other hand, thinks in terms of the return on his labor. If he can get more return from a given expenditure of labor by cultivating additional land than by intensifying cultivation on a given piece of land, he will do so, even though the yield per acre is not high. An example of this point was a program in Sukumaland administered by the trusteeship government of Tanganyika before independence in 1961. The agricultural officers tried to persuade the farmers to raise their cotton yields and avoid erosion by tie-ridging their fields to conserve water and avoid run-off. At the same time, new land was made available to the tribe through a program of clearing out bush, eliminating the tsetse fly, and providing water supplies. The Sukuma, comparing their advantages, preferred to expand into the new area, and the program of intensified cultivation was a failure. The same experience has been repeated in other parts of Africa. When people emigrate from areas where the distribution of human and livestock populations makes intensive agriculture desirable to areas where pressure on the land is less intense, they revert to extensive agriculture. Similarly, if to avoid soil erosion takes too high a cost now in relation to the return over the next few years—or if it is possible to move on to new land instead—it is useless to try to persuade farmers to expend labor on anti-erosion works.

It is also necessary to know where the real bottlenecks are in the allotment of time to specific agricultural tasks. Usually the most critical factor affecting the size of a crop is the timing of the planting; but a farmer's failure to observe the recommended planting dates is usually due, not to stubborn conservatism or laziness, but to an inability to cope with the work load, given the tools available or, as we have discussed before, a desire to maximize security rather than output. It is useless to tell farmers to plant immediately upon the advent of rains, for instance, when they have been unable in advance to break the hard dry ground with their work hoe or ox plow, or when they must interrupt the planting in order to cope with weeds in fields that were sown earlier.

## AGRICULTURAL EXTENSION SERVICES

An important governmental instrument for transforming African agriculture by passing on new knowledge to the farmers is the extension service. Unfortunately, when the colonial powers departed, the services they had established were still in their infancy. Paradoxically, while political independence has improved the African farmers' receptivity to the services' advice, the departure of "expatriates" before Africans had been trained to replace them has weakened the effectiveness of the services.

In the past, tribal societies emphasized conformity to established customs and practices and deference to established authority, particularly to the elders. This tendency discouraged any serious deviations from the accepted way of doing things and made the "progressive farmer" an object of suspicion and hostility, unless he himself happened to be a person of authority in the society.

During the colonial period, the Belgians in particular and the British in some areas gave preference, when educating the Africans, to chiefs and sons of chiefs, in this way attempting to get influential leaders of the next generation on the side of change. When the various colonial territories became independent, nationalist leaders, parties, and movements took the "progressive farmers" as their own and made them status-holders. In Malawi, the contrast is particularly striking: before independence, the progressive farmer was often regarded as a pariah; since independence, he has often been singled out as a success symbol for the other farmers. The new favor with which the progressive farmer is viewed should have a good effect on the level of productivity in many African countries—as long, of course, as the nationalist movements do not become dizzy with success and try to leap forward faster than knowledge of and conditions in the environment permit.

In some cases, reliance on individual farmers to move ahead of the group is unsatisfactory, and it is necessary to work with an entire rural population to achieve any success at all. In the cotton-growing area of Kenya's Central Nyanza, progressive farmers discovered that if they followed advice and planted cotton before planting maize and sorghum, these latter crops, when grown by farmers who did not follow the new schedule, harbored and encouraged the multiplication of cotton pests which attacked the cotton. Further, the progressive farmers got their cotton crops in early, but if the rest did not, the gins would not be open when they harvested and they would have to store the cotton in the interim. Also, it is necessary for everyone to pull up and burn cotton stalks after the harvest; if some do not, the remaining stalks will harbor pests into the next season.

In central Africa in the mid-1950's, the cotton-boll worm appeared. For some years in Rhodesia, this wrecked the promising development of cotton as an additional cash crop on African and European farms. In what was then Nyasaland, however, the boll weevil was defeated by all the farmers' simultaneously switching the season—reversing the time of planting and harvesting. Such a program could not be carried out in Rhodesia, reportedly because the Agriculture Department was not able to secure the voluntary cooperation of the European farmers.

## AGRICULTURAL CREDIT

Adequate agricultural credit systems are essential to the rapid development of agricultural output. Credit is needed to give a farmer the capital he needs to increase output in advance of the time necessary to finance himself through building up his savings.

Properly used, capital helps the farmer to achieve an output surplus sufficient not only to repay the borrowed capital and the interest on it, but to give him something beyond this to add to his income.

The only safe way to provide credit to farmers who are still deficient in managerial ability is in combination with managerial assistance—that is, the credit must be supervised by informed professionals who can ascertain that there is a proper need for the credit, that it will be spent on what it was secured for, and that it will be used to secure higher output. To safeguard the extension services' day-by-day relationships with the farmers, however, the services cannot get involved in loan repayment collections. Cooperatives, when properly administered, have proved to be an excellent alternate device for the allocation and collection of credits. So far, however, there have been few good examples of credit programs in African agriculture. The most successful ones have followed these general principles.

So far, commercial banks have not been very helpful in meeting the credit needs of African agriculture. In most areas without land titles, they are practically barred from even trying. In any case, they have difficulties in assessing the credit needs of small farmers and in controlling disbursements of loans, and have dealt more successfully with the larger commercial farmers and the cooperatives. It may be that they will be able to work out ways to finance members of cooperatives. In most countries, however, it is fairly certain that some sort of government credit agency is needed.

COOPERATIVES

Farmers and governments alike (particularly in Tanzania) have had enough experience with cooperatives to show that they can be an important means of agricultural development in Africa. Cooperatives fit in well with the existing social structure; they are naturally most successful when based on existing kinship or social groups, so that both the members' feeling of identification with the organization and the management's feeling of responsibility to the members are encouraged.

Cooperatives have done well in Africa in the buying, bulking, grading, storing, and simple processing of their members' produce. But it is yet to be demonstrated that cooperative farms, where the land is farmed in common and the produce is shared, can be operated successfully. Farms where some of the operations are performed for all the members—i.e., mechanical plowing of all the fields—but where the produce of the individual plots goes to each individual farmer might well be successful in appropriate circumstances.

The continued, successful operation of cooperatives appears to require government supervision, inspection, and audit of accounts, as well as government advice on management. This service again was badly hurt by the exodus of "expatriates" after independence. Another problem is the pressure applied by some governments, including Tanzania's, to proliferate and expand cooperatives more rapidly than available personnel can ensure a reasonable chance of success. In spite of such temporary problems, however, cooperatives should be one of the strong points in the expansion of African agriculture.

## LARGE-SCALE SCHEMES

So far in this chapter, I have mentioned primarily programs and policies for increasing the output of existing African farms. Even the schemes in Kenya, though they involved hundreds of thousands of farmers, were well grounded on either existing African farms or on formerly European farms settled by African farmers. But a number of governments believe that they must decide whether to try to increase the national output by improving, helping, or even reorganizing existing farms or by undertaking large-scale schemes for the development of unutilized or underutilized land—between concentrating on and trying to increase production within existing areas of agricultural production, or putting resources into large-scale agricultural projects such as resettlement or irrigation.

There is no easy answer for a government faced with this decision, although theoretically it is just a matter of comparing the yield of investment in alternative projects (including both private and social costs and benefits in the calculation). Unfortunately, not enough of the elements are known to demonstrate clearly what the answer should be. Under these circumstances, the large schemes, with the greater risks of loss, are a dubious choice. There is a tendency, just the same, to prefer them—in part because they are more spectacular and make a greater effect in a development plan, and in part because when they succeed, it is easier in these schemes to demonstrate the benefits deriving from government action than when the benefits are scattered over the mass of a farming population.

It was for reasons such as these that the British government decided to launch the ill-fated scheme costing some $80 million to increase the supply of peanuts in Tanganyika, rather than to help Nigerian farmers to increase production and improve the marketing arrangements for their groundnuts. The White Paper advocating the Tanganyika scheme said: "No significant increase in the present output of oilseeds can be achieved . . . by the existing methods of peasant production. Nothing but the most highly mechanical agricultural methods, on a vast scale never previously envisaged, will result in any appreciable amelioration of the present disastrous food position." (*A Plan for the Mechanized Production of Groundnuts*, p. 18.) It is obvious, with hindsight, that if only a small fraction of the money wasted on the groundnut scheme had been used in Nigeria to improve rail transport, peasant production of groundnuts would have been increased by more than the Tanganyika scheme hoped to achieve.

The Tanganyika scheme was only the most notorious of a number of failures of this kind in various parts of Africa. Another example is the South Busoga development scheme started in Uganda in 1947 to use mechanical cultivation to increase food supplies for Jinja, where it was anticipated that industrialization would create a demand that the small African farmer could not hope to supply. By 1954, the scheme had to be written off as a complete failure, while the farmers demonstrated that they could meet all increased demands for food without major difficulty.

The same seductive attractions of large-scale schemes are enticing some of Africa's independent governments today. In the Western Region of Nigeria, the 1962–68 development plan provided for large-scale settlements of young farmers—200 farmers per 5,000–7,000 acres, with each farmer debited with a capital cost of £2,400 to be repaid over fifteen to twenty years. In Tanzania, a large number of village and settlement schemes are planned, although not one has yet proved successful.

One type of large-scale scheme of particular importance is concerned with irrigation projects. With a climate favorable to reproduction and growth, there is a good possibility of developing a prosperous farming community, *if* an adequate supply of water can be assured and applied to soils whose characteristics are thoroughly understood. Wherever a good supply of water can be found in the arid and semi-arid regions of Africa, irrigation is a possibility worth exploring. So far, however, only the large Gezira irrigation scheme in the Sudan has successfully overcome the sociological and administrative obstacles. (See below, pp. 159–61.) The Office du Niger scheme in Mali and the Richard Toll scheme in Senegal, to name only the most conspicuous, have not shown any outstanding economic success. In 1970, the Office du Niger, after some forty years of existence and an investment of around $180 million, was not yet providing any return on capital.

It is clear that, for a large-scale project to be successful, a great deal must be known about the natural conditions; a pilot project should be operated for some years to discover the practical answers to the challenges they present. But governments are often too impatient to move as slowly as necessary. Secondly, a sufficiently large cadre of skilled agricultural technicians and extension agents is needed to provide guidance and control for the mass of farmers involved. But governments have been unwilling to wait until one develops. Thirdly, it is important to assign responsibility for preparing and administering the scheme to a quasi-governmental entity, outside of and independent of the regular governmental administration—on the example of TVA, or the Gezira Board. Finally, the farmers must be ready to accept and follow the advice proffered. Again, farmers have frequently not been ready to adopt new methods wholesale, and the government is unwilling to be tough with those who will not.

With these difficult major conditions for success, it is not surprising that at this time in Africa and for some time to come, the most practical and economic approach to achieving a sizable increase in agricultural productivity and output would be to enhance the efficiency of the existing agricultural economy, not to attempt large-scale transformation projects. Unfortunately, the unhappy experience of the past is cheerfully overlooked, and it is a rare development program in Africa that does not include substantial investment in large-scale untried transformation, "resettlement," or "mechanical cultivation" schemes.

## THE GEZIRA SCHEME

The Gezira irrigation and cotton-growing scheme was an outstanding exception to the record of failures of large-scale projects in Africa. Thanks to good management and some good luck, the Gezira scheme was able to avoid most of the difficulties that ruined other such projects. To begin with, of course, the Sudanese had many centuries' experience with irrigation from the Nile. The actual idea for this scheme dated back to a 1907 pilot irrigation project for water pumped from the Nile, a project handled by a British company, the Sudan Plantations Syndicate, which was already farming in the Sudan. This project was successful and was gradually expanded with more pumps until, in 1925, the Sennar Dam was completed and gravity irrigation became possible. The project was then expanded rapidly to new areas. In 1950, the Sudanese government took over the concessions, and the management was taken over by the Sudan Gezira Board, an autonomous public authority, whose personnel had been trained over the preceding twenty-five years. With some 850,000 hectares under irrigation, the completion of the Roseires Dam, under the Nile waters agreement with Egypt is permitting the Sudan to use more water and thus both bring more land under cultivation and intensify production of already cultivated land.

The Gezira scheme has been operated on a partnership basis: the government provides the water and the land, which has been purchased or rented (if necessary, compulsorily) from the original landlords; the board administers the scheme and does the research, allocates the tenancies, supervises and finances the tenants, mechanically cultivates the land, provides cotton seed and fertilizer, undertakes pest control, transports gins, and markets the cotton; the tenants provide the labor. The net proceeds of the cotton sales are divided among the tenants, government, and board in the ratio 48:40:10. The remaining 2 per cent goes to the local government. The land is under cotton only a quarter or a third of the time, depending on the area; other crops raised belong in their entirety to the tenant. In recent years, the tenants have numbered around 80,000; their average annual share is about $500. The board also employs directly 10,000 workers, and there have been in addition about 250,000 laborers working for the tenants. The government gets 5–15 per cent of its total revenues from the Gezira scheme directly, and probably an equivalent amount indirectly from import taxes levied on goods bought by consumers whose incomes derive from it. The Gezira is responsible for around 8 per cent of the Gross Domestic Product of the Sudan and around 16 per cent of the product of the modern sector; it is the source of 35–40 per cent of total foreign-exchange earnings. Over the last fifteen years, the direct return to the government on its investment in the Gezira has averaged 20 per cent per year.

A reappraisal of the Gezira scheme was undertaken for the government by a special mission from the World Bank in 1965, headed by Leonard Rist, since the government felt that the original scheme suffered from several drawbacks. No action has been taken to reorganize the scheme by the several governments that have come into power since. Among the elements that keep the scheme in its present form, below its full economic potential, are the following: With the intensified cropping possible after completion of the Roseires Dam, more area is now under the noncotton crops (wheat, groundnuts, sorghum, vegetables) than under cotton. These new crops are not supervised, nor does the Board or government get any share of the proceeds. The tenants have increasingly withdrawn from direct labor in the fields, and about three quarters of the field work is done by paid field labor, with some loss in incentive and efficiency in farming. The system of sharing proceeds well after the cotton crop is in weakens the direct incentive between a farmer's level of output and his earnings; the farmer in addition is not fully appreciative of the benefits he gets from the services provided by the Board. A direct payment by him would be more economic.

### The Small Farmer vs. the Plantation

During the colonial period, the issue of whether a particular country should develop its agriculture on the basis of plantations or small farms came up at different times, and was as often as not decided as much on political or social grounds as on economic grounds. The alternatives are still posed today.

Prior to World War I, the British colonial office, for example, in considering a request by Unilever to establish oil palm plantations in Nigeria, decided against plantations, because they did not want to create a large landless agricultural proletariat, and Unilever moved to the Belgian Congo instead. This was the origin of the vast Huileries du Congo Belge plantations, still important today.

At present, the principal plantation products are rubber in Liberia and Congo (Kinshasa); oil palm in the Congo; sisal in Tanganyika and Kenya; sugar in Uganda, Kenya, Tanganyika, Mauritius, and Natal; bananas in Cameroon, Somalia, and the Ivory Coast; tea in Malawi and Uganda; coffee in Kenya, Ivory Coast, and Angola; coconut palm in Mozambique.

The newly independent nations of Africa are now free to reconsider the methods they want to employ for agricultural development. There seems to be a tendency to experiment: Nigeria and Ghana have begun to try out plantations or the equivalent of plantation systems; Tanzania and Kenya are trying small-holder production of what were formerly plantation crops. Social and political considerations probably justify the bias toward small-farmer production, if this is an economic alternative. It provides a more even distribution of income and power and avoids the concentration of wealth and power in a small group, whether private or public. Economically too, small farms can be said to have a number of advantages over large-scale production: their owners have a stronger incentive to work harder themselves and to work their families; the innumerable managerial decisions that must be taken day by day, hour by hour, are hard to organize by a management having to deal with large areas and many workers, etc. Farming in Africa is exactly the opposite of large-scale factory output, where conditions can be completely controlled and the cycle of production is set and repetitive. It is not surprising, consequently, that for production of most crops in Africa, plantations failed when in competition with small farmers.

Yet, plantations have been successful in competing with small farmers in raising certain products where the following advantages are critically important: command of a large amount of capital, greater technical knowledge, better work discipline where timing of operations is important, greater knowledge of and better trade contacts with foreign markets. Throughout the world, indeed, smallholders have been least successful in production of tea and sisal.

In sisal, for example, the minimum scale of feasible operation is already very large. The decorticator, the machine that strips the sisal fiber out of the leaf, has a minimum economic capacity of around 1,200 tons annually—requiring an area of 2,700 acres (one ton of fiber per acre per year over a productive period of four years, three years to come to maturity): mature sisal, 1,200 acres; immature, 900; annual planting, 300; fallow, 300. Second, sisal requires a precise, well-timed transport organization. Only 2-5 per cent of the leaf yields fiber, and it is therefore necessary to transport to the processing machines a great weight of what is essentially waste in order to get a small amount of product; this processing has to be done within forty-eight hours of cutting to prevent the plant juices from becoming gummy; the waste materials must then be discarded. Large amounts of water, too, are needed. Consequently, one has what amounts to an industrial operation—large-scale organization of transport on a tight schedule to feed a large unit.

In tea, the decisive matter is taking very good care of the tea plant, plucking the right leaves at the right times, and getting the leaves to the processing plant quickly. For successful growing of tea, it is necessary to inculcate and to maintain a rather high level of skill and rhythm of work.

In principle, it is not impossible to organize even the main "plantation" crops on a small-holder basis. The government, or a cooperative, or a private enterprise could handle the processing and marketing part of the operation. The crucial point is the technical and sociological level reached by the farmer—whether he is able to maintain sufficient self-discipline to perform his part of the operation or not. If the farmers in a particular country or area have not yet reached this level of development, small-holder production of crops that requires it will fail.

Plantations can be much more than instruments of agricultural output. They could be a center for radiating modern techniques into the surrounding economy: a place where the local population is taught skills and habits of methodical work and acquires supervisory experience. In short, a plantation could be, like a mining development or a large-scale industry, a nucleus for development of the whole economy.

In actual fact, this has not yet happened in Africa. In the past, this was because the plantations, while depending on African migratory labor, reserved the key jobs for non-Africans; Africans received little or no training and acquired few valuable skills. Today, the governments tend to eliminate existing plantations for anti-colonialist reasons (with the exception of Uganda, where the sugar plantations are used as centers from which development can spread), rather than use them as places to train skilled African workers and managers. It would be better to keep these golden geese than to kill them.

### Marketing Boards

Another important institution in African agriculture is the marketing board. Marketing boards, or *caisses de stabilisation*, were set up during and after World War II to control the marketing of some of the most important export crops in a number of countries: cocoa in Ghana and Nigeria; coffee in Ivory Coast, Uganda, Kenya; cotton in Uganda and Nigeria; peanuts in Senegal and Nigeria, etc. There were a number of reasons for doing so, some of which were not completely formulated at the time and some of which may have been quite contradictory. In some cases, the boards were designed to maintain purchases of the farmers' crops at a time when world markets were closed because of the war; in other cases, the boards were designed to eliminate the middlemen in the sale of crops and to provide stable prices for the farmers. Generally, however, as world prices went up in the postwar period, the prices received by the crop-growers in the English territories did not follow suit; in the French territories prices received tended rather to exceed what the world market price would justify. Some of the differences between the world market prices and the prices paid to the farmers by the marketing boards was set aside in price reserve funds, parts of which were later taken over or borrowed by the governments for development plans. (Part of the export proceeds was also directly taken by the governments in the form of export taxes and used to finance capital and current expenditures.)

In the early postwar years, there was some justification for the policy of building up large price reserve funds, in that the supply of commodities the farmers could buy was limited anyway, and giving them extra money would simply have resulted in their bidding up prices against themselves. But, once this first period of scarcity was over, the issue was clearly joined. As the East African Royal

Commission and a number of economists pointed out, in sharp criticism of the marketing board policy, economic development would progress faster if the African farmers received the full benefit of the higher prices than it did with the government's use of the money: (*a*) in benefiting from the higher prices, the farmers would have made greater efforts, producing greater output of the commodities concerned; (*b*) the farmers would have saved more, and used the funds to develop, improve, and even transform their farms; (*c*) the higher purchasing power in rural areas would have stimulated other forms of economic development—e.g., African traders and backyard industries; (*d*) the marketing boards insulated the farmer from world market prices, hindering the development of an entrepreneurial sense and leading the farmer to believe that the way to change low prices was to put pressure on the government; (*e*) government expenditures, both current and capital, were enabled to increase rapidly through the higher availability of funds to the government (much of the money went into assets, such as educational and research assets, with a very slow yield; but much was probably wasted in extravagance).

This is a formidable indictment. Unfortunately, no thorough research has been done either to prove or to disprove these points. There is some possibility that research will throw light on the main point of whether higher incomes for farmers do have the beneficent results claimed for them—by making a comparative study of the results obtained in Ghana, where a policy was followed of taxing cocoa producers quite heavily, with that in some of the ex-French nations, where France made part of her aid available in the form of prices above what would be justified by world market prices. Not all economists agreed, or agree, with the main critique of the marketing boards as given above. In view of the lack of any real data, one's attitude toward what the marketing boards did or did not accomplish is largely a matter of judgment. The World Bank Economic Survey missions of Nigeria and Uganda, after making as thorough an assessment as they could of the policies followed and their results, concluded that on balance the way the export proceeds were used did contribute effectively to the national development. In Nigeria, the mission said, "On the whole, the operations of the Marketing Boards have benefited the producers of the controlled crops and the Nigerian economy in general." It pointed out that under any stabilization scheme, a period of rising prices is the time for the formation of reserves. Setting relatively low producer prices greatly mitigated the severity of inflationary pressures at a time when no other machinery for anti-inflationary action existed. And the accumulated stabilization reserves were large enough not only to assure producers the direct benefit of reasonable and relatively stable prices for many years, but also to enable the boards to lend large sums to the government for development purposes. Helleiner agreed with this conclusion:

> Can it be said that the uses to which the trading surpluses earned by the Nigerian Marketing Boards were put were superior to those to which the peasant farmers would have put them had they been given the opportunity? Since a much larger proportion of the increase in peasant income would have been consumed than that which was actually consumed out of Marketing Board trading surpluses, the rates of return on peasant investments would have had to be much greater than those on Marketing Board ones if peasant uses of the funds in the aggregate were really to have been considered superior. The disposition of Marketing Board surpluses may not have been perfect, but the rates of return from their investments in research, roads, agricultural schemes, universities, modern manufacturing plants and so forth are unlikely to have been any lower than those on housing, sewing machines, land clearing and the other small-scale outlets for peasant funds discussed above, let alone so much lower as to offset the difference between consumption ratios. It can therefore unambiguously be stated that Nigerian development has been aided through the device of channelling a portion of its export earnings via the Marketing Boards away from the producer to other (governmental) decision-makers. (Helleiner, p. 603.)

In Uganda, the World Bank survey mission of 1960–61 felt that the marketing boards and export tax arrangements had made a useful contribution in financing a large growth of the infrastructure and of most of Uganda's modern economy outside of agriculture; in view of the very high prevailing cotton and coffee prices, the predominant position of these two crops in the Uganda economy, and the fact that Africans were exempt from income tax, the government had no choice but to tap this tax source. But it is also true that the export tax introduced an element of inequality: cotton and coffee growers became subject to a rather heavy tax burden while the producers of other crops and livestock paid no similar tax.

A similar practical conclusion is advanced for most developing countries:

> For an underdeveloped country that is seriously trying to achieve economic progress, the requirements for investible funds and government revenue seem certain to outstrip the supply except in those countries which have large earnings from petroleum or mineral exports or particularly favorable access to foreign capital. The sheer size of the agricultural sector in an underdeveloped country points to its importance as a source of capital for over-all economic growth. (Johnston and Mellor, p. 348.)

It is now generally agreed that marketing boards and *caisses de stabilisation* should be regarded as multi-purpose institutions, not merely as stabilization devices. In general, the stabilization sought is of the national income, not necessarily of the price paid to producers. In some cases, it is possible to act to stabilize the national income by using the marketing board resources elsewhere than to increase prices to producers. The boards also perform useful technical and commercial services for the small farmers, protect them against collusive buying by middlemen, and often finance effective technical aids to production.

### Selected Bibliography

ALLEN, W. *The African Husbandman.* New York: Barnes & Noble, 1965.

CLAUSON, G. *Communal Land Tenure.* (Agricultural Studies No. 17.) Rome: Food and Agriculture Organization, 1953.

DUMONT, R. *Afrique Noire, Développement Agricole.* Paris: Presses universitaires de France, 1962.

————. *False Start in Africa.* London: Andre Deutsch; New York: Frederick A. Praeger, 1966.

EAST AFRICA ROYAL COMMISSION. *1953–55 Report.* (Cmd. 9475.) London: H. M. Stationery Office, 1955.

*The Economic Development of Nigeria.* Baltimore, Md.: The Johns Hopkins Press, for the International Bank for Reconstruction and Development, 1955.

*The Economic Development of Uganda.* Baltimore, Md.: The Johns Hopkins Press, for the International Bank for Reconstruction and Development, 1962.

EICHER, CARL K. "The Dynamics of Long-Term Agricultural Development in Nigeria," paper presented at annual meeting of the American Farm Economic Association, Guelph, Ontario, August 13–16, 1967, pp. 1–20.

FRANKEL, S. H. "The Tyranny of Economic Paternalism in Africa," supplement to *Optima* (Johannesburg), December, 1960.

GAITSKELL, A. *Gezira.* London: Faber & Faber, 1959.

GOUROU, P. *Les Pays Tropicaux.* Paris: Presses Universitaires de France, 1947.

HELLEINER, G. K. "The Fiscal Role of the Marketing Boards in Nigerian Economic Development 1947–1961," *The Economic Journal,* LXXIV, No. 295 (September, 1964), 582–610.

JAVABU, N. *Drawn in Colour.* London: John Murray, 1960; New York: St. Martin's Press, 1962.

JOHNSTON, B. F. "The Choice of Measures for Increasing Agricultural Productivity: A Survey of Possibilities in East Africa," *Tropical Agriculture* (London: Butterworths, for University of West Indies), XLI, No. 2 (April, 1964), 91–113.

JOHNSTON, B. F., and MELLOR, J. W. "The Nature of Agriculture's Contribution to Economic Development," *Food Research Institute Studies* (Stanford University), I, No. 3 (November, 1960).

JONES, W. O. "Food and Agricultural Economics of Tropical Africa," *Food Research Institute Studies,* II, No. 1 (February, 1961).

———. "Increasing Agricultural Productivity in Tropical Africa." Paper presented at Nyasaland Economic Symposium, 1962. Mimeo.

LA RUUE, E. A. DE, BOURLIÈRE, FRANÇOIS, and HARROZ, J. P. *The Tropics.* New York: Alfred A. Knopf, 1957.

LEE, D. H. K. *Climate and Economic Development in the Tropics.* New York: Harper & Bros., for the Council on Foreign Relations, 1957.

MCKELVEY, J. J., JR. "Agricultural Research," in R. A. LYSTAD (ed.), *The African World: A Survey of Social Research.* New York: Frederick A. Praeger, 1965, pp. 317–51.

MCLOUGHLIN, PETER F. M. "Some Aspects of Land Reorganization in Malawi (Nyasaland) 1950–1960 and Their Pertinence to Present Day Development," Spring, 1968, Ms. pp. 1–14.

MASEFIELD, G. B. "Agricultural Changes in Uganda: 1945–1960," *Food Research Institute Studies,* III, No. 2 (May, 1962), 87–124.

OKURUME, G. E. "Interdependence Between Food Production and Export Production in Nigerian Agriculture," May 23, 1968, Ms. pp. 1–25.

PHILLIPS, J. *Agriculture and Ecology in Africa: A Study of Actual and Potential Development South of the Sahara.* London: Faber & Faber, 1959; New York: Frederick A. Praeger, 1960.

———. "Certain Criteria for Application to Large-Scale Irrigation Projects in the Developing Countries." Unpublished paper, 1965.

————. *The Development of Agriculture and Forestry in the Tropics: Patterns, Problems, and Promise.* London: Faber & Faber; New York: Frederick A. Praeger, 1961.

"A Plan for the Mechanized Production of Groundnuts in East and Central Africa." (Cmd. 7030.) London: H.M. Stationery Office, 1947.

POGUCKI, R. J. H. *Land Tenure in Ghana.* Accra: Lands Department, 1957.

RAEBURN, J. R. "Some Economic Aspects of African Agriculture," *The East African Economic Review,* V, No. 2 (January, 1959), 45.

SCHROO, H. "The Three Pillars of Agriculture in the Tropics," reprinted as "Soil Fertility" in *Weekly News* (Nairobi), No. 2005 (July 17, 1964), pp. 40–41.

THOMPSON, V., and ADLOFF, R. *The Emerging States of French Equatorial Africa.* Stanford, Calif.: Stanford University Press; London: Oxford University Press, 1960.

VAN DER HORST, S. T. "Africans on the Land," review article, *The South African Journal of Economics* (Johannesburg), XXXIII, No. 3 (September, 1965), 237–47.

WICKIZER, V. D. "The Smallholder in Tropical Export Crop Production," *Food Research Institute Studies,* I, No. 7 (February, 1960).

WILDE, J. C. DE. *Experiences with Agricultural Development in Tropical Africa.* Baltimore, Md.: The Johns Hopkins Press, for the International Bank for Reconstruction and Development, to be published 1967.

WORTHINGTON, E. B. *Science in the Development of Africa.* London: CCTA and Scientific Council for Africa South of the Sahara, 1958.

YUDELMAN, M. *Africans on the Land.* Cambridge, Mass.: Harvard University Press, 1964.

# VI

# Mineral Development

*The dynamite works get into production and deliver to*
*the miners who blast, the mule drivers, engineers and*
*firemen on the dinkies, the pumpmen, the rope riders,*
*the sinkers and sorters, the carpenters, electricians and*
*repairmen, the foremen and straw-bosses,*

*They get out the ore and send it to the smelters, the*
*converters where by the hands and craft of furnace*
*crushers and hot blast handlers, ladlers, puddlers,*
*the drag-out man, the hook-up man, the chipper, the*
*spannerman, the shearsman, the squeezer,*

*There is steel for the molders, the cutlers, buffers,*
*finishers, forgers, grinders, polishers, temperers—*

*This is for the sake of a jack-knife in your pocket or*
*a shears on your table.*

CARL SANDBURG, The People, Yes

The exploitation of mineral resources has been and will probably continue to be, for at least the next decade, the only way available to some African countries to bypass the slow and laborious process of economic growth through agricultural development. (In Chapter VII, I shall attempt to demonstrate why industrialization in most of Africa will probably also continue to be slow and halting, especially in the countries that do not have mineral resources.) Under present conditions in Africa, only through the development of mineral resources can a state multiply its export earnings, national income, and government revenues within a few years.

In general, a successful new mining complex requires bulk transport facilities and leads to the building of new railways, which, while not so efficient as highways in opening up new country, do provide transport facilities that help agricultural producers to find a way to markets. Further, the export of minerals requires a port, to which general cargo wharves can be added, thereby promoting other exports. Mines also require an infrastructure of other public services: the Kariba power project on the Zambezi River, built in the late 1950's and completed by 1960, was necessary at that particular stage because of the growing demand for power from the Zambian copper belt, which could no longer be met economically by thermal plants burning imported coal from Southern Rhodesia or America. Mines provide, lastly, an enclave of modern technology in the empty spaces of Africa where Africans can be trained, learn to improve their productivity, and move into the machine civilization.

If large enough, the mining sector is often an effective leading or propulsive sector of the economy: it provides a direct demand for manufactured products: the incomes it generates stimulate demand for consumer goods; and, through the multiplier process, it tends to raise output and incomes generally in the economy. In some cases, mining groups not only engage in the industrial processes of mining proper, like refining, but move on into other industries. (In Australia, the iron and steel producer BHP was initially a mining concern. When its zinc mine ran out, BHP looked around for something else in which to invest its organization and capital, and, deciding that Australia was ready for a modern iron and steel industry, set to work to create one—now among the most economic in the world.) In Zambia, the British South Africa Company (BSA), the Anglo-American Corporation, and the Roan Selection Trust joined to finance and subsidize the first modern (and first tolerable) hotel in the capital city of Lusaka as a means of encouraging other foreign investors. BSA also financed several trucking concerns. In Rhodesia, Anglo-American was involved in creating a fertilizer industry and a ferro-chrome industry.

The modern economic development of South Africa was, of course, sparked by the discovery of its mineral wealth—beginning with the discoveries of diamonds at Kimberley in 1867 and of gold on the Witwatersrand in 1886. Mining required, and the income derived from mining made possible, the railways that opened up the whole country; financed the government and its aid to agriculture; provided the market and stimulus for industrialization; and earned most of the foreign-exchange income of the country. Even though mining is no longer South Africa's dominant economic activity, it still earns the foreign exchange to pay for the imported machinery, fuel, and raw materials that South African manufacturing requires.

In Zambia, the output of the copper, lead, and zinc mines, valued at around $1,100 million a year, furnishes two thirds of the gross domestic product; the mines provide almost all the exports and nearly three quarters of the government revenue to finance both current and capital expenditures. The Congo (Kinshasa) also now produces about $600 million of minerals a year; Nigeria, $500 million; Liberia, $200 million; Southern Rhodesia, Ghana, Sierra Leone, Mauretania, Angola, Gabon, and Tanzania, $50-100 million; Kenya, Uganda, Rwanda, and Swaziland, $10-30 million. In Mauretania, the new Miferma iron-ore mine is such a large part of the economy that in 1962, when its development was at its height, gross investment was at the absurdly high level of 70 percent of GDP! Angola, Gabon, and Tanganyika produce $20–$30 million a year, and Kenya, Uganda, Rwanda, and Swaziland about $10 million.

Obviously, not all countries can use mining as a propulsive sector. This depends first and foremost on having and finding exploitable minerals; second, on exploiting them; and, finally, on ensuring that the general development of the country benefits as much as possible from the mineral development.

Unfortunately, even though there is still much to learn about the geology of Africa, it is already certain that the useful mineral deposits are unevenly distributed—some countries are likely to be very fortunate and some comparatively poor in mineral resources. Apart from South Africa and Libya, which are already success stories in this regard, Algeria, Nigeria, Gabon, and Angola clearly possess the mineral potential that, if used wisely, can make successful and rapid economic development possible. Libya, starting from nothing, by the beginning of the 1970's had become the fourth largest oil producer in the world, after the United States, the Soviet Union, and Iran. Her reserves are among the world's largest, and the inflow of income from the exploitation of her resources already puts her in the middle-income bracket of the nations of the world. Algeria, although she started before Libya, has fallen considerably behind in the discovery and exploitation of reserves: her output of about 40 million tons in 1970 was only one fourth that of Libya. Nigeria, south of the Sahara, appears also to possess large oil and natural-gas reserves. Production recovered quickly after the end of the civil war in 1970, and at around 60 million tons a year surpassed that of Algeria by around 50 per cent. With continued stability, the income from the growing oil output, and exploitation of her large natural-gas resources, Nigeria should be able by 1975 to mount a large economic-development effort out of her own earnings.

Gabon, with a half-million inhabitants by 1970, has manganese, uranium, and oil (5 million tons a year). During the 1970's the very rich and large (over 800 million tons of reserve proved) Mekambo iron-ore deposits should begin to be exploited. Angola has likewise proved to have reserves of oil (around 10 million tons of output from offshore Cabinda and the mainland in 1970), diamonds, iron ore, and copper. All were under exploitation in 1970, and plans for further expansion of output were well under way.

There are other nations whose mineral potential, while not so spectacular as Gabon's or Nigeria's, still provides a solid volume of export earnings as a developmental base: Mauretania, Guinea, Sierra Leone, Liberia, Congo (Kinshasa), Zambia, and Rhodesia. Ghana could move into this group; she now exports manganese, diamonds, and, in a somewhat less solid position, gold, and has large deposits of bauxite. With the successful exploration for oil offshore in Nigeria, Gabon, and Cabinda, there is a considerable probability that oil may also be found in the continental shelf below the sea off Ghana, Togo, Dahomey, and Cameroon.

### The Search for and Exploitation of Minerals

By now, the major features of the geology of Africa are known, but, aside from a few areas like the Witwatersrand in South Africa and the Katanga-Zambia copper belt, most of the continent has not been investigated in great detail. In any case, mineral wealth is hard to assess even in areas (like the United States) where a very great deal is known about the geology—as the experience of the 1950's showed, in the many discoveries of rich uranium deposits feasible for mining that were made when a determined effort was mounted by governments to encourage prospecting for that element. And the chances of finding minerals have been increased in recent years with the improvement in prospecting methods due to new techniques of geophysics and geochemistry. These are particularly important in Africa, where direct geological research is difficult and expensive because of the forest cover or the sand or laterite over-burden in many areas.

The "mineral solution" to development in any one area of Africa should not be discounted out of hand. While blind optimism is foolish, one can also go far wrong in being pessimistic about mineral resources, as can be seen in the following remark from a book written in 1952 by a deservedly noted geographer: "The conditions favoring the accumulation of oil in quantity, in folds among the sedimentary rocks on the margins of great sedimentary basins, do not exist in Africa." Quite clearly, the chances of finding a particular mineral vary from area to area—oil is not likely to be found in the pre-Cambrian rocks of inland Cameroon or a diamond pipe in the Niger Delta. But, as the demand for particular minerals grows in the world, there is a good chance that different regions of Africa will be discovered to possess these minerals in economically exploitable quantities and conditions.

Whether a particular deposit is "exploitable" or not depends on the economics of its possible use. The iron mountains near Fort Goraud, in Mauritania, have been known since the 1920's but were uneconomic to exploit until the 1950's. Again, developments during World War II and after, when techniques of moving large volumes of materials at low cost were revolutionized, have improved Africa's chances. Materials that once could not be feasibly mined because of prohibitive costs of transport are now able to compete. (These techniques are applicable not only to Africa. For example, in the last few years they have made it possible to open up vast new iron-ore deposits for exploitation in the wastelands of western Australia.)

The greatly improved methods in prospecting and in exploitation have underlined the fact that there is no such thing as an absolute scarcity of mineral resources in the world; there are only costs involved in finding exploitable new deposits. All the continents of the world have many usable mineral resources. All other things being equal, which deposit in which continent is developed will depend first on which is known, and on the general environment in which the mining operation will have to take place. High on any government's list of economic priorities, therefore, should be continuing study of and search for minerals.

There is little justification for the theory governments express occasionally that exploitation of a mineral resource should be held back on the ground that it is "a wasting asset." When there are so many possibilities of finding a good mineral deposit elsewhere in the world, a government or company that sits on a resource too long may find in the end that it has no value. By the time it was finally decided to exploit the Tonkolili iron-ore deposit in Sierra Leone, for example, it was no longer feasible to do so—other deposits in Africa and Australia had been discovered in the meantime that were much more economic. If South Africa had hesitated in 1950 and 1951 to make contracts to sell its uranium from the gold-mine tailings, she would have never succeeded in doing so, since interest in them would have vanished as richer resources were discovered in North America. With modern technology, moreover, it is always possible that some invention or process will alter the whole economics of an industry, and the kind and quality of raw materials it needs. If a resource is already being exploited, it may be able to continue to compete; if it is not, interest in it may disappear.

Before the search for minerals can begin, there are certain prerequisites that must be filled. The nation must have appropriate mineral-resources legislation which provides security to the mining enterprises, exploration incentives, and a suitable institutional framework. It is useless to invite prospectors into the country if, when they wish to follow a promising lead, they have to negotiate with every petty chief to get access to the land.

Aside from these conditions, and aside from direct government support of research on the country's basic geological structure and mineral wealth, an important contribution can in many cases be made by the mining companies themselves and by individual prospectors. The creation of conditions encouraging both prospectors and the large mining companies to search for minerals is often the best line of action for governments to take. This is shown by the cases of Canada, Australia, and South Africa.

In fact, a government that can capture the interest of one of the large mining companies or groups in its country has an asset of great value. Any mining group will give priority in its search for minerals to the country where it is already operating, to take advantage of economies of scale for the existing organization. And a routine part of the on-going mine operations is the continuous establishment of new reserves by drilling, which often results in the discovery of new minerals as well as in additions to the knowledge of the country's geology. Finally, while there are certainly outstanding exceptions, the large mining companies or groups nowadays are in the main very conscious of their responsibility to aid in every way in the develop-.ment of the countries in which they operate. This does not mean that hard bargaining with them is no longer necessary, but it pays off best when coupled with the recognition that most of these groups are willing to go beyond their immediate economic interests to help the national development. The initiatives taken by the Roan Selection Trust group of companies in Zambia to finance agricultural research on the Kafue flats; in breaking the color bar in the mines; in making, together with the Anglo-American Corporation, what was in essence a grant contribution of $28 million toward the financing of the Kariba power project as well as a large loan of $56 million for the same purpose; and in financing secondary school construction in the copper belt—these are all examples of an enlightened policy a government can hope to encourage.

The large mining groups are in addition an important channel for bringing foreign capital into Africa. The international private capital markets have largely dried up for Africa. (See below, chap. IX.) The one section of the investment community that is still willing to take risks is that composed of the mining investors. The international groups that have entered Africa, particularly since World War II, are among the most important in the world; maintaining their interest in the future development of Africa, as against other continents, should be among the top economic-policy priorities of African governments. This is a matter of economic pragmatism and not of ideology. Most African governments have been well aware of this: the lead was in fact taken by such ideologically sensitive leaders as Sekou Touré in Guinea and Nkrumah in Ghana, who encouraged aluminum producers to invest in the development of their resources.

Also, as noted earlier, a mining group often will branch out into other activities. And the indirect influence of these mining complexes must also not be underrated. Their educational value, in affecting Africans moving from an age-old subsistence agriculture into a world of modern technology, is bound to be profound.

(While small mining operations do exist in Africa, in general, as seems to be true of other underdeveloped areas, profitable mining evidently requires large mining groups. This is probably due to the fact that mineral deposits in Africa are usually found far from the coast or in such difficult terrain that only a large-scale operation has hopes of making a go of the enterprise.)

A major problem in the exploitation of any African nation's mineral resources nevertheless continues to be the negotiation of the terms with the mining group or groups involved. While most mining corporations may take a long-term view of their interests and be conscious of the need to give a fair share of the benefits to the country concerned, this does not obviate the need for hard bargaining on the part of the government. All mining groups are not equally enlightened, for one thing. In any case, a government that drives a hard bargain is not so repelling to potential investors as one that does not keep its side of a bargain once it is made and harasses a concern by changing the conditions under which it must operate.

The African countries now have at their disposal a variety of aids in their negotiations that were not available or as easily accessible in earlier eras. A study of a proposed project by the U.N. Development Program (formerly Special Fund) or World Bank (granted under certain circumstances, e.g., possible World Bank participation in the financing) can provide a completely objective analysis of the project, including the basic financial parameters involved. The World Bank study of the Volta Project, for example, gave a basis for Ghana's negotiations with private aluminum companies on the smelter they were to build to use power from the Volta Project—analyzing as it did what the financial impact would be of different sizes of smelter, different rates charged for the power, etc. And the World Bank also advises on such matters as whether a consulting firm a country is thinking of appointing is suitable. There are also other sources of such help: an oil-producing country can take advantage of the technical information that has been acquired by the Organization of Petroleum Exporting Countries (OPEC) over the years; the Economic Commission for Africa and the United Nations have both made comparative studies of mining legislation in various countries. The major copper-producing countries—Congo (Kinshasa), Zambia, Chile, and Peru—have also created an organization, CIPEC (Conseil Intergouvernemental des Pays Exportateurs de Cuivre), to safeguard their interests, with a primary concern to study the world copper market to try to find a way to stabilize the price of copper.

In short, there is no reason why an African government confronted with a large international mining group need feel handicapped. A government should be able to secure the full benefits available to it from mineral exploitation and need have no inferiority complex about or resentment against "enclave investment."

Beginning in the Congo (Kinshasa) in Africa—and before that in Chile—the developing countries have experimented with acquiring a majority share in the large mining concerns operating within their borders. The typical arrangement reached (described in more detail below, in the section on African mining companies) is as follows: (1) the African government secured 51 per cent of the shares in the company, with the payment to the former shareholders to come out of dividend income of the company; (2) the management of the mines continued to be carried out by the international mining group; and (3) the marketing of the product continued to be handled by the international mining group. In brief, under this arrangement the African government became the majority owner of the mines but continued to take advantage of the managerial, technical, and sales competence of the international mining group. As far as the latter was concerned, if the arrangement operated as a genuine partnership of interests it would have the advantage of providing a stable and politically secure environment under which to operate. It remains to be seen whether the new arrangements will both provide sufficient gain to the countries concerned and sufficient security for the mining groups to encourage further mineral development in the 1970's.

## Africa's Minerals

In the past, the main African minerals of any economic importance were gold and diamonds. Indeed, gold—an African export since time immemorial—has become more and more a primarily African commodity. South Africa's share of world production outside the Soviet Union has been steadily increasing and by 1970 was at $1.2

billion a year, about 90 per cent. (The Soviet Union, the world's second largest producer, may have an output of $200–$300 million— far below that of South Africa.) Rhodesia, Ghana, and the Congo (Kinshasa) together produce under $100 million. Africa also produces 80 per cent of the world's diamonds—Brazil and the Soviet Union being the only other significant producers. Diamonds are a leading South African export, and the South African de Beers Company, with its related companies, still controls the world diamond-selling monopoly. Diamonds are the main export of Sierra Leone and the Central African Republic and a significant one for the Congo (Kinshasa), Ghana, South West Africa, and Angola. They also figure in the export earnings of such countries as Tanzania and Congo (Brazzaville).

Copper became an important African export between the wars. It is now the main export (around 800,000 tons a year in 1970, to go to 860,000 tons in 1974) of Zambia, second only to the United States in production, and is also important in the Congo (Kinshasa), which produces more than 300,000 tons. Uganda's copper output, only about 2 per cent of Zambia's, is still its most important mineral export. Among other minerals, most of the world's cobalt comes from the Congo, Zambia, and Morocco; manganese from Ghana, South Africa, Congo (Kinshasa), and Gabon, which provide about one fourth of the world's supply; a third of the world's chrome ore and of its vanadium ore, and one fifth of its asbestos come from South Africa and Rhodesia. The uranium for the world's first atomic bombs came from a mine in Katanga that has since been exhausted. South Africa was an important world producer of uranium from gold-mine tailings during the 1950's but has since decreased in importance as lower-cost sources were found in the United States and Canada. Gabon has been the main source for France's uranium. New deposits have been found and are being developed by European and Japanese firms in the Central African Republic and Niger. By 1973, C.A.R.'s exports may have a gross value of around $50 million and Niger's around $20 million—both sizable additions to total exports. Africa is also believed to have some 60 per cent of the world's thorium reserves (of over 0.01-per-cent oxide content)—mainly in South Africa, Madagascar, Malawi, Nigeria, and East Africa.

Iron ore became economically important after World War II, as the steel industries of Europe and America outran their raw-material base. Before the war, the United States was self-sufficient. Now, with its highest-grade ores used up, it must look to Canada, Latin America, and Africa for at least one quarter of its present consumption. In Europe, Great Britain has depended on imported ore since the 1930's; the Common Market countries used to be self-sufficient, but by 1960, they were importing a quarter of their total consumption; by 1970, half.

Iron-ore deposits have been known, mined, and processed into iron in Africa for centuries. Most of the large, economically exploitable deposits of today were discovered in the last fifty years. With the markets opening up for them, large-scale mining began essentially after World War II. The major expansion took place in the 1960's. A brief account of the development of some of these deposits may bring out more clearly the pattern mineral development in Africa takes.

Iron ore was discovered in West Africa about sixty years ago near Conakry, in Guinea, during the building of the Niger railway. Systematic study of the deposits was made before World War I and after, but the ore, with less than 50-per-cent iron content, could not be exploited and marketed economically until the 1950's. Less than a million tons a year are now exported from the port of Conakry (which can only take ships of under 25,000 tons). In Sierra Leone, iron ore of 56-per-cent iron content was discovered by the government's Geological Department at Marampa, within forty miles of Freetown, one of the best natural harbors in Africa. It was therefore economic to exploit, and in 1933, the Sierra Leone Development Company, formed by private Scottish investors (Baird's) to develop the deposit, became the first exporter of iron ore from West Africa. The mine now has a capacity of more than 2.5 million tons a year. Another deposit, at Tonkolili, about 100 miles from the sea, has ore of around 56-per-cent iron content but with high moisture and alumina content. After intensive study, the company concluded in 1962 that the competition from better ores in other African countries would not allow an economic return on the $90 million or so that would be required to build the necessary railway and ore-mining installations.

In Liberia, the Bomi Hills deposit was first reconnoitered in the 1930's by Dutch interests, but they could not find sufficient financial backing to undertake development. In 1944, the U.S. Geological Sur-

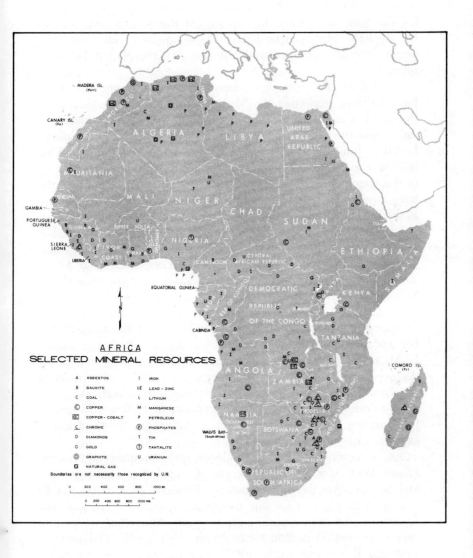

# AFRICA
## SELECTED MINERAL RESOURCES

| | | | |
|---|---|---|---|
| A | ASBESTOS | I | IRON |
| B | BAUXITE | l-Z | LEAD – ZINC |
| C | COAL | L | LITHIUM |
| Ⓒ | COPPER | M | MANGANESE |
| Ⓒ̄ | COPPER – COBALT | P | PETROLEUM |
| C̲ | CHROME | Ⓟ | PHOSPHATES |
| D | DIAMONDS | T | TIN |
| G | GOLD | Ⓣ | TANTALITE |
| Ⓖ | GRAPHITE | U | URANIUM |
| | NATURAL GAS | | |

Boundaries are not necessarily those recognized by U.N.

0   200   400   600   800   1000 MI.

0   200  400  600  800  1000 KM.

vey, working with the Liberian government, thoroughly explored the deposit, and in 1949, L. K. Christie, who founded the Liberian Mining Company to develop the deposit, got the needed support from the Republic Steel Corporation to begin mining. Three other deposits were also explored and are now being exploited by other interests.

The largest and, now, most important of these is the LAMCO–Joint Venture, exploiting the Mount Nimba deposits, which lie at the point where Liberia, Guinea, and the Ivory Coast meet 170 miles from the sea. The deposits go across the border into Guinea. LAMCO–Joint Venture, with an investment so far of around $300 million, is the largest single mining project undertaken in Africa up to the present time. The project is financed by a partnership of the large Swedish company Grängesberg (75 per cent of the total) and Bethlehem Steel (the remaining 25 per cent). In 1955, the Swedish government had bought Grängesberg's holdings in the Swedish Lapland iron-ore mines and Grängesberg, looking around for a new source of iron ore and having the money to invest, came to Africa. The LAMCO project includes the development of the mine (with known ore reserves of about 250 million tons of around 66 per cent iron content), construction of a U.S. standard-gauge railway (4'6", compared to Africa's standard gauge of 3'6"), and the artificial harbor and port of Buchanan (which can handle 60,000-ton ships). LAMCO has built a $50-million plant at Buchanan to concentrate the ore further into pellets before export. In 1966, the capacity of the Nimba mine was raised to 10 million tons a year. With the other mines, Liberia's total iron-ore capacity in 1970 was 20 million tons, making it the largest producer in Africa and the third largest exporter in the world.

Other important African iron producers are Mauretania and Namibia (South West Africa), with an output of roughly 8 million tons each, and Senegal, Angola, and Swaziland. Rhodesia used to convert its iron ore into pig iron for sale to Japan. Tunisia, Algeria, and Morocco have also been exporting ore for years. Altogether, Africa now exports around 50 million tons of iron ore annually, and provides from one fifth to one quarter of Western Europe's iron-ore supplies.

Of the other African countries, the most important *potential* iron-ore exporter is Gabon, with its Mekambo deposit of around 800 million tons of proven ore of 60-per-cent or higher iron content. This deposit is, however, 400 miles from the sea, near the border of the Central African Republic. The French government announced in May, 1970, that it would help to finance the building of the railway line to make it possible to mine this deposit. The line is expected to cost about $160 million and to have an initial capacity of 8 million tons of iron ore and one million tons of timber a year for export. Guinea has two large deposits also well inland—one in the Mount Nimba area, which is to be developed in conjunction with the Liberian one. Undeveloped iron-ore deposits are also present in Ghana, which have become accessible with the creation of the new Volta Project lake, and in Nigeria, where there are plans to use them for a domestic industry. Dahomey, Mali, Niger, Togo, Cameroon, Congo (Brazzaville), Zambia, Tanzania, Somalia, Ethiopa, and the Sudan also have deposits, but most of these are still insufficiently proven, have too low iron content, or are still too inaccessible to good harbors to be serious contenders for development over the next five to ten years.

It must be remembered, however, that since World War II, the search for new sources of iron ore has not been restricted to Africa. Canada has become a major exporter to the United States and Great Britain. Both Brazil and Venezuela have also become large-scale exporters. And, within the last few years, billions of tons of high-iron-content ore have been found in western Australia. These finds have coincided with the continued trend to huge super-ore carriers of upwards of 100,000 tons, which, if ports can take them at both ends of their voyage, reduce the cost of transport so much that Australian ores are able to compete effectively in any market, even in Western Europe. To stand up to Australia's competition, the African ores also have to be transported in the huge ships, which means added large investments to create the necessary harbors and ports. In this connection, Australia's proven political stability gives her an intangible advantage which may weigh heavily with corporation managers who must decide where they should commit hundreds of millions of dollars in one sizable lump of investment.

The mining of bauxite, the raw material for aluminum, the fastest growing nonferrous metal in consumption, is another potentially very important African industry. For, so far as is known, Africa has the largest and best unexploited reserves of bauxite in the world. (Large reserves competitive with those of Africa have been staked out in northern Queensland, Australia, and in northern Brazil. Nevertheless, Africa remains in a favorable competitive position, all else being equal.) In addition, Africa possesses the greatest and most economic unutilized hydroelectric potential in the world. (See below, chap. VIII.) With sufficient political stability, she therefore has the basis for becoming one of the largest centers of aluminum production.

At present, bauxite ore is exported from Guinea, Sierra Leone, and Ghana. In Guinea, with the help of World Bank loans to build a new port and railway, a bauxite mine at Boké is to begin producing in 1972 and is scheduled to reach an output of nearly 10 million tons for export by 1978. Sierra Leone's production of around 400,000 tons a year is the major source of bauxite for the alumina plants of Alusuisse, the Swiss aluminum company. In Guinea, the first stage in the process of transforming bauxite into aluminum has been developed for some years, with a large plant at Fria, in operation since 1956, converting bauxite into alumina at a rate of 500,000 tons a year (to be increased to 700,000 tons in 1971). In Edea, in Cameroon, the first aluminum smelter in Africa is already producing 50,000 tons of aluminum annually. In Ghana, an aluminum smelter owned by the American Kaiser and Reynolds companies with an initial capacity of around 115,000 tons, began production in April, 1967, using electric power from the Volta Project. It is the biggest smelter in the world outside North America. It is to expand to 150,-000 tons by 1972 and could go to 185,000 tons in 1977.

Production of phosphate for fertilizer in Africa is also important—until recently, mostly in North Africa, in Morocco (the world's second largest producer, at 9 million tons a year) and Tunisia. Since 1961, rich deposits have been developed in Togo, with exports of one and a half million tons making phosphate one of Togo's main exports. Senegal has also become an important exporter. Rich deposits have also been discovered in the Spanish Sahara (estimated at over 1 billion tons). A 60-mile-long conveyor belt to a new seaport is being built by the Spanish government's company Enminsa to exploit the deposit. Exports are to begin in 1971.

Rich deposits of potash also needed for fertilizer were found during the 1960's in Congo (Brazzaville) near the coast in the course of drilling for oil. With the help of the French government's Alsatian potash company and a World Bank loan, export of potash had begun to be a source of foreign exchange for Congo (Brazzaville) by 1970. The Malagasy Republic, profiting from the favorable market resulting from sanctions against Rhodesia's chromite, found and started extraction of this mineral in 1969 and reached a level of output of 120,000 tons in 1970.

Among the most important mineral discoveries in recent years for the country concerned have been the nickel-copper and diamond deposits in Botswana. Botswana, among the last of African countries to achieve independence, with its area largely desert or semi-desert, has been extremely poor. The United Kingdom has had to finance almost half the current expenditures of the government, and the government has been entirely dependent on external sources to finance any capital investment. In the course of its mineral prospecting, the Roan Selection Trust, based in Zambia, discovered a rich nickel-copper deposit in Botswana. With the help of the U.N. Development Fund, other U.N. agencies, and the World Bank Group, a mine is to come into production in 1973 with an annual output of some 37,000 tons of copper-nickel matte and some 125,000 tons of sulphur recovered from the refining process. Meanwhile, De Beers Consolidated Mines discovered one of the largest diamond pipes in the world. Production of diamonds is expected to start in 1971 and to reach about 3 million carats by 1975. With the revenue from the nickel-copper and diamonds, Botswana should be able not only to become independent of subsidies for its current expenditures but to begin to finance some of its investment requirements.

The end of the 1960's and the beginning of the 1970's saw a significant new factor emerge in African mineral development. The rapid growth of Japan made her an increasingly large consumer of minerals and led her to look for new sources of minerals in new areas. Japan was already a significant consumer of African minerals by 1970 and potentially a new major market. By 1970, Japan was purchasing the whole of the iron-ore output of Swaziland—in fact, it was only the Japanese contract that justified developing these resources. Japan had also contracted to buy the whole output of Uganda's Kilembe copper mine and almost half of Sierra Leone's iron-ore-concentrates exports to the end of 1979 (making it necessary to increase the capacity of the iron-ore export port of Pepel to accommodate ships of at least 90,000 tons cargo capacity). In addition, the Japanese Nippon Mining Company has begun to venture its own capital and technology to help develop minerals resources in Africa. A joint Congo government–Japanese firm (Société Développement Industriel et Minière du Congo) has taken over two large areas in the Katanga near the Zambian border. Mining operations are to start in 1971 with an objective of an output of 60,000 tons of copper by 1973. Another copper mine is to be developed in the Malange district of northern Angola. The Japanese Sumitomo Investment Bank jointly with the Portuguese has developed an iron-ore mine at Namapa in northeast Mozambique.

### African Mining Companies

The important mining groups operating in Africa are still few, and most of them are in southern Africa, where mineral development first occurred on the continent. The richest of these groups is probably the Anglo-American Corporation of South Africa, Ltd. Anglo-American is mostly owned in South Africa and the United Kingdom; American shareholdings are negligible. It has large interests in gold and coal mines and in electrical manufacturing and chemicals in South Africa; it manages the Wankie coal mine in Rhodesia and has some industrial interests there too; in Zambia, it controls the lead and zinc output at Broken Hill and is a partner with the Zambian government in mines, producing just under half of the output of the copper belt. It produces 40 per cent of the gold of South Africa— i.e., about one third of total world output. In partnership with Imperial Chemicals, Anglo-American owns the largest explosives manufacturer in the world—African Explosives. Anglo-American is also closely associated with de Beers, the diamond-monopoly interests of South Africa marketing the bulk of the world's diamonds, which also has an interest in and manages the Williamson diamond mine in Tanzania and is developing the diamond mine in Botswana. It is also, with Charter Consolidated, developing a new copper mine, Bakel Akjoujt, in Mauretania.

The Roan Selection Trust (RST) manages the mine that produces the other half of Zambia's copper and is developing the nickel-copper mine in Botswana. RST is largely owned by American, British, and French investors; American Metal Climax (AMAX) of New York is the largest shareholder. AMAX also has interests in Tsumeb, a lead-zinc mine in South West Africa and, along with other companies, in the new Palabora copper mine being developed in the Transvaal.

The British South Africa Company, organized by Cecil Rhodes, which administered both the Rhodesias until 1923 and 1924, continued to own all the mineral rights in Zambia to the eve of that country's independence in October, 1964. It continues to have interests in some of the other mining operations in the former Rhodesias, and in some industrial and transport companies. It has since merged with other interests into a new concern, Charter Consolidated Ltd., which has been mentioned earlier.

Tanganyika Concessions, Ltd., which has nothing to do with Tanganyika, was organized in 1889 and was given the right systematically to prospect the Katanga. When Union Minière du Haut-Katanga was organized in 1906, it was a pooling of the interests of Tanganyika Concessions, the Société Générale of Belgium (Belgium's leading financial group), and the Comité Spéciale du Katanga (the concessionaire group which had been given the right to administer the Katanga by the Congo Free State). Tanganyika Concessions now owns about 15 per cent of Union Minière and 90 per cent of the Benguela Railway Company, which owns the rail line that runs from Katanga through Angola to the sea. Among its major stockholders are understood to be Anglo-American, the Société Générale, the Belgian Banque Lambert group, and Lazard Frères.

The principal interests in Katanga are all, then, closely associated with the Société Générale through the latter's shareholdings and financial guidance in the Union Minière, Forminière (the foremost producer of industrial diamonds in the world), and the BCK (Bas Congo–Katanga) Railway, which serves the Katanga and the power companies. The main shareholder of Union Minière is the Democratic Republic of the Congo, which now owns 18 per cent of the shares and has a voting power of 24.5 per cent, Tanganyika Concessions, the Société Générale, and the Katanga Company. (*The Economist* [London], June 19, 1965, p. 1453.) The Union Minière's assets in the Katanga were nationalized in 1967 by the Congo government. They are managed by the Société Générale des Minerais, another affiliate of the Société Générale.

The Consolidated African Selection Trust and its sister company, African Selection Trust, owned the diamond mines in Ghana and Sierra Leone. They are related to RST in Zambia through the Brit-

ish Selection Trust (organized by Sir Chester Beatty), as well as
to the Tsumeb Corporation in South West Africa, AMAX, Bikita
Minerals (lithium) in Rhodesia, and several gold-mining ventures
in South Africa.

Union Carbide, an American concern, operates chrome mines in
Rhodesia and the manganese mine in Ghana. Other large American
iron, steel, and aluminum companies have an interest in African
minerals. Republic Steel has interests in the Liberian Mining Company. Bethlehem is not only part of the group exploiting the Mount
Nimba deposits in Liberia but holds interests in the eventual development of the Mekambo deposits in Gabon. U.S. Steel is a
principal shareholder (with French interests [Mokta-el-Hadid] and
the French government's Bureau Minier, charged with mineral exploration and development in Africa) in the Comilog manganese
mine in Gabon.

Of American aluminum companies, Kaiser and Reynolds are
owners (90 per cent and 10 per cent, respectively) of the large new
Valco aluminum smelter in Ghana; Olin Mathiesson is a partner in
the 500,000-ton Fria alumina plant in Guinea (responsible for some
two thirds of Guinea's total foreign-exchange earnings); and Harvey
Aluminum has the concession for the rich Boke bauxite deposits in
Guinea originally held by Aluminium Ltd. of Canada through its
French affiliate, Bauxites du Midi. The large French aluminum
concern Pechiney is also a partner in Fria, as well as the owner of
the first aluminum plant constructed in Africa, the 50,000-ton
smelter at Edea, in Cameroon.

Among the other important mining groups in Africa there is
Compagnie de Mokta, a French mining group, which wholly owns
the Grand Lahou Mining Company in the Ivory Coast and has a
19-per-cent share in Comilog. Mokta also has a 50-per-cent share in
the Compagnie des Mines d'Uranium de Franceville in Gabon and
a 10-per-cent interest in Les Mines de l'Air, the new uranium mining
company in Niger.

Although it is a conglomerate, the Lonrho Group of London is
worthy of mention, if for no other reason than that it is one of the
very few investment groups that has been willing to expand its stake
in Africa substantially in recent years. It took over the Ashanti Gold-
fields Company in Ghana in 1968. It has bought John Holts, an
important trading firm in West Africa and, through Whiteheads, a

British textile firm, it controls Kaduna textiles in Nigeria. In Congo (Kinshasa) in 1968, through one of its subsidiaries, it gained control of Cominière, which incorporates more than twenty medium-sized concerns operating in the Congo, such as Agrifor, a timber concern, and Vicicongo, a narrow-gauge railway in Orientale Province. It also owned the oil pipeline from Beira to Umtali in Southern Rhodesia.

## Mining Nationalizations

As mentioned above, several of the most important mining concerns in Africa have been nationalized. The term "nationalized" probably overstates the position in most cases. Essentially, what has happened is that several of the governments have become partners in the major mining enterprises in their territory. The Liberian government, in fact, as noted above, has had a 50-per-cent equity in LAMCO from the beginning. In LAMCO, as in the nationalizations, the management and the marketing continue to be in the hands of the foreign partner. For both, the foreign partner is essential, since no African country at present has either the technical and managerial personnel or the access to world markets that the international mining groups have. The main elements of the nationalizations that have taken place are described below.

At the beginning of 1967, the properties of the Union Minière du Haut Katanga (UMHK), valued by UMHK at $800 million, were vested by the Congo government in a newly formed, state-owned corporation, Générale Congolaise des Minerais (GECOMIN). In September, 1969, an agreement was reached under which the Société Générale des Minerais (SGM), essentially UMHK under another name, would operate the mines (as it had been doing after the nationalization) and market the minerals for a management fee of 6 per cent of the value of the minerals sold for fifteen years. Since it had been receiving 4.5 per cent from the nationalization, the additional 1.5 per cent might be regarded as compensation. At the end of fifteen years, the total amount paid to SGM is to be reduced to 1 per cent to cover technical cooperation and related expenses.

In August, 1969, Zambia announced that it intended to acquire a 51-per-cent interest in the two copper-mining groups, Roan Selection Trust and Anglo-American. In November, 1969, agreement was reached according to which the Zambian government's Industrial Development Corporation (INDECO) took over 51 per cent of the equity and appointed six out of the eleven directors as from January 1, 1970. The mining groups in question provide management and act as sales agents under contracts which run for a minimum of 10 years. They will receive fees for these services equivalent to 1.5 per cent of gross sales plus 2 per cent of profits, calculated after payment of the minerals tax but before income tax. The total value of the Zambian participation in the companies was set at $112.5 million in Roan Selection Trust and $179.5 million in Anglo-American. These amounts are to be paid by INDECO in negotiable tax-free government-guaranteed bonds denominated in U.S. dollars and bearing an interest rate of 6 per cent; the bonds are to be paid off over eight years for Roan Selection Trust and over twelve years for Anglo-American. In both cases, there is provision for more rapid repayment if two thirds of the dividends paid on INDECO's share of the equity exceeds the installments due in any year.

The mining companies are to pay a minerals tax of 51 per cent of net profits and a regular company tax of 45 per cent on the balance, resulting in a total tax payment of about 73 per cent, or about what the companies have been paying. As a result of the dividends paid to INDECO, Zambia should get an additional 5 per cent of the over-all gross profits, and this figure will rise to 13 per cent once compensation is completed. Roan Selection Trust and Anglo-American will form new external companies to hold their share of the equity. Dividends paid to these companies are exempted from any special Zambian taxation, exchange controls, or restrictions on dividend remittances for a minimum period of ten years.

In December, 1969, Sierra Leone announced that it would take control of 51 per cent of the shares of the four mining companies. Payments for the shares will be made from the future dividends. The government will appoint the majority of directors in each case. The government stated that when it had paid for its stock, tax rates would be reduced to offset revenues coming to it through its shareholdings. It will also consider reducing taxation as a mine reaches the end of its life. The companies concerned are Sierra Leone Selection Trust, a wholly owned subsidiary of Consolidated African Selection Trust, which mines diamonds in Ghana and of which Selection Trust has a 36.8-per-cent holding; Sierra Leone Development Company, which mines iron ore, a subsidiary of William Bairds of Glasgow, with a 5-per-cent holding by United Africa Company; Sherbo

Minerals, which mines rutile, in which Pittsburgh Plate Glass of the United States holds 51 per cent preference and 80 per cent ordinary shares, the balance being held by British Titan Products, in which Rio Tinto and Imperial Chemicals have substantial holdings; and Sierra Leone Ore and Metal Company, mining bauxite, wholly owned by Alusuisse of Zurich, a Swiss holding company for a group holding internationally owned mines and aluminum plants. The last two companies are still so new in Sierra Leone that they are enjoying the income-tax holiday—an incentive given to induce foreign capital to invest in Sierra Leone. By mid-1970, the government had decided to restrict nationalization to the first two companies.

### Selected Bibliography

COLLIER, J. L. "West Africa and Its Iron Ore: the Present and the Future." Unpublished paper, School of Advanced International Studies, Johns Hopkins University, 1966.

KIMBLE, G. H. T. "The Mineral Realm," in *Tropical Africa*. New York: The Twentieth Century Fund, 1960, pp. 289–370.

KUN, N. DE. *"The Mineral Resources of Africa*. Amsterdam: Elsevier, 1965.

McKINNON, D. "Minerals, the Key to Progress in Africa," *Optima* (Johannesburg), XIII, No. 2 (June, 1963), 73–81.

MOUSSA, P. *Les Chances économiques de la Communauté franco-africaine*. Paris: Colin, 1957.

OSTRANDER, F. T. "The Place of Minerals in Economic Development." Address to the Council of Economics, American Institute of Mining, Metallurgical and Petroleum Engineers, Dallas, Texas, February 27, 1963.

OSTRANDER, F. T., and KLOMAN, E. "The Corporate Structure of Rhodesian Copperbelt Mining Enterprise." Unpublished paper, August 31, 1962.

PRAIN, SIR RONALD. "Copper and its Place in the World," *Horizon* (publication of Roan Selection Trust), April, 1964, pp. 22–28.

PRÉ, R. "Problems of the African Mining Economy," in E. A. G. ROBINSON (ed.), *Economic Development for Africa South of the Sahara*. London: Macmillan, 1964, pp. 588–608.

*A Review of the Natural Resources of the African Continent*. Paris: UNESCO, 1963.

STAMP, L. D. *Africa. A Study in Tropical Development*. New York: John Wiley; London: Chapman & Hall, 1953.

WOLFE, A. W. " 'The Team' Rules Mining in Southern Africa," *Toward Freedom* (Chicago), XI, No. 7 (January, 1962), 1–3.

# VII

# Industrialization

Is it fear of the wasteland at my back
That keeps me looking ahead
Or the lame struggling will to do the
work?
Am I past the middle of the river
And therefore must go on?

KWESI BREW

Aside from the Republic of South Africa, no African country has taken more than the first steps leading to industrialization. South Africa, however, already produces a quarter of its GNP in manufacturing, and the addition of mining, which is also highly mechanized, brings the total to around 40 per cent. She is, in fact, beginning to move into the final stages of industrialization—the production of capital goods and equipment for her industries. Insofar as such comparisons are valid, she is now at roughly the same stage of development that Italy was at in 1950. Like the Italy of that period, but even more so, she still has large sections of her population that derive little benefit from the modern economy.

If one takes as an indicator of industrialization the value added in manufacturing, the following figures present a comparison of the stage of industrialization reached by some of the African countries in 1966:

VALUE ADDED IN MANUFACTURING, 1966

| | As Percentage of Value Added in Total Commodity Production | Per Capita in U.S. $ |
|---|---|---|
| United States | 73 | 1,054 |
| Japan | 58 | 219 |
| South Africa | 44 | 122 |
| Central African Republic | 14 | 10 |
| Congo (Kinshasa) | 34 | 14 |
| Ghana | 24 | 47 |
| Kenya | 21 | 12 |
| Liberia | 6 | 11 |
| Malawi | 8 | 3 |
| Senegal | 27 | 27 |
| Southern Rhodesia | 35 | 15 |
| Togo | 15 | 13 |
| Tunisia | 23 | 14 |
| Uganda | 9 | 7 |
| Upper Volta | 7 | 6 |

Although industry contributes a relatively unimportant part of the total GNP, many countries, as these figures indicate, already have a number of small enterprises of many kinds. These include, first of all, food-processing industries producing for the local market: flour mills, bakeries, soft-drink plants, breweries, and even distilleries. Building materials are produced in most countries—bricks, cement, window-frames, paint, etc. Shoes, cigarettes, textiles, and other consumer goods typical of the first stage of industrialization are also widely produced in West Africa—in Senegal, Ghana, and Nigeria, for example.

The impact of the automotive industry has been felt throughout Africa. Among the first industries to be considered feasible in many countries are tire retreading and the making of simple spare automobile parts. And, as the number of motor vehicles has increased, it has begun to be economic to import them in components and to have the final stage of assembly in the country. Truck-assembly plants and automobile-assembly plants have been established in a number of countries.

Then too, with the growing markets for gasoline and oil, the large oil companies have become concerned to get a stake in them, although it is clear that for a long time to come not more than one oil refinery per country will be economically justifiable. The desire to be the company owning that one refinery is usually very strong and has tended to outweigh the consideration that, at present, hardly any African market outside of South Africa, Nigeria, and the East African common market is large enough to justify an economic size of refinery (roughly one million tons of annual throughput). Stimulated by the demands from the governments and the particular competition from Italy's government-owned oil company, E.N.I., the large international oil companies in the early 1960's raced to be the first to build the refineries—a race made possible by their large capital resources and their experience in coping with political risks in all parts of the world.

The result is that refineries have been built all around the coasts of Africa. In 1962, there were four refineries south of the Sahara, two of which were in South Africa; in 1970 there were about twenty outside of South Africa. Hardly any major port is without its refinery, usually one which is below the optimum minimum size. Still, only one (in Tanzania) is below 500,000 tons capacity, and, in most cases, the additional cost resulting from building a small refinery is not too great to be borne, given the long-term benefits Africans will derive from becoming trained in the refinery's highly technical and complex operation. For the oil companies, with long experience in operating in developing countries, have definite policies favoring local training and aid to local enterprises.

Small iron and steel mills have already been built in Rhodesia, Kenya, and Uganda; Nigeria is likely to have one before 1975. But the potentially most important African metal industry is aluminum. (See above, chap. VI, p. 143.) With an output of 50,000 tons in Edea, Cameroon, and a smelter of 115,000 tons in Ghana, Africa is just beginning to exploit its potential in this regard.

### The Goal of Industrialization

The desire of most African governments to industrialize their nations as rapidly as possible is essentially well based. Unfortunately, the range of possibilities open in the immediate future is not very great. Industrialization lies a considerable distance off in the future for most African countries. But this does not obviate Africa's need to make as much progress toward this goal as possible. It is only in manufactured goods and services that human beings appear to have almost limitless wants; it is only in these fields, therefore, that nations can count on demand rising at the same pace with or faster than the rise in incomes—i.e., demand for manufactures is income elastic. One study on industrial growth and world trade concluded that, looking ahead to 1970-75, the developing countries' exports of primary products (other than oil) are unlikely to rise more than two thirds as fast as the total real incomes of the industrial countries. (Maizels.) Since income growth in the African countries in particular is closely related to export incomes, this means that the already large gap between their incomes and those of the industrial countries is likely to increase not only absolutely but relatively. (A widening absolute gap is inevitable in any case: a 1-per-cent increase in American per-capita GNP is more than $40; if African per-capita incomes grew at a rate of 10 per cent a year, which they do not, this would be an increase of $10 [assuming a per-capita income of $100]. Even with a 10-per-cent increase in African per-capita income and a 1-per-cent increase in American incomes, the absolute gap would continue to widen yearly.)

African countries at present export mainly agricultural products, and most of these are foods—coffee, cocoa, bananas, edible oils. Over-all and in the long run, demand for food follows Engel's Law— that is, as income rises, the proportion of it spent on food declines. (As a rule of thumb, the long-term income elasticity of demand for primary foodstuffs can be taken as below 0.7.) Even within this context, there is considerable opportunity for some food producers to prosper. With a rise in income, demand for a "superior" food can be elastic over a considerable range, as consumption of it increases at the expense of an "inferior" food. That is, consumption of chocolate will increase at the expense of sugar candy, meat at the expense of potatoes or bread. There is also the possibility that changing habits or new habits will result in an increase of consumption of a particular food more rapid than the increase in population or even income— e.g., the jump in the amount of coffee drunk in the United States when the coffee-break became a widespread habit during and after World War II. Again, if a nation is exporting a food with only a slowly growing demand, it can still, by winning a larger and larger part of the market, improve its GNP more rapidly than the over-all demand position for its products would seem to permit. And, in fact, many African countries since World War II have done just this—at the expense of Asian, particularly Indonesian, and Latin American producers of tropical products. Similarly in the nineteenth century, American development was greatly aided by American grain producers' taking over much of the European market from European farmers.

But, while a country can do quite well for a considerable time by taking advantage of these possibilities, for the food producers as a group the fact remains that their over-all market position will ultimately hamper their attempts to improve their standards of living; certainly it will hamper them in any attempt to catch up and keep up with the developed countries.

Producers of industrial agricultural products—e.g., raw cotton—and minerals confront similar fundamental problems. Again, total demand for these products does not rise as rapidly as incomes in the industrialized societies. For one thing, while no one has expounded it as yet, there is an industrial law equivalent to Engel's Law, which would read: As the value of a particular manufactured product goes up with its further improvement, the proportion of total cost represented by the raw materials used tends to go down; in other words, the higher the price of a manufactured good, the more likely it is that the high price represents the cost of the manufacturing process or the value added to the raw-material components. The automobile or airplane of today uses more raw materials than that of yesterday, but the raw materials are a smaller fraction of the total cost.

Further, with the rise in incomes in industrialized societies, the proportion spent on services goes up, and services use little if any raw materials.

Another set of causes holding down the rate of increase of demand for raw materials stems from the progress of technology: many technological improvements are directed to economizing in the use of raw materials; another main objective is to produce inexpensive synthetic substitutes for raw materials. The process that made it possible to tin-plate steel with tin only a molecule thick, for example, prevented any substantial growth in the demand for tin for a good decade and more; synthetic fibers cut into the demand for cotton and wool, etc.

As in the case of the market for foods, these various factors bear unequally on different products and different countries. In particular, there is the possibility that an underdeveloped country can take the market for minerals away from a developed country as the latter's richest deposits are exhausted, become unable to meet the growth in demand, or even prove to be uncompetitive with newer and richer mines. The exhaustion of American and European iron-ore mines and their inability to meet growing demands, for example, has led to widespread interest in African iron ore in the last twenty years. This excellent possibility of winning away from the industrial countries a larger share of the growing market tends to make minerals in particular a potential propulsive sector for many countries in Africa.

Whatever the main product a country exports, however, whether food, agricultural raw materials, or minerals, that country is likely to find that its export earnings are far more vulnerable to price fluctuations than is the case with countries that sell a variety of industrial products. (See chap. IV.) With the heavy reliance African economies now have on the export sector, the magnitude of such fluctuations presents major problems to the government and people. This alone is a powerful reason for trying to increase industrialization as much as is economically possible, so as to mitigate the vertiginous ups and downs in the economy.

Some theorists hold that, over the long run, terms of trade develop adversely against primary producing countries. But they usually overlook the fact that the quality of the industrial goods whose prices they are comparing over the period has changed. The price of an industrial good may have gone up, but the service it renders may be quite different from that formerly given by the commodity; i.e., a pound of copper today is essentially the same as a pound of copper was in 1914, but an automobile of today provides a more comfortable and carefree ride than the auto of 1914. The phonograph of today may cost more than the gramophone of yesteryear, but the music reproduction is infinitely superior.

There is another series of reasons for favoring industrialization. As I have tried to make clear in earlier chapters, progress in agriculture is bound to be slow in Africa. We still know relatively little about the best methods of improving tropical farming and of changing the attitudes and increasing the productivity of subsistence farmers. In industry, on the other hand, a great deal of the necessary skill and technology is easily transferable from the advanced countries to Africa: there is little real difference in the technical processes of textile manufacture between a factory in Europe and one in Uganda. The catch is, of course, that this presupposes the use of or the importation of scarce entrepreneurial talent, skilled workers, and capital. Difficulties arise if reliance must be placed on the local supplies of these factors, which are very scarce or nonexistent.

### The Problems of Setting Up Industries

There are many self-reinforcing constraints on getting industries started in any underdeveloped country. Probably the most important is a market that is too small. Only two countries in Africa outside of South Africa (Nigeria and Morocco) have a total market for manufactures as large as $1 billion equivalent. The three East African countries (Kenya, Tanzania, and Uganda) together reach this class. The others vary from around $900 million for Ghana, $600 million for Zambia, $500 million for Congo (Kinshasa), to less than $100 million for Central African Republic, Chad, Rwanda, Somalia, etc. The size of the market for manufactures grows more rapidly than per-capita income. A country like the Netherlands, with 13 million inhabitants, has a gross national product not quite so large as Middle Africa's, but its market for manufactures, around $20 billion equivalent a year, is about twice that of all the Middle African countries together.

Now, since the size of the market in most African countries depends primarily on the incomes of farmers, who make up the overwhelming mass of the population, it follows that, as stated by the Uganda Economic Development Committee in 1958, "the most effective steps which can be taken to secure development of manufacturing industry in Uganda, paradoxical though it may seem, are steps which will have the effect of increasing agricultural production. The committee *recommended* that government's economic strategy should be determined accordingly." In a World Bank report of 1962 on the economic development of Uganda, the essence of the policy recommendations remained the same (although there was a subtle change in emphasis): that "everything that is administratively and economically feasible be done in the next five years to increase output in manufacturing, mining and agriculture. . . . It is quite obvious, however, that in spite of doing everything possible in manufacturing and mining, the main opportunities for economic growth in Uganda in the next five years are in agriculture."

These factors, of course, are self-reinforcing. As manufacturing and towns grow, the internal market for agricultural products also grows. The internal market can then gradually provide more and more of the propulsive impulse that export markets still provide in Africa.

The chances for successful industrialization obviously will increase (up to a point) as the market area increases. There is, of course, the possibility of manufacturing for export to the growing markets of the industrialized countries. Unfortunately, for most African countries this solution is out of the question at this time. For their manufactured goods to compete successfully on equal terms in the industrialized countries, a degree of skill in design, of uniformity in quality, and of response to market conditions is required that is beyond reach. Even South Africa, with over a generation of industrial experience, has not yet been able to export manufactured products successfully in any appreciable volume outside of Africa. The penetration of the markets in industrial countries on any scale is tending to become more difficult, rather than easier, as the varieties of commodities produced and consumed there depart further and further from the simple goods a country embarking on industrialization is able to produce.

The trend in industrialized countries toward more complicated capital-intensive production may, however, open up the market for simple, cheap, mass-produced commodities (the kind Japan used to produce but has abandoned) for those developing countries that are able to produce them. To enter this market, Africa must be able to compete against Taiwan, mainland China, Hong Kong, Singapore, Korea, and India—all of which are likewise interested in and penetrating these markets, and all of which have a head start in terms of number of entrepreneurs, trained technicians, and skilled and semi-skilled labor. However, if increased African political unity results in some intra-Africa economic cooperation, African countries may be able, by protection of their markets, at least to win them from competing Asian producers.*

There is also always the possibility of the Africans' attacking the problem of how to develop industrial production at both ends of the

* The foregoing applies to Middle Africa. North Africa, Tunisia in particular, has the potential, by uniting European enterprises and indigenous labor (already considerably skilled, through centuries of artisan work and experience in European manufacturing enterprises), to produce and compete successfully in European markets.

manufacturing–trade–distribution process—by taking, at one end, materials they produce and processing them further before export, and, at the other, by completing the last stages of manufacture on commodities they import. If a given raw material or product is reduced substantially in weight or size through processing, there will be an added advantage in lowered transport costs if it is processed on the spot or in the country of origin; and, at the other end, if a manufactured commodity is bulkier than the materials of which it is made—such as furniture, or assembled cars and trucks—there may be advantages in lowered transport costs here too if the last stages of assembly or finishing are done in or close to the ultimate market. In both cases, it helps if these steps in the production process are labor-intensive—i.e., if wages are a high proportion of the production cost. For, with low-cost labor in the developing country, the savings in wage costs can then be added to the savings in transport costs (assuming that the labor is sufficiently productive to ensure that low wages mean low costs).

A lot of progress has already been made in Africa in the first type of "nibbling" at the process of industrialization, and further movement down the production process should be possible as time goes on. Copper, for example, is no longer exported as ore but in the form of blister and, in recent years, more and more as electrolytic copper—that is, as practically pure metal. Gold, too, is refined on the spot. Iron, manganese, and chrome are still exported mainly in the form of ore, although processing into ferrochrome is becoming important in Rhodesia. Rhodesia also successfully exports pig iron rather than iron ore. African cotton is always ginned and separated into cotton fiber and cotton seed before being exported, and the next steps, spinning the fiber into thread or even weaving finished fabric and processing the seed into cake and cotton oil, are becoming economically feasible in some countries.

Whether further processing of raw material is economically feasible or not depends not only on the productivity of the local labor force—the technical skills available, etc.—but even more on how the processing will affect transport costs and the costs of the next stage in the production process. Processing electrolytic copper into copper wire before exporting it, for example, would not reduce the weight or save any significant amount on labor costs, and it would add, because of more awkward packing sizes, more to transport costs than could be saved by the processing.

At the other end of the industrial process, similar considerations apply. It is cheaper to import tin plate for cans in flat strips than to import the cans, which take up a lot of space. The same is true of lumber vs. furniture and of metal components vs. car and truck bodies. As time goes on and African markets grow, it will become more and more economic to make the parts for such finished goods; this process has already gone far in South Africa.

### Other Industrialization Problems

Many of the difficulties that African countries face in industrialization are common to the rest of the world. The following report could just as easily be a story of an African factory, and every weakness mentioned is typical of ones found in African industries:

#### POST MORTEM ON A FURNITURE FACTORY

The National Seating and Dimension Company was started in 1962 as a way to help industrial development of the area. It bought the newest and most modern equipment and got the bulk of the finance on favorable terms from the government. It created more than 100 jobs but never paid its way and was closed in November, 1964.

Among the difficulties it experienced was bad management. At one point administrative control was so bad that a load of damaged or imperfect parts, though labeled plainly as scrap, was shipped out to customers as good products. Products often came unglued when received by customers.

Holding and finding key personnel was another problem: the supervisor of maintenance for the milling machines, the production manager, and the general manager left and were not immediately replaced. The company failed to procure sufficient working capital to carry it over the difficult teething period. The secretary of the corporation blamed "a few union troublemakers" for bad labor morale. Finally, he mentioned a thought that haunts the . . . officials who are trying to inject new life into the region—that Appalachia's people do not want to work. (Ben A. Franklin, "First Plan to Aid Appalachia Fails," *The New York Times*, November 25, 1964, pp. 1, 24.)

The difficulties faced by this factory in Appalachia, in the United States, and similar difficulties faced in Zambia, Mali, and Tanzania are due to the same lack of experience; they are all soluble with patience, effort, and time. The techniques for achieving success are by now well known. Entrepreneurs are developed: in part from the trading community, by the government's encouraging (and sometimes pushing) them to convert to industry; in part from active and energetic individuals working for large foreign firms, by encouraging them to set up as parts suppliers or subcontractors; in part from skilled workers and foremen trained in public-works and railway workshops, by encouraging and helping them to set up on their own. Government industrial advisory services and industrial development-finance companies are set up to aid small entrepreneurs with advice, guidance, and funds. Governments create industrial estates where many of the problems of new industries are already solved, such as obtaining various governmental permits, land set aside for manufacturing, public utilities laid on,* transport facilities, and often buildings provided. By various tax and financial incentives, governments invite foreign investors to enter the country and encourage new industries by offering them protection from competing imports through tariffs, quotas, rebates, or subsidies—as may be justified. Then, the whole environment is made as encouraging as possible to industrialization— an atmosphere of political stability, government aid in the search for and encouragement of exploitation of natural resources, education and training programs for children and adults, etc.

## LABOR AND UNEMPLOYMENT

There are a few specifically African problems in the matter of industrialization, however. There is first of all the problem of "non-committed" or migrant labor. (See above, chaps. III and V.) It is important to note that the experience during the beginning

---

* The availability of electric power, railways, or roads is often a necessary pre-condition for industry, but is by no means a sure-fire stimulant to it. Aside from a few industries that absolutely require it (the electrochemical or electro-metallurgical industries, for example), cheap electric power is not a significant factor in the economics of most industries, reliability and adequacy of the power supply being more important, and most industries being able, if necessary, to generate their own power using diesel plants. The formula that industrialization is called forth by cheap electric power is much too simplistic, therefore, as Uganda found when she built a power project at Owen Falls in the early 1950's, which industry did not use to capacity for another ten years. The Russians made the same mistake when attempting to follow Lenin's famous dictum "Electric power plus Soviets equals Communism."

of the Industrial Revolution in Great Britain has not occurred in Africa. (Elkan, *Migrants and Proletarians*.) In England, the people from the countryside who settled in the cities as the new industrial proletariat were not farmers but agricultural laborers who had no property stake in the land. But most African wage-earners are not landless, and their economic calculus is consequently different. In most of Africa, existing land tenure and market arrangements do not give land *per se* a money value. The only way a man can secure benefit from his claim to land is by keeping his family on it and working it. Land provides social security against unemployment, sickness, and old age, but the individual cannot use it for these purposes if he does not preserve his claim to it. Thus, he himself has a constant incentive to quit an industrial job for (longer or shorter) periods to return to his family and land.

Given the prevalence of migrant labor, industries that need semiskilled or skilled African labor find it difficult to become efficient and survive. In other words, progress in industrialization, like agricultural advance, may be closely related to the slow change in land-tenure systems and in the relationship of men to the land.

A major change in this respect is currently taking place in many African countries (notably Ghana and Nigeria). The major earlier educational drive in these countries is turning out large numbers of "school-leavers" who would prefer clerical jobs but are unable to find them, since their number far exceeds the number of such jobs available. These school-leavers are reluctant to return to the country and are, therefore, soon ready and willing to become committed industrial workers. These countries are now finding themselves, consequently, with a ready-made proletariat available for employment and training in new industry. In Ghana and Nigeria, these potential industrial workers already number in the tens of thousands. Schools in other countries, where the increased educational effort came later— Uganda, Kenya, Ivory Coast—are also now turning out thousands of unemployed school-leavers.

There is another special aspect to the labor-supply problem in Africa which, while it is present in other parts of the world, is so important there as to seem peculiarly African. This is the infinite elasticity of supply of unskilled labor—or, more bluntly, the unlimited supply of labor. The parts of Africa that have developed modern economies are still so small in relation to the sea of subsistence activities that surrounds them, and the mobility (intranational and transnational) of labor is so great that, within a reasonable wage range, the supply of labor can be considered virtually unlimited. What, then, determines the level of wages for unskilled labor?

Before World War II, Ida Greaves concluded that wages paid to an unskilled worker had to be high enough to overcome the strength of the tradition that binds him to customary tribal practices. (Wages, therefore, could be used by an anthropologist to measure the strength of tribal tradition.) In the 1950's, W. Arthur Lewis went further, and concluded that the floor, or minimum-level, of wages paid was set by the subsistence income an African could earn on the land, while the ceiling was set by this income plus the necessary incentive to go into wage labor. (Lewis, "Development with Unlimited Supplies of Labour.")

Not all African governments have fully appreciated the implications of this analysis. For example, what happens if wage rates are raised by minimum-wage legislation, union action, or other influences above the wage "ceiling" as thus defined? Clearly the wage will then attract labor from the subsistence economy into the urban areas even after there is no longer any need for more workers. The result may be that the number of urban unemployed will increase until the average real income of urban wage workers is reduced (by their having to support some of their unemployed tribal brothers) or the capacity of the urban center to sustain the unemployed (housing limitations, police action, petty jobs available, etc.) is reached. Given the forces holding nominal wages up, the level of unemployment then would be like a pressure gauge, the exact level of which would be set by the pressure of the movement of people from the land into towns against the counter-pressure of the absorptive capacity of the towns. (See also above, chap. III, p. 77.)

The growth of this unemployment in Africa has been sufficiently great to lead the African Advisory Committee of the International Labour Office to state:

> The employment problem is now the most serious problem facing African countries. Unemployment and underemployment put a brake on economic and social development and constitute a threat to the social and political stability of society. It is essential to take concerted measures with a view to their progressive elimination.

Priority should therefore be given to providing productive and remunerative employment for all those capable of work, since this is the only way in which to speed up development and to achieve the progressive improvement of the standard of living of the masses of population, whether they are wage earners or not. (I.L.O., 1969, p. 1.)

There is no question that the unemployment problem is great and growing in Africa, but it is, as I hope I have shown, something quite different from what the concept usually means in an industrialized country, where large-scale unemployment results from a deficiency of demand. In Africa, the problem is structural, not cyclical. It is, in fact, a fundamental part of the development problems of Africa. For counter-measures against unemployment, African governments have to re-examine the structure of urban incomes in relation to rural incomes and the whole gamut of their other policies.

The emphasis on encouraging industrialization has resulted often in policies that tend to bias investment decisions against labor-intensive methods. For instance, tax concessions offered to new private investors and comparable tariff concessions on imported capital equipment are generally designed to lower capital costs in order to stimulate private investment. These concessions either contain some bias against labor-intensive methods, as in the case of accelerated depreciation allowances, or are neutral as regards capital-saving versus labor-saving methods, as with most tariff concessions. The technical departments of governments often have a strong bias in favor of using capital-intensive methods. These methods minimize problems of labor mobilization and organization, and the technicians usually prefer to use the latest technique.

Preference for capital-intensive methods often arises from the shortage of skilled labor. Through the use of machinery, the use of skilled labor may be minimized. There is a reluctance on the part of employers to recruit labor which would not only need on-the-job training but may also be without much previous experience in regular wage employment. The use of machinery avoids the difficulties encountered in the organization of training and the development of disciplined work habits.

As mentioned above, much of the problem is due to the fact that it takes time to alter expectations. In the past, when only a handful of children completed primary school, clerical jobs were available for all of them. This set up the expectation that schooling leads to a well-paid, non-agricultural job. This expectation cannot be fulfilled when most children finish primary school. The interval before expectations change is one of painful frustrations. As the number of secondary-school-leavers goes up, many occupations now manned largely by primary-school leavers—such as nurses, typists, clerks, etc.—will in the future have to be filled mainly by secondary-school-leavers, who at present tend to look down on such jobs. The same problems are also beginning to be felt at university levels in some countries. In Nigeria, a new university graduate expects to be paid as much as four miners or ten farmers, whereas in the United States a new university graduate may not be paid as much as a miner and may never make as much money as a successful farmer—who, in fact, is also a university graduate.

A "solution" adopted by some countries to cope with unemployment is to bar foreign Africans and even to expel some who have been living in the country for years. Such policies have been enacted in Tanzania, against the Kikuyu from Kenya; in the Ivory Coast, against Ghanaians; in Ghana, against people from Upper Volta, Togo, Dahomey, and Nigeria; in Gabon, against Congolese; in South Africa, against Africans from north of the Limpopo River; etc. These policies may retard the general growth of the economy otherwise by raising wage costs and preventing the establishment of some industries, but they do reduce competition for existing jobs at the expense of the foreign Africans.

## NON-AFRICAN ENTREPRENEURS

Another problem which may be present rather more in Africa than in other developing areas is the presence of foreign entrepreneurs. In East Africa, most of the groups from which industrial entrepreneurs should logically emerge—in commerce, among skilled workmen and foremen—are non-African, mostly Asian, in origin; in West Africa, many of these people are Syrians, Cypriots, and Lebanese; in northern Nigeria, many were Ibos from southeastern Nigeria. They are successful traders not because they adopt unfair methods but because they are willing to work long hours, to save and reinvest, to please their customers, and to pay their creditors. This "culture of immigration," as Sir Arthur Lewis calls it, in fact describes what a successful entrepreneur in industry needs. In actual fact, this should not become a problem unless it becomes one politically. For industrialization is a snowball process: if an Asian creates a new industry in Nairobi, he is not reducing but, in the long run, augmenting the opportunities for other (African) industrial entrepreneurs. Problems develop only if governments and politicians, continuing an existing bias from commerce, believe they must encourage African entrepreneurship by discouraging non-African entrepreneurs.

So far there are no indications that development in Africa will be held up by Africa's inability to produce sufficient entrepreneurs. The emergence of enough entrepreneurs may take time, and a country may therefore be justified in relying for a considerable period on immigrant entrepreneurs, as in Liberia and the Ivory Coast. But there is also a danger that the creation of local entrepreneurship may be discouraged for too long. Various studies of entrepreneurship in the developing countries suggest that as people have experience with market-oriented activities, given favorable economic opportunities, entrepreneurs do come forth. As development proceeds and the monetary economy spreads and deepens, the supply of potential entrepreneurs increases, and they begin to take advantage of the opportunities opening to them.

## Land Tenure

Another specifically African problem is, like some of the labor problems, related to the land-tenure situation. In some countries, the communal land tenure may make it difficult for infant industries to secure the land they need. Governments can intervene to acquire the land, directly or through the creation of industrial estates, although the acquisition of land will still be a time-consuming and discouraging process, but the problem created by the lack of land-collateral is not so easily avoided. With tribal or communal land tenure, one of the ways in which small businesses in other areas of the world acquire loan capital and grow big is shut off. Elsewhere, a man who wishes to borrow money to enlarge his business can use his (or a relative's or friend's) land as security for a bank loan; land is often, indeed, the best security. Not being able to do this will continue to handicap industrialists in Africa.

REGIONAL ECONOMIC INTEGRATION

Regional political federations, customs unions, free-trade areas, common markets, or industry-preference agreements * among African countries, on the other hand, would unquestionably facilitate and speed up industrialization—certainly for the area concerned as a whole, although the economic benefits for a given individual state might be slight or even negative. A tariff area as a whole will benefit industrially from protection since protection may encourage the development of industry and so enlarge the size of the market that it justifies the original decision to set up the industry. And the social benefits of new industry—in the form of trained workers and entrepreneurs, and the boost it gives to the indigenous economy—may be great enough to warrant imposing a tariff that permits the industry to operate at a private profit.

But the benefit from tariffs may, on the other hand, be unevenly distributed. A customs union that joins together a relatively developed and a relatively underdeveloped country will benefit the former; Country A, which already has more industry than Country B, has considerable advantages in attracting still further industrial investment, some of which might not come into the area at all in the absence of the larger market provided by the union but some of which might have been located in Country B if the union had not existed (in which case Country B could have raised a tariff to protect the industry from Country A's competition).

Jacob Viner, in his authoritative work on customs unions, regarded the common market in East Africa as a good example of how a customs union worked to the detriment of the less developed part of the union—i.e., Tanganyika and Uganda vis-à-vis Kenya. The East African Fiscal Commission (Raisman Commission), in a report of February, 1961, and the World Bank's economic survey mission to Uganda in 1962 also examined the East African common market from this standpoint. They agreed that the East African common

---

* A customs union is an arrangement among countries whereby trade moves freely from one to another and they have a common tariff against outsiders. In a free-trade area, trade moves freely among the countries concerned, but each country continues to maintain its own tariff against outsiders. In a common market, there is not only freedom of trade but also freedom in the movement of capital and labor. An industry-preference agreement provides for free trade among the countries concerned only in the products specifically named.

market had resulted in special benefits to Kenya, and that there should be some special compensation to Kenya's partners in the market to offset it. (See above, chap. II, for a description of the present arrangements in East Africa.)

With the Federation of Rhodesia and Nyasaland—made up of the present states of Southern Rhodesia, Zambia (formerly Northern Rhodesia), and Malawi (formerly Nyasaland)—a customs union and a political federation were created at the same time. The economic benefits of this union have been studied closely, most notably by Hazlewood and Henderson. Their basic conclusion was that the Federation did contribute to economic development but not as much as some analysts have implied. The contribution it did make was due mainly to the fact that government expenditures and investment were higher than they would otherwise have been, since tax revenues from the copper belt in Northern Rhodesia were used for the Federation as a whole, whereas otherwise they would have reduced or eliminated the Northern Rhodesian government's need to borrow. Most of the advantages accrued to Southern Rhodesia, which, as the region most attractive to investors, probably drew industries that without the common market might have gone to Nyasaland or Northern Rhodesia. In addition, tariff changes were made to the detriment of Nyasaland consumers but in the interests of Southern Rhodesian industry. Since Nyasaland was not able to set tariffs to protect industry from Southern Rhodesia's competition, this may also have kept her industry from developing—a trend that could have been offset with a policy of other inducements to industry, but this was not done.

The main advantages of the Federation for Nyasaland were that she received more government revenue and that employment opportunities for Nyasas in the Rhodesias increased.

It cannot be taken for granted, then, that a particular country will or will not benefit from participating in a common market, customs union, or federation. The answer must depend on an economic analysis within the framework of the political and constitutional decisions that determine how the economic benefits can be distributed.

It should be noted, though, that the economist may look at the problem of a federation from two different points of view. From the vantage point of a particular country, he may conclude that a proposed federation is against its interests. On the other hand, from the vantage point of the development of Africa or the particular area of Africa involved, he may legitimately conclude that it is economically advantageous. Similarly, in any consideration of the allocation of revenues and expenditures within a federation, an economist advising a constituent part of the federation can legitimately propose a transfer of revenues from the richer to the poorer sections, while, on the federal level, he might advise that the over-all economic interest in achieving rapid growth of gross national product required concentrating on the development of the already richer section. (This also applies, of course, to multiracial countries, where there is no necessary coincidence between policies that result in the most rapid growth of total gross national product and those that raise the standard of living of a particular race most rapidly.)

The general approach of economic theory is that a customs union will be beneficial if on balance it is "trade-creating"; it will be harmful if on balance it is "trade-diverting." The removal of tariffs on intra-union trade will tend to increase trade among the countries forming the union. Whether or not the union is beneficial will depend on whether the intra-union trade is, on balance, the result of "trade creation" or "trade diversion." If union causes a member to replace its own previous high-cost production of a commodity with imports from other members of the union that have lower costs, this is "trade-creating." Trade creation is likely when there is union among countries that differ in their comparative advantage for the various products. After union, competition will lead to a pattern of specialization whereby each country produces and supplies to the other members of the union the products in which it has comparative advantage. The high-cost industries in each country will tend to be displaced by the low-cost competitors among other members of the union. Through the creation of intra-union trade, each member will be supplied from the lowest-cost source within the union; consequently, the countries will tend to be better off. If, on the other hand, the effect of the union is to cause members to switch their purchase of a commodity from a low-cost external source to high-cost sources within the union, there is "trade diversion." The union will not have been beneficial because it will have caused a shift of resources into less efficient uses.

(Trade creation is likely to be dominant in a customs union among countries in which a small proportion of total expenditure is on imports and a high proportion of external trade takes place among the member countries. The less important the external trade with non-union countries, the smaller will be the effect of union in diverting imports to higher-cost sources within the union. The more important domestic trade is in total expenditure, the more the union is likely to create intra-union trade by displacing high-cost domestic production. This is the conventional theory.)

According to the conventional theory, customs unions are practically irrelevant in Africa: there is little manufacturing, the countries are very dependent on foreign trade, they trade mainly with the developed industrial countries. But, in actual fact, for Africa conventional economic theory is wrong in this respect. In Africa, customs unions (or free-trade areas or common markets or any measures that unite African markets) are important means of economic development: they provide not only larger markets for the few existing enterprises but also incentives for the creation of new enterprises in manufacturing industry. The whole purpose of a customs union is to secure changes that are condemned by the conventional theory— that is, diversion of trade from extra-union to higher-cost intra-union sources. However, the effects of such a switch in the allocation of resources are far less important than its effect on stimulating growth by creating a new larger market for manufactures.

The creation of a customs union will help industrialization in Africa, but it is not a sufficient condition, of course. The union of several economically small countries may not result in making many more industries feasible simply because even the combined market may be smaller than the economic size for most industries. As mentioned above, with the low per-capita incomes in Africa, the range of commodities people can buy is small: a customs union may add a substantial number of buyers for some commodities, but it may increase the market for others very little.

Another important obstacle is the familiar transport difficulty. If tariffs are removed between two countries that have no roads or railways between them, the absence of tariff barriers will have little impact since the real barrier to trade is high transport costs.

There are substantial dangers for the future of Africa if integration is delayed and countries establish industries in which economies of scale are great and, therefore, cannot operate effectively within a market confined by national boundaries. Fragmentation of the market and duplication of productive units are already serious problems in Latin America. Africa can still escape this dead-end, but the progress of integration must not be long delayed. Once industries are established, however inefficient they are and however poor their prospects, governments are unwilling to see them destroyed. The solution is to integrate before resources are wasted in the establishment of inefficient industries and before vested interests in them are entrenched.

As discussed above, a difficulty with customs unions in which market forces are allowed to operate freely is that the benefits are likely to be unequally distributed among the associated states. Some countries may even lose from integration, although the area as a whole clearly benefits. For customs unions to survive, it will be necessary in most cases to have a "regulated" union (rather than "laisser-faire"). That is, measures have to be taken to correct inequalities which would develop within a laisser-faire union. For a country pursuing a policy of protection of its own infant industries, lower revenue from customs duties is the price it must pay for the industrial development stimulated by the protective tariff. But in a customs union, the less fortunate countries are likely to find themselves losing revenue (since they no longer collect customs duties on the imports coming in from their partners' industries) in the interest of development of industry in other countries. A second difficulty is the polarization of development in some members of the union. The simplest form of regulation is the payment of fiscal compensation for the inequitable operation of the market (as was done under the Raisman recommendations in the East African Common Market), but this is probably not enough. Countries want revenue, but they also want development. Other regulators are more difficult to devise and to operate.

Fiscal redistribution does not attempt directly to affect the location of economic activity. It is concerned to redistribute its benefits. With other measures the choice between equity or efficiency is harder. To promote an equitable distribution of industry among the countries, should governments prevent some industries from locating where they would be most efficient? The answer must be yes, but the cost cannot be completely ignored: it must be borne in mind that internal economies of scale deriving from the size of the market may not be realized in the absence of external economies arising from location in large industrial complexes. Even if an industry has free access to a large market, it may be unable to operate efficiently in an isolated location remote from a major industrial center.

The most obvious regulation is the erection of barriers to intra-market trade to protect the industries of the weaker members in competition with those that are larger. (The East African Common Market has such a provision, for example—see above, chap. II.) Such measures, if carried too far, would destroy the customs union. Another arrangement would be for the slower countries to offer fiscal or tax inducements to industry that the other members of the union agree to forego. But these deprive the country offering them of a revenue, and this is usually the country that can least afford loss of revenue. Another means would be to build up the infrastructure of the slower countries to make them more attractive. This means that they would have to do more than the leading country—i.e., that an outside lender or donor would make this possible, since the slower countries are unlikely to have more savings of their own—or, as in East Africa, that the leading country would agree to a re-distribution of its investment resources to the other countries. (In East Africa, Kenya does this through the East African Development Bank.)

A regional development policy—that is, supranational planning—is theoretically the best answer to the problem of regulating a common market. But this is hardly likely in the absence of a political federation: the fundamental difficulty is the surrender of autonomy that is involved.

An allocation of industries has often been suggested and some-times attempted. It has never really worked (according to Hazle-wood, pp. 1–25). The minimum necessary condition is that there are enough industries to go around. What is needed is a very long list of industries that are economical and are coming in so that each country can have a large absolute addition to its industry while, if necessary, the less-developed countries are allocated more than the rest. The difficulty is that the number of industries that are, at least initially, likely to be economic and interested in coming into the market is very small. There is no guarantee that an industry allocated to a country will actually be created.

In short, creation of an effective customs union (free-trade area or common market) is not easy in the absence of a strong political will to create a political unity that can with less difficulty (but not neces-sarily easily!) reconcile opposing interests within the framework of a single government and a single political unit.

## Selected Bibliography

BYL, ADHEMAR, and WHITE, JOSEPH. "The End of Backward-Sloping Labor Supply Functions in Dual Economies," *Cahiers Economiques et Sociaux*. Lovanium, IV, No. 1 (March, 1966), 38–41.

ELKAN, W. "Criteria for Industrial Development in Uganda," *East African Economic Review*, January, 1959, pp. 50–57.

———. *Migrants and Proletarians*. London and New York: Oxford University Press, 1960.

EWING, A. F. *Industry in Africa*. London, New York, Ibadan, Nairobi: Oxford University Press, 1968.

GEIGER, T., and ARMSTRONG, W. *The Development of African Private Enterprise*. (Planning Pamphlet No. 120.) Washington, D.C.: National Planning Association, 1964.

GREAVES, IDA C. *Modern Production Among Backward Peoples*. London: Allen & Unwin, 1935.

HAZLEWOOD, A. "Problems of Integration Among African States" in A. Hazlewood (ed.), *African Integration and Disintegration*. Oxford University Institute of Economics and Statistics and Royal Institute of International Affairs. London, New York, Toronto: Oxford University Press, 1967.

———, and HENDERSON, P. D. "Nyasaland: The Economics of Federation," *Oxford University Institute of Statistics Bulletin*, XXII, No. 1 (February, 1960), 1–91.

International Labor Office. *Employment Policies in Africa*. Third African Regional Conference. Geneva: I.L.O., 1969.

———. *Minimum Wage Fixing and Economic Development*. Geneva: I.L.O., 1968.

LEWIS, W. A. "Development With Unlimited Supplies of Labour," *The Manchester School*, XXII (May, 1954), 139–92.

———. *Industrialization on the Gold Coast*. Accra: Government Printer, 1953.

———. *Some Aspects of African Development*. London: George Allen & Unwin; Ghana: Ghana Publishing Corporation for University of Ghana, 1969.

MAIZELS, A. *Industrial Growth and World Trade*. Cambridge: Cambridge University Press, 1963.

MASON, E. S., *et al. The Economic Development of Uganda*. Baltimore, Md.: The Johns Hopkins Press, for the International Bank for Reconstruction and Development, 1962.

MIKESELL, R. F. "The Theory of Common Markets as Applied to Regional Arrangements Among Developing Countries," in R. HARROD and D. HAGUE (eds.), *International Trade Theory in a Developing World*. London: Oxford University Press, 1963.

Moussa, P. *Les Nations Prolétaires.* Paris: Presses universitaires de France, 1959.

Nyhart, J. D. "The Uganda Development Corporation and the Promotion of Entrepreneurship." Paper delivered at a conference of the East African Institute of Social Research, Kampala, Uganda, December, 1959.

Staley, E., and Morse, R. *Modern Small Industry for Developing Countries.* New York: McGraw-Hill, 1965.

Todaro, Michael P. "A Model of Labor Migration and Urban Unemployment in Less Developed Countries." *The American Economic Review,* LIX, No. 1 (March, 1969), 138-48.

Walker, D. "Criteria for Industrial Development in Uganda: A Comment," *East African Economics Review,* July, 1959, pp. 58-66.

# VIII

## Infrastructure

> *The most valuable of all capital is that invested in human beings.*
> ALFRED MARSHALL,
> Principles of Economics

The economic infrastructure is, essentially, the basic services, or public utilities, necessary to the commodity-producing sectors of a nation. Provision of these basic services is essential to, but not sufficient for, the growth of these sectors, and, in time, particular needs for basic services not only grow but change in character.

In general, it has come to be regarded in Africa (as elsewhere) as almost axiomatic that governments are responsible for providing this infrastructure, but it is a responsibility inherited almost by default. In the early years of the twentieth century, chartered companies, concessionaires, and other private interests generally provided whatever modern infrastructure there was. The control of the Benguela railway in Angola by Tanganyika Concessions and the important role that missionaries continue to play in education in some countries are relics of the earlier arrangements. But most governments everywhere in the world (with the exception of the United States in railroads and power) hold themselves responsible, and are held responsible by their citizens, for developing these sectors of the economy.

The introduction of modern transport means into Africa was completely financed from abroad. And, generally speaking, dependence on foreign sources of capital to finance a substantial part of the infrastructure has continued throughout the twentieth century, even though national governments and not foreign interests in time came to provide these services. This heavy dependence on outside sources of finance is a unique characteristic of African development of infrastructure; no other region of the world is in a similar position.

There is no completely satisfactory measure of the development of the economic infrastructure in sub-Saharan Africa. Because the economic infrastructure is there to serve the rest of the economy, physical measures are not of great use to establish a standard of its adequacy. If one compares the number of miles of railway per square mile in two countries, the fact that Country A has a lesser railway density than Country B does not mean that its railway network is less adequate. In fact, if Country A's railways are running at less than capacity, it may be that they have actually been overbuilt. In other words, a proper appraisal of an economic infrastructure's adequacy can be made only in relation to the economic needs of a given country. I will not try to present such evaluations here but will, rather, be content to make a *tour d'horizon* of the subject.

## Transport

Until late in the colonial period, the main impediment, not only to economic development in Africa, but to her development in most fields of human endeavor, was lack of transport, and consequent impossibly high transport costs. (Wrigley, *passim.*) To raise the African standard of living above a bare subsistence level, it was necessary for Africans to be able to produce a surplus of commodities, and to transport and sell them abroad, so that they could purchase, in exchange, the products of industrial societies and the skilled services of foreign technicians and administrators. Transport had to be cheap enough so that African products could reach world markets and could sell for a price that, after paying for it, would leave an adequate return. And this could not be provided for most of Africa before railways had been built.

The threshold to development represented by transport obstacles, then, that the Africans had to surmount was too high for them to climb over it on their own—help from outside was needed.

The transport of goods was impeded, first, by difficulty of access to the continent, caused by the scarcity of good natural harbors and deep inlets of the sea. On the entire African coast south of the Sahara, the really good natural ports can almost be counted on the fingers of one hand: Dakar, Bathurst, Libreville, Cape Town, Durban, Lourenço Marques, Mombasa. The plateau formation of much of the continent,ending near the coast, results in the rivers ending in falls or rapids and prevents their use as routes into the interior. Once a landing was made, therefore, penetration into the interior almost always depended on land transport. Internal trade routes were difficult to establish, however, because of the impossibility in much of Africa of using draft or pack animals—due to trypanosomiasis, carried by the tsetse fly, and to other animal diseases; because of the presence of dense forests, swamps, deserts, or steppes; and in many cases because of the resistance of the local people. Reliance therefore had to be placed on the wholly inadequate transport capacity of human carriers.

Modern economic development of Africa, then, had to await the coming of the "iron horse" immune to the tsetse fly and other natural enemies. "The bulk of the African resources lay inland and their development could not begin until the railroads made it possible." (Van Dongen, p. 3.) But the railway is a capital-intensive activity *par excellence*, requiring amounts of investment that no primitive economy can hope to muster. It came to tropical Africa, therefore, only when the colonial countries were ready to turn from their own railway building in Europe and North America, and looked abroad to the Argentine, Australia, and Africa. The main railway-building effort in Africa was from about 1885 to about 1914.

Aside from South Africa, where mineral development in large part necessitated the building of railways, in Africa they were built for strategic military or imperial reasons. Often, they were pushed ahead well before the area they served had developed enough to make them economic. The railways were built first, then attempts would be made to find ways of making them pay. Only after the Kenya-Uganda railway was built was the idea of finding settlers to farm along its route to provide traffic put forward. Cecil Rhodes's British South Africa Company began in the 1890's to push a railway north from the Cape Colony through Bechuanaland, to avoid the Boer states, and through Southern and Northern Rhodesia. While the railway securities were sold to investors on the basis that the railway would be the means of tapping the mineral wealth of Southern and Northern Rhodesia, Rhodes was probably motivated more by his dream of acquiring Central Africa for the British Empire and having a Cape-to-Cairo railway all on British territory. Exploitation of the mineral wealth of Northern Rhodesia did not really begin until the 1930's.

Highways began to take over the function of railways as a means of opening up new areas for development while Africa was still getting its first railways. (Since World War II, the airplane has also taken on some of this task.) The automobile, truck, and highway perform this task much better than railroads, in fact, being more flexible and less capital-hungry. Investment in transport can now proceed in stages, beginning with a dirt or gravel road with a few trucks and building up to a modern highway with an enormous volume of traffic, so that the territory opened up can largely pay for the investment as its needs grow. A highway, moreover, allows development to take place all along its length, whereas a railway concentrates development at its stations.

In industrialized countries, rail networks are tending to shrink as highways and airways absorb large amounts of what was formerly rail traffic.* In Africa, however, there is still a tendency carried over from colonial times to associate railways with development and to underrate highway and air transport. In some cases, of course, building new railways is justified—particularly to carry heavy, low-value, bulk traffic over long distances. Africa continues to be the only region in the world where there is actually a justifiable reason for a large-scale building of railways (though this does not imply that all the railways recently built or projected are really needed).

During the 1950's, the Belgians constructed a Kamina-Kabalo link in the Katanga to bring the rail network of southern Africa (South Africa, Rhodesia, Zambia, Angola, Mozambique, and Congo) into

---

* In air transport, Africa at least started on a par with the rest of the world. In fact, since government subsidy of airlines is general practice, Africa suffers a smaller absolute economic loss from the uneconomic, overly rapid development of air travel than other countries do, since she has less investment in other forms of transport to lose in the process. The *relative* size of this loss is another matter, however, and cannot easily be estimated.

contact with the rail system of East Africa across Lake Tanganyika. At present, the southern African network, with African standard gauge (42 inches), cannot, however, exchange rolling stock with the East African system, with meter gauge, but officials of the latter have been working toward an eventual changeover to standard gauge. In the meantime, the East African railway, which once consisted of two separate systems, has linked the whole together with a line opened in 1963 from Kenya to Tanganyika. It has also pushed a line north through Uganda to the Nile River within 70 miles of the Sudanese border, thus giving the southern Sudan shorter access to the sea than by way of the Sudanese rail system.

In December, 1965, east and west Cameroon were linked by rail; the railway was being extended across the entire country in 1970, to Ngaoundéré in northeast Cameroon. It is planned eventually to reach Chad.

A United Nations Development Program (UNDP)–World Bank study concluded late in 1969 that there was economic justification for another link from the Trans-Cameroon Railway to be built toward the Central African Republic (CAR), eventually to be extended to Nola in CAR. A railway link was also opened in 1970 to connect the Malawi Railways with a railway in Mozambique leading to the port of Nacala, some 700 miles north of Beira, the former main port serving both Malawi and Southern Rhodesia. Since Nacala is a somewhat better natural port than Beira, with its continuous dredging problems, and can take ore carriers of around 30,000 tons, this new link may encourage the development of the so-far-untouched bauxite deposits of Malawi or the mineral resources of northwest Mozambique, on the other side of Malawi from the port.

As a part of the development of the large Boke bauxite deposits in Guinea, a 140-kilometer railway is clearly needed and was being built in 1970.

By far the biggest railway project contemplated in the 1970's is the 1100-mile Tan-Zam Railway to link Zambia's copper belt with the port of Dar es Salaam in Tanzania. On November 4, 1969, the two African countries and Mainland China signed an agreement by which Mainland China would build and finance the railway, estimated to cost about $400 million inclusive of rolling stock and to take about five years to build. During 1970, Chinese surveyors were busy studying the alignment and design on the ground. Since the

TABLE 1
RAILWAYS, AFRICA
(1968)

| Country | Length (in track miles) |
| --- | --- |
| North Africa | |
| Algeria | 3,071 |
| Libya | 115 |
| Morocco | 1,837 |
| Tunisia | 2,276 |
| Total | 7,299 |
| | |
| Middle Africa | |
| Angola | 2,074 |
| Cameroon | 630 |
| Congo (Brazzaville) | 587 |
| Congo (Kinshasa) | 3,702 |
| Dahomey | 395 |
| Eritrea | 221 |
| Ethiopia | 523 |
| Ghana | 799 |
| Guinea | 542 |
| Ivory Coast | 817 |
| Kenya, Tanzania, Uganda | 4,370 |
| Liberia | 251 |
| Malagasy Republic | 628 |
| Malawi | 303 |
| Mali | 428 |
| Mauretania | 454 |
| Mozambique | 1,895 |
| Nigeria | 2,666 |
| Réunion | 40 |
| Senegal | 736 |
| Sierra Leone | 338 |
| So. Rhodesia, Zambia | 2,780 |
| Sudan | 3,372 |
| Swaziland | 150 |
| Togo | 310 |
| Zambia | 820 |
| Total | 29,831 |
| | |
| South Africa | 19,563 |
| | |
| Total | 56,693 |

SOUCE: *Jane's World Railways*, 1969–70.

economic justification for building the railway vs. improving the other transport routes between the two countries appears to be somewhat dubious, whether the decision turns out to be wise or will take its place as a horrible example alongside the notorious Tanganyika groundnut scheme will be watched with interest.

The difficulties of getting rid of an uneconomic railway, a common experience in recent years in the developed countries, are no less great in Africa. In Sierra Leone, the narrow-gauge railway from Freetown has for years been unable to meet its recurrent expenses, and governments have understood that it should be completely replaced by road transport. By 1970 the branch line had been phased out, and the main line was to be phased out before the end of 1972, thus ending a continuous drain on government finances. The iron-ore railway in Sierra Leone, however, is economic and will continue to exist.

Railroad development notwithstanding, the main expansion in ground transport in Africa, as elsewhere, has come to be in roads; road-building as an important part of the investment plan has become a worldwide phenomenon.

Statistics on road milage in Africa are unfortunately not very good; a reasonable estimate is that there are about 60,000 miles of road in tropical Africa. Table 2 gives the number of vehicles by country and provides some insight into the development of road transport. The total is about three quarters that of South Africa.

In relation to this highway development, it should be noted that oil-marketing companies have become major investors in sub-Saharan Africa. In this respect, Africa is like the industrialized countries: the gasoline service stations that are scattered across Africa are duplicates of the stations in the United States and Europe. The ultimate economic and cultural effect of this development will no doubt be staggering.

Most African countries have also had to make large investments in ports, often to make up for the deficiencies of nature in providing shelter and deep anchorages. Ghana's two ocean ports, for example, Takoradi and Tema, are both artificial. (The latter, Africa's largest artificial port, cost £17 million to build.) Since 1939, an enormous effort has been made to build or expand existing ports all around Africa. Nouadhibou, in Mauretania; Conakry, in Guinea; Port Harcourt and Lagos, in Nigeria; Matadi, in Congo (Kinshasa); Lourenço Marques and Beira, in Mozambique; Dar es Salaam, in Tanzania; and Mombasa, in Kenya, have been expanded. And the new ports of Abidjan, in the Ivory Coast; Cotonou, in Dahomey;

TABLE 2
MOTOR VEHICLES IN CIRCULATION, 1967
(in thousands)

| Country | Passenger Cars | Commercial Vehicles | Total |
|---|---|---|---|
| **North Africa** | | | |
| Algeria | 98 | 80 | 178 |
| Libya | 63 | 30 | 93 |
| Morocco | 178 | 71 | 249 |
| Tunisia | 57 | 32 | 89 |
| Total | 396 | 213 | 609 |
| **Middle Africa** | | | |
| Angola | 56 | 22 | 78 |
| Cameroon | 24 | 25 | 49 |
| Central African Republic | 5 | 7 | 12 |
| Chad | 3 | 6 | 9 |
| Congo (Kinshasa) | 44 | 33 | 77 |
| Dahomey | 8 | 5 | 13 |
| Ethiopia | 27 | 9 | 36 |
| French Somaliland | 6 | 1 | 7 |
| Gabon | 5 | 5 | 10 |
| Gambia | 2 | 2 | 4 |
| Ghana | 29 | 19 | 48 |
| Guinea | 8 | 12 | 20 |
| Ivory Coast | 42 | 30 | 72 |
| Kenya | 79 | 14 | 93 |
| Malagasy Republic | 38 | 25 | 64 |
| Malawi | 8 | 6 | 14 |
| Mali | 5 | 5 | 10 |
| Mauretania | 3 | 3 | 6 |
| Mauritius | 12 | 5 | 17 |
| Mozambique [a] | 53 [a] | 12 [a] | 65 [a] |
| Niger | 3 | 5 | 8 |
| Nigeria | 73 | 31 | 104 |
| Senegal | 32 | 20 | 52 |
| Sierra Leone | 15 | 6 | 21 |
| Somalia | 7 | 8 | 15 |
| Southern Rhodesia | 111 | 42 | 153 |
| Sudan | 21 | 18 [a] | 39 |
| Tanzania [b] | 36 [a] | 12 [a] | 48 [a] |
| Togo | 5 | 4 | 9 |
| Uganda | 33 | 6 | 39 |
| Upper Volta | 5 | 6 | 11 |
| Zambia | 50 | 20 | 70 |
| Total | 804 | 398 | 1,202 |
| *South Africa* | 1,313 | 342 | 1,655 |
| Total | 2,513 | 953 | 3,466 |

Note: [a] 1966.     [b] Tanganyika only.

SOURCE: *United Nations Statistical Yearbook*, 1968.

TABLE 3
INTERNATIONAL PORT TRAFFIC
(in millions of tons)

| Country | 1964 | 1966 | 1968 |
|---|---|---|---|
| *North Africa* | | | |
| Algeria | 24.7 | 28.4 | 46.7 |
| Libya | 42.8 | 74.3 | 127.9 |
| Morocco | 15.3 | 14.6 | 16.3 |
| Tunisia | 7.0 | 8.2 | 8.1 |
| Total | 89.9 | 125.5 | 199.0 |
| *Middle Africa* | | | |
| Angola | 3.6 | 3.3 | 5.9 |
| Cameroon | 1.1 | 1.2 | 1.7 |
| Congo (Brazzaville) | 1.9 | 2.3 | 2.5 |
| Congo (Kinshasa) | 1.2 | 1.4 | 1.3 |
| Dahomey | 0.3 | 0.4 | 0.4 |
| Ethiopia | 0.8 | 0.9 | n.a. |
| French Somaliland | 1.9 | 2.2 | n.a. |
| Gabon | 1.9 | 2.3 | 5.1 |
| Gambia | 0.1 | 0.2 | n.a. |
| Ghana | 4.8 | 4.5 | 4.6 |
| Guinea | 2.2 | 1.9 | n.a. |
| Ivory Coast | 3.6 | 4.3 | 5.1 |
| Kenya | 4.1 | 5.1 | 5.2 |
| Liberia | 12.6 | 17.0 | n.a. |
| Malagasy Republic | 0.8 | 1.0 | 1.4 |
| Mauritius | 1.3 | 1.2 | 1.4 |
| Mozambique | 8.2 | 11.0 | 19.2 |
| Nigeria | 11.7 | 24.4 | 5.0 |
| Senegal | 3.5 | 3.9 | 4.1 |
| Sierra Leone | 3.0 | 3.2 | 3.7 |
| Somalia | 0.5 | 0.4 | 0.5 |
| Sudan | 2.4 | 2.3 | 2.5 |
| Tanzania | 1.6[1] | 2.3 | 3.2 |
| Togo | 1.0 | 1.1 | 1.7 |
| Total | 71.4 | 97.8 | (98.0)[2] |
| *South Africa* | 21.9 | 23.1 | 21.0 |
| Total | 183.2 | 246.4 | 318.0[2] |

[1] Tanganyika only.
[2] Estimate.
n.a.  Not available.

SOURCES: *United Nations Statistical Yearbook,* 1968.
*United Nations Monthly Bulletin,* February, 1970.

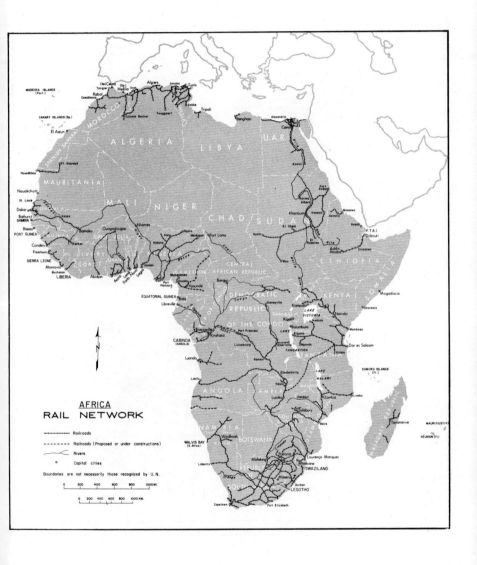

AFRICA
RAIL NETWORK

- ┄┄┄┄┄ Railroads
- ╍╍╍╍╍ Railroads (Proposed or under constructions)
- ～～～ Rivers
- ○ Capital cities

Boundaries are not necessarily those recognized by U.N.

0   200   400   600   800   1000 Mi.

0   200  400  600  800  1000 KM.

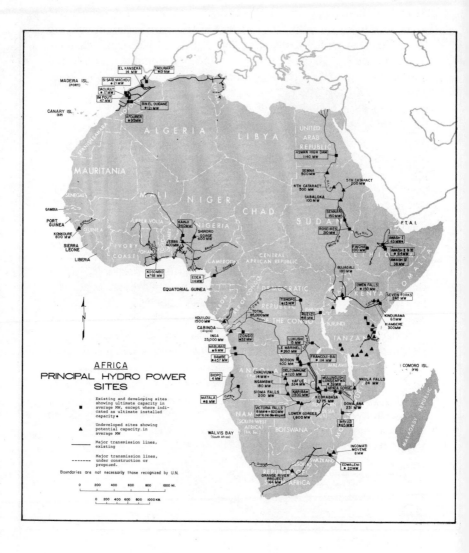

AFRICA
PRINCIPAL HYDRO POWER
SITES

■ Existing and developing sites
showing ultimate capacity in
average MW, except where indicated as ultimate installed
capacity ●

▲ Undeveloped sites showing
potential capacity in
average MW

——— Major transmission lines,
existing

------- Major transmission lines,
under construction or
proposed

Boundaries are not necessarily those recognized by U.N.

0    200  400  600  800  1000 MI.

0   200  400 600  800  1000 KM.

MADEIRA ISL.
(PORT.)

CANARY ISL.
(SP.)

EL KANSERA
14 MW
SI SAID MACHOU
● 21 MW
DAOURAT
● 17 MW
IM FOUT
47 MW
TAOURART
●13 MW
BIN EL OUIDANE
●121 MW
AFOURER
● 95 MW

ALGERIA            LIBYA          UNITED
                                  ARAB
                                  REPUBLIC
MAURITANIA                        ASWAN HIGH DAM
                                  1140 MW
MALI    NIGER      CHAD           SEMNA
                                  500 MW
                                  4TH CATARACT    5TH CATARACT
                                  500 MW          200 MW
SENEGAL                           SABALOKA
                                  100 MW
GAMBA                             S U D A N         F.T.A.I.
PORT                              SENNAR
GUINEA    GUINEA   UPPER VOLTA    150 MW
KONKOURE  NIGERIA                 ROSEIRES        AWASH I
800 MW    KAINJI                  210 MW          43 MW
SIERRA    960MW                   FINCHA          AWASH II & III
LEONE     SHIRORO                 100 MW          ●64 MW
LIBERIA   GORGE                                   AWASH IV
          600 MW                                  38 MW
          JEBBA                   BUJAGALI
          400 MW                  180 MW
IVORY     CAMEROON  CENTRAL       OWEN FALLS   SEVEN FORKS
COAST                AFRICAN       ● 150 MW     240 MW
          KOSSOMBO    REPUBLIC                  KINDURAMA
          ● 768 MW   EDEA                       60 MW
          EQUATORIAL 114 MW       K E N Y A     KIAMBERE
          GUINEA                                300MW
                    TSHOPO
                    ●12 MW        RUZIZI
                                  ●48 MW
KOUILOU   TOTAL                   BURUNDI    TANZANIA   COMORO ISL.
1500 MW   85,000MW                                      (FR)
CABINDA                           LUKUSHI
(Angola)  INGA      ZONGO         15 MW
          25,000 MW ●32 MW        LE MARINEL
MABUBAS                           ●260 MW      MULUNGUSHI   NKULA FALLS
● 6 MW                            BODSON       LUNSEMFWA    24 MW
BAMBE                             400 MW       ● 39 MW
●457 MW                           FRANCQUI-BAI MPATA GORGE
BIOPO     CHAUVUMA   DELCOMMUNE   ●114 MW      KEBRABASA
4 MW      14 MW●     120 MW                    2,775 MW    DONA ANA
          NGAMBWE   KAFUE                                  23 MW
MATALA    180 MW    334 MW        KARIBA●                  MAVUZI
●8 MW     SIOMA FALLS             1500 MW                  ●65 MW
          200 MW    LOWER GORGES
          VICTORIA FALLS 1,800 MW
          6 MW●620 MW
          not to be developed
ANGOLA                                         INCOMATI
                                               MOVENE
NAMIBIA                                         8 MW
(SOUTH-WEST                        SWAZILAND   EDWALENI
AFRICA)                                        ● 20MW
(So. Tar.)          BOTSWANA
WALVIS BAY
(South Africa)

                    Orange    ORANGE RIVER   REPUBLIC
                              PROJECT        OF
                              164 MW         SOUTH
                                             AFRICA

MALAGASY
REPUBLIC

Lomé, in Togo; and Monrovia, in Liberia, deserve special mention. After less than ten years, at the end of the 1960's Abidjan needed to be complemented by another new port, San Pedro in western Ivory Coast. Another artificial port in Liberia, Buchanan, was completed in 1964 to handle iron-ore shipments from new mines and now moves over 10 million tons. Somalia, which had no deep-water port, by 1970 was well on the way to having three: Berbera in the north had been built by the Russians, Chisimaio had been built by the Americans, and the World Bank was financing study of a deep-water port at Mogadiscio. Indeed, tropical Africa has moved ahead more rapidly in the provision and use of ports than in inland transport. Table 3 demonstrates the rapid growth principally in mineral exports from Africa. The leveling off from 1966 to 1968 is due solely to the drop in Nigerian exports because of the civil war.

African nations are likely to put a higher proportion of their total investment into transport than industrialized countries do, for a number of reasons. First, investment in roads, bridges, and ports has gone on for 2,000 years in Europe (in Cyprus, for example, expansion of the port at Kyrenia changed the contour of a port, established by the Venetians, to one that takes advantage of a break-water left by the Romans); the African patrimony of infrastructure goes back scarcely seventy years. Secondly, the African populations are usually spread very thinly over enormous areas, which means there is a relatively high investment per head in the increased transport facilities required as internal production gradually changes from subsistence to the market. Also, topography and climate cause difficulties, and the investment in providing a given level of transport must consequently be greater; thus, the Kenya-Uganda railway from Mombasa to Kampala has to climb from sea level to 7,600 feet, descend to 6,000 feet in the Rift Valley, rise again to 9,000 feet, and finally reach Kampala at an altitude of 4,000 feet. Transport must also be emphasized because commodities make up a much larger share of gross national product than in industrialized areas, where services are more important. And, finally, the commodities to be transported in Africa are mostly primary products, which are bulkier in relation to value than fabricated industrial products.

Of World Bank Group loans and credits of $2.7 billion in Africa from 1950 to the end of 1970, almost half went to develop transport facilities. (In the rest of the world, World Bank loans for transport were less than a third of the total.)

## Electric Power

Though adequate transport infrastructure must remain an indispensable part of economic development, the word "infrastructure" has a broader meaning. Africa's earlier needs were essentially for transport facilities; African farmers, or European concessionaires or miners, required little else than the means to get their products to market. Until World War II, Lugard's comment was essentially true: "The material development of Africa may be summed up in one word—transport." But, as the economy of Africa broadened and the first stages of industrialization and urbanization began, the necessary infrastructure also broadened. Electric power became essential, if products were to be processed in Africa itself. Assuring electric power for industry has thus come to be generally accepted as one of the basic services that governments hold to be their responsibility.

Electric-power output has been growing rapidly in Africa. Between 1951 and 1960, it more than doubled; to 1970, it more than doubled again. This rate of increase is higher than the world average, even though the absolute level reached is still low. The very great unevenness in the production of power by different countries (see Table 4) is an indication of unevenness in the degree of industrialization or mining development reached by them; in the Republic of South Africa, power production was almost triple that of the total of the other countries in the early 1960's but only about double by the end of the decade.

Hydroelectric power is peculiarly important to Africa. For it appears likely that tropical Africa is not rich in coal—the basic source of energy for Western countries when they industrialized. (The most important coal deposits are in South Africa. Aside from the Wankie coalfield in Rhodesia, the Tete field in Mozambique, some inferior coal found in northern and eastern Nigeria, and a coalfield in Zambia being exploited only to reduce Zambia's dependence on Rhodesian coal, no other coal is being exploited in sub-Saharan Africa. Coalfields in Tanzania have not yet been found economically exploitable.) For Nigeria, Gabon, and Angola, oil and possibly gas may become main sources of energy, but for the rest of the continent, for domestic sources of energy, attention must be turned to hydroelectric power at this stage of knowledge. (Nuclear energy may eventually prove to be economic for such relatively small markets as

# TABLE 4
## ELECTRIC-POWER PRODUCTION IN AFRICA
### (in millions of kilowatt hours)

| Country | 1963 | 1965 | 1966 | 1967 | 1968 |
|---|---|---|---|---|---|
| *North Africa* | | | | | |
| Algeria | 1,092 | 1,116 | 1,116 | 1,118 | 1,308 |
| Libya | 140 | 190 | 220 | 255 | 300 |
| Morocco | 1,140 | 1,284 | 1,344 | 1,344 | 1,536 |
| Tunisia | 307 | 368 | 450 | 488 | 545 |
| Total | 2,679 | 2,958 | 3,130 | 3,275 | 3,689 |
| *Middle Africa* | | | | | |
| Angola | 220 | 317 | 350 | 373 | 475 |
| Burundi | 14 | 15 | 15 | 16 | 17 |
| Cameroon | 1,127 | 1,100 | 1,012 | 998 | 1,016 |
| Central African Republic | 17 | 21 | 25 | 28 | 35 |
| Chad | 13 | 18 | 22 | 26 | 31 |
| Congo (Brazzaville) | 42 | 42 | 46 | 48 | 54 |
| Congo (Kinshasa) | 2,407 | 2,686 | 2,928 | 3,000 | 3,500 |
| Dahomey | 18 | 22 | 23 | 23 | 25 |
| Ethiopia | 175 | 246 | 277 | 320 | 365 [2] |
| Gabon | 32 | 42 | 49 | 56 | 60 [2] |
| Gambia | 7 | 7 | 8 | 11 | 13 [2] |
| Ghana | 470 | 528 | 588 | 1,560 | 2,588 |
| Guinea | 156 | 177 | 186 | 198 | 202 |
| Ivory Coast | 155 | 220 | 176 | 314 | 372 |
| Kenya | 263 | 328 | 346 | 338 | 380 |
| Liberia | 182 | 278 | 342 | 468 | 480 |
| Malagasy Republic | 125 | 153 | 157 | 181 | 200 |
| Malawi | 40 | 53 | 68 | 85 | 102 |
| Mali | 21 | 28 | 31 | 33 | 35 |
| Mauritius | 88 | 103 | 113 | 120 | 127 |
| Mozambique | 240 | 260 | 280 | 300 | 325 |
| Niger | 14 | 16 | 20 | 22 | 25 |
| Nigeria | 893 | 1,177 | 1,279 | 1,122 | 1,109 |
| Rwanda | 11 | 14 | 21 | 25 | 30 |
| Senegal | 175 | 204 | 222 | 240 | 247 |
| Sierra Leone | 72 | 106 | 109 | 125 | 144 |
| Somali Republic | 9 | 12 | 13 | 15 | 16 |
| Southern Rhodesia | 3,369 | 4,116 | 4,212 | 4,956 | 5,580 |
| Sudan | 163 | 174 | 262 | 318 | 385 |
| Tanzania [1] | 186 | 214 | 252 | 282 | 320 |
| Togo | 22 | 34 | 40 | 48 | 60 |
| Uganda | 497 | 572 | 635 | 704 | 732 |
| Upper Volta | 16 | 20 | 22 | 22 | 23 |
| Zambia | 740 | 660 | 600 | 600 | 648 |
| Total | 11,979 | 13,963 | 14,729 | 16,975 | 19,720 |
| *South Africa* | 27,828 | 32,773 | 34,752 | 37,872 | 40,944 |
| Total | 42,486 | 49,694 | 52,611 | 58,122 | 64,353 |

[1] Tanganyika only.     [2] Estimates.

SOURCES: 1963—*U.S. Agency for International Development, Economic Data Book Africa.* 1965–68—*United Nations Monthly Bulletin of Statistics,* February, 1970.

the African countries are likely to be for some time. But this is not probable for another perhaps twenty or thirty years. Until then, nuclear power will be economic only in large units and only where it provides a portion of the total power output.)

Hydroelectric potential appears to be one of Africa's most important natural assets. Indeed, the geographical formation that kept Africa isolated for millennia—the great central plateau with the rivers plunging off it to the coast—gives Africa the greatest hydroelectric potential of any continent in the world: an estimated 200 million kilowatts, or about two fifths of the total world potential, more than Europe and the two Americas put together. (The Inga site alone on the Congo River near its mouth has a potential equal to that of North America.) Now, with most of the sites in North America and Europe where cheap hydropower can be produced already utilized, what was once a handicap for Africa has become an attractive asset for the rest of the world.

The greatest hydroelectric potential in Africa is in Congo (Kinshasa) (500 billion kwh annually), Angola (200 billion kwh), Malagasy Republic (100 billion kwh), and Cameroon (100 billion kwh). Congo (Brazzaville), Central Africa Republic, Gabon, and Liberia also have significant potential, especially in relation to the size of their populations.

The problem, however, is to find uses for this potential electric power. While cheap available electric power is an important aid to industry, it is not an irresistible attraction. Uganda discovered this the hard way when she built a power station at Owen Falls in 1954 with an ultimate capacity of 150,000 kw, which was not sufficiently utilized to pay its way until 1962. The *market* for electric power, as in industry proper, is the key. With a domestic market that is too small, the solution is often to look to export—either of the power itself or of industrial commodities that are highly intensive users of electric power, like aluminum or the products of electro-chemical industries.*

So far, the expectation of export has usually been the rationale for building large-scale hydroelectric power projects in Africa. Owen Falls, the first of these, eventually paid its way by adding to growing

* The kw hours of electricity required to produce a ton of metal are as follows for selected metals: titanium, 40,000; aluminum, 17,000; electrolytic manganese, 11,000; ferrochromium, 7,700; electrolytic copper, 2,500.

domestic consumption the export of power itself to Kenya, and by the use of its electricity to refine exportable copper from the Kilembe mines. The Kariba Dam and power plant on the Zambezi River border between Rhodesia and Zambia—which began operations in 1960 with an initial capacity of 705,000 kw (four times the size of Owen Falls), one of the world's largest stations, with the dam forming the world's largest man-made lake—was based on the need for power in the mines and electrolytic copper refinery of Zambia's copper belt and for power in Rhodesia's factories and mines (including an electrolytic ferrochrome plant that came into existence only because cheaper power from Kariba made it economically possible). By 1970, growth of consumption in the copper belt in Zambia justified the beginning of the construction of an additional power house, Kariba North, with an initial capacity of 600,000 kw, to be completed in 1975. A 600,000-kw station on the Kofue River in Zambia is scheduled to be completed in 1971, but since this has little storage, firm output will be little more than 200,000 kw. By the end of the 1970's, it should be necessary to increase the Kofue power development to 900,000 kw of firm capacity by increasing the generators and building a storage barn.

And the Volta Dam Project in Ghana, officially inaugurated in January, 1966, with an initial capacity of 588,000 kw (and creating an enormous lake the size of Lake Kariba), depended completely for its construction on the decision to commit a large bloc of its power to a huge aluminum refinery to be built, based on the use of Volta power. In 1969, it was decided to expand Volta to its ultimate capacity of 882,000 kw by putting in more generators. The increased power, available in part from 1971, is to be exported to Togo and Dahomey over a new 180-mile transmission line and to be used for consumption in the expanded aluminum smelter. By 1977, it is expected that the Volta power will be fully utilized, and additional sources of power will have to be developed.

By 1970, another large hydroelectric project had been started in tropical Africa. A beginning at harnessing the enormous potential at Inga in Congo (Kinshasa) was underway. A small (relative to the potential) first stage of 300,000 kw capacity and a transmission line of 300 miles to Kinshasa, at a cost of around $60 million, were begun in 1969 by diverting part of the lower stream of the Congo River.

Plans have also been worked out for constructing a large project, even bigger than Kariba, on the Zambesi downstream from Kariba at Cabora Bassa in Mozambique, with a potential capacity of 4 million kw and costing in the neighborhood of $500 million. Work began on the dam in October, 1969. The basic justification of the project is to export power some 850 miles to the power network in Pretoria, South Africa, with the first power to be delivered in 1975. Essentially, this project has become possible as a result of the advances in technology during the last decade that made it feasible and economical to transport power over such long distances.

### Communications and Public Utilities

The spread of modern governmental administration into Africa brought with it the need for better public communications systems— post office, telephones, and telegraphs. Growth in the African economies is often hampered by deficiencies in the facilities for communications. Having to start almost from scratch in this field may turn out to be an advantage in the long run for the African countries, however. The newer technologies in this field are much more capital-saving than older systems of communications based on stringing wires on poles across hundreds of miles of empty spaces. Instead, the telecommunications network in a country can now be built around the construction of a microwave network, and the external communications can develop using the new international satellite communication that will be set up during the 1970's.

In 1968, the first telephone link, using high-frequency radio, was installed between East and West Africa (Ethiopia and Ivory Coast). For the first time since Africa's independence it became possible for Africans to communicate directly with each other across the continent, without having to make connections through Europe.

The growth of Africa's cities has made water supply and sewerage essential public utilities, although over most of Africa individuals and companies still make their own provision for these; they are yet to become fully a part of the economic infrastructure.

### Education

Education was not always considered a part of the economic infrastructure: in economic terms, it was regarded more as an expensive consumer good than as a necessary prerequisite of economic growth. It is not possible to make a reasonable estimate of education's *economic* effects; it is difficult to distinguish, that is, what part of the cost of education can reasonably be assessed as the cost paid for increased productive capacity.

Concern with modern education occurred in Africa really only in the twentieth century; at first, education was left to the missionaries to handle. In the 1920's, however, governments in Africa began to take an active interest in the education of Africans, although the missionaries remained dominant. This government activity in education was increasingly emphasized after 1950. But many Africans still had a suspicion and a fear of education. Then suddenly in the early and mid-1950's, their attitude changed; African parents began to express a great desire for education for their children, and the children too seemed enthusiastic. Since 1960, the high *economic* yield of expenditures on education has also been widely recognized, and investment plans are influenced by this fact.

In Africa, there has been a special reason for this. During the first decade after World War II, the general approach of government policy-makers in Africa on the subject of economic development was that the provision of economic infrastructure, strictly defined, was the main essential. It is true that the capacity of the infrastructure in many African countries then was the major bottleneck holding back economic development, since the infrastructure had been neglected during the depression of 1930's and during World War II. With the world market for African products growing after World War II, investment in infrastructure was imperative to get these products to market. And it has continued to be the decisive element in many countries. But in many others, once the infrastructure caught up with or even ran ahead of the needs of the rest of the economy, governments were faced with the central task of stimulating the growth of the commodity-producing sectors directly—that is, with the need to increase agricultural production through the voluntary action of millions of small farmers and to develop entrepreneurial, managerial, and skilled-worker groups where none had existed. It is understandable that governments began to consider investment in education as a means of achieving this.

The development of the educational infrastructure in Africa was no less uneven, however, than in the other fields we have considered.

At a conference at Addis Ababa in 1961, sponsored by UNESCO and the U.N. Economic Commission for Africa, the African govern-

TABLE 5

ENROLLED STUDENTS AS A PERCENTAGE OF THE SCHOOL-AGE
POPULATION, 1960 AND 1965

| Country | Elementary [1] 1960 | Elementary [1] 1965 | Secondary [2] 1960 | Secondary [2] 1965 | Elementary and Secondary [2] 1960 | Elementary and Secondary [2] 1965 |
|---|---|---|---|---|---|---|
| *North Africa* | | | | | | |
| Algeria | 28 | 41 | 8 | 9 | 26 | 37 |
| Morocco | 27 | 34 | 7 | 13 | 29 | 38 |
| Tunisia | 44 | 42 | 15 | 20 | 45 | 63 |
| *Middle Africa* | | | | | | |
| Angola | 9 | 9 | 3 | n.a. | 7 | n.a. |
| Botswana | 41 | 67 | 2 | 4 | 37 | 61 |
| Burundi | n.a. | 24 | n.a. | 2 | n.a. | 22 |
| Cameroon | 57 | 82 | 5 | 9 | 48 | 70 |
| Central African Republic | 22 | 37 | 3 | 4 | 19 | 32 |
| Chad | 14 | 18 | 1 | 2 | 10 | 15 |
| Congo (Brazzaville) | 58 | 79 | 7 | 15 | 49 | 69 |
| Congo (Kinshasa) | 43 | 42 | 3 | 6 | 39 | 39 |
| Dahomey | 18 | 23 | 2 | 5 | 15 | 20 |
| Ethiopia | 5 | 6 | * | 2 | 4 | 6 |
| French Somaliland | 16 | n.a. | 6 | n.a. | 13 | n.a. |
| Gabon | 49 | 60 | 6 | 11 | 42 | 52 |
| Gambia | 10 | 16 | 5 | 10 | 10 | 16 |
| Ghana | 40 | 62 | 3 | 44 | 29 | 61 |
| Guinea | 13 | 22 | 3 | 6 | 13 | 21 |
| Ifni | 4 | n.a. | 8 | n.a. | 5 | n.a. |
| Ivory Coast | 31 | 38 | 4 | 6 | 26 | 33 |
| Kenya | 49 | 59 | 4 | 6 | 41 | 50 |
| Lesotho | 78 | 89 | 5 | 5 | 66 | 76 |
| Liberia | 16 | 24 | 2 | 5 | 15 | 23 |
| Malagasy Republic | 34 | 44 | 5 | 9 | 26 | 39 |
| Malawi | 41 | 48 | 1 | 3 | 29 | 40 |
| Mali | 6 | 12 | 1 | 4 | 5 | 12 |
| Mauretania | 6 | 9 | 1 | 2 | 5 | 8 |
| Mauritius | 69 | 72 | 36 | 42 | 81 | 86 |
| Mozambique | 26 | 26 | 2 | 2 | 26 | 26 |
| Niger | 4 | 7 | 1 | 1 | 3 | 6 |
| Nigeria | 35 | 29 | 5 | 6 | 30 | 26 |
| Rhodesia | 60 | 70 | 12 | 17 | 62 | 74 |
| Rwanda | 22 | 53 | 1 | 2 | 9 | 44 |
| Senegal | 20 | 30 | 5 | 9 | 18 | 27 |
| Sierra Leone | 14 | 19 | 3 | 6 | 11 | 16 |
| Somalia | 4 | 4 | 2 | 3 | 4 | 5 |
| Spanish Equatorial Africa | 46 | n.a. | 3 | n.a. | 33 | n.a. |
| Spanish Sahara | 13 | n.a. | 6 | n.a. | 11 | n.a. |
| Sudan | 11 | 15 | 6 | 7 | 12 | 16 |
| Swaziland | 53 | 65 | 6 | 10 | 54 | 68 |

TABLE 5 (*Cont.*)

| Country | Elementary[1] 1960 | 1965 | Secondary[2] 1960 | 1965 | Elementary and Secondary[2] 1960 | 1965 |
|---|---|---|---|---|---|---|
| Tanzania | 19 | 25 | 2 | 2 | 17 | 21 |
| Togo | 29 | 36 | 4 | 6 | 25 | 31 |
| Uganda | 32 | 29 | 6 | 8 | 33 | 31 |
| Upper Volta | 6 | 9 | 1 | 2 | 5 | 8 |
| Zambia | 48 | 55 | 2 | 6 | 37 | 43 |
| *South Africa* | n.a. | n.a. | n.a. | n.a. | 69 | n.a. |

[1] Unadjusted.
[2] Adjusted.
* Less than 0.5%.
n.a. Not available.

SOURCE: International Bank for Reconstruction and Development, World Tables, 1968.

ments set forth their objectives in the field of education. In 1960, only 16 per cent of the primary- and secondary-school-age children in Africa were in school—with great variation among countries, of course. The conference set goals for 1980 of universal, compulsory, and free primary education; for 10 per cent of the primary-school-leavers to go on to general academic secondary schools and 20 per cent to vocational, technical, or teacher-training schools; for 20 per cent of the pupils completing secondary school to go on to higher education. UNESCO subsequently outlined the following Second Development Decade targets for 1980 for the various regions of the world:

| | Enrollment (%) Africa | Asia | Latin America |
|---|---|---|---|
| Primary | 100 | 100 | 100 |
| Secondary | 23 | 36 | 46 |
| Third level | 1.5 | 5.0 | 6.4 |

The goals set for Africa are lower than those for the other regions, at least partly on the basis of the estimate that for Africa to accomplish these goals would represent a greater sacrifice than would be true elsewhere. In 1965, Africa was estimated to be already spending 4.7 per cent of its GNP on education, compared to 4.2 per cent in Latin America and 3.1 per cent in Asia. Assuming growth of GNP by 6 per cent a year (the Second Development Decade target), Africa would be spending, according to the UNESCO projections, $2.6 billion a year in 1980 on education for these targets, or 6 per cent of GNP as compared to 4.7 per cent in Latin America and 4.3 per cent in Asia.

Table 5 shows how far most countries in Africa were from the UNESCO targets. A few (Tunisia, Ghana, Mauritius), however, were either close to or had surpassed the 1980 targets by 1965. An OAU/UNESCO Conference of African Ministers in Nairobi in July, 1968, found that well over two thirds of the newest generation of Africans were still destined for illiteracy. Taking the African countries as a whole, in 1965, out of the six million children of starting-school age, only 1.33 million would finish primary school.

What this means for a particular African country can be seen from the experience of the Ivory Coast, which can be taken as a median African country in this respect. In 1927, the Ivory Coast had 2,600 pupils in primary school, and a large proportion of these were non-Africans. In 1947, there were 22,000; in 1959, just before independence, 165,000; in 1968, 410,000. By 1968, 45 per cent of all children in the Ivory Coast of primary-school age attended school. At the secondary level, the number of pupils went up from 5,000 in 1958 to 40,000 in 1968. Further increase has been delayed by the shortage of qualified teachers, most of whom still have to come from abroad. Of the total of 898 secondary-school teachers on the job in 1965, the sources were as follows:

| | |
|---|---:|
| Ivory Coast | 117 |
| French technical assistance | 468 |
| Individual contract, mostly French | 269 |
| U.S. Peace Corps | 44 |
| | 898 |

In 1964, the University of Abidjan was inaugurated, taking over from the teaching center established in 1958 by the University of Paris. The university now has some 2,000 students of whom half are other Africans and French; 1,200 Ivory Coast students, in addition, are in universities overseas.

Even with the help provided by foreign aid, the financial burden on the Ivory Coast for education is very large: the percentage that education represents of the government budget went up from 12½ per cent in 1960 to 18 per cent in 1968, and 40 per cent of all civil servants are employed in education.

Insufficient attention has been paid to educating the bulk of the population, the adults, who have never had formal schooling. The purpose of education can be earning as well as learning, and the former goal has been much neglected in Africa. The content of African education was until recently geared to people who were uninterested in practical affairs. "It is only now, with independence, that it is realized that the basic problems of tropical agriculture, the social organization of a society still based on the tribe and the extended family, and the cultural traditions of the African nations themselves have been neglected in favor of producing people who could enter the Sorbonne or Oxford without difficulty." (Vaizey, p. 353.)

What kind of education the Africans devise for themselves will probably determine the future of their continent. Certainly, if the African economy is to develop, it will be necessary to train children in rational modes of thought and in an objective, empirical attitude toward nature and society. Problem-solving abilities must be developed, rather than the knowledge of how to pass examinations. The Japanese example is probably not a bad one to follow, for the educational system of Japan is largely responsible for the extraordinary adaptability of its economy. Aside from ensuring a good supply of entrepreneurs and technicians, it has promoted mobility and versatility and encouraged inventiveness. "More generally, it is not unreasonable to ascribe, in part at least, to the character of the education systems some of the intense loyalty to their country and of their eagerness for work, which are notorious among Japanese people." (Hicks, p. 28.)

While continued economic development in Africa ultimately depends on the education of the African peoples, the immediate impact of rapid expansion of schooling in many areas is an increase in unemployment among school-leavers. This phenomenon can appear at any point in time since it is the result of a discrepancy between the gross school output and the rate of growth of job opportunities in the modern sector. In part, this is a transitional problem for primary-school-leavers. When schools first begin, school-leavers with a little education usually find it easy to get "good" jobs. As the school output grows rapidly, this can no longer occur, and unemployment on a large scale takes place. Finally, when everyone goes to primary school, it will be accepted that all work requires primary-school training, and the problem of unemployment of the primary-school-leaver as such will disappear. However, the more general problem of unemployment (as discussed above, chap. VII) may persist or a similar problem may arise with secondary-school or university graduates if the wrong skills are produced in relation to the economy's needs.

The World Bank Group is now the most important external source for financing the capital cost of educational development—that is, providing financing for school construction and equipment. The Bank has aimed specifically to fill serious gaps in the education system, especially at the level of secondary schooling. It has pressed for improvements in the quality of education, especially by helping to increase the number of qualified teachers at both primary and secondary level, and by conditioning loans on the modernization of curricula. It has also tried to achieve increased efficiency of education systems as a means toward keeping cost levels within the limits of available resources. The Bank's entrance into financing education was stimulated by the needs of its member countries in Africa. In April, 1960, addressing the U.N. Economic and Social Council, the President of the Bank indicated that the International Development Association, when it came into existence as a part of the World Bank Group, would enter the field of educational financing, especially to meet the needs of the new countries of Africa. Just over 50 per cent of the Bank Group's educational commitments (around $300 million by the end of 1970) are, consequently, in Africa. And among the sources of aid to education, the World Bank Group is probably going to continue to increase its support faster than any other.

The educational systems of Africa are still far from ready to contribute what is needed to build the new African states and economies. Discovering and developing physical resources, with all its difficulties, is relatively simple compared to training human resources. Although the knowledge of how to design the right kind of educational system for economic development is still very limited, it is possible to indicate in some respects how the educational system that the Africans inherited on independence was lacking.

## Selected Bibliography

HAEFELE, E. T., and STEINBERG, E. B. *Government Controls on Transport: An African Case.* Washington, D.C.: The Brookings Institution, 1965.

HICKS, U. "The Economics of Educational Expansion in Low-Income Countries," *Three Banks Review*, No. 65 (March, 1965), pp. 3–29.

HUNTER, G. "Education and Manpower," in *The New Societies of Tropical Africa.* London and New York: Oxford University Press, 1962.

IVORY COAST, GOVERNMENT OF. *Ivory Coast Year V: Education.* 1965.

LEWIS, W. A. "Education and Economic Development," *Final Report*, Conference of African States on Development of Education. (UNESCO/ED/181.) New York, 1961.

MASLAND, JOHN W. *Educational Development in Africa: The Role of United States Assistance.* Occasional Report No. 4. New York: Education and World Affairs, 1967.

SCHNEYDER, P. "Les Problèmes Africains de l'Energie," *Problemes Economiques, Notes Rapides* (Institut National des la Statistiques et des Etudes Economiques), No. 855 (May, 1964), pp. 13–17.

SILVEY, JONATHAN. "Unwillingly from School: The Occupational Attitudes of Secondary School Leavers in Uganda" in A. R. Jolly (ed.), *Education in Africa: Research and Action*, Nairobi: East African Publishing House, 1969.

*Situation, Trends and Prospects of Electric Power Supply in Africa.* (U.N., E/CN.14/EP.3/Rev.1.) New York, 1965.

VAIZEY, J. "Education in African Economic Growth," in E. A. H. ROBINSON (ed.), *Economic Development for Africa South of the Sahara.* London: Macmillan, 1964. pp. 340–55.

VAN DONGEN, I. S. *The British East African Transport Complex.* (Research Paper No. 38, University of Chicago, Department of Geography.) Chicago, 1954.

WRIGLEY, C. "Economic Problems of Development," *Proceedings, Conference on Research in West Africa.* Ibadan, March, 1961.

# IX

## Foreign Investment and Aid Programs*

*If you find any Island or maine land populous, and that the people hath need of cloth, then you are to devise what commodities they have to purchase the same withall. If they be poore, then you are to consider the soile, and how by any possibilities the same may be made to enrich them, that hereafter they may have something to purchase the cloth withall.*

Instructions given by RICHARD HAKLUYT to merchants of the Moscovie Company, 1580

*Their gain shall be the knowledge of our faith, and ours such riches as the country hath.*

SIR FRANCIS DRAKE, speaking of the American Indians

The time period in which there has been substantial foreign lending and investing in Africa is not long—for most of the continent,

---

* The help of Badri Rao and Dina Driva in assembling much of the material used in this chapter is gratefully acknowledged.

considerably less than the sixty-odd years since a significant economic contact was established with the rest of the world.*

There are two aspects to any provision of capital by foreign private investors: the private investor must expect to get a return adequate to induce him to invest; and the receiving country must expect that the investment will make a net contribution to its gross national product.

Let us consider first the financial return to lenders. Formally, this consists of interest and amortization. If we accept this as a working basis, and assuming the bond or the loan is made at par, the amortization is the repayment of the original capital; the interest is the return on the capital. But this assumes that there is no risk involved and that no risk premium is included in the interest. In foreign lending, though, risk is always involved, and the return to the lender must include not only a return on the capital but a differential payment for the particular risk taken. In addition, the lender will usually have administrative costs that have to be covered. Until quite recently, the make-up of the World Bank's interest rate, for example, was explicit on this point: it was made up, grosso modo, of the cost of money to the Bank—the rate the Bank was paying on money it borrowed at a given time—plus ¼ of 1 per cent for administrative expenses and 1 per cent for a Special Reserve against losses; that is, it explicitly combined the return on capital, administrative costs, and the risk premium. (The Bank now no longer sets its rate in this mechanical fashion but, taking all these factors and other policy considerations together, sets a final rate without attempting to break it down into the various elements.)

The return to foreign *investors*, companies or people making direct investments in a foreign country, is even more complicated, including some similar elements (return on capital, payment for risk premium) and also payments for the services of management, super-

---

* Until about 1860 in West Africa and 1900 in East Africa, the bulk of foreign investment was devoted to the slave trade. Very little is known about the returns on this investment. Presumably, the slave trade was very profitable, else the large losses in men and ships would not have been borne for so many centuries. It was certainly an important part of the commerce in England, western Europe, and the New World. And the Arab slave trade in the Indian Ocean must also have paid handsome returns.

vision, and technicians (engineers, accountants, salesmen, etc.). It can also consist of something much more: of profits, in the Schumpeter sense—that is to say, of profits made by a foreign entrepreneur because his knowledge of the business and techniques learned in his own economy are in advance of those available in the host country, enabling him to produce at lower cost than the local producers.

The direct investment made by foreign entrepreneurs takes advantage of their access to know-how, managerial techniques, or capital equipment superior to the local entrepreneurs'. The sector of the economy which they control may expand quite rapidly and, if it has tariff protection or transport-cost protection, it will keep most of the benefit of the high productivity for quite a time, rather than pass it on to local consumers. In essence, such enterprises gain from exploiting a type of quasi-rent—which in some cases lasts for a long while, until the indigenous population adopts similar techniques, methods, or organization, or until other foreign investors come in. The degree of difference in the levels of technique between the foreign firm and that of the indigenous economy helps to determine how long it will take before the catching up occurs and the quasi-rents are wiped out—in the case of Africa, it could be a very long time. The persistence of the gap varies inversely with the openness of the country to imports and the entrance of additional foreign investors. (In Australia, however, the data appear to show that there is now no marked divergence in earning rates between foreign-owned companies in general and domestic companies, probably as a result of both a large amount of competitive foreign investment and improvement in Australian competitiveness.)

A somewhat similar quasi-rent arises from the exploitation of natural resources in any underdeveloped country. At Africa's present stage of development, it is a far more important factor than the quasi-rent discussed above. Investors in developing countries very often stand to gain most by providing the missing cooperating factors—transport, technical knowledge, management, or the command over capital—without which it is impossible to exploit an important natural resource. In Africa, the natural obstacles to mining development are so great, and the exploitation of most mineral resources requires so much capital and so many managerial and technical resources, that the indigenous population cannot possibly do the job unaided. For the investor, then, where it is possible to buy resources at prices corresponding to their value in their present uses and then to turn them over to other more profitable uses, which the rest of the local economy is at present in no position to exploit, large gains can be made—gains that provided and provide one of the main inducements to invest in the first place. And one of the chief benefits of foreign investments in African development is that they make it possible to secure an economic use for natural resources, for which before there was none, and thus to convert objects without economic value into economic resources. (Lachmann, pp. 698–713.)

This discussion so far has assumed that the returns on investments can be measured solely in terms of the money made. But direct investment is often motivated by other, less easily measurable expectations. One important reason for investing in the development of iron-ore and bauxite resources in Africa has been the desire to have a sure source of raw materials. And a good part of the foreign investment in manufacturing plants in South Africa, Rhodesia, East Africa, and Nigeria was made in the hope of gaining a foothold in a market that was likely to be (or was being) otherwise cut off by tariff barriers. Some machinery manufacturers make direct investments as a result of their sales of machinery: as a partial return, they take an equity in the factory. There are other motives, too: for example, the "empire-building" instinct in corporate managers who want to run a far-flung corporation.

The philanthropic motive is not unimportant. The Uganda Company, which has contributed a great deal to the development of Uganda through spreading improved agricultural techniques in Uganda and encouraging new crops, was organized around the turn of the century under the inspiration of the Church Missionary Society as a practical way to help the people of Uganda. (*The Economic Development of Uganda*, p. 16.) Much of the impetus to accelerate the development of what is now Zambia and Rhodesia through intensified search for investment opportunities, backed up with the money to put into them, came from Sir Ernest Oppenheimer, Chairman of Anglo-American, de Beers, British South Africa Company, etc., and his wish to make a personal contribution to the development of southern Africa. (Source: conversations with the author, Johannesburg, 1955, 1956.)

### Investing in Africa

It is not possible to make a comprehensive study of the returns on private foreign investment in Africa—much of the information is inaccessible or impossible to collect. But I have been able to get together enough information, which I believe is fairly representative, to present a fairly consistent story.

In Africa south of the Sahara (except in South Africa, which we shall discuss separately), major investments prior to World War I were made through the chartered companies. Most of these companies tried mainly to exploit existing resources—simply going into a territory and taking out what could be easily taken out, such as ivory or gold—and to invest as little as possible. (See, in particular, Conrad, *Heart of Darkness*, and Gide, *Voyage au Congo*.) There were some exceptions—like the East Africa Company, set up to build a railway to Uganda and abolish the slave trade in East Africa. But, as it happens, there are little in the way of *easily* exploitable riches in Africa. By World War I, one after another, nearly all of the companies went bankrupt or ran into such financial difficulties that the European governments then controlling the African territories had to take them over as bankrupt or buy them out.

In French Equatorial Africa, a few remained in existence into the 1930's. The British South Africa Company (BSA) survived longer. After it lost the last of its privileges (mineral rights in what is now Zambia) on the eve of Zambia's independence in October, 1964, it merged with two other mining companies with interests in other parts of Africa and the world, forming a new company, called Charter Consolidated. The three Belgian charter companies (the most important being the Comité Speciale du Katanga [CSK]), established in 1901, 1902, and 1928, after the Congo ceased to be the personal property of King Leopold, still exist. By agreements made in February, 1965, between Belgium, the Democratic Republic of the Congo, and the companies themselves, the Congolese government took over the portfolio of the former Belgian Congo, consisting in part of shares in the chartered companies, and the companies lost their remaining concession-granting privileges as well as rights to royalties from the mines. (Kredietbank, *Weekly Bulletin*, Brussels, April 24, 1965.)

The chartered companies that went out of existence before World War II in no case had given positive returns on the invested capital. In some cases, the investors were able to get a short-lived return while the territory was initially exploited, but very soon, most of these companies found themselves unable to pay dividends. The BSA did not pay any substantial dividends until World War II.* And even then, the rate paid by BSA was very small: the dividends of £400,000 paid in 1940 represented 5 per cent of the company's book value at that date. Of the three Belgian chartered companies in the Congo, the Comité Speciale du Katanga, with the rich mineral resources of the Katanga to exploit, appears to have become quite profitable as early as the 1920's, but the other two did not become prosperous until after World War II.

South Africa was an early and important exception to the history of frustrated hopes of foreign investors. Like the investments in the CSK and the BSA which finally began to pay off, the profitable investments in South Africa were in mining, showing fairly good returns mostly in the range of 6–8 per cent, which in fact was nothing particularly spectacular for most investors, especially when one remembers that this was the average return of a *successful* company. (Frankel, pp. 96–97.) The contrast between South Africa and the rest of the continent is indicated in Frankel's classic study, which showed that in 1936 the largest share of direct foreign investment in Africa south of the Sahara had taken place in South Africa.

But, in general, outside of South Africa and of mining in particular, returns on direct investment were very low before World War II. The experience of Lever Brothers (now Unilever) in Africa prior to World War II is instructive in this regard. (Wilson, *Unilever*.)

### Unilever and United Africa Company

Unilever is the second biggest corporation in Europe. It is prob-

---

* The BSA and the three Belgian companies differed from other chartered companies in that they did make substantial investments in permanent productive facilities. BSA built the railway from South Africa through Bechuanaland and the Rhodesias to the Congolese border, as well as the one connecting Southern Rhodesia with Beira, in Mozambique. The Belgian companies opened up and exploited mineral resources in the Katanga, established plantations in Kivu, and built the rail connection between the Congo River at Stanleyville and Lake Tanganyika.

ably the biggest single factor in the world oils-and-fats market; in 1965, for example, it bought nearly a quarter of the 10 million tons moving in international trade. (*The Economist*, April 30, 1965, p. 525.)

Since before World War II, Unilever has been, and still is, the single largest foreign direct investor (outside of the mining companies) in Africa, the biggest single foreign industrial interest (outside of South Africa), and the biggest trading, farming, and transport complex in Africa. In its subsidiary, United Africa Company (UAC), and directly, Unilever employs over 40,000 men and women in more than thirty African countries, with the largest number located in English-speaking West Africa. Among the companies in the group are African Timber and Plywood (the plant at Sapele is the biggest industrial enterprise in Nigeria); Kingsway Stores, operating department stores; West Africa Cold Storage of Nigeria; and the trading companies of G. B. Ollivant and Swiss African Trading Company. Altogether, the group owns about a hundred factories in Africa, including breweries, textile, auto and truck assembly plants, and plantations in the Congo. Unilever directly owns new palm-oil and rubber estates in Nigeria.

In 1906, Lever Brothers was Great Britain's leading soap manufacturer. Its growth had been of a fairly simple "vertical" type, encompassing the entire manufacturing process from raw-material production to output of soap. Because imported vegetable oils were required, William Lever was particularly conscious of the importance of foreign supplies—and he feared being "squeezed" by merchants and brokers who, he thought, conspired against the manufacturers; he also feared that other manufacturers might take competitive action to secure their own raw materials.

Because of the British colonial policy of refusing to alienate African land for the establishment of plantations, Lever was unable to get land in West Africa as a secure raw-material source. (He did, however, buy trading companies in Nigeria, Sierra Leone, and Liberia.) In 1911, therefore, he established the Société Anonyme des Huileries du Congo Belge to buy wild-palm oil and grow oil palms in the Congo. The Belgian government empowered Lever's company to establish communications and other facilities (which were to be made available to others) and required it to provide schools and hospitals and to pay a guaranteed minimum wage to labor in the areas it controlled: the Société, in fact, like the chartered companies of the period, was almost more of a government than a business. The original concession covered 1.8 million acres leasehold, of which about 500,000 eventually became freehold. Lever also acquired some 6 million acres from a French concessionaire, the Compagnie Propriétaire du Kouilou Niari (CPKN), in the French Congo. But on closer investigation it turned out that only 10,000 acres of this were suitable for planting and this proved a total loss.

A second product of the oil palm is palm kernels, and Lever decided to have them crushed on the spot, for palm-kernel oil, to save on transport costs. But he found that shipping the oil alone was more expensive, since the valuable by-product, the cake, had no market in Africa. (This industry has still not shown itself economic in Africa.)

The Huileries du Congo Belge, the single largest enterprise that Lever had undertaken, ran into difficulties almost immediately. The available manpower was not sufficient for the double task of collecting wild-palm oil and constructing new plantations. Costs were high and progress was slow. By 1914, about £1.5 million had been sunk in the African businesses. The CPKN was a dead loss; the Congo operations showed no profit; the oil mills lost more than £50,000 in 1913 alone.

The war years proved prosperous for Lever Brothers in general, but the African investments were evidently a burden on the rest of the business. Ordinary dividends of 10 per cent were declared in 1914, 15 per cent in 1917, and 17.5 per cent in 1918. The years 1919–29 were difficult. In 1919 Lever Brothers took on the Niger Company (this had been the Royal Niger Company prior to 1900, when it both traded and governed in the Niger River areas) and in 1929 merged it with other companies in Africa into the United Africa Company (UAC). (In 1929, after the merger of Margarine Unie with Lever Brothers into Unilever, UAC also acquired Margarine's West African trading companies.)

For years, UAC was in severe financial trouble and did not declare any dividends. Unilever's Congo plantations, now closely associated with the UAC, were producing palm oil at a cost higher than market price—and the latter was a little more than a third of the value of palm oil when the original concession had been secured. But, because of its investments, Unilever felt compelled to continue to use African oils rather than other, possibly cheaper, products. By the autumn of 1931, banks and finance houses were pressing UAC to cut its commitments, but Unilever found the £3 million of liquid capital that UAC required and decided to stay in Africa—a decision reached by looking hopefully at Africa and her resources rather than by looking at balance sheets. Better management and rising commodity prices served to improve UAC's prospects between 1932 and 1936. But commodity prices broke again in 1937, bringing new trouble.

After World War II, with continuing world prosperity and higher primary-product prices, UAC did much better. However, it does not appear to have done so well as other parts of Unilever. In 1957, for example, 25 per cent of Unilever's capital was invested in Africa, but only 13 per cent of the profits came from there. Unilever's policy seems to have been to reduce UAC's relative share in total investment by limiting fresh investment in Africa to the cash flow of depreciation charges on existing assets. It has been reorienting its activity in such a way as to withdraw from politically sensitive areas, such as the buying of African agricultural produce, and to expand in manufacturing by building factories, itself or in partnership with other local or foreign investors. By 1967, Unilever had reduced the share of its capital invested in Africa to 13 per cent, and this earned 10 per cent of total group profits.

According to a number of comprehensive estimates of private investment in the Belgian Congo before and after World War II, total private investment in the Congo in 1939 equalled about $800 million; for 1953, the estimate was almost $2 billion. (Banque Centrale du Congo Belge, *Bulletin*, August, 1955.) Of this latter amount, half derived from non-African sources and the other half was ploughed-back profits on the foreign investment. In a 1958 study, the Banque Centrale calculated that the dividends payable abroad by Congolese enterprises averaged between 11.6 per cent and 13.1 per cent during the years 1951–56. If one adds to this the "allocations to reserves," total profits ran at 30–35 per cent during the early 1950's, admittedly years of unusually high primary-product prices. The Banque Centrale's conclusion that firms in the Congo had much greater returns than firms in Belgium during those years, certainly appears justified.

The Banque Centrale also compared the capital/net-domestic-output ratio in Belgium (1950) and the Congo (1953); with a total capital-investment figure of $2.2 billion equivalent in the Congo, it found a ratio of 3 to 1, and, to its surprise, it found the same ratio in Belgium. The implication here is that the productivity of capital in the two countries must have been roughly the same. (Banque Centrale du Congo Belge, *Bulletin*, January, 1958.)

### U.S. Investment in Africa

Before World War II, direct investment by the United States in Africa consisted of little more than the Firestone rubber plantation in Liberia, the beginnings of the copper mines in what is now Zambia, and mining investments in South Africa. After World War II, the mining groups in copper, iron ore, and manganese, the petroleum companies, and manufacturing companies began to take an interest in Africa. Over a billion dollars of investment ("book value") * was first reached in 1961, the second billion was achieved in 1966, and (although the figures are not yet available) probably the third billion was reached by 1970. To put these figures in context: only about 4 per cent of total worldwide U.S. direct foreign investment is in Africa.

The bulk of American direct investment in Africa is in petroleum (about 60 per cent). Mining used to receive the second largest share at around 15 per cent, but in recent years it has been passed by manufacturing. South Africa used to have about half of total American investment in Africa but with the rapid growth of oil investment in Libya and Nigeria and mining elsewhere, South Africa in 1968 was only about a quarter of the total. (See Statistical Appendix.) The total American direct investment in all the countries of Middle Africa was about $1.2 billion.

The rates of return shown on the total American investments in Africa in the late 1950's and early 1960's tended to run lower than the roughly 11 per cent shown on American investment in the world as a whole. Since 1964, the African investments have tended to show a return about double the return elsewhere. This change is due mainly to the fact that in the earlier period the oil companies were

---

* The data are those gathered and published by the U.S. Department of Commerce. Direct investments abroad are given at book values, which represent the cumulative amounts invested less liquidations or losses; they may be more or less than current market values.

running losses while they were looking for oil and now, as the oil is being produced, they are recouping their losses. In mining and smelting, there has been little change between the two periods. The rate of return shown on African investments in this sector has been and continues to be several percentage points higher than on U.S. investments in the sector taking the world as a whole. In manufacturing, trade, and public utilities, the rate of return has dropped since the earlier period, but it is still higher than elsewhere.

Probably these figures cannot be taken completely at face value. Different tax laws in different countries can influence the way in which multinational corporations show their profits. However, the differences do fall the way one would reasonably expect them to: investing in Africa is more risky for a foreign investor than investing in western Europe or Australia, for instance. There are more unknowns, and the risk of loss from expropriation in at least some countries is greater; some risk premium is therefore necessary to induce foreign investors to come in.

## Other Countries' Investments in Africa

Outside of the United States, no governments publish official statistics on direct investments of their nationals. Based on the available information, it can be estimated that British direct investment in South Africa is around $3 billion and that the investments of France, Germany, Switzerland, and the Netherlands probably total over $500 million. In the French-speaking countries, French private investment is dominant, and the same is largely true of British investment in the English-speaking countries in Africa. "It seems entirely reasonable to conclude that, if U.S. direct investment in 'black Africa' totals $1 billion, then British, French, Belgian, and West German investment must total perhaps three to five times that figure." (Ostrander, p. 41.)

By the end of the 1960's, Japan was becoming interested in Africa: in large part for investment in sources of raw materials, but also as a possible field for investment in manufacturing. Among the most important investments made so far have been the following:

In 1968, in Zambia, a deal was arranged through Anglo-American Corporation involving $72 million by way of loans and deferred payments for machinery and equipment. In return, Japan is guaranteed 100,000 tons of finished copper annually for 10 years at prevailing market prices. In the Congo, the NIPPON Mining Company has ventured into the Katanga, taking over two huge areas of mineral exploration fields near the Zambian border at Sakania. A new company with a capital of $200,000 was formed to exploit these rights, with the Congolese government and NIPPON Mining holding equal shares. Mining operations are expected to start by 1971 and, it is hoped, will achieve an annual production of 60,000 tons of copper by 1973. Similar investments are being worked out in Mozambique and Angola.

Japanese industrial firms have also ventured into textile manufacturing in Nigeria, the Sudan, and Ethiopia, usually in partnership with the International Finance Corporation of the World Bank Group and local interests.

## SIFIDA

As a means of encouraging private foreign investment in Africa, the African Development Bank (ADB) sponsored the formation in 1970 of a multinational investment corporation for this purpose. The new organization, Société Internationale Financière pour les Investissements et Développement en Afrique (SIFIDA), was set up in July, 1970, with a capital of $12.5 million provided by a consortium of leading banks from all the major industrial countries of the world outside of the Sino-Soviet group. Its purposes are to find and develop opportunities for profitable private ventures in Africa. The success of the ADB in interesting banks in setting up this company augurs well for the company's ability to act as a catalyst in mobilizing capital and management for any investment it may find with a suitable return.

### Loans to Africa

Until World War II, the main sources for loans to Africa were the private and institutional bond buyers in the capital markets of London and Paris, and the main borrowers were the governments of Africa. Today, most lending to African, as to other developing countries, is done by governments or their official agencies or by international development institutions. Of the developing nations selling public issues in the major private capital markets of the world in the first twenty years after the war, only the English-speaking African countries were successful. Since 1960, the free, independent African states have not been able to secure any appreciable amounts in this way. The British government, like the French, has replaced the private capital market as the main source of external funds.

Because information on the French record is less known, and because France's policy orientation on this issue has led the way for other countries, the French experience is particularly interesting.

## THE FRENCH TERRITORIES

Before World War II, most of the funds needed for capital works in the French colonies of Africa were raised on the French market and in almost all cases carried the guarantee of the French government. (A few loans were made directly by government agencies such as the Caisse des Dépôts et Consignations and the Caisse de Garantie des Assurances Sociales.) Because French government credit was involved, in order to raise a loan on the market, the borrowing colony first had to get a special act passed by the French parliament and had to submit its total budget to the parliament for approval.

From 1900 to World War I, the total of these loans amounted to some 315 million francs, the equivalent of a little over $60 million at the time—all but 35 million francs of which went to French West Africa and Madagascar. Most of these loans were paid off after World War I at depreciated franc rates; the investors lost from two thirds to four fifths of their original investment.

From 1919 to 1931, only 510 million francs were raised (all by French West Africa and French Equatorial Africa), or about $20–$30 million. During this period, too, interest rates went up. One part of the loans to French Equatorial Africa was issued at a rate of more than 8 per cent; this was a loan a large part of which was devoted to what was then a somewhat dubious project—the construction of the first railroad in French Equatorial Africa, from Brazzaville to Pointe Noire, which duplicated the existing Belgian line from Léopoldville to the sea.

In 1931, the French parliament passed laws authorizing new loans for public works in all of France's overseas territories. For the first time, a general program—the Maginot Program—was spelled out for the development of the colonies, but no direct financial aid was granted other than the usual guarantee. By the end of 1939, about 3 billion francs had been issued, at interest rates which rose steadily from 4 per cent to 6.25 per cent. During World War II, new authorizations of more than a billion francs (around $150 million at the exchange rates of the time) were made to those colonies not adhering to free France, these advances being made by the French Treasury in view of the unpropitious market conditions. Again, of this capital, the investors have since lost 80–90 per cent of the capital value.

The total capital lent by French investors to Africa prior to World War II came thus to the equivalent of perhaps $200–$250 million (pre–World War II dollars). According to a calculation made by the French National Institute of Statistics, investment in bonds between 1914 and 1940 gave a negative yield of minus 3 per cent to minus 7 per cent. ("L'Intérêt du capital.") Since World War II, the bulk of the external capital provided to the public sector in the ex-French areas of Africa has been provided by the French Government on a grant basis, with only a small amount extended in the form of loans (and this mostly in soft loans). Since 1957, the governments of other European Economic Community members have also contributed.

## The Belgian Territories

By 1920, private investors had lent a total of some 170 million (1914) francs (equivalent to about $35 million) to the Belgian Congo government; another $4 million equivalent was lent by 1939. Again, as in the French case, most of the value of the loans was wiped out by the inflation connected with World War II, and the net return to investors was definitely negative. ("Les Investissements . . . du Congo.")

Between the wars, the Belgian government had found it necessary to finance the Congo directly. From 1921 to 1925, it advanced 17 million gold francs equivalent. In principle, these were repayable, but repayment was never demanded. Then, beginning during the depression and until 1940 and the German occupation, it provided 104 million gold francs to meet the Congo budget deficits. Altogether, from the beginning of the Congolese Free State until 1951, the Belgian government had to pay some 209 million gold francs net (around $140 million foreign-exchange equivalent as of 1965) as grants or non-reimbursed advances. (*La Belgique et l'aide économique,* p. 191.)

## THE BRITISH COLONIES

On the conclusion of World War II, the British government began an expanded program of grants to the colonies under the Colonial Development and Welfare Acts (CD & W), and created the Colonial Development Corporation (CDC) to make direct investments in the colonies and the Overseas Food Corporation for investment in food production. This last ceased to exist after several disastrous investments; the CD & W became irrelevant to the African countries as they gained their independence. But the British government gradually recreated a substitute for it: first, by setting up Commonwealth assistance loans with interest rates geared to the government's own borrowing cost; then, by waiving interest charges on some loans for an initial seven-year period; and, since July, 1965, by making interest-free loans in appropriate cases. (See Statistical Appendix, Table 8, pp. 320–21.) The CDC, at first not permitted to operate in independent countries, has since been renamed the Commonwealth Development Corporation and is now allowed to function in the English-speaking African countries.

### The Flow of Capital Funds

Based on figures provided by S. H. Frankel, I have estimated that the total foreign capital invested in Africa south of the Sahara before World War II was around $6 billion; of this, about half was borrowed by the public sector of the African territories on private capital markets, mostly in London and Paris; about half was private. From 1945 to 1960, probably another $6 billion (at current prices,) came in from private sources and around $10 billion in public funds. At varying dates in much of Africa, and certainly since 1960 for all of Africa south of the Sahara, it has not been possible for the African public sector to secure an appreciable amount of funds from private lenders or investors at a reasonable range of return. Official sources—that is, governments and the international-development institutions—have therefore been the main providers of funds at concessional rates. In the 1960–69 period, the total net inflow of public capital was around $10 billion, with a net inflow of private capital (including ploughed-in profits) of perhaps $2.5–3 billion. The flow of official financial resources (net of amortization payments on loans) to Middle Africa from the principal donor nations has gradually increased in total over the decade of the 1960's from less than $700 million to almost twice that figure in 1969.

## Aid Programs

Until World War II, economic aid to Africa was sporadic and was never included as a part of the over-all foreign economic policies of the metropolitan or industrialized powers. After the war, both the British and French governments started aid programs to their dependent territories—so did Portugal, on a much smaller scale—and since those territories won their independence, the aid programs have continued, without interruption by the French; after a pause by the British. Indeed, the largest single aid program in Africa is still France's bilateral program to her former colonies (supplemented since 1957 by the Economic Development Fund of the European Economic Community (EEC). These countries have received foreign aid amounting on the average to around 6 per cent of GNP (with the range between 4 per cent and 9 per cent) and to about half of gross investment (which averages around 12 per cent of GNP in these countries). Their volume of aid per capita is typically around $10 equivalent. In the rest of sub-Saharan Africa, aid is only about half so important to the economy, averaging over the whole area about $4 per capita and about 4 per cent of GNP. Since 1963, however, French policy has been gradually to reduce dependence on bilateral aid, in order, presumably, to encourage self-reliance and independent action on the part of the African aid recipients and to free French resources for use elsewhere in the world. (*La Politique de Coopération.*)

The United States came on the African aid scene for a brief period during the Marshall Plan and after, mostly because of the use of local-currency counterpart funds generated in the European aid programs. The amounts of the American aid contribution are lost

## TABLE 1

### THE NET FLOW OF FINANCIAL RESOURCES FROM MULTILATERAL AGENCIES AND THE FLOW OF OFFICIAL BILATERAL NET CONTRIBUTIONS FROM INDIVIDUAL OECD MEMBER COUNTRIES TO SUB-SAHARAN AFRICA (EXCLUDING SOUTH AFRICA)

(in millions of dollars)

| | 1960 | 1961 | 1962 | 1963 | 1964 | 1965 | 1966[4] | 1967[4] |
|---|---|---|---|---|---|---|---|---|
| *Multilateral Agencies* | | | | | | | | |
| World Bank Group | 48.7 | 51.9 | 44.0 | 8.3 | 24.3 | 61.0 | 50.80 | 74.44 |
| Other U.N. Agencies[1] | 16.0 | 39.9 | 29.5 | 36.0 | 49.4 | 35.0 | 22.32 | 22.32 |
| EEC | 3.3 | 15.2 | 51.3 | 58.9 | 77.4 | 97.0 | 101.74 | 94.77 |
| Total Multilateral | 68.0 | 107.0 | 124.8 | 103.2 | 151.1 | 193.0 | 174.86 | 192.03 |
| *Bilateral* | | | | | | | | |
| France | 280.1[2] | 275.7[2] | 288.1[2] | 294.0[2] | 281.0[2] | 319.0[2] | 327.0 | 386.0 |
| United Kingdom | 123.6 | 228.0 | 172.5 | 163.5 | 211.3 | 210.0 | 191.6 | 176.6 |
| United States | 39.0 | 75.0 | 197.0 | 159.0 | 161.0 | 248.0 | 276.0 | 221.0 |
| Belgium | 86.0 | 70.5 | 63.4 | 75.8 | 76.5 | 96.0 | 59.7 | 63.1 |
| Germany | 5.3 | 13.4 | 59.2 | 54.1 | 41.4 | 61.0 | 95.8 | 74.2 |
| Portugal | 36.6 | 32.4 | 40.7 | 51.1 | 61.9 | 21.0 | 22.4 | 46.4 |
| Italy | 16.6 | 18.5 | 12.5 | 22.5 | 16.4 | 27.0 | 22.9 | 57.5 |
| Other[3] | 20.8 | 27.5 | 33.8 | 35.2 | 14.9 | 23.0 | 35.1 | 50.0 |
| Total Bilateral | 608.0 | 741.0 | 867.2 | 855.2 | 864.4 | 1,005.0 | 1,030.5 | 1,075.0 |
| Grand Total | 676.0 | 848.0 | 992.0 | 958.4 | 1,015.5 | 1,198.0 | 1,205.36 | 1,267.03 |

[1] Disbursements net of subscriptions payments for UNICEF, UNWRA, U.N. High Commissioner for Refugees, the U.N. Fund for the Congo, the U.N. Special Fund, and the U.N. Technical Assistance Programs.

[2] Excluding aid to French overseas territories.

[3] Including funds from Australia, Austria, Canada, Denmark, Japan, Netherlands, Norway, Sweden, and Switzerland.

[4] Geographical Distribution of Financial Flows to Less Developed Countries (Disbursements), OECD, 1969.

SOURCES: Organization for Economic Cooperation and Development and the World Bank.

or obscured in the intricate accounting of these counterpart funds—particularly in France, where a strict division was not maintained between the use of funds in France and overseas. Since during this period France and the U.K. were receiving aid from America and simultaneously extending aid and exporting capital to their currency areas, it is admittedly arbitrary to identify one final user as the "recipient" of aid. But in any case, about half a billion dollars of real resources made available to France and the United Kingdom under the Marshall Plan were passed on to Africa. Most of this went to North Africa, but as much as $100 million of the French and British aid to sub-Saharan Africa might at least be ascribed to the Marshall Plan. That is, the $100 million is essentially an accounting estimate of the amount of counterpart funds generated by Marshall Plan aid that were made available to sub-Saharan French and English colonies. In general economic terms, one could just as well argue that the aid given to African countries by Britain and France during this period was a marginal use of resources, and that if the Marshall Plan aid had not been received in the first place, there would have been no aid to Africa. On this basis, one could label all the French, British, and Portuguese aid to Africa during this period as indirect American aid.

It was essentially after the African territories became independent that the United States began to give aid directly to Africa. Although the American program at first extended to virtually every independent country, around the middle of the 1960's it began to concentrate on only a few countries where development prospects looked brightest or where there appeared to be an especially severe need for U.S. aid—e.g., Nigeria, Tunisia, Congo (Kinshasa), Somalia, and Ethiopia. In March, 1970, the United States government issued a statement designed to guide United States policy toward Africa in the 1970's. It read as follows:

> The United States will continue to provide assistance to those nations which have been given emphasis in the past. . . . We will to the extent permitted by legislation also provide limited assistance in other African countries to projects which contribute significantly to increased production and revenues. . . . We will continue to emphasize aid to regional programs and projects. . . .
> We wish to do more to strengthen African economic institutions including the U. N. Economic Commission for Africa, the African

Development Bank, the OAU's Scientific Technical and Research Commission, and subregional organizations. . . . We will utilize food aid to advance economic-development objectives and to help tide nations over emergency food shortages. . . . We will more and more orient the program of the Peace Corps to meet the technical, educational, and social-development needs of African nations. . . . We will concentrate our economic assistance in the coming years in the fields of agriculture, education, health including demographic and family planning, transportation and communications. . . . We intend to provide more assistance to Africa through international institutions and multidonor arrangements. We contribute 40 per cent of the budget of the U. N. Development Program; 40 per cent of its program is now being directed to Africa. We also contribute 40 per cent of the budget of the International Development Association; in the past year its loans to Africa have risen substantially, to 20 per cent of all its loans, and the prospect is that this proportion will continue to rise. . . . We are seeking a substantial increase in the absolute amount of United States contributions to these institutions. The United States is now engaged in discussions with other members of IDA, under the leadership of the World Bank, which we hope will lead to larger contributions by all donor members of IDA. We have proposed to Congress an increased contribution to UNDP.

The Soviet Union and Eastern European countries also began aid programs to Africa, starting in 1958. From the beginning, they concentrated on particular countries—mainly Ghana, Guinea, Ethiopia, Mali, Somalia, and Tunisia. Communist China came on the scene first in North Africa, with help to the Algerian nationalists, and then in 1964 south of the Sahara, with aid to Guinea, Kenya, Mali, Somalia, and Tanzania. While no detailed reports are available on aid programs from the Soviet Union, Eastern Europe, or China, from the information available on actual agreements, and given the exceptional slowness of disbursements under them, we can conclude that total disbursements are unlikely ever to have averaged as high as $100 million. Total commitments came to $1.6 billion through 1968, but this figure includes $112 million committed to Ethiopia in 1959, of which less than a third had been disbursed a decade later. (See Statistical Appendix, Table 13.) The Soviet Union's economic-aid programs to Africa seem to have tapered off in recent years. Mainland China appears to be mostly interested in carrying out the Tan-Zam railway. (See chap. VIII above.)

Looking toward the 1970's, the bilateral aid programs in Africa that appeared most likely to expand rapidly were those of West Germany; the Scandinavian countries, especially Sweden (in East Africa and Tunisia); the Netherlands, and Canada. Israel's program of technical assistance was also of considerable importance in a number of countries.

Multilateral-assistance programs are of growing importance to Africa. The European Economic Community's Economic Development Fund has been an important contributor to the eighteen African Associate Members. (See chap. IV above and the Statistical Appendix, Table 12.) The World Bank Group (including the International Bank for Reconstruction and Development, the International Development Association, and the International Finance Corporation) should become of increasing importance in the 1970's. The growing pace of commitment of loans and credits by the World Bank Group during 1970 was beginning to match or surpass the level of capital funds provided by France, otherwise the largest source of capital to Africa.

Of course, not all of the amounts we have mentioned should properly be called "economic aid"—i.e., funds made available on a subsidized basis, below market cost, to help a nation's economic development.* Certainly some of these funds were provided for political or military ends—to influence the political orientation of the recipient country or to secure military bases. Some funds were provided and accepted for cultural reasons. (The President of the Central African Republic, David Dacko, stated in a speech to his legislature, "Our countries have been rebuilt in the image of the West, and we have agreed to keep the French language here; it is because we have learned this language that we have adopted French civilization. We are called upon to build in the heart of Africa a nation in the image of France.") Also, some part of these funds were supplier or exporter credits designed primarily to sell machinery or equipment—in some cases, machinery that was basically unsuitable or uneconomic to use in the country to which it was sold. Probably only the international

---

* Economic aid might more precisely be defined as the residual left to the borrower after subtracting the present value of the debt service installments (discounted by the rate of yield on the investment made with the funds). A loan at 2 per-cent interest "invested" in a prestige project with no return would have no aid element in it.

and multilateral aid programs can be described without reservation as being wholly devoted to economic development. But capital made available for other ends can be helpful to economic development— even aid to military forces, through the army's construction of roads, the training of soldiers in useful skills, etc.

A substantial part of the aid programs in Africa provides technical assistance; indeed, Africa receives a greater volume of technical assistance in both relative and absolute terms than any other region of the world; almost half of France's contribution is in technical assistance; almost a third of all aid to Africa south of the Sahara consists of expenditures on or is connected with technical assistance.* In Africa, technical assistance in the form of trained personnel is often even more important than additional capital, and in most African countries, the ability to absorb capital depends on the amount of technical assistance received.

During 1965, there were 38,000 technical-assistance personnel stationed in Africa south of the Sahara—over 40 per cent of the total provided to developing countries by the OECD. There were 28,000 technical-assistance personnel in North Africa. Seventy-two per cent of all technical-assistance personnel and 88 per cent of the teachers (i.e., 28,000) serving abroad provided by the OECD countries were in Africa. Of a total of some 66,000 publicly financed technical-assistance personnel working in Africa in 1965, 61 per cent came from France, 19 per cent from the United Kingdom, 10 per cent from the United States, 5 per cent from Belgium, and the remainder from a number of other countries. The situation was roughly the same in 1970.

The foregoing figures do not include Soviet or Chinese technicians. In 1966, there were estimated to be 4,000 Soviet technicians in Africa, mostly in Algeria, Mali, and Guinea. The largest number of Chinese technicians is in Tanzania, where several hundred were

---

* The great importance of technical assistance in Africa is indicated by the following figure: bilateral technical-assistance personnel from the OECD nations form about 1 per cent of the university teaching staffs of all developing nations; in Africa, however, *three-quarters* of the university teachers come from this source. "The total input of foreign personnel probably represents about 2.2 per cent of the high-level manpower of developing countries and about the same fraction of middle-level manpower. . . . [But] in Africa south of the Sahara, the majority of the high-level skills are possessed by foreigners." (Maddison, pp. 18–19.)

working in 1970 surveying the proposed route of the Tan-Zam Railway.

A notable aspect of French aid to Africa is the high quality and effectiveness of its agricultural technical assistance based on a number of semi-public French institutions outside of the civil service, including research, advisory, and executive functions. In Dahomey, for example, where agricultural conditions are difficult, the patient work of these institutions together with the Dahomeans is succeeding in getting the economy out of its relative stagnation to a moderate rate of growth.

In the period since 1962, IRHO (Institut de Recherche pour les Huiles et Oléagineux) has helped a Dahomean public corporation, Sonader(Société Nationale pour le Développement Rural), build up 18,000 hectares of industrial plantations of high-yielding oil palms. Substantial progress has also been made in cotton. With technical assistance provided by CFDT (Compagnie Francaise pour le Développement des Fibres Textiles), Dahomean farmers increased cotton production from 6,500 tons in 1965–66 to around 35,000 tons in 1969–70. Two other "societés d'intervention" (SATEC: Société d'Aide Technique et de Coopération and BDPA: Bureau pour le Développement de la Production Agricole) are also giving leadership for agricultural-development work in other parts of Dahomey. With all this, agricultural exports are likely to grow in value over 80 per cent from 1965–67 to 1975, or 7 per cent yearly. GDP, at near-stagnation from 1960–65, should grow by at least 4 per cent annually.

The distribution of French personnel among the African countries varies in intensity from country to country. It is seven times higher per million Africans in the Ivory Coast than in the Congo (Brazzaville), for example. In general, the higher the per-capita income, the greater the intensity, so that Senegal and Ivory Coast each receive four times as much assistance as Upper Volta, for example. (Upper Volta's population is greater than either, but its per-capita income is about a quarter or a fifth that of the others.) This certainly is not the criterion on which the assistance is made available—the criterion being rather the ability of a country to use the assistance well and its desire for it—but it is clear that the more resources a nation has and the more developed it is, the more help it can use to accelerate its growth. After a certain point, it will obviously be able to cut back on technical assistance. But this point is not likely to come before the

0 The Economics of African Development

African countries have multiplied their present per-capita income several times and are at least semi-industrialized.

Consideration of the French-speaking countries in this regard is particularly revealing, since it represents what amounts to a controlled experiment. Because of the French government's generosity in paying for technical assistance and because of its willingness to meet almost any reasonable request, we can safely say that French aid before 1963 was close to being the maximum amount that could be usefully employed in the recipient countries. That this assistance appears to have varied directly with the country's level of development is therefore particularly significant. It should be possible for a country, in the course of its development, to reduce its use of technical assistance—and this appears to have happened among the English-speaking nations of Africa—and still maintain a favorable growth rate. But, when technical assistance is available on favorable terms and is politically acceptable, the nation's capacity to substitute its own manpower in activities that were once foreign technical-assistance programs apparently, as in the French-speaking countries, makes it possible to absorb and use still more technical assistance, and to secure an accelerated rate of growth in this way.

In conclusion, then, economic development in Africa clearly does not depend solely on the flow of aid from non-African sources, but, just as clearly, aid is very important. Insofar as it is possible to disentangle them, the main outlines of present policies and actions concerning the principal sources of capital and aid appear as follows:

Aid from bilateral donors is beginning to level off. France and the United States are cutting back, the United Kingdom is increasing its aid but at a slow pace; Belgium, Canada, Germany, the Netherlands, and Sweden are growing quite rapidly. The Communist aid programs, after an initial flurry of commitments, are unimportant in actual disbursements and economic effectiveness and are likely to proceed cautiously.

Aid from multilateral and international sources shows considerable possibility of growth. The European Common Market's FED and the European Investment Bank are increasing their activities, but the funds allocated to Africa are only slightly above those available in the past. The World Bank Group in 1964 assigned a representative to Addis Ababa to work with the Economic Commission for Africa and the Ethiopian Government; in 1965, it opened two regional offices (in Nairobi for eastern and southern Africa and in Abidjan for western Africa) to help African governments to prepare projects for finance. (The Abidjan office is also helping in the organization of the African Development Bank.) In 1970, offices were also opened in Nigeria and Congo (Kinshasa). While all this activity should result in a considerable increase in the World Bank's role in Africa, the amounts depend mainly on a substantial increase in IDA funds made available to the Bank Group. (The IDA, or International Development Association, provides money on concessionary terms to developing countries. The source of these funds is contributions made by the principal developed countries who are members of the Bank.) Few African countries are in a strong enough economic and financial position to take on a substantial volume of foreign debt on conventional terms; consequently, the World Bank Group has to provide a large proportion of the loans to African nations on IDA terms. (In 1970, these were 50 years; 10-year initial period of no principal repayments; 0.75 per cent service charge per year.)

Another source of funds for the African countries is the International Monetary Fund (IMF), among whose functions is the provision of short-term finance to help a country in temporary balance-of-payments difficulties. At the beginning of 1970, the size of the IMF quotas (which controls the amount of help a country can receive from the IMF) was enlarged, adding $316 million to the quotas of the Middle African countries and $139 million to the quotas of the North African countries. At the same time, the setting up of the Special Drawing Rights (SDR) system in essence gave the African countries increases in the foreign-exchange reserves that they could freely use (up to 70 per cent of their holdings) for international purchases, if necessary. The SDR's created on January 1, 1970, amounted to $139 million for the Middle African countries and $34 million for North Africa. According to plan, SDR's will also be created in 1971 and 1972, providing about $120 million each year for Middle Africa and $30 million for North Africa.

The African Development Bank (ADB) proposed in November, 1966, that an "African Development Fund" be set up which would receive convertible currency contributions from developed countries as grants. The initial size was fixed at $214 million. The administration was to be vested in a joint administrative council of the Bank and the representatives of the countries contributing to the Fund. While a number of countries indicated their willingness to contribute, the Fund had not yet been set up by mid-1970: With a new president of the ADB more willing to work with the industrialized countries than the first president, it is possible that the new fund will come into existence as a new African source of aid in the early 1970's.

## Conclusion

No large-scale increase in private foreign investment is likely to occur in Africa in the foreseeable future, although some individual countries may do quite well, while only a moderate increase in the supply of public capital is in sight. There is much to be done in Africa that is beyond the capacities of the local economies at present; yet, at the same time, the Africans' eagerness to move ahead and their receptivity to new ideas and techniques puts their continent in a unique category among developing regions. A major effort in research, education, training, institution-building, and investment—at this point in history, when the Africans are still not weary or disillusioned—could bring about a real breakthrough in economic development.

But aside from the lead given by the World Bank Group for an increase in its lending, there are no major new initiatives at present and no coherent approach to the problems of the continent. The drive necessary to galvanize support and action to help Africa. An organization coordinating all the principal donor countries and economic agencies, with African participation and a strong Secretariat to focus on African economic and financial problems, is needed to stimulate and coordinate new provision of aid. Only such a stimulus would make it possible to get the African aid programs out of the rut, to assess and correct the deficiencies in the various sectors where action is needed, and to coordinate the programs and approaches in an effective attack on Africa's problems.

## Selected Bibliography

BANQUE CENTRALE DU CONGO BELGE ET DU RUANDA-URUNDI. *Bulletin* (Brussels, Léopoldville), IV, No. 8 (August, 1955); VII, No. 1 (January, 1958).

*La Belgique et l'aide économique aux pays sous-développés.* Brussels and The Hague: Nijhoff, for the Institut Royal des Relations Internationales, 1959.

*Colonial Development and Welfare.* (U.K., Secretary of State for the Colonies [Acts, Cmd. 672, February, 1959].) London: H.M. Stationery Office, 1959.

CONRAD, J. *Heart of Darkness.* London: J. M. Dent & Sons, 1902.

*The Flow of Financial Resources to Less Developed Countries, 1956–1963.* Paris: OECD, 1964.

FRANCE, MINISTÈRE D'ETAT CHARGÉ DE LA RÉFORME ADMINISTRATIVE. *La Politique de Coopération avec les pays en voie de Développement.* Report of the Jeanneney Study Group, 1963.

FRANKEL, S. H. *Capital Investment in Africa.* London and New York: Oxford University Press, 1938.

GIDE, A. *Voyage au Congo.* Paris: Gallimard, 1927.

HAILEY, LORD. *An African Survey, Rev. 1956.* London and New York: Oxford University Press, 1957.

"L'Intérêt du capital de 1914 à 1965," *Études et Conjoncture* (Paris, Institut Nationale de la Statistique et des Études Économiques), XX, No. 10 (October, 1965), 47–64.

"Les Investissements Belges et Étrangers au Congo," in Banque National de Belgique, *Bulletin d'information et de documentation,* I, No. 3 (March, 1952), 174–81.

LACHMANN, L. M. "Investment Repercussions," *Quarterly Journal of Economics,* LXII (1948), 698–713.

LITTLE, I. M. D. *Aid to Africa.* Oxford: Pergamon Press; New York: Macmillan, 1964.

MADDISON, A. *Foreign Skills and Technical Assistance in Economic Development.* Paris: Development Center of the OECD, 1965.

MASON, E. S., *et al. The Economic Development of Uganda.* Baltimore, Md.: The Johns Hopkins Press, for the International Bank for Reconstruction and Development, 1962.

OSTRANDER, F. TAYLOR. "U.S. Private Investment in Africa," *Africa Report,* XIV, No. 7, January 1969, 38–41.

*Private Overseas Investment in Australia,* supplement to the Commonwealth of Australia Treasury *Information Bulletin,* (Canberra), May, 1965.

U.S. DEPARTMENT OF COMMERCE. *Survery of Current Business* (Washington, D.C.), various issues, various years.

U.S. DEPARTMENT OF STATE. "U.S. and Africa in the '70's," Press Release, No. 105, March 27, 1970.

WILSON, C. *The History of Unilever.* 2 vols. London: Cassell, 1954.

# X

## Economic Plans
## and Planning in Africa

*Other things being equal, fortune is
always with him who plans.*

MACHIAVELLI

Africa is the continent of economic plans. Every country in
Africa (except South Africa) has had at least one since World War
II, and most have had several. The preparation of economic plans
began under the colonial regimes and under the stimulus of the
colonial powers. Both the British and the French decided that aid
to their colonial territories after the war had to be provided within
the context of development plans, worked out for each colony by the
territorial governments themselves with help from London in the
case of the British colonies and by Paris for the French colonies.

Perhaps the one point in colonial history upon which everybody
now agrees is that these development plans were defective: they were
prepared by administrators with little or no economic background;
coordination of the investments in various sectors was largely non-

264

existent; there was no consistent development strategy. In short, the plans were "no more than lists of projects."

Yet, it must be said (nostalgically) that these plans did have one virtue: they were usually carried out. They did represent something that was actually planned to take place, and the probability was high that it would take place. And when, to the preparation and execution of these plans, an economic intelligence was added to influence government policy (as in the case of the Rhodesias during C. H. Thompson's tenure as Economic Adviser, 1951–58, or in Nigeria after the 1953 World Bank Economic Survey Mission), the results were probably as close to the economic optimum as one could have reasonably expected to attain.

In Africa during the 1960's, the highest rate of economic growth may well have been reached in the production of plans—increasingly more "comprehensive" and sophisticated plans. *The Plan* had become a symbol of independence, and a great deal of public attention was devoted to, and praises sung over, the plan document.

The planning process was in many countries depressingly similar: An expert or team of experts arrived to prepare a plan. They set to work to construct or fill in a model of the economy, build up intersectoral input-output tables, develop a system of equations, and present an internally consistent over-all development plan complete with capital/output ratios; marginal savings coefficients; import, consumption, and production functions; investment; savings; and import gaps. A plan was worked out for the whole economy which laid down a growth rate, sectoral targets and allocations of funds, and a balance-of-payments projection showing the need for foreign aid. The plan was turned over to the government; the visiting experts departed. At that point, the government may have simply filed the plan away on a shelf (as Upper Volta did, in one case); adopted it with great fanfare and a year or so later requested someone else to prepare another one (as happened in Sierra Leone and Senegal); or, as in most cases, continued to give lip service to the plan but otherwise paid little or no attention to it. "The majority of the plans . . . are only vaguely operational in the sense that decisions with respect to investment and other policy matters are often made by the government without respect to the plan's objectives and priorities." (Forrest, p. 6.)

But when the government tried to carry out the plan, it often found it to be of not much help. In Guinea, for example, the Three-Year Development Plan 1960–63, devised by two foreign advisers, had as objectives: decolonization and economic independence by restructuring the economy; accelerated growth as far as possible within the framework of collective property of the means of production, with the state sector and cooperatives playing a dominant role in all domains; amelioration of the standard of living of the population; etc. The plan was unrealistic, its stated goals completely out of line with the administrative capacity of the government and the existing information on the resources and problems of Guinea. The government tried valiantly to carry out the plan, however; with the help of substantial foreign aid, it got investment to well over 20 per cent of GNP. But the GNP grew more slowly than the population, so that the per-capita standard of living went down; foreign aid and voluntary domestic savings were insufficient to finance the investments, so the central bank had to print money, resulting in a rise in prices and a discouragement to export; export earnings (outside of the foreign-owned mines) went down.

On the other hand, the plans in Kenya and the Sudan (and, in North Africa, Tunisia) were certainly of help—perhaps, to greater or lesser degree, in other countries as well. But in general, an objective observer must inevitably conclude that for most of Africa the plans have so far made little or no contribution to economic development. As Robert Gardiner, Executive Secretary of the Economic Commission for Africa, said in summarizing the conclusions of the December, 1967, conference of African planners: "There had been much more success in drawing up plans than implementing them. Plans represented high hopes and sour performance."

The improvement of planning in Africa depends in part on some general factors, and in part on some specifically or especially African characteristics.

I would venture to say that a general consensus on planning has arisen among most economists who have had extensive experience in development planning: A. K. Cairncross, W. Arthur Lewis, E. S. Mason, G. M. Meier, and the World Bank economic advisers give roughly similar advice in this field. What matters most, they all say, is not whether a plan is well coordinated or internally consistent, although those are desirable, but whether it is based on good economic judgment and reasoning. Uncoordinated decisions are bad, but so may be coordinated ones: even if the Tanganyika groundnut project of the Overseas Food Corporation had been perfectly coordinated, it would have been a disaster, for the original decision to grow peanuts in Tanganyika by large-scale mechanization was wrong. A plan should be a focus, not a substitute, for decision-making.

In fact, an economic plan is nowhere near so important as the process by which a government makes economic and financial decisions. It is much better to have a good planning process in this sense than to have a good plan. As Albert Waterston puts it:

> Development planning as a process involves the application of a rational system of choices among feasible courses of investment and other development actions based on a consideration of economic and social costs and benefits. Planning as a process is an indispensable precondition for the formulation of effective development policies and measures. A plan can play an important part in the planning process when it makes explicit the basis and rationale for planning policies and measures. But if a plan is prepared before the process has begun in earnest or if it is unable to generate the process, it is likely to have little significance for development. (Waterston, p. 5.)

The pressure that international aid agencies have exerted on governments to prepare national plans and the priority that the governments have given these plans are, then, misapplied. The priority belongs to building up a proper economic policy-making machinery and using it effectively. What is important is not setting a target in a document called a plan, but establishing the right economic policies and targets and then deciding on the action to carry them out. Once these are secured, an effective and realistic plan can be easily produced. It is really useless, for example, to produce a plan for a nation that has not yet succeeded in preparing and administering a proper government budget—as is true of one African country now launched on its Second Five-Year Plan.

Perhaps one of the biggest wastes in developing countries is in the way economists are used. It is not at all unusual to find the scarce economic talent available segregated in a planning office, working on a sophisticated macro-economic model, while policy decisions that are shaping the economic future of the country are made without benefit of economic analysis or advice.* What makes the whole matter worse is that the model and plan being constructed often bear little relation to reality. This is not a defect peculiar to Africa: "The latest Turkish plan, according to one observer, is a workmanlike job, complete with intersectoral input-output tables. But it has one defect: the underlying statistics are either unreliable or absent." (Watson and Dirlam, note 4, p. 187.) But if the time and effort spent on such unrealistic exercises were devoted to improving basic statistical and economic information, economic development in Africa would be speeded up.

In other words, an African government would be well advised to use its own and any available foreign economists as advisers in the Prime Minister's or President's office and the principal economic ministries, and in strengthening the statistical services—*before* it turns to the problem of providing personnel to build ultra-refined econometric models.

It is true that the economists and foreign advisers involved may find it easier to play with models and write papers than to engage in the demanding task of finding out the real facts of the nation's economic problems, working out the policy solutions, and trying to persuade a ministry or government to adopt them. The kind of talent required is exactly that described by Keynes:

> The amalgam of logic and intuition and the wide knowledge of facts, most of which are not precise, which is required for economic interpretation in its highest form is, quite truly, overwhelmingly difficult for those whose gift mainly consists in the power to imagine and pursue to their furtherest points the implications and prior conditions of comparatively simple facts which are known with a high degree of precision. (*Essays in Biography*, pp. 191–92.)

That is to say, what is required is an economist who understands how the economy really works in the African context and what broad

---

* Colin Leys goes so far as to say: "While the influence of planning economists may well have improved some decisions, it is possible that in many cases the actual performance of policy-makers has been impaired by the planning process. Not only have scarce administrative and technical resources been used in the preparation of plans which never even began to be implemented, they were prevented from concentrating on assuring some more rudimentary rationality in the flow of decision-making on short-term policy matters, with the result that an unnecessarily irrational pattern of decision-making has often flourished behind the medium-term plan facade." p. 3.

institutional forces affect it. Unfortunately, in today's scientific environment, governments too often believe that an economist-mathematician, if sufficiently incomprehensible, is the best planner. That this results, in Keynes' phrase, in losing "sight of the complexities and interdependencies of the real world in a maze of pretentious and unhelpful symbols" is considered not a drawback but a virtue. This is because plans are regarded as "magic"—pointed to with pride, expected to result in growth, but not regarded as a guide to action.

"Much in the same way as the governments of the underdeveloped countries succumb to the lure of the 'steel mills' embodying the most advanced and capital-intensive type of Western technology, many development economists have succumbed to the lure of the intellectual 'steel mills' represented by the latest and most sophisticated theoretical models. This is where, I believe, the greatest mischief has been done. This is why I have always maintained that a good development economist should also be something of an applied historian of economic thought." (Hla Myint, p. 73.)

Aside from the proper use of economists, the planning process should be realistic in regard to what is administratively feasible in the country concerned. "A due regard for these considerations would limit the size of the public investment sector in a development program to dimensions capable of effective administration; it would counsel against the imposition of controls whose implementation lies outside the competence of existing public services; it would emphasize the importance of training programs and of necessary changes in government procedures." (Mason, p. 72.)

In addition, planners all too often spend their time on the aggregates and never get to the sectors or projects. For development to occur, concrete investment plans for individual projects must have been prepared—investigating technical feasibilities, computing the costs and benefits, and dealing with problems of administration and management. It does no good to be told that investment of x amount is necessary on roads. What roads, going from where to where, what quality, costing how much, saving how much in road-user costs and conferring how much in development benefits?

A major constraint, in other words, is what Hirschman calls the shortage of "the ability to make and carry out development decisions." It is illusory to think in terms of complex plans in countries where the administrative structure is in disarray. This was obvious in countries like the Congo (Kinshasa) after independence. But even in a number of other African countries that did not go through the same disastrous experience, the rapid departure of "expatriate" government officers and their replacement by inexperienced local people meant that even normal administrative tasks were difficult to carry out; much less was it possible to carry out bold new plans. In Tanganyika in 1962, I was told that an AID project for town water supplies was proceeding exceptionally slowly—because it was necessary to dig up the streets to find out where the existing pipes were, the turnover in personnel having been so great that no one was left who knew how to find the files that had the information!

Even without the special disruptions of the independence process, "the ways in which economic policy is formed and institutions are adopted are . . . much messier than is normally . . . acknowledged by economists. Since these changes are part of economic progress *and yet are not fully determined by it,* the process of development is by implication far too complicated to be fitted into the elegant (or should one say naïve) fantasies of the model builders." (Seers, p. 159.)

The colonial governments were governments by bureaucrats, men trained to be good administrators, but with little or no economic training. For such men, the transition was easy from issuing directives to the administration to issuing directives to the economy. Even the public utilities were run as government departments instead of as business enterprises having to meet the economic test of profit and loss.

This tendency to administer the economy by directive has been inherited by the independent African governments, and it is reinforced by an easy perversion of "comprehensive" planning, which is always believed to be more desirable than something that sounds as incomplete as "partial" planning. In any case, it does make sense to prepare plans for the public sector in terms of and within a framework of comprehensive estimates and forecasts for the structure and evolution of the entire economy; it also makes sense to include the policy plans and instruments the government intends to use to help, persuade, and induce the private sector to develop. But it is easy to go too far, especially among the African governments, whose neo-colonialist tendencies to indulge in government by directive are strong, and to attempt also to plan the private sector in detail. This is not an ideological mistake but simply a matter of ineffective development tactics.

Perhaps the most telling criticism of bureaucratic or centralized economic planning was made by Trotsky, when he foresaw the dead end that Stalinist planning policies would lead to. As we now know, bureaucratic planning can secure growth for a time, but with such inefficiency and sacrifice that eventually they are insupportable. As Trotsky put it:

> If there existed the universal mind that projected itself into the scientific fancy of Laplace; a mind that would register simultaneously all the processes of nature and of society, that could measure the dynamics of their motion, that could forecast the results of their interreactions, such a mind, of course, could a priori draw up a faultless and exhaustive economic plan. . . . In truth, the bureaucracy often conceives that just such a mind is at its disposal; that is why it so easily frees itself from the control of the market and of Soviet democracy. . . . The innumerable living participants of the economy, State as well as private, collective as well as individual, must give notice of their needs and of their relative strength not only through the statistical determination of plan commissions but by direct pressure of supply and demand. The plan is checked, and, to a considerable measure, realised through the market. . . . Economic accounting is unthinkable without market relations. (*The Soviet Economy in Danger*, pp. 29–30, 33. Quoted in Lerner, pp. 62–64.)

For the African countries to achieve a satisfactory rate of growth will not be easy. It is much more difficult than in developed countries, where growth may be stimulated or induced by manipulating the macro-economic variables—increasing the rate of investment by appropriate tax measures, or increasing total gross national expenditure by a budgetary deficit, or shifting the relationship between the domestic cost-price structure and the international one by changing exchange rates, etc. One is able to rely on the law of large numbers and, therefore, on the statistical equations that describe economic behavior and the relationships in the economy. But to use this approach in Africa, and to use it as the main analytical policy guide, leads to meaningless and irrelevant conclusions.

At this stage development planning in Africa does not require elaborate statistical exercises. The main problem is to identify the development potentialities—unexploited minerals, fertile soils, water supplies, commercial crops, technological improvements, and opportunities for import substitution. Mathematical models are needed by countries where the growth of internal demand is the engine of development, since full identification of the possibilities then requires demand projections and input-output analysis of inter-industry transactions. In Africa development planning is primarily an exercise in detecting new opportunities; its tool is not mathematics, but lavish expenditure on surveys and research. (Lewis, "Aspects of Economic Development," p. 9.)

In developed countries, one can safely assume that the behavior from input-output tables is almost linear. In developing countries, at the level the African countries are at, structural changes make the system nonlinear and discontinuous.

Successful development in Africa will consist in large part of discontinuities—not of even movement along a curve but of kinks in the curve, jumps from one production function to another. It will proceed not so much in the form of small increases in industrial output, for example, but of a whole new industry getting started, or a new mineral resource suddenly becoming economic. Even in agriculture, where progress is more likely to be slow, jumps will occur—when the answer is found to a plant pest or a new hybrid is developed. (In Ghana, cocoa production, after remaining on a plateau for a quarter of a century, shot up by 50–70 per cent in the space of a few years in the 1960's.)

Macro-economic models imported from the developed world also suffer from another defect as far as Africa is concerned: they emphasize investment. "It is one of the weaknesses of development programming generally, and one based on aggregative investment targets specifically, that it may concentrate the attention too much on tangible investment as the only method of raising incomes." ("Problems Concerning . . . African Countries," p. 32.) Obviously, investment is important and necessary, but often a greater contribution to development can be made by governmental economic policies. In Ethiopia, for example, reform of the feudal land-tenure system, which would give farmers the incentives to improve agricultural practices, would increase the national income more rapidly than the various power and road projects, etc., now under way—even though these latter may be economically justifiable. The very important role of the government in African economies notwithstanding, most economic activities take place *outside* the public sector. Economic growth in Africa can to some extent be measured by the shrinkage of the public sector's importance as agricultural, industrial, and mineral production grows. It is, therefore, of prime importance for governments to maintain policies that encourage private investment. It helps greatly, too, if a government provides the environment for growth: honest and efficient housekeeping of its own affairs and finances, political and legal security for private investors and producers, etc.

Macro-economic models often rest on the rather questionable assumption that capital/output ratios (or capital coefficients) or the technical coefficients of an input-output table remain stable in a developing economy. But much of the problem of development is precisely to increase the output per unit of capital per worker. The model will be even more questionable if the parameters are often not even taken from the economy in question but are imported from quite different ones. (Again, this does not mean they are not useful rule-of-thumb checks; but to rely on them is dangerous.) What makes the whole process often somewhat ridiculous is that in an African economy, where the bulk of the output comes from farming, much of the investment carried out by the farmer is not even included in the GNP estimates! A more relevant model for African economies would emphasize not the capital/output ratio but a coefficient that measured the effort made to raise the general level of skills and broaden the average African's horizons in relation to output—including recurrent government expenditures on education, extension services, radio, libraries, and some part of the political-party expenditures, etc.

Another danger of building economic plans in a developing country solely on macro-economic models is that it has an anti-economic effect in the real sense of the word "economics." It ignores or does not emphasize to governments that it is most important to make the most efficient possible use of scarce resources. The implication of a macro-economic approach is that *any* investment will produce output, whereas what really matters to a development plan is that some investment will have a much higher yield than others—that some, indeed, may have a negative yield. The main problem is to find and take advantage of high-yield opportunities, not to ensure that all in-

put requirements in the model have been accounted for and that
there is an exact matching of domestic resources and requirements
and of foreign - exchange requirements and capabilities. In the
economies of Western Europe and the United States, this problem
does not matter, for the government can assume that the private enterprises whose behavior is described in the aggregative model will
operate to maximize profits. But in a centralized planned economy,
or in a developing country where the government may be taking the
initiative in investment, it is a matter of top priority to keep firmly in
the foreground what yield can be expected from each investment.
"We can allow the investment of capital to remain at the center of
the picture; but we must insist, while we do so, that economic
growth is not merely a matter of investment as such, but of investment in ways that are sufficiently productive." (Hicks, p. 177.)

Lastly, it should be emphasized that in Africa, noneconomic factors are at least as important as purely economic ones in the achievement of economic development. Yet the more "advanced" and
rigorous a mathematical model is, the less likely it is to take into
account the noneconomic factors. We have seen how complex the
problem of African development is and how important some of the
noneconomic characteristics of the society are in this regard. Planning which excludes such factors or throws them into a simple variable is simply not relevant, for economic development in Africa
depends on the transformation of a society, and this must always be
kept fully in mind.

In conclusion, then, the first importance is in staffing and organizing the government to improve day-to-day economic management of
the government and the economy. Any plan for development should
flow out of and be based on this work, with the following points
firmly adhered to:

1. The planners—with a thorough understanding of the economy's
resources and problems, including the main institutional, sociological,
anthropological, and political factors involved—should study the
impediments and opportunities for growth, sector by sector, and
the international market possibilities.

2. Inventory should be made of the costs and benefits of public-
sector investment projects already under way, and as much information as possible should be gathered on private investment under way
or planned.

3. A rough forecast of how the economy will grow without further action should be prepared.

4. A policy program should be prepared of recommendations for action required to stimulate a faster rate of growth, sector by sector and over-all. Where possible, the costs and yields of each should be calculated.

5. Based on a rough financial forecast, which should include the fiscal impact of the plan and be governed by an estimate of administrative capacity (and, where applicable, the constraints of construction or contracting capacity) and by a realistic growth assumption, a public-sector program should be prepared. The projects in it would not need to be fully worked out at first, but one should have a rough idea of their costs and benefits. The program should include projects and programs *affecting* the private sector but not the projects *of* the private sector (i.e., provision of capital to industrial or agricultural development financing agencies, industrial estates, etc.). A check should then be made of the private sector, where appropriate, to see how its plans would be modified by the proposed public-sector policies. The program would then be reworked to be made internally consistent.

6. The decision in each sector to accept projects should be made on the basis of a partial equilibrium model. That is to say, it should be based on a calculation of the costs, forecasts of demand and prices (in the light of a realistic forecast of GNP growth and making whatever adjustments are necessary wherever market prices clearly do not reflect actual social costs), and calculation of yield. The latter would be the determining factor. No attempt should be made to screen projects on the basis of capital/output ratio, input-output matrixes, or any other kind of general equilibrium model.

7. The resulting economic plan should be regarded as a working plan, a stage in a process and not a blueprint. It should be reviewed constantly and revised periodically.

## Selected Bibliography

CAIRNCROSS, A. K. *Factors in Economic Development.* London: Allen & Unwin, 1962; New York: Frederick A. Praeger, 1963.

CLARK, P. G. "Towards More Comprehensive Planning in East Africa," *The East African Economics Review*, XX, No. 2 (December, 1963), 65–74.

FORREST, O. B. *Financing Development Plans in West Africa.* Cambridge, Mass.: Massachusetts Institute of Technology, Center for International Studies, 1965.

HICKS, J. R. "National Economic Development in the International Setting," *Essays in World Economics.* London: Oxford University Press, 1959, pp. 161–95.

HIRSCHMAN, A. O. *The Strategy of Economic Development.* New Haven, Conn.: Yale University Press, 1958.

HLA MYINT. "Economic Theory and Development Policy," in THEODORE MORGAN and GEORGE W. BETZ, *Economic Development Readings in Theory and Practice.* Belmont, Calif.: Wadsworth Publishing Co., 1970, pp. 71–80.

JULIENNE, R. "L'Afrique à l'heure des plans," *La Documentation Africaine* (Paris, Penant), January, 1964, pp. 1–26.

LERNER, A. P. *The Economics of Control.* New York: Macmillan, 1946.

LEWIS, W. A. "Aspect of Economic Development." Background paper for the African Conference on Progress through Cooperation, Makerere University College, Kampala, 1965. Mimeo.

———. "On Assessing A Development Plan," *The Economic Bulletin* (Accra, Economic Society of Ghana), III, No. 6–7 (June–July, 1959).

LEYS, COLIN. "A New Conception of Planning." Paper presented at Crisis in Planning conference at Institute for Development Studies, University of Sussex, June 29–July 10, 1969.

MASON, E. S. "Economic Planning in Underdeveloped Areas: Government and Business." (The Millar Lectures, No. 2, 1958.) New York: Fordham University Press, 1958.

———. "On the Appropriate Size of a Development Plan." Unpublished paper: Cambridge, Mass., 1964.

MEIER, G. M. "The Development Decade In Perspective." Background paper for the Cambridge Overseas Studies Committee Conference, 1965. Mimeo.

*Problems Concerning Techniques of Development Programming in African Countries.* (U.N. Economic Commission for Africa, E/CN 14/42/Add 1.) Addis Ababa, December, 1959. Mimeo.

SEERS, D. Review of *Journeys Toward Progress: Studies of Economic Policy-Making in Latin America,* by A. O. Hirschman, in *American Economic Review,* LIV, No. 2 (March, 1964), 157–60.

VINER, J. *International Trade and Economic Development.* (Lectures delivered at National University of Brazil, 1953.) Oxford: The Clarendon Press, 1953.

WATERSTON, A. *Development Planning: Lessons of Experience.* Baltimore, Md.: The Johns Hopkins Press, 1965.

———. "What Do We Know About Planning?," *International Development Review*, VII, No. 4 (December, 1965), 2–9.

WATSON, A. M., and DIRLAM, J. B. "The Impact of Underdevelopment on Economic Planning," *Quarterly Journal of Economics*, LXXIX, No. 2 (May, 1965), 167–94.

WILSON, T. *Planning and Growth*. London: Macmillan, 1964.

# XI

# Economic Development, Politics, and Diplomacy

> *No country can reasonably be expected to cut its own throat.*
> DR. HASTINGS BANDA, President
> of Malawi

The economic forces and economic structure of a country are major factors in its domestic politics and foreign policy. Very simply, to survive you must eat. What an individual or nation must do to get food and other needed commodities is bound to be an important influence; the extent of this influence, however, cannot be so easily explained as some Marxists or other economic determinists would have us believe. It depends on the strength of the economic forces at work, on the awareness in the government leaders and among other leading elements of the economic factor, and on the strength of other forces such as nationalism, cultural objectives, etc.

In some cases, economics may be determinant, as seems to be true in Malawi's refusal to take drastic action against Portuguese Africa. Even though there is no doubt of Dr. Hastings Banda's solidarity with and commitment to the African independence movement, the influence of the economic factor is clear in his continued reliance on the routes across Portuguese Africa for Malawi's trade.

In most cases, however, the economic factor is not so overridingly important or it may not be so well appreciated, or other factors may be given more weight. Economic considerations were clearly deemed of secondary importance, for example, in the Moroccan government's insistence that the United States remove its air bases from Moroccan soil, even though these provided a considerable income to Morocco and gave employment to thousands of Moroccans. (In addition, the air bases undoubtedly gave the United States a special interest in giving Morocco priority in economic aid.) On the other hand, these considerations may have influenced the slowness with which the bases were finally "phased out." (Elsewhere in Africa, the financial and economic advantages of foreign military bases were more appreciated. When France reduced her armed forces in Africa from 40,000 to 6,000 between 1963 and 1965, the decision was regretted by almost all countries where troops had been stationed. Senegal estimated that it had enjoyed the equivalent of $40 million a year from the French military establishments at Dakar and Thies, and their loss was a severe economic blow.)

The economic forces affecting politics and foreign policy stem from (*a*) the structure and nature of the domestic economy, and the nation's external economic and financial relationships; (*b*) the objectives of the government and people as to the kind of economy and foreign economic relationships they want; and (*c*) the tension between the first and second—that is, the tension between "what is" and "what ought to be."

## The Structure of the Economy

As we have seen, African economies are heavily dependent on the outside world for capital; external markets are the main propulsive force for their growth, etc. And we have seen that it is their *market* or *money* economy—the economy of the future—which is dependent on the outside world, so that the dynamic parts of the economy and the people most interested in change are the ones who must be oriented to foreign affairs.

Indeed, most of Africa is still at that stage of development where the main engine of economic growth is growth in export earnings. Consequently, the richer a country, the higher the relative per-capita importance of its foreign trade; the richer a country, the more it depends on other nations for the continuation of its existing economy and for further economic growth. (South Africa is an exception because it has passed beyond this stage and, at its present phase of development, depends more on an increased internal market than on an increase in exports.)

African nations also, as we have seen, depend heavily on imported capital and on key trained personnel from non-African sources. African countries receive more finance from abroad, on the average, than countries in other parts of the world—around $4 per capita of capital annually (Tunisia and Swaziland received more than $15 per capita of net capital imports in 1968), as opposed to rather less than $3 in developing countries elsewhere. In many African countries, almost all of the recorded investment is financed from abroad; in most, the size and pace of inflow in investment funds makes the difference between rapid economic growth—as in the Ivory Coast, for instance, with a 10 per-cent growth or more in the last few years—or very slow growth or near stagnation. (Here again, South Africa is an exception, being now practically independent of inflows of capital from abroad.)

Although the rest of the world is vital economically for the African countries, African trade and investments are of little importance outside of the continent. Even if the African countries were organized in a bloc, which they are not, they could not use their economic power as a bludgeon to serve their political interests in the world arena. They simply do not have that much economic strength. They are, rather, in the position where it makes more economic sense to use their political power—for example, in their votes and influence in the U.N.—to serve economic ends.

Still, it is difficult to argue that any nation has or can have decisive economic influence. Even the United States with its enormous economic power cannot successfully wield its economic power alone to force another country to adopt policies or programs that the latter wants strongly to resist (*vide*, Cuba). Today, nations are bound closer together economically, and, at the same time, any one nation has only a small degree of economic influence over others. Certainly no developing nation or group of developing nations can exercise decisive international economic power.

## The New International Economic Environment

In the 1930's, many small countries were forced into separate face-to-face bargains over trade with a larger economic power. And it is not surprising that many of them fell into the economic clutches of a dominant great power. Today, with international economic affairs (except for some remnants of bilateral relations, preserved mostly by the Soviet countries) based on multilateral trade and convertible currencies, a small country has a multiplicity of markets and suppliers to choose from, and it can choose on the basis of the economic advantages in each individual transaction. Developing countries, which usually produce only a few commodities, and primary products at that, do not have the flexibility and alternatives open to developed nations in this regard, but the present situation is still an immense improvement over the prewar world.

The growth of international economic and financial organizations since World War II has resulted in more and more international economic and financial decisions being made through negotiations—in organizations like the World Bank, the International Monetary Fund, the General Agreement on Tariffs and Trade, and the new U.N. Trade and Development Board—than through unilateral imposition by any one nation or group of nations. In these instances, no one country is dominant, and decisions are reached more by consensus than by vote; the African states are able to exercise a legitimate influence and get a hearing for their needs and aspirations.

### African Aid Options

The economic ends which African countries strive to achieve in the present international economic and financial context are, usually, the best paying markets, stable remunerative prices for their exports, and the most generous provision of economic aid and technical assistance. An African country, in some cases but not all, may have the option to develop close relations with a particular donor nation or group in order to gain the optimum benefit; or to maneuver among various donor countries, perhaps playing one off against the other; or, thirdly, to play the "multilateral game." Most of the ex-French colonial countries have chosen the alternative of working closely with France. From the *economic* point of view, it is hard to argue that they have been wrong; essentially, they were offered no comparably generous alternative. The two countries which did not initially follow this pattern, Guinea and Mali, have in recent years re-established relations with France. (Mali remained an associate member of the European Common Market and has rejoined the franc zone.)

Other newly independent African countries did not receive from other Western powers the kind of treatment the French provided their former colonies, and most of them were quick to learn that close ties with the Communist countries are not an adequate substitute. And to play the field successfully—that is, to play potential givers of aid off against one another—requires a large cadre of diplomatic and financial negotiators that only two or three countries in Africa possess. In general, African nations, in most cases from choice, have made no attempt to use political maneuvers as a means of securing aid, but have remained politically true to the principles of nonalignment.

On this score, Ghana was temporarily successful, but by the end of Nkrumah's regime, aid to Ghana from both East and West was drying up. Tunisia was probably most successful in securing aid from a whole range of sources, in both the West and the East, while at the same time eliminating the vestiges of its former dependent status and becoming no country's client. (She has been given economic aid by France, the United States, West Germany, the Netherlands, Sweden, Italy, Switzerland; the U.S.S.R., Poland, Czechoslovakia, Bulgaria; Yugoslavia; and the World Bank Group— including the Bank, the International Development Association, and the International Finance Corporation, the U.N. Special Fund, and the U.N. Expanded Program of Technical Assistance.)

By 1970, the possibility of playing Mainland China, the Soviet Union, and the United States against one another was very slight in most of Africa. The United States and the Soviet Union did not place that high a value on their interests in Africa, and Mainland China had not the resources to do much. Per-capita income in China is actually below that of most of the African countries. Moreover, there must always be present in any African consideration of relations with China the fact that China alone of the three powers is densely populated and could have an interest in securing territories for settlement.

### African Trade Options

The eighteen African associate members of the European Economic Community—with free entry for their products into the Common Market—have a direct interest in trying to preserve this rapidly growing market for themselves as against Asian, Latin American, and other African producers of the same products. For they could in this way secure more rapid growth in exports and, therefore, in their economies than if they had to gear production to the slow over-all growth of the total world consumption of primary products. The other African producers have two alternatives in this situation: one is to try to join with Latin American and Asian producers to persuade the Common Market to eliminate or to reduce the preferences given to associate members; the other alternative is to attempt to have the preferences extended to their products too. It is also possible to try to operate on both fronts simultaneously. The nations of East Africa, which are strongly affected, have negotiated with the EEC for an agreement permitting entry of their products into the Common Market on some basis of equality with the African associate members. Tunisia, Morocco, and Algeria have also worked out acceptable relations with the Common Market. (It is not at all surprising that these African countries appoint some of their ablest economic negotiators as their diplomatic representation in Brussels.)

The bulk of African trade is now with western Europe. North America is a poor second—except in the case of a few countries, notably Liberia and Ethiopia—although coffee exports from Uganda, Angola, etc., to the United States are important. The Soviet bloc is a very poor third, yet the Communist bloc presents the biggest potential unexploited market for Africa's primary producers. These countries' consumption of coffee, cocoa, palm oil, etc., in relation to their per-capita income levels, is only a fraction of the western figure; if they bought tropical products in the same proportion to per-capita income as the West Europeans or Americans do, the African producers could sell another $3 billion or $4 billion of exports—i.e., African exports and the African standard of living could rise by almost 50 per cent, and the opening up of this large market could provide an important propulsive force for the next decade or two.

This "import gap" of the Sino-Soviet countries has many implications for African-Soviet relations in particular and for African international relations generally, and both the Africans and the Soviet Union know it. The Soviet Union's announcement that it had abolished custom duties on tropical products on January 1, 1965, is one indication of this, but this decision has remained meaningless for Africa—exports have not risen rapidly.

In the Soviet Union's centralized economy, the decision to buy or not to buy African products is not taken by consumers, who might be influenced by the price they must pay—which would be affected by whether a customs duty was levied. The decision to import a particular product is a bureaucratic decision made by the government's foreign-trade monopoly. The fact that a customs duty may be levied when a product is passed on to a government sales organization has little influence on the monopoly's original decision to buy that product (assuming that the demand for the product at a price including the tariff was already greater than the quantity permitted to enter when the duty was imposed; under the Soviet system, in any case, the internal price may or may not be related to the foreign-exchange price paid). It is simply that if the foreign-trade monopoly, under a bilateral agreement, can "sell" Soviet machinery (which is not easily salable for foreign exchange elsewhere) in exchange for African products (which are), it will make good business sense to do so. Or if the price at which Soviet equipment is sold, in terms of the world market value of the African products received in exchange, is higher than the price at which it can be sold elsewhere, it makes sense to trade it for African products and then sell the latter in world markets. Both Egypt and Ghana discovered that cotton or cocoa sold to the Soviet bloc against purchases of Soviet goods wound up for sale in western Europe, in competition with cotton and cocoa coming directly from Africa. (For this reason, the African countries in UNCTAD have insisted that the Soviet Union agree not to resell abroad primary products purchased originally from the developing countries. If, however, the Soviet Union and other Eastern European nations evolve toward a more decentralized economy—as indications are that they might—with buying decisions determined more and more by price and by the consumers themselves, the elimination of customs duties would increase the volume of African exports.

On the other hand, at present there is little potential for the growth of Chinese-African trade in the near future. The simple manufactured products that China itself is trying to export are in fact of the type that African countries themselves hope soon to export; and the Chinese standard of living is, and is likely to remain for a long time to come, too low to provide much of a market for present African exports; in addition, China is likely to exclude them in order to save foreign exchange for purchase of machinery. China's purchase of raw cotton or tea from time to time can only be momentary phenomena resulting from crop failures or ad hoc political decisions.

### Africa's Interests as a Primary-Product Exporter

As exporters of primary products, African countries have a common cause with developing countries everywhere to try to secure cooperative international action that would control the market in such a way as to assure favorable prices and minimize fluctuations. As the most dynamic and lowest-cost producers in many primary commodities, however, their economic interest is in many cases to try to get a larger share of the market away from producers in Asia or Latin America—and to secure a more rapid economic growth in this way than the general sluggish growth of demand for most of the commodities they produce would otherwise permit. Consequently, in regard to international commodity agreements (except concerning commodities where they already dominate the market, as in cocoa), the intelligent thing for African countries to do may be to remain outside the agreement as long as possible to take advantage of the price umbrella created and maintained by the other producers. Once they are within the agreement, their interest may be to secure flexibility in quotas so that they can get a growing share of the market as time goes on. (In the International Coffee Organization, it is precisely the African producers who have applied the most pressure for increased quotas and who have been the most restless with the quotas they have. The long-range coffee situation can be summed up in a few statistics: the Brazilian share of the world coffee market decreased from 70 per cent before World War I to 33 per cent in 1970; the African share has increased from 1 per cent in 1909–13, 8 per cent in 1934–38, 16 per cent in the 1950's, to 33 per cent in 1970.) Finally, it may be in their interest to have the prices set by international commodity agreements at a level low enough so that high-cost producers elsewhere will not be encouraged to stay in production or go into production, and to discourage production of synthetic substitutes.

These interests, of course, may, in specific cases, put Africans into direct conflict with other world producers. But Africans have a long-term interest in allying themselves with other primary producers to get more favorable treatment in the markets of the developed world. In particular, the semi-industrialized or industrializing nations of Latin America and, to some extent, India and Pakistan are endeavoring to find markets for their new manufacturing industries in Europe and North America—through liberalized tariff treatments, preferential markets, etc. To the extent that these semi-industrialized countries can succeed and their economies become more industrialized, it will be easier for them to move over and allow the African countries to take over a larger share of the world markets for the primary products.

### Intra-African Relations

While the most important economic relations of African states are with non-African nations, some states have important ties to other African countries. For the land-locked African state that depends on another for access to the sea, for example, this dependence can be a dominant factor in its diplomatic as well as economic relations. Malawi has no choice but to use routes through Mozambique to the sea, so good relations with Mozambique are vital, as Dr. Banda has indicated. Uganda, Rwanda, Burundi, the Central African Republic, Chad, Niger, Mali, and Upper Volta each have two or more feasible routes to the sea, and their situation is somewhat more flexible. The degree of flexibility may be severely curtailed, however, because of the costliness of shifting trade from one route to another; and the degree of costliness may be a determining factor in foreign policy. In the case of Zambia, not only does its main rail connection to the sea lead through Rhodesia, but still another important factor links it to Rhodesia; that factor is power. Most of the electric power consumed in Zambia is produced by the Kariba hydro-power project, situated at the dam straddling the Zambezi River between the two countries. (This power is especially vital to the continued operation of the copper mines in northern Zambia, which produce Zambia's main export.) Unfortunately, the first powerhouse to use the Kariba potential was built on the south, or Rhodesian, bank. This fact became one of the central issues in the drama of Rhodesia's unilateral announcement of independence in late 1965 and early 1966. Zambia repeatedly asked that British troops enter Rhodesia to take over custody of the Kariba power project in order to safeguard Zambian power supplies, which it feared Southern Rhodesia's rebel government would curtail or cut off. (The power was not cut off, and by 1970, the decision had been made to construct a station on the north bank to produce power for Zambia alone.)

Clearly, this situation, and the fact that the Rhodesian Railways are Zambia's major route to the sea, were severe constraints on Zambia's freedom to pursue the kind of policy she might have wished vis-à-vis Southern Rhodesia's declaration of unilateral independence. The vital importance of these services was clearly acknowledged by President Kenneth Kaunda when he told the Zambian parliament that if Rhodesia interfered with Zambia's railway services or supply of power to Zambia, "it would be a declaration of war, and I would not hesitate to order my country into action." (Lloyd Garrison, "Zambian Warning Given to Britain," *The New York Times*, December 10, 1965, p. C.7.)

Another important economic link among African countries is the international movement of labor. To citizens of Lesotho, Swaziland, Botswana, and Mozambique, job opportunities in South Africa are important, if not vital. "None of this means that Africans like apartheid. It simply means that countries held in South Africa's economic thrall, like Basutoland, cannot afford to declare political war upon it." (*The Economist* [London], May 8, 1965, p. 622.) On the other hand, South Africa's need for this labor is considerably less acute than the need of the labor-supplying countries to have the job opportunities in South Africa.

Their citizens' need to continue to be able to work in another country is also an important economic factor for Malawi vis-à-vis Rhodesia, Rwanda vis-à-vis Uganda, Niger and Chad vis-à-vis the Sudan, and northern Nigeria and Upper Volta vis-à-vis Ghana and the Ivory Coast. In most cases the need for jobs is more important to the "proletarian" country than the labor is to the "employer" country. For example, Ian Smith, Prime Minister of Southern Rhodesia after her declaration of independence in November, 1965, in-

jected the issue of the migrant labor force directly into Rhodesian
foreign policy: with more than half of the African wage-labor force
in Rhodesia made up of migrants from other African countries (200,-
000 from Malawi, 120,000 from Mozambique and Angola, and 70,000
from Zambia), Smith warned those countries that, if economic sanctions against Rhodesia caused unemployment, the foreign workers
would be the first to be dismissed. (Dispatch from Salisbury, "Smith
Warns He Will Expel Foreigners If Sanctions Cause Job Shortage,"
*The Washington Post*, December 9, 1965, p. A 18.)

A third important link among African nations is created by the
need to have large markets. Aside from Nigeria, the Congo (Léopoldville), South Africa, and to some extent Algeria, none of the
African countries has or is likely to have in the near future a market
large enough to permit industrialization to get under way. Only by
several countries' joining together in a customs union or free-trade
area, pooling their purchasing power in a single market, can this be
accomplished. But only if the gains—new industries made possible by
the larger size of the common market—are clearly beneficial and the
distribution of benefits is skillfully carried out will the common market hold together. Politically, the distribution of benefits and allocation of compensations are easier to handle if they are done within the
context of a common government. Consequently, the hopes of maintaining common markets in Africa are usually brighter if they are the
result of a federation or union of states than if they are only negotiated agreements among sovereign states.

The problems of locating industries have important political implications in the common-market context and in other areas as well
(see above, pp. 198-201). There is, for example, the question, where
slaughterhouses handling cattle from Niger which are destined for
Nigeria should be located—a question whose political implications
increase when analysis of the economic costs and benefits involved
shows that there is no clear-cut economic advantage to one or the
other country. The location of natural resources is another such
factor. In areas where a frontier is in dispute or there are irredendist
claims, an agreed solution may be much more difficult to come by if
there are rich natural resources involved. The belief that there might
be oil in Kenya's northeast corner reinforces its reluctance to consider
concession of this area to Somalia. The discovery of oil in the Sahara
made both Moroccan and Tunisian claims to parts of the area under
Algerian control politically more important.

Economic aid may also be a factor in the political relationships among African states. The financial contribution that the Ivory Coast has been making since 1959 to the other states of the Conseil d'Entente (Upper Volta, Niger, Dahomey, and Togo) helps the Ivory Coast to be recognized as the leader among them.

### The Colonial Inheritance

Some African countries inherited what might be called a complete "colonial" economic structure. Unskilled African labor faced big foreign mining or plantation concerns; African farmers producing export crops confronted small groups of foreign-owned exporting and processing firms who monopolized the market (although in most countries the colonial governments themselves, after World War II, had set up marketing boards or *caisses de stabilisation*); and, as consumers, they faced the same group of import-export firms selling or distributing imported commodities. In many countries, finally, a middle stratum has grown up between the big European firms and the local population—made up of Asians in East Africa, of Syrians and "Coast Africans" in West Africa.

The political effect of these patterns has been significant. Many African governments either have tried to set up "countervailing power" to the strategic power of the big concerns—through encouraging labor unions and increased government controls—or have nationalized them.

The United Africa Company in recent years has shifted out of trade into manufacturing, which should help to avoid the hostility that is natural in the colonial trade pattern when a farmer sells his produce to a foreign company or individual trader at a price he feels is too low and buys commodities from the same trader at prices he easily can come to believe are too high. In those countries where no major change in this "colonial" structure has taken place, the potential for political difficulties continues. Particularly when domestic action to change the status of Europeans, Indians, Pakistanis, Lebanese, or Syrians (as the case may be) in key positions of the economy is not under control, disputes with the nations whose citizens or companies are involved are bound to occur.

A related problem concerns the relationship of African governments to large international corporations—particularly the mining companies. When an African government negotiates with an international mining group whose worldwide net profits are as large as the national income, it may naturally feel the negotiations are not on an equal basis.

While there are ways of equalizing the bargaining capabilities (see above, chap. VI), there may also be a case for international cooperative action. The Economic Commission for Africa has helped to prepare a uniform investment code applicable to foreign investment; oil-producing and copper-producing nations have organized protective associations on matters of mutual interest. There is still considerable potential for additional ties of this type among African nations.

## Conclusion

By the beginning of the 1970's, it was becoming clear that the African states were not going to become or remain in the long run dominated by any of the major powers outside of Africa. They had not opted for either the pure capitalistic or the Soviet socialistic system but were experimenting with mixed economies of various types. At the same time, as European control over most of Africa receded, some of the older African economic-political patterns began to become evident again. Perhaps the most important of these was the antagonism between the Sudanic, originally animal-herding peoples and the agricultural peoples farther south that has been appearing in many areas as a conflict between Islamic and non-Islamic peoples, either within or between states. The civil war in the Republic of the Sudan, guerrilla warfare in Eritrea in the Ethiopian Empire, civil war in the Chad, the shiftas (Somali guerrillas) in the northeast province of Kenya, and even the coups and civil war in Nigeria were manifestations of this ancient fault-line running across the continent that was again exposed as European influence waned. Mastery of this conflict in many areas is becoming an important precondition for economic development.

Finally, we must consider the "revolution of rising expectations." There is a tremendous, largely invisible, but important change going on in Africa—the slow growth throughout the continent of the monetary economy. With it, there is an enormous increase in the demands of the African peoples. This is coming from the impact of education, of the experiences of migrant laborers, of the transistor radio, movies, and now television. Everything and everybody is influenced, whether or not this is immediately evident, and this change in people is accelerating. The modern economy—with its amazing power to create wealth, to control disease, to satisfy material desires—is becoming desired by Africans throughout Africa. The traditional outlook, with its more passive attitude toward the ups and downs of life, is being discarded. People realize that they are poor, and that something can be done about it; sickness and early death are seen as avoidable; burdensome tribal discipline and responsibilities are no longer tolerable. The new African governments are very much aware of these growing demands and new attitudes, but also of their inability to achieve something quickly.

When European officials enjoyed a high standard of living in colonial Africa, this was resented as part of the whole colonial system. Now, the first generation of independent Africa's governing elite enjoy the benefits formerly held by Europeans. More and more people feel that they should qualify as members of the elite, and even those who may not feel qualified see no reason why they should not have radios and automobiles. (The contrast between the educated elite already in power and those outside can take several forms; there is also the struggle between the "petite" and "grande" intelligentsia— i.e., between school and university graduates—and the struggle between the first-generation graduates in power and the second university generation, who feel shut out.) But the economic reality is that Africa cannot yet afford to extend the elite's standard of living to the masses. In many cases, it is questionable whether they can afford it for the elite and still have the necessary savings and investment to grow on. On the one hand, these benefits should act as an incentive to greater efforts, but on the other hand, the high consumption of the elite may restrict the amount of savings. (And the wrong lesson may be drawn: that the rewards are made not for economic effort but for political effort.)

Political problems also arise when a government, cognizant of the desirability of cutting down the cost of special privileges for civil-service and government workers, tries to do so. In January, 1966, when the President of Upper Volta proposed a 20-per-cent salary cut for the civil service, the civil-service union struck and there were riots in the streets. To restore order, the army seized power and rescinded the salary cut. This pattern has been repeated in other countries. Only President Nyerere, in Tanzania, has been successful in substantially reducing the privileges of the governing elite.

In brief, Africa's modern governing elites are faced with demands for the benefits of the Western economy, but with an unawareness of the costs that must be paid to produce these benefits. People are converted to new wants and aspirations more rapidly than their earning capacity or the national income can be increased. People begin to desire "the American way of life for themselves," with all the products they see on television and in the movies; they also desire social-security schemes, unemployment insurances, old-age pensions, etc., which their leaders, acquainted with these things from their experience of England and France, have promised them. Unfortunately, the African countries came to independence only after governments in the West had taken on the responsibility of providing a welfare state: America as late as 1932 did not regard itself as obliged to look after the poor, the aged, and the sick. "It would . . . be a crowning point of irony if some backward countries were to turn towards Communism through an excessive fondness for the American and British ways of life." (Hla Myint, p. 132.)

When through economic development the African countries create a large middle class, this may become a stabilizing force, but the creation of the middle class is often highly destabilizing.

> Typically, the first middle-class elements to appear on the social scene are intellectuals with traditional roots but modern values. They are then followed by the gradual proliferation of civil servants and army officers, teachers and lawyers, engineers and technicians, entrepreneurs and managers. The first elements of the middle class to appear are the most revolutionary; as the middle class becomes larger, it becomes more conservative. (Huntington, p. 289)

Another danger hovers in the background—exemplified by the case of Haiti, independent for almost two centuries, but with less economic progress than any of the newly independent African countries —the danger that the modernizing elite will lose its power to govern and control, and that a country will lose all its gains and slip back into a situation far worse than the nineteenth-century tribal society from which it has ostensibly liberated itself. Such a retrogression might come in many ways: the elite may be displaced by leaders who pander to the masses and promise them the benefits of modern life, while they remove the pressure to make the changes that are the preconditions for a modern economy; the elite may use the state machinery merely to provide themselves with a "good life" while letting the economy and administration slip backwards; or, on the Haitian pattern, some soldier, remarkable only for his command of violence, may seize and retain power. (That it is possible for a small band of military men to overthrow a government in Africa has been shown in several instances: in Togo, President Olympio's assassination in January, 1963, by a small group of soldiers; and, notably, the coup executed by "Field Marshal" Okello, an ignorant but ruthless freebooter from Uganda, that overthrew the centuries-old Sultan's government of Zanzibar in December, 1963. But that there is resistance to such schemes seems also to be shown by the way in which the abler political leaders eased Okello out of power and out of Zanzibar; by the military coup against Nkrumah that led to the reestablishment of constitutional government in Ghana, etc.) So far in Africa—and this is a good omen—all threats of substantial regression have been successfully mastered.

In brief, economic development in Africa is, almost inevitably, creating a situation of high political and social tension. African leaders are confronted with a conflict between the overwhelming desire for change, and the feeling that the social and individual costs involved are close to unbearable, and the obstacles overpowering and perhaps insurmountable. It is not at all surprising that they should turn to the developed countries for sympathy and help, nor that the pressures on them from their citizens to produce quick results become the dominant factors in their relations with the rest of the world.

## Selected Bibliography

HANCE, W. A. "Efforts to Alter the Future: Economic Action," in A. C. LEISS (ed.), *Apartheid and the United Nations.* New York: Carnegie Endowment for International Peace, 1965.

HUNTINGTON, SAMUEL P. *Political Order in Changing Societies.* New Haven and London: Yale University Press, 1968.

MOUSSA, P. *Les Etats-Unis et les nations prolétaires.* Paris: Editions du Seuil, 1965.

———. *Les Nations Prolétaires.* Paris: Presses universitaires de France, 1959. (3d ed., 1963.)

MYINT, H. "An Interpretation of Economic Backwardness" in A. N. AGARWALA and S. P. SINGH (eds.), *The Economics of Underdevelopment.* London and New York: Oxford University Press, 1963.

PREST, A. R. and STEWART, I. G. *The National Income of Nigeria, 1950–51.* (Colonial Research Studies No. 11.) London: H. M. Stationery Office, 1953.

STOLPER, W. F. "Politics and Economics in Economic Development," *Revista di Politica Economica* (Rome), LIII, third series, No. 6 (June, 1963), 851–76.

# XII

# The Prospects
# for Economic Development

*Come il viso mi scese in lor più basso,*
*mirabilmente apparve esser travolto*
*ciascun tra il mento e 'l principio del casso:*
*Che dal reni era tornato il volto,*
*ed indietro venir gli convenia,*
*perche il veder dinanzi era lor tolto.*
DANTE, Inferno, Canto XX,
lines 10–15

Dante's belief that forecasters belong in Hell was based not only on the idea that it is sacrilegious to try to predict the future but also on his perception that predictions can change the future and, therefore, interfere with God's plans.

Economic forecasts in particular run this danger. In some cases, economic forecasts may be self-realizing—this is largely true of the successful "indicative plans" in the industrialized market economies. In the late 1950's, the Vanoni Plan forecast a rapid growth in the Italian economy. Industrialists assumed this would happen and invested on that assumption; their belief in the forecast made it come true. In other cases, economic forecasts may be self-frustrating: by calling attention to the disastrous future an economy is heading

295

toward, it may stimulate government or other action to make sure the forecast does *not* come true.

This chapter is primarily an attempt to forecast the future economic development of the African countries on the assumption that present and probable future trends will continue. Based on this assumption, it attempts to highlight those areas where action could be taken to make the future other than it now appears it will be.

*An Economic Forecast*

The economic test I am applying in this chapter is the achievement of a per-capita GNP of $400. This is not to imply that the figure represents happiness or any other noneconomic state. Even on economic grounds, $400 is essentially an arbitrary target, chosen because at that level, with any sort of reasonable management, and without special foreign aid, a country's standard of living can continue to grow. (In some cases, the capacity to grow without special aid can develop at lower income levels, but it is virtually assured at the $400 per-capita level—with, at most, the help of foreign loans at conventional interest rates.)

Moreover, the U.N. Research Institute for Social Development has found that between $400 and $500 per-capita GNP appears to be a threshold of rapid change between social and structural factors, on one hand, and economic production factors, on the other. That is, the most rapid gains in social development and in the structure of an economy occur as a country's per-capita GNP rises toward $400; afterward the gains are much slower. For example, longevity rises rapidly to an average expectation of life at birth to over 60 years at around this $400 level. Afterwards, longevity rises very slowly as income rises.

In the African context, the speed with which this goal is attained is important. Until recently, this did not matter much; for most of Africa, it was fairly simple to keep the economy growing at pace with or even a little faster than the population growth. But nowadays this is no longer enough; as a minimum to maintain stability, people must feel that their standard of living is rising perceptibly. What this implies in terms of a GNP growth rate has not been established; it probably varies from country to country and group to group. (As a working figure, I have finally adopted a minimum 7-per-cent GNP growth rate, as will be seen later in this chapter.) As a first assumption, I have arbitrarily begun with a target of a per-capita GNP of $400 by 1980–that is, by the end of the second Development Decade.

For some African countries, this goal is not overly ambitious. The Republic of South Africa has already considerably exceeded it. By 1980, indeed, at its present rate of growth, it is possible that its per-capita GNP will be at a level with that of Western Europe's in the late 1950's (i.e., around $1,000). If the economic benefits of the South African economy were evenly distributed, all the nation's races would then enjoy a good standard of living; on the present basis, the people of European origin will continue to have one of the highest standards of living in the world, while the Africans do better than most of the other African nations but not so well as the highest income countries.

Of the other African countries, Libya already in 1970 had over $1,000 GNP per capita, and Réunion, Gabon, and the French Territory of Afars and Issas were well over $400. Algeria, Tunisia, Ivory Coast, Mauritius, and Swaziland appear to be within striking distance of this objective. To attain it, they would need a per-capita growth of GNP of about 5 per cent yearly, or, assuming a population increase of 2 per cent yearly, a 7-per-cent GNP growth rate. This is a high rate—higher than was sustained by the present industrialized countries in their developing stages. But it has been maintained or surpassed for long periods since World War II by some countries (Japan, Taiwan, Israel, Southern Rhodesia during the 1950's, Gabon and Libria in 1960–65, and Ivory Coast during the 1960's).

But for most of the continent, the attainment of a per-capita GNP of $400 by 1980 would require a rate of growth two or three times as high—and such rates extended over so long would be unprecedented and, I believe, practically impossible. But if a 7-per-cent rate could be reached and maintained, all Africa would reach the $400 per-capita level by the year 2000.* This would be no mean achievement: Africa would have made as much progress in a century as it took Europe more than 1,000 years to accomplish. A 7-per-cent growth

* In a statement drafted by, among others, the African experts R. H. Green, Gerald Helleiner, Richard Jolly, and H. M. A. Onitiri, and subscribed to by ninety-nine participants in the Columbia University Conference on International Economic Development (held in Williamsburg, Virginia, and New York City, February 15–21, 1970), it was laid down that the essential target to be sought for the developing countries should be "a minimum average per-capita income of $400 to be reached by all countries not later than the end of the century."

rate is also desirable politically: it means doubling the GNP in ten years or, with a 2-per-cent rate of population growth, doubling per-capita income in less than 15 years—that is, in less than a genera-tion; this would mean an appreciable gain in income every year and would give parents confidence that their children would be better off than they. (Seers suggests that a 7-per-cent growth rate is a neces-sary condition for political stability in Africa.)

Whether Africa can and will achieve these growth targets depends on a large number of factors: the favorable conditions and the ob-stacles offered by the natural environment; the cultural readiness and receptiveness of Africans to economic growth; the interplay of politics and economics; and the opportunities and constraints pre-sented by the rest of the world to African economic growth.

ENVIRONMENT

The natural environment is still the dominant factor in African economics. To a large extent, development represents mastery over it or escape from its limitations. The fact that man has still not mastered the tropics is Africa's biggest restraint on economic develop-ment. But there is always the exciting possibility that the potentials for progress in Africa are greater than anywhere else in the world. For example, in the temperate areas, the gains from increasing a man's efficiency through reducing disease are, while appreciable, nowhere near so great as they would be in the tropics. Bilharzia, for example, is a disease that may persist in a person for years before it kills him and is currently debilitating tens of millions of Africans. Since African agricultural production is set by the amount of labor that can be mustered at peak periods (sowing and harvest), the eradication of bilharzia could result in a 50-per-cent increase in out-put with no increase in agricultural investment.

Satisfactory measurement of the economic cost of malnutrition is still to be made. There is enough evidence, however, to suggest that malnutrition is a substantial economic drain. Malnutrition in early life is directly or indirectly responsible for more deaths among chil-dren in Africa than all other causes combined. This means that a large percentage of national income is required to rear chil-dren who do not live long enough to make a productive contribu-tion. Of those who survive, some are physically retarded, and this must affect their labor productivity. This is clearly so in cases of physical handicap, such as the blindness caused by Vitamin A deficiency. Similarly, the amount of energy a person has must have a relationship to productivity, even though so far this relationship has not been quantified in economic terms. A major need of the African countries is an alert, creative, and intelligent citizenry. Whether malnutrition has a permanent impact on learning ability or not, certainly during the years that the children are undernourished, they fall behind during the most critical years of learning.

Since World War II, the volume and quality of research on the tropics and on Africa in particular has risen, although suffering a severe setback with the political turmoil of the 1960's. But it is reasonable to expect that this factor will make a more and more important contribution to African development. Research, especially in agriculture, takes a long time—first to show results and then to be applied. While it is impossible to quantify the contribution research will make, it is safe to say that it will exert a fairly gentle upward push on economic growth during the next fifteen years, growing in intensity as time goes on.

But all this notwithstanding, some natural handicaps are not likely to be overcome in this century. The lack of rainfall in the deserts, the unevenness of mineral distribution—such factors cannot be offset by research, and they will lead to an uneven development among the African nations. On this basis alone (barring any presently unforeseen discovery of oil, *à la* Libya), the task of economic development appears very difficult indeed in countries like Upper Volta, Niger, Chad, Central African Republic, Somalia, Botswana, and Lesotho.

## CULTURAL AND POLITICAL FACTORS

The new African governments have, if anything, accentuated the emphasis on and the desire for material goods. The monetary economy has continued to erode the subsistence culture, economy, and fatalistic philosophy of life. The spread of education, the transistor radio, and now television is resulting in an accelerating rate of social change—a difficult and painful process. With its uneven incidence on individuals and generations, its vast political and social tensions, the surprise is that there has been so little unrest in Africa. But the logic of African economic development, the "anguish of disintegration and adjustment," must continue, and at a pace that is often "too urgent for patient reflection and wise action." (de Kiewiet, p. 86.)

The breakdown of law and order in the Congo in the early 1960's

demonstrated the importance of political life for economic development, the fragility of the political structure left behind in some cases
by colonialism, and, happily, the large capacity for political recovery
in African countries. Development cannot take place without a certain minimum of security and without the provision and maintenance of basic government administrative services. Slow progress,
while these are built up on a Congolese basis, is therefore inevitable
for the immediate future. This political and administrative factor
will be a determining one in the Congo for the next fifteen years.

But the Congo only dramatized a situation that in less acute form
is typical of other African countries. I. R. Sinai, in his analysis of
what happened in some Asian countries that preceded Africa to independence by a decade or more (*The Challenge of Modernization*),
points out that  western imperialism provided no more than a top-
dressing of modernization—a tiny intellectual elite, developed ex-
port-import sectors, a few big cities and communications geared to
foreign trade, little industry, and no transformation of farming for
local consumption. Modernity could become an ambition in such
countries, but not a reality. Behind the façade of modernity, there
was slow retrogression, as the old ways reasserted themselves. Administration became confused and incompetent; corruption spread;
there was an irresistible tendency to confuse talk with action and to
blame the rest of the world for domestic shortcomings.

This is a somber picture, and it reveals real dangers for many
countries in Africa. It may not be possible for an African government, no matter how well intentioned or how able its leaders, to
avoid retrogression. The difficulty in some cases is that too little real
modernity was left behind by the colonizing power. Many of the
ex-French colonies are now trying to cope with this problem by
continuing to import vast numbers of French technicians and teachers—in a race to shift the balance to the modern world before it is
too late. But such a policy requires on the one hand a considerable
modern elite and strong enough political leadership to hold on while
the transformation continues, and on the other, large-scale foreign
assistance. Even in some of the French-speaking countries, the latter
does not obtain; the volume of technical assistance available or ab-
sorbed in Upper Volta, Niger, and Chad is less than in the Ivory
Coast and Senegal; Guinea and Mali are even worse off. Various
new programs providing technicians and teachers from the United
Kingdom, the United States, and some of the West European coun-

tries are helping, but they are not anywhere near large enough to eliminate these dangers.

Another widespread political problem that is already interfering with economic progress in Africa is a more sociological one: the yet unfinished problem of nation-building. In most of the new African nations, there are large sectors, often a majority, of the population who regard themselves first as members of a tribe or ethnic group and as citizens of the new country secondarily, if at all. In some cases, there are large groups who still regard themselves as subject peoples, subject no longer to the British or French but to the dominant tribe who inherited the colonists' position. Whether this is justified or not, the fact is that the tension or fighting between southern Sudanese and the government, between Somalis in northern Kenya and in Ethiopia and their respective governments, drains the resources of these governments and makes development that much more difficult.

Finally, it is necessary to take special note of the spread of corruption in some of the new African states. The position in Nigeria before the January, 1966, military revolt was described as follows: "Corruption was widespread. It was almost axiomatic that all members of the government were rich. It was considered standard practice for a federal or regional minister to get a percentage of any new loan on contract being negotiated. Tips or 'dash' greased the wheels of a cumbersome bureaucracy. It was the system and everyone played along. For the average Nigerian, a politician was expected to take 'dash.' He wasn't hated for it. He was envied." (Donald H. Louchheim, *The Washington Post*, January 23, 1966.)

Aside from any economic ill effects, it could certainly be demonstrated that corruption has an undesirable effect on the whole quality of African life. And corruption can certainly destroy a society's chance for economic development. By causing decisions to be made on the basis of the rake-off to the decision-maker, rather than of what pays best for the enterprise or economy, corruption can result in such a misuse of resources that the economy stagnates or retrogresses. If limited, corruption will simply make the economy a little less efficient; this is probably true in the United States, where corruption in the form of expense-account entertainment used to influence decisions taken on other than purely economic bases not only is legal but is actually encouraged by the tax laws.

Corruption can also in some situations make a positive economic contribution: in inefficient, slow-moving governments, where the bureaucracy attempts to control the economy in every detail, corruption may make it possible for the economy to move. It may also result in the government's making major new policy decisions and thus allowing profitable new opportunities to be exploited more rapidly. Corruption may also serve as an efficient—if inequitable—means of capital accumulation, if the capital is invested at home and not in Switzerland.

In the African context, the prevalent one-party systems of politics and government encourages the spread of corruption, for the checks provided by a vigilant opposition and by the threat of losing power are not present. And, whenever "African Socialism" manifests itself in the attempt to regulate the economy in minute detail, when the government tries to make all the important economic decisions, and this is beyond the effective capabilities of the administration, corruption is inevitable. It becomes one of those compromises that are common to all governments: laws and regulations are passed regulating economic activity to satisfy the mass of the people, while the persons or enterprises regulated are enabled, through the judicious use of bribery, to pursue their interests unhindered. (In more sophisticated societies, these compromises are reached within the law: income-tax rates are made progressively high to satisfy the mass of the electorate, but sufficient loopholes are left to allow the rich to avoid the high brackets.)

An important argument against corruption is that it is a handicap to foreign aid and investment. Representatives of the aid-giving countries lose their enthusiasm for giving aid when they observe ostentatious living by the ruling few financed by their rake-off on contracts and credits in countries where the masses of people are still living in the utmost poverty.

The full economic effect of corruption, in the nature of things, is hard to evaluate since the phenomenon itself is not statistically measured. What one can say is that "productive" corruption—i.e. that which helps to get things done that need to be done—very soon turns into counterproductive corruption—which results in getting things done that ought not to be done (for example, the enormous growth of suppliers' credits in some countries; not all of these are corrupt or uneconomic, but a very large portion of them are). Eliminating or reducing corruption is not solely a moral or ethical problem: probably the greatest progress can be made by reducing the number of administrative decisions that have to be made by an overstrained civil service.

The foregoing discussion is closely related to that of socialism in the African context:

> At Oxford, the London School of Economics, and the Sorbonne, the British and French trained the elites of their erstwhile empires to a deep faith in socialism. To this was later added a practical case. Much of the capital for development in new countries comes from abroad as publicly organized aid. Or, it is raised locally, not from voluntary savings of individuals and corporations, but from domestic taxation or other public sources. It has seemed plausible that the state should invest publicly raised funds in publicly owned firms. And private entrepreneurs of requisite competence and responsibility have not always been abundant.
>
> The public enterprises have not been accorded autonomy. Here the socialist faith has been thought to require parliamentary control, the right to examine budgets and expenditures, review policies. Technical personnel are less experienced than in the older countries, organizations less mature; these lead to error and suggest to the parliamentarians and civil servants the need for careful review of decisions by hiring presumably more competent authority. Poverty makes nepotism and favoritism in letting contracts both more tempting and more culpable than in a rich country. This calls for further review. The effect of this denial of autonomy and the ability of the organization to accommodate itself to changing tasks has been visibly deficient operations. Further, social control, in particular, is applied to two decisions which are of the greatest popular interest: the prices charged the public and the wages paid to the workers. This has the effect of keeping prices lower and wages higher than the organization can stand. It eliminates net earnings and therefore this source of savings. The poor country which most needs capital is thus denied the resource on which the rich countries must rely. (Galbraith, pp. 101–3.)

In addition to burdening a state machinery that is already over-worked and overstrained in trying to cope with the normal governmental tasks with the job of overseeing the new state organizations in the economy, the nationalizations weaken one of the most potent forces of economic development, the scope for action of the ingenuity and creativity of the individual African. For the process of industrialization to operate vigorously, a great diversity of economic organizations and individuals is required. Development of new products is a matter of trial and error. Even when the result is successful, it is often a surprise, not what was actually being sought. One of the important conditions for economic development is the possibility for an individual to change drastically his own kind of work as he sees an opportunity open up to him. Trying to bring about industrialization through large state-controlled organizations alone is inevitably going to be a slower, costlier process in Africa.

Probably the greatest contribution the political sector could make to economic development is in the creation of larger political and, therefore, economic units. For the preservation of bigger markets where they already exist, as in Nigeria, or the creation of them elsewhere is the *sine qua non* for substantial industrial growth in Africa. But there is no indication at present that African politicians and statesmen will be able to make a substantial contribution of this kind in the next fifteen years.

EXTERNAL CONSTRAINTS

There is still a great deal that African countries can do (and are doing) to increase their output and improve their standard of living without regard to the outside world—in the improvement of food production, the creation of industries for the home market, the construction of an infrastructure that is not primarily intended for the use of foreign trade, such as electricity for domestic consumption, etc. But these activities cannot result in a good growth rate if the countries cannot at the same time improve their ability to purchase foreign goods. Practically every one of these activities requires imported equipment, tools, spare parts, books, paper, etc. The need for more foreign exchange, either through increased exports or foreign aid, is still one of the most important constraints on African growth.

In the past, Africa's GNP has grown roughly in line with the growth of her export earnings—over the last fifteen years, at around 4 per cent per year. The gross domestic product of the industrialized countries of the world, outside of Eastern Europe, grew at a 4.8-percent rate during the 1960's. This rate is projected by OECD to go up to over 5 per cent in real terms during the decade of the 1970's. (This rate of growth is roughly equal to an addition each year to total GDP of the OECD countries of around $90 billion a year in the early 1970's and around $180 billion around 1980—assuming a price-increase rate of 2½ per cent a year.) Secondly, the East European countries are beginning to increase consumption of tropical products to a rate commensurate with their per-capita incomes. Consequently, a higher estimate for African export earnings growth, perhaps around 4 per cent, now appears more reasonable. While African terms of trade (i.e., export prices compared to import prices) improved in the last years of the 1960's, they are likely to deteriorate somewhat in the 1970's.

With proper development policies, the African countries may be able to increase GNP somewhat faster than export earnings—conceivably to 4.5 or 5 per cent a year. These figures, however, are based on the assumption that there will be no change in the flow of aid and technical assistance, which, at around $1.5 billion a year during the 1960's to the whole of Africa, facilitated growth in the African economies. If the growth rate of GNP is to be lifted from 4.5–5 to 7, an increase in capital and technical assistance seems necessary. A 2-per-cent increase in African GNP (excluding South Africa) is equivalent to $800–$900 million a year. Assuming a capital-cum-cost of technical assistance/output ratio of 3 to 1, which may be a reasonable over-all rule of thumb for Africa, an increase in the growth rate would appear to require an increase in the annual volume of expenditure on investment and technical assistance to around $2.4–2.7 billion. There are some countries that could increase their own savings, while many, like the Ivory Coast and Uganda, are already saving over 20 per cent of gross national product—an impressive ratio for countries at their per-capita level of GNP. Probably, therefore, most of the increase—say, $1.5–2.0 billion—would have to come from foreign-capital inflow and technical-assistance expenditures. If the rate of population growth could be slowed down to 1 per cent per year (rather than the 2 per cent assumed), the required increase in investment and technical skills could be halved, or the rate of increase of GNP could be increased by the same percentage-point amount as population increase drops. Such a drop in population growth is hardly likely to be achieved during the 1970's; the prospects are, rather, that the rate of population growth will continue to go up.

Obviously, these are very rough calculations, based on daring assumptions, but they may provide some indication of the order of magnitude of the problem. In actual fact, of course, the prospects and possibilities differ radically from one African country to the next. In any case, a broad distinction should be drawn between mineral producers and the agricultural exporters. As earlier chapters have tried to make clear, the former tend to have brighter prospects than the latter.

Of the mineral producers, Algeria, Gabon, Guinea, Liberia, Zambia, Nigeria, Congo (Kinshasa), and Rhodesia already clearly have the potential to reach or surpass a 7 per-cent GNP rate of growth. Congo (Brazzaville), with potash and possibly bauxite and iron-ore deposits; the Sudan, a very large and practically unexplored area; and Ghana, if it handles its opportunities from the Volta power and aluminum project wisely—may also belong in this select group. Most of the other African countries depend mainly on agricultural exports, and here the external constraints apply. But this still does not mean that particular countries cannot be successful—especially if others, by mishandling their affairs, open up the opportunities to get a bigger share of a limited market. Among the possible candidates for such success are the Ivory Coast, Kenya, Morocco, Uganda, and the Sudan.

By 1970, several new opportunities had opened up for African development. For the North African countries, their associate membership in the European Economic Community provided the possibility of their becoming exporters of manufactures to Europe. With reasonable political stability, their capable labor force and location on the borders of Europe could provide an attraction for the movement of industries there to produce for the European market. Another new economic activity is the rapid growth of tourism to Africa. In Tunisia, Morocco, and Kenya, it has already become the largest single foreign-exchange earner. The other East African countries, like Senegal, Sierra Leone, and Ivory Coast, could also profit in varying degrees from the continued rapid growth of international travel. Some of the land-locked countries could also profit in lesser degree.

Finally, there is the possibility of labor migration to Europe. By 1970, there were six million migrant workers in western Europe, mostly from the southern European countries but also from the North African countries. The Economic Commission for Europe has estimated that in the 1970's with the low rate of growth of the European labor force, another two million will be needed. In the countries that have been mostly providing the workers—Greece, Italy, and Spain—growing prosperity at home will reduce the numbers looking for work abroad. Portugal, Turkey, and Yugoslavia have been providing an increasing number of workers, but they too are likely to level off or decline during the 1970's. More workers can come from North Africa, but there is now also a possibility that Middle Africa may be able to provide some workers. Senegalese, in fact, already do go to work in France. With suitable arrangements negotiated between governments for their reception and treatment in Europe, such a flow could become a substantial economic opportunity for hundreds of thousands of Africans and for their governments. In addition to the revenues the workers would bring or send home, they would have an unrivaled opportunity to learn modern industrial skills and habits that would be a valuable base for future industrialization at home.

## Conclusion

In the course of this discussion, it has been possible to identify several African countries where, even with a continuation of existing trends, the chances are good that a satisfactory rate of growth can be achieved. Some others, with substantial improvement in political and economic policies, also stand a good chance. For the rest, it appears clear that there will have to be drastic changes in existing trends —certainly including the lifting of the whole aid and technical-assistance effort to a considerably higher level and planning and coordinating it through some new international effort—if they are to be able to move ahead at a proper pace. New development techniques may also be required. Perhaps it will be possible to work out a generation-long contract between an international or bilateral aid agency and the recipient country, through which the necessary transformation of the country's economy from top to bottom could be systematically and thoroughly carried out. Greater aid efforts should certainly include more investment in research on African problems. Perhaps, even more important, this research should be organized on a more permanent basis, in the form of internationally sponsored research institutes, along the line of the new International Institute of Tropical Agriculture in Ibadan, Nigeria, and be better coordinated and directed toward a coherent set of targets.

Finally, major political changes creating larger economic units would greatly improve the prospects for the African economies.

The next decades are not likely to be easy ones for Africa. The final solutions are certainly not in sight; we are not even sure that the problems have been fully and accurately ascertained. Most of the agony in the process of development is still ahead. Nevertheless, I am confident that for most of Africa the economic future before the end of the century can be bright. The environmental difficulties that held Africa back for so long have not yet been fully overcome but, with the right help from abroad, they can be. In the last analysis, economics, like politics, largely depends on people. The Africans have the will to learn and the talent to make good use of the opportunities offered them.

## Selected Bibliography

ANDRESKI, STANISLAV. *The African Predicament: A Study in the Pathology of Modernisation.* London: Michael Joseph, 1968.

BERG, ELLIOT J. "Socialism and Economic Development in Tropical Africa," *Quarterly Journal of Economics,* LXXVIII, No. 4 (November, 1964).

DE KIEWET, C. W. *The Anatomy of South African Misery.* (The Whidden Lectures, 1956.) London and New York: Oxford University Press, 1956.

GALBRAITH, JOHN KENNETH. *The New Industrial State.* Boston: Houghton Mifflin, 1967.

LOUCHHEIM, D. H. "Premier Balewa's Body is Discovered," *Washington Post,* January 23, 1966, pp. 1 and 18.

NYE, J. S. "Corruption and Political Development: A Cost-Benefit Analysis," *American Political Science Review,* LXI, No. 2 (June, 1967).

SEERS, D. "International Trade and Development—The Special Interests of Africa," in I. G. STEWART and H. ORD (eds.), *African Primary Products and International Trade.* Edinburgh: Edinburgh University Press, 1965, pp. 19–25.

SINAI, I. R. *The Challenge of Modernisation: The West's Impact on the Non-Western World.* London: Chatto & Windus, 1964.

TOYNBEE, A. J. "Africa: Birth of a Continent," *Saturday Review,* December 5, 1964, pp. 27–29, 87–88.

WRAITH, RONALD, and EDGAR SIMPKINS. *Corruption in Developing Countries.* London: George Allen & Unwin, 1963.

# APPENDIXES

# TABLE 1

## The Independent African Countries

| Country | Date of Independence | Area (in million sq. km.) | Estimated population at mid-1969 (in millions) | Density of population (per sq. km.) | Annual growth rate of population 1961–67 | GNP 1 (in millions of U.S. $) | Per capita GNP, 1967 (U.S. $) |
|---|---|---|---|---|---|---|---|
| **NORTH AFRICA** | | | | | | | |
| Algeria | 7/ 3/62 | 2.4 | 13.3 | 6 | 2.9 | 2,583 | 250 |
| Libya | 12/24/51 | 1.8 | 1.9 | 1 | 3.7 | 1,030 | 720 |
| Morocco | 3/ 2/65 | 0.5 | 15.0 | 30 | 2.8 | 2,376 | 190 |
| Tunisia | 3/20/56 | 0.2 | 4.8 | 30 | 2.3 | 864 | 210 |
| **MIDDLE AFRICA** | | | | | | | |
| Botswana | 9/30/66 | 0.6 | 0.6 | 1 | 3.0 | 33 | 90 |
| Burundi | 7/ 1/62 | 0.03 | 3.5 | 11.7 | 2.0 | 151 | 50 |
| Cameroon | 1/ 1/60 | 0.5 | 5.7 | 11 | 2.2 | 585 | 130 |
| Central African Republic | 8/13/60 | 0.5 | 1.5 | 3 | 2.8 | 154 | 120 |
| Chad | 8/11/60 | 1.3 | 3.5 | 3 | 1.5 | 211 | 70 |
| Congo (Brazzaville) | 8/13/60 | 0.3 | 0.9 | 3 | 1.4 | 144 | 190 |
| Congo (Kinshasa) | 6/30/60 | 2.3 | 17.1 | 7 | 2.2 | 934 | 90 |
| Dahomey | 8/ 1/60 | 0.1 | 2.7 | 25 | 2.9 | 175 | 80 |
| Equatorial Guinea | 10/12/68 | 0.03 | 0.3 | 10 | 1.8 | 66 | 240 |
| Ethiopia | Time Immemorial | 1.2 | 24.4 | 20 | 1.8 | 1,282 | 60 |
| Gabon | 8/17/60 | 0.3 | 0.5 | 2 | 0.9 | 178 | 410 |
| Gambia | 2/18/65 | 0.01 | 0.4 | 40 | 2.1 | 29 | 90 |
| Ghana | 3/ 6/57 | 0.2 | 8.6 | 43 | 2.6 | 1,795 | 200 |
| Guinea | 10/ 2/58 | 0.2 | 3.9 | 20 | 2.5 | 276 | 90 |
| Ivory Coast | 8/ 7/60 | 0.3 | 4.2 | 14 | 2.3 | 913 | 230 |
| Kenya | 12/12/63 | 0.6 | 10.6 | 18 | 3.0 | 861 | 120 |
| Lesotho | 10/ 4/66 | 0.03 | 0.9 | 30 | 2.9 | 47 | 60 |
| Liberia | 1847 | 0.1 | 1.2 | 12 | 1.9 | 236 | 190 |
| Malagasy Republic | 6/25/60 | 0.6 | 6.7 | 11 | 2.4 | 551 | 100 |
| Malawi | 7/ 6/64 | 0.1 | 4.3 | 36 | 2.5 | 216 | 60 |
| Mali | 8/22/60 | 1.2 | 4.9 | 4 | 1.9 | 280 | 80 |
| Mauretania | 11/28/60 | 1.0 | 1.1 | 1 | 2.0 | 133 | 130 |
| Mauritius | 3/12/68 | 0.002 | 0.8 | 400 | 2.5 | 155 | 220 |
| Niger | 8/ 3/60 | 1.3 | 3.7 | 3 | 2.7 | 232 | 70 |
| Nigeria | 10/ 1/60 | 0.9 | 53.7 | 60 | 2.7 | 4,684 | 80 |
| Rwanda | 7/ 1/62 | 0.03 | 3.5 | 117 | 3.1 | 121 | 60 |
| Senegal | 4/20/60 | 0.2 | 3.9 | 20 | 2.5 | 730 | 190 |
| Sierra Leone | 4/27/61 | 0.1 | 2.5 | 25 | 1.5 | 334 | 140 |
| Somalia | 7/ 1/60 | 0.6 | 2.8 | 5 | 3.4 | 124 | 50 |
| Sudan | 1/ 1/56 | 2.5 | 15.2 | 6 | 2.8 | 1,311 | 90 |
| Swaziland | 9/ 6/68 | 0.02 | 0.4 | 24 | 2.9 | 102 | 280 |
| Tanzania (excluding Zanzibar) | 12/ 9/61 | 0.9 | 12.9 | 14 | 2.9 | 843 | 80 |
| Togo | 4/27/60 | 0.05 | 1.8 | 36 | 2.4 | 159 | 100 |
| Uganda | 10/ 9/62 | 0.2 | 8.3 | 35 | 2.5 | 744 | 100 |
| Upper Volta | 8/ 5/60 | 0.3 | 5.3 | 18 | 2.0 | 258 | 50 |
| Zambia | 10/24/64 | 0.8 | 4.2 | 5 | 3.1 | 678 | 180 |
| **SOUTH AFRICA** | | | | | | | |
| South Africa | 1910 | 1.2 | 19.6 | 16 | 2.4 | 10,7013 | 5903 |

1 GNP at factor cost (1964 U.S. dollars)—latest available year.
2 Latest year available for each country.
3 South Africa GNP, GNP per capita and growth rate includes South West Africa.
— Not available.

310

| | | Industrial Origin of GDP [2] | | | | | | | | |
|---|---|---|---|---|---|---|---|---|---|---|
| Annual growth rate of GNP 1961–67 | Annual growth rate of per capita GNP 1961–67 | Agriculture | Mining | Manufacturing | Construction | Electricity, gas, and water | Transport and communication | Trade and finance | Public Administration and defense | Other branches |
| −1.4 | −3.5 | 16.8 | 17.5 | 7.5 | 3.9 | 1.8 | 3.1 | 21.8 | 19.0 | 8.6 |
| 25.9 | 21.4 | 3.9 | 54.3 | 2.4 | 7.5 | 0.2 | 4.5 | 7.6 | 11.1 | 8.5 |
| 3.1 | 0.3 | 27.9 | 5.1 | 12.5 | 5.2 | 2.6 | — | 18.8 | 11.2 | 16.7 |
| 3.7 | 1.4 | 16.2 | 4.0 | 15.4 | 9.1 | 2.0 | 10.0 | 13.3 | 17.0 | 13.0 |
| | | | | | | | | | | |
| 3.7 | 0.7 | 46.9 | 0.1 | 7.5 | 5.4 | 0.8 | 7.8 | 13.0 | 4.1 | 14.4 |
| 1.9 | −0.1 | 60.0 | 7.0 | — | — | — | — | — | — | — |
| 2.8 | 0.6 | 37.3 | — | 11.4 | 3.7 | 1.0 | 7.6 | 22.0 | 13.4 | 3.6 |
| | | | | | | | | | | |
| 1.5 | −1.0 | 49.0 | — | 12.0 | — | — | — | — | — | — |
| 0.9 | −0.6 | 54.1 | — | 4.0 | 4.1 | — | 1.1 | 19.9 | 13.6 | 3.2 |
| 3.2 | 1.7 | 23.4 | — | 17.0 | — | — | 34.2 | — | 25.4 | — |
| 1.6 | −0.5 | 21.5 | 6.4 | 15.9 | 2.6 | 0.9 | 6.4 | 16.1 | 18.1 | 12.0 |
| 3.1 | 0.2 | 45.9 | — | 2.8 | 5.5 | 0.6 | 6.9 | 18.8 | 15.0 | 4.5 |
| 6.6 | 4.7 | — | — | — | — | — | — | — | — | — |
| | | | | | | | | | | |
| 4.7 | 2.7 | 63.8 | 0.3 | 6.9 | 3.0 | 0.4 | 3.4 | 8.4 | 4.9 | 8.9 |
| 4.3 | 3.5 | 22.9 | 18.1 | 5.9 | 8.8 | — | 9.7 | 10.0 | — | 24.6 |
| 4.3 | 2.3 | — | — | — | — | — | — | — | — | — |
| 2.6 | −0.1 | 51.4 | 2.5 | 19.2 | 4.4 | — | — | — | 7.4 | 15.1 |
| 5.3 | 2.5 | 53.8 | 8.9 | 2.6 | 1.0 | 1.0 | 3.0 | 4.8 | 12.6 | 12.3 |
| 8.4 | 5.4 | 33.7 | 0.5 | 9.4 | 5.5 | 3.7 | 8.5 | 22.6 | 10.5 | 5.6 |
| 4.0 | 1.1 | 35.7 | 0.4 | 11.1 | 4.4 | 2.0 | 8.4 | 14.7 | 12.3 | 11.0 |
| 4.1 | 1.2 | 65.3 | 1.6 | 0.8 | 1.9 | 0.6 | 1.0 | 4.7 | 9.9 | 14.2 |
| 3.2 | 1.5 | 25.4 | 29.4 | 5.1 | 5.1 | — | 6.0 | 11.4 | 9.0 | 9.6 |
| 1.9 | −0.5 | 31.7 | — | 10.9 | — | — | 10.3 | 18.4 | 20.1 | 8.6 |
| 5.7 | 3.2 | 46.7 | — | 4.6 | 5.3 | 1.1 | 6.0 | 15.7 | 4.9 | 13.1 |
| 2.8 | 0.7 | 54.0 | — | 6.0 | 5.0 | 1.0 | 5.0 | 15.0 | 11.0 | 3.0 |
| 8.9 | 6.9 | 37.7 | 27.2 | 1.0 | 2.0 | — | 2.0 | 13.5 | 11.5 | 5.1 |
| 0.5 | −2.0 | 24.0 | 0.1 | 15.2 | 6.6 | 2.8 | 12.5 | 12.6 | 5.7 | 20.5 |
| 3.1 | 0.1 | 62.0 | — | — | — | — | — | — | 7.0 | — |
| 3.5 | 1.1 | 55.7 | 3.0 | 7.4 | 4.9 | — | 6.0 | 12.2 | 8.5 | 2.3 |
| 4.9 | 1.7 | 69.0 | 2.0 | 14.0 | — | — | — | — | 7.0 | — |
| 2.3 | −0.1 | 33.1 | 2.5 | 14.0 | 2.7 | — | 4.5 | 34.4 | 17.5 | 7.6 |
| 2.6 | 1.3 | 31.4 | 19.2 | 6.3 | 3.6 | 0.8 | 7.7 | 15.0 | 5.2 | 10.8 |
| 2.4 | −1.6 | — | — | — | — | — | — | — | — | — |
| 3.1 | 0.2 | 54.3 | 0.1 | 5.6 | 5.8 | 0.5 | — | 15.1 | 10.3 | 8.3 |
| 18.7 | 15.4 | 36.0 | 14.0 | 1.0 | — | — | — | 14.0 | — | 35.0 |
| | | | | | | | | | | |
| 4.4 | 1.9 | 53.5 | 2.6 | 5.0 | 3.1 | 0.9 | 4.5 | 14.1 | 7.0 | 9.3 |
| 3.1 | 0.5 | 44.9 | 9.2 | 4.5 | 3.3 | 2.2 | 6.0 | 18.3 | 7.1 | 4.5 |
| 3.7 | 1.2 | 58.5 | 2.3 | 7.8 | 1.9 | 1.6 | 3.0 | 10.5 | 4.1 | 10.3 |
| 1.6 | −0.6 | 58.0 | — | 2.0 | — | — | — | — | — | 40.0 |
| 4.6 | 1.6 | 9.5 | 37.2 | 7.9 | 10.0 | 1.1 | 5.0 | 13.1 | 5.9 | 10.3 |
| | | | | | | | | | | |
| 6.3[3] | 3.9[3] | 10.2 | 12.2 | 22.4 | 3.3 | 2.5 | 9.5 | 17.6 | 9.4 | 12.9 |

SOURCES: Population Reference Bureau, April, 1960.
United Nations Demographic Yearbook, 1967.
IBRD World Tables, December, 1968.
United Nations Yearbook of National Accounts Statistics, 1968, Volume II.
Statesman's Yearbook, 1969–70.
World Bank Atlas, 1969.

## TABLE 2

U.S. DIRECT INVESTMENTS BY AREA, 1929–68
(in millions of dollars)

| Year end | Total | Canada | Other Western Hemisphere | Europe | Africa | Asia | Other |
|---|---|---|---|---|---|---|---|
| 1929 | 7,700 | 2,000 | 3,600 | 1,400 | n.a. | n.a. | 700 [1] |
| 1940 | 7,300 | 2,100 | 2,600 | 1,900 | n.a. | n.a. | 700 [1] |
| 1945 | 8,400 | 2,500 | 3,100 | 2,000 | n.a. | n.a. | 800 [1] |
| 1950 | 11,788 | 3,579 | 4,735 | 1,720 | n.a. | n.a. | 1,753 [2] |
| 1956 | 22,177 | 7,460 | 7,373 | 3,520 [3] | 659 | 1,106 [4] | 2,059 [5] |
| 1960 | 32,778 | 11,198 | 9,271 | 6,681 | 925 | 2,291 | 2,412 |
| 1961 | 34,667 | 11,602 | 9,190 | 7,742 | 1,064 | 2,477 | 2,593 |
| 1962 | 37,226 | 12,133 | 9,474 | 8,930 | 1,271 | 2,500 | 2,918 |
| 1963 | 40,686 | 13,044 | 9,891 | 10,340 | 1,426 | 2,793 | 3,193 |
| 1964 | 44,386 | 13,796 | 10,205 | 12,109 | 1,685 | 3,112 | 3,478 |
| 1965 | 49,328 | 15,223 | 10,836 | 13,985 | 1,918 | 3,569 | 3,797 |
| 1966 | 54,711 | 16,999 | 11,448 | 16,209 | 2,074 | 3,896 | 4,085 |
| 1967 | 59,486 | 18,097 | 12,044 | 17,926 | 2,273 | 4,289 | 4,856 |
| 1968 [6] | 64,756 | 19,488 | 12,989 | 19,386 | 2,673 | 4,693 | 5,526 |

[1] Including undistributed.
[2] Including Western European dependencies.
[3] Western Europe only.
[4] Middle East only.
[5] Including the Far East.
[6] Preliminary figures.

n.a. Not available.

SOURCES: U.S. Department of Commerce, *Survey of Current Business*, issues of 1929; 1940; 1945; November, 1949; 1936; December, 1950; 1952; and November, 1954. Figures for 1956–65 were obtained from either the August or September issues; figures for 1966–68 were obtained from the October issues.

## TABLE 3

### U.S. DIRECT INVESTMENTS IN AFRICA, BY COUNTRY
(in millions of U.S. dollars)

| Country | 1929 | 1943 | 1950 | 1959 | 1960 | 1961 | 1962 | 1963 | 1964 | 1965 | 1966 | 1967 | 1968[p] |
|---|---|---|---|---|---|---|---|---|---|---|---|---|---|
| **NORTH AFRICA** | | | | | | | | | | | | | |
| Libya | — | — | — | — | — | — | — | — | 402 | 428 | 389 | 451 | 678 |
| **MIDDLE AFRICA** | | | | | | | | | | | | | |
| Congo (Kinshasa) | + | 4 | 8 | 17 | * | * | * | * | * | * | * | * | * |
| East Africa | — | 4 | 12 | 43 | 46 | 56 | * | * | * | * | * | * | * |
| Ethiopia | * | * | 5 | 1 | * | * | * | * | * | * | * | * | * |
| French Equatorial Africa | — | — | 4 | 8 | * | * | * | * | * | * | * | * | * |
| French West Africa | 1 | 3 | 11 | 76 | * | * | * | * | * | * | * | * | * |
| Ghana | — | — | — | 9 | * | * | * | * | * | * | * | * | * |
| Liberia | 5 | 18 | 16 | 115 | 139 | 160 | 184 | 197 | 189 | 204 | 207 | 174 | 174 |
| Nigeria | — | 5 | 11 | 16 | * | * | * | * | * | * | * | * | * |
| Rhodesia and Nyasaland | — | 18 | 26 | 72 | 82 | 85 | 83 | no longer exists → | | | | | |
| Other Countries | 19 | 27 | 54 | 163 | 372 | 454 | 647 | 818 | 628 | 758 | 878 | 982 | 1,130 |
| Total | 25 | 79 | 147 | 520 | 639 | 755 | 914 | 1,015 | 817 | 962 | 1,085 | 1,156 | 1,304 |
| **SOUTH AFRICA** | 77 | 50 | 140 | 323 | 286 | 309 | 357 | 411 | 467 | 529 | 600 | 666 | 692 |
| Total | 102 | 129 | 287 | 843 | 925 | 1,064 | 1,271 | 1,426 | 1,685 | 1,918 | 2,074 | 2,273 | 2,673 |

+ Less than $500,000.
* Not separately shown.
ᵖ Preliminary figures.

Note: Totals may not agree owing to rounding.

SOURCES: Department of Commerce, U.S. Business Investment in Foreign Countries, 1960, p. 92. Survey of Current Business, August issues of 1962–64, September issues of 1965–67, and October issues of 1968 and 1969.

# TABLE 4

U.S. FOREIGN DIRECT INVESTMENT [1] AND EARNINGS, [2]
BY SECTOR AND PERCENTAGE OF EARNINGS ON TOTAL INVESTMENT, 1958–68

(in millions of U.S. dollars)

| Year | Total | | | Mining and Smelting | | |
|------|-------------|----------|----------------------------------------|-------------|----------|----------------------------------------|
|      | Invest- ment | Earn- ings | Per cent of earnings to in- vestment | Invest- ment | Earn- ings | Per cent of earnings to in- vestment |
| ALL COUNTRIES | | | | | | |
| 1958 | 27,075 | 2,954 | 10.9 | 2,856 | 219 | 7.7 |
| 1959 | 29,735 | 3,255 | 10.9 | 2,858 | 315 | 11.0 |
| 1960 | 31,865 | 3,566 | 11.2 | 2,997 | 394 | 13.1 |
| 1961 | 34,717 | 3,815 | 11.0 | 3,094 | 362 | 11.7 |
| 1962 | 37,276 | 4,235 | 11.4 | 3,244 | 372 | 11.5 |
| 1963 | 40,736 | 4,587 | 11.3 | 3,419 | 388 | 11.3 |
| 1964 | 44,480 | 5,071 | 11.4 | 3,665 | 512 | 14.0 |
| 1965 | 49,474 | 5,460 | 11.0 | 3,931 | 571 | 14.5 |
| 1966 | 54,777 | 5,702 | 10.4 | 4,365 | 659 | 15.1 |
| 1967 | 59,486 | 6,034 | 10.1 | 4,876 | 746 | 15.3 |
| 1968 p | 64,756 | 7,010 | 10.8 | 5,370 | 789 | 14.7 |
| AFRICAN COUNTRIES | | | | | | |
| 1958 | 789 | 69 | 8.8 | 234 | 37 | 15.8 |
| 1959 | 843 | 56 | 6.6 | 255 | 38 | 14.9 |
| 1960 | 925 | 33 | 3.6 | 247 | 61 | 24.7 |
| 1961 | 1,017 | 28 | 2.8 | 285 | 44 | 15.4 |
| 1962 | 1,246 | 80 | 6.4 | 307 | 34 | 11.1 |
| 1963 | 1,426 | 170 | 11.9 | 349 | 31 | 8.9 |
| 1964 | 1,685 | 346 | 20.5 | 358 | 38 | 10.6 |
| 1965 | 1,918 | 376 | 19.6 | 354 | 61 | 17.2 |
| 1966 | 2,074 | 417 | 20.1 | 368 | 78 | 21.2 |
| 1967 | 2,273 | 421 | 18.5 | 400 | 74 | 18.5 |
| 1968 p | 2,673 | 671 | 25.1 | 387 | 69 | 17.8 |

| | Petroleum | | | Manufacturing | | | Other | | |
|---|---|---|---|---|---|---|---|---|---|
| | Invest-ment | Earn-ings | Per cent of earnings to in-vestment | Invest-ment | Earn-ings | Per cent of earnings to in-vestment | Invest-ment | Earn-ings | Per cent of earnings to in-vestment |
| **ALL COUNTRIES** | | | | | | | | | |
| | 9,681 | 1,307 | 13.5 | 8,485 | 873 | 10.3 | 6,053 | 555 | 9.2 |
| | 10,423 | 1,185 | 11.4 | 9,692 | 1,129 | 11.6 | 6,762 | 626 | 9.3 |
| | 10,810 | 1,302 | 12.0 | 11,051 | 1,176 | 10.6 | 7,007 | 694 | 9.9 |
| | 12,190 | 1,476 | 12.1 | 11,997 | 1,203 | 10.0 | 7,436 | 774 | 10.4 |
| | 12,725 | 1,695 | 13.3 | 13,250 | 1,307 | 9.9 | 8,057 | 861 | 10.7 |
| | 13,652 | 1,824 | 13.4 | 14,937 | 1,541 | 10.3 | 8,728 | 834 | 9.6 |
| | 14,328 | 1,808 | 12.6 | 16,935 | 1,852 | 10.9 | 9,552 | 899 | 9.4 |
| | 15,298 | 1,830 | 12.0 | 19,339 | 2,022 | 10.5 | 10,906 | 1,037 | 9.5 |
| | 16,200 | 1,868 | 11.5 | 22,078 | 2,104 | 9.5 | 12,134 | 1,071 | 8.8 |
| | 17,404 | 2,120 | 12.2 | 24,167 | 2,055 | 8.5 | 13,039 | 1,112 | 8.5 |
| | 18,835 | 2,466 | 13.1 | 26,354 | 2,514 | 9.5 | 14,196 | 1,242 | 8.7 |
| **AFRICAN COUNTRIES** | | | | | | | | | |
| | 276 | —19 | — 6.9 | 139 | 23 | 16.6 | 140 | 28 | 20.0 |
| | 338 | —27 | — 8.0 | 120 | 17 | 14.2 | 130 | 28 | 21.5 |
| | 407 | —77 | —18.9 | 118 | 19 | 16.1 | 152 | 30 | 19.7 |
| | 491 | —84 | —17.1 | 113 | 19 | 16.8 | 180 | 50 | 27.8 |
| | 627 | — 6 | — 1.0 | 141 | 32 | 22.7 | 171 | 20 | 11.7 |
| | 702 | 65 | 9.3 | 177 | 43 | 24.3 | 198 | 31 | 15.6 |
| | 883 | 227 | 25.7 | 227 | 43 | 18.9 | 216 | 35 | 16.1 |
| | 1,029 | 240 | 23.3 | 292 | 42 | 14.4 | 234 | 37 | 5.8 |
| | 1,104 | 259 | 23.5 | 333 | 43 | 12.9 | 270 | 34 | 12.6 |
| | 1,219 | 268 | 22.0 | 370 | 46 | 12.4 | 285 | 31 | 10.9 |
| | 1,567 | 501 | 32.0 | 400 | 42 | 10.5 | 319 | 58 | 18.2 |

1 Position at the end of period.
2 Per year. Earnings is the sum of the U.S. share in the net earnings.
p Preliminary figures.
Note: Detail may not add to total due to rounding.

SOURCE: U.S. Department of Commerce, *Survey of Current Business,* (For specific issues, see Table 8.) Data for "All Countries" 1960–1968, October, 1969. Earnings percentage calculated from U.S. Department of Commerce data.

## TABLE 5

### FOREIGN DIRECT INVESTMENT IN SOUTH AFRICA, OFFICIAL AND PRIVATE SECTORS
(in millions of rands)

| Country | Grand Total | | | | Official Sector | | | | Private Sector | | | |
|---|---|---|---|---|---|---|---|---|---|---|---|---|
| | 1965 | 1966 | 1967 | 1968 | 1965 | 1966 | 1967 | 1968 | 1966 | 1967 | 1968 | 1969 |
| *STERLING AREA* | 1,595 | 1,765 | 1,864 | 2,144 | 133 | 164 | 166 | 191 | 1,463 | 1,601 | 1,698 | 1,953 |
| Great Britain | 1,484 | 1,636 | — | — | 119 | 140 | — | — | 1,365 | 1,495 | — | — |
| Other | 111 | 129 | — | — | 14 | 24 | — | — | 98 | 106 | — | — |
| *DOLLAR AREA* | 368 | 438 | 445 | 529 | 9 | 7 | 8 | 6 | 358 | 431 | 437 | 523 |
| United States | 306 | 363 | — | — | 9 | 6 | — | — | 297 | 356 | — | — |
| International Organizations | — | — | — | — | — | — | — | — | — | — | — | — |
| Other | 62 | 75 | — | — | — | 1 | — | — | 61 | 75 | — | — |
| *WESTERN EUROPE* | 276 | 332 | 362 | 394 | 18 | 28 | 31 | 14 | 260 | 306 | 331 | 380 |
| Germany (Fed. Rep.) | — | 70 | — | — | — | 3 | — | — | — | 68 | — | — |
| Belgium and Luxembourg | 16 | 15 | — | — | 2 | 1 | — | — | 14 | 14 | — | — |
| France | 86 | 96 | — | — | 3 | 3 | — | — | 84 | 93 | — | — |
| Switzerland | 72 | 82 | — | — | 5 | 4 | — | — | 67 | 78 | — | — |
| Other | 102 | 69 | — | — | 8 | 17 | — | — | 95 | 53 | — | — |
| *OTHER AREAS* | 16 | 14 | 17 | 28 | 6 | 2 | 2 | 13 | 10 | 11 | 15 | 15 |
| Total | 2,255 | 2,549 | 2,688 | 3,095 | 166 | 201 | 207 | 224 | 2,091 | 2,349 | 2,481 | 2,871 |

SOURCE: *Quarterly Bulletin of South African Reserve Bank*, September, 1967, March, December, 1968, December, 1969.

## TABLE 6

FOREIGN AND INTERNATIONAL BONDS ISSUED BY AFRICAN COUNTRIES

| Issuing Country | Year | Market | Amount | Total All Markets |
|---|---|---|---|---|
| Algeria | 1966 | United States | 15.0 | 15.0 |
| East African Community | 1968 | United Kingdom | 16.8 | 16.8 |
| Gabon | 1962 | France | 2.0 | 2.0 |
| | 1963 | United States | 3.8 | 3.8 |
| | 1964 | France | 2.0 | 2.0 |
| | 1966 | France | 2.4 | 2.4 |
| | Total | | | 10.2 |
| Ivory Coast | 1961 | France | 8.1 | 8.1 |
| | 1963 | France | 6.3 | 6.3 |
| | 1965 | France | 6.1 | 6.1 |
| | 1968 | France | 6.1 | 16.1 |
| | 1968 | Eurobond Market | 10.0 | |
| | Total | | | 36.6 |
| Liberia | 1965 | United States | 6.0 | 6.0 |
| Malagasy Republic | 1968 | France | 4.1 | 4.1 |
| Senegal | 1968 | France | 6.1 | 6.1 |
| South Africa | 1962 | Switzerland | 11.6 | 11.6 |
| | 1965 | Others | 12.5 | 12.5 |
| | 1966 | Eurobond Market | 25.0 | 25.0 |
| | 1967 | Eurobond Market | 62.5 | 62.5 |
| | 1968 | Switzerland | 13.8 | 68.8 |
| | 1968 | Eurobond Market | 55.0 | |
| | 1969 | Eurobond Market | 25.0 | 25.0 |
| Total | | | | 205.4 |

TABLE 7

## UNITED STATES AID COMMITMENTS IN AFRICA

| Country | Total Fiscal Year 1967 | Appropriation Category Development Loans | Supporting Assistance | Technical Cooperation Grants | Total Fiscal Year 1968 |
|---|---|---|---|---|---|
| **NORTH AFRICA** | | | | | |
| Algeria | 94 | — | — | 94 | — |
| Morocco | 3,939 | 2,900 | — | 1,039 | 14,933 |
| Tunisia | 25,634 | 23,225 | — | 2,409 | 13,007 |
| *Total* | 29,667 | 26,125 | — | 3,542 | 27,940 |
| **MIDDLE AFRICA** | | | | | |
| Botswana | 34 | — | — | 34 | 65 |
| Burundi | 197 | — | — | 197 | 36 |
| Cameroon | 1,000 | — | — | 1,000 | 359 |
| Central Africa | 413 | — | — | 413 | 223 |
| Chad | 538 | — | — | 538 | 559 |
| Congo (Kinshasa) | 20,301 | 2,500 | 17,200 | 601 | 16,065 |
| Dahomey | 1,169 | 850 | — | 319 | 345 |
| Ethiopia | 13,638 | 5,800 | — | 7,838 | 6,850 |
| Gabon | 406 | — | — | 406 | 325 |
| Gambia | 201 | — | — | 201 | 36 |
| Ghana | 24,059 | 22,000 | — | 2,059 | 16,846 |
| Guinea | 1,081 | — | — | 1,081 | 1,084 |
| Ivory Coast | 845 | — | 275 | 570 | 159 |
| Kenya | 2,801 | 350 | — | 2,451 | 2,624 |
| Lesotho | 143 | — | — | 143 | 50 |
| Liberia | 7,379 | 1,890 | — | 5,489 | 5,638 |
| Malagasy Republic | 2,322 | 2,000 | — | 322 | 296 |
| Malawi | 1,493 | — | — | 1,493 | 8,137 |
| Mali | 628 | — | — | 628 | 1,105 |
| Mauretania | 50 | — | — | 50 | — |
| Mauritius | — | — | — | — | 50 |
| Niger | 822 | — | — | 822 | 1,055 |
| Nigeria | 21,562 | 6,000 | — | 15,562 | 21,334 |
| Rwanda | 448 | — | 106 | 342 | 100 |
| Senegal | 318 | — | — | 318 | 322 |
| Sierra Leone | 1,469 | — | — | 1,469 | 1,104 |
| Somali | 15,470 | 13,220 | — | 2,250 | 3,708 |
| Sudan | 10,677 | 3,900 | — | 3,077 | 337 |
| Swaziland | — | — | — | — | — |
| Tanzania | 3,138 | 900 | — | 2,238 | 2,508 |
| Togo | 423 | — | — | 423 | 147 |
| Uganda | 6,792 | 4,950 | — | 1,842 | 2,050 |
| Upper Volta | 422 | — | — | 422 | 348 |
| Zambia | 964 | — | — | 964 | 1,214 |
| Cent. W. A. Reg. | — | — | — | — | — |
| East Afr. Reg. | 2,467 | 125 | — | 2,342 | 3,251 |
| Africa Regional | 29,641 | 7,200 | 1,100 | 21,341 | 30,447 |
| *Total* | 173,308 | 71,685 | 18,681 | 79,142 | 128,777 |
| Total | 202,975 | 97,810 | 18,681 | 82,684 | 156,717 |

| Appropriation Category | | | | Appropriation Category | | | |
| Development Loans | Supporting Assistance | Technical Cooperation Grants | Total Fiscal Year 1969 | Development Loans | Supporting Assistance | Technical Cooperation Grants | Contingency Fund 1967–1969 |
|---|---|---|---|---|---|---|---|
| — | — | — | — | — | — | — | — |
| 13,000 | — | 1,933 | 9,524 | 8,000 | 156 | 1,368 | — |
| 10,265 | — | 2,742 | 9,052 | 6,719 | 223 | 2,110 | — |
| 23,265 | — | 4,675 | 18,576 | 14,719 | 379 | 3,478 | — |
| | | | | | | | |
| — | — | 65 | 65 | — | — | 65 | — |
| — | — | 36 | 14 | — | — | 14 | — |
| — | — | 359 | 87 | — | — | 87 | — |
| — | — | 223 | 76 | — | — | 76 | — |
| — | — | 559 | 46 | — | — | 46 | — |
| — | 15,325 | 740 | 4,257 | — | 3,000 | 1,257 | — |
| — | — | 345 | 157 | — | — | 157 | — |
| 1,000 | 300 | 5,550 | 17,218 | 13,000 | — | 4,218 | — |
| — | — | 325 | — | — | — | — | — |
| — | — | 36 | 23 | — | — | 23 | — |
| 15,000 | — | 1,846 | 4,469 | 2,738 | 119 | 1,612 | — |
| — | — | 1,084 | 757 | — | — | 757 | — |
| — | — | 159 | 65 | — | — | 65 | — |
| — | — | 2,624 | 2,260 | — | 133 | 2,127 | — |
| — | — | 50 | 74 | — | — | 74 | 100 |
| 525 | — | 5,113 | 10,623 | 5,625 | 279 | 4,719 | — |
| — | — | 296 | 454 | 300 | — | 154 | — |
| 7,000 | — | 1,137 | 1,237 | — | — | 1,237 | — |
| 855 | — | 250 | 89 | — | — | 89 | — |
| — | — | — | — | — | — | — | — |
| — | — | 50 | 50 | — | — | 50 | — |
| 900 | — | 155 | 98 | — | — | 98 | — |
| 9,700 | — | 11,634 | 43,603 | 7,200 | 24,441 | 10,062 | 1,900 |
| — | — | 100 | 69 | — | — | 69 | — |
| — | — | 322 | 260 | — | — | 260 | — |
| — | — | 1,104 | 203 | — | — | 203 | — |
| — | — | 3,708 | 2,570 | — | — | 2,570 | — |
| — | — | 337 | 151 | 151 | — | — | 3,700 |
| — | — | — | 50 | — | — | 50 | — |
| — | — | 2,508 | 1,314 | — | — | 1,314 | — |
| — | — | 147 | 204 | — | — | 204 | — |
| — | — | 2,050 | 5,173 | 3,200 | 73 | 1,900 | — |
| — | — | 348 | 90 | — | — | 90 | — |
| — | — | — | 8,037 | — | 36 | 8,001 | — |
| 600 | — | 2,651 | 4,504 | 350 | — | 4,000 | — |
| 13,000 | 1,000 | 16,247 | 25,935 | 17,500 | 1,121 | 8,315 | 200 |
| — | — | 1,214 | — | — | — | — | — |
| 48,580 | 16,625 | 63,372 | 135,284 | 50,064 | 29,203 | 54,117 | 5,900 |
| 71,845 | 16,625 | 68,047 | 153,860 | 64,783 | 29,582 | 57,595 | 5,900 |

SOURCE: U.S. *Annual Report to the Congress on the Foreign Assistance Program*, 1967, 1968, and 1969.

## TABLE 8

### BRITISH FINANCIAL AID TO AFRICA, BILATERAL DISBURSEMENTS (GROSS), BY COUNTRY
#### (in £ thousand)

| Country | 1945-1960 Grants | Loans | Total | 1960-1965 Grants | Loans | Total | 1966 Grants | Loans | Total | 1967 Grants | Loans | Total |
|---|---|---|---|---|---|---|---|---|---|---|---|---|
| **NORTH AFRICA** | | | | | | | | | | | | |
| Libya | — | — | — | — | — | — | + | — | + | 9 | — | 9 |
| Morocco | — | — | — | — | — | — | 2 | — | 2 | 8 | — | 8 |
| Tunisia | — | — | — | — | — | — | 23 | — | 23 | 3 | — | 3 |
| *Total* | — | — | — | — | — | — | 25 | — | 25 | 20 | — | 20 |
| **MIDDLE AFRICA** | | | | | | | | | | | | |
| Botswana | 4,560 | 2,351 | 6,911 | 9,520 | 1,256 | 10,776 | 3,995 | 669 | 4,695 | 4,793 | 769 | 5,562 |
| Burundi | — | — | — | — | — | — | 10 | — | 10 | 9 | — | 9 |
| Cameroon | 1,730 | — | 1,730 | 1,753 | 1,350 | 3,103 | 116 | — | 116 | 130 | — | 130 |
| Central African Republic | — | — | — | — | — | — | — | — | — | 44 | — | 44 |
| Chad | — | — | — | — | — | — | 1 | — | 1 | 13 | — | 13 |
| Congo (Brazzaville) | — | — | — | — | — | — | 8 | — | 8 | 8 | — | 8 |
| Congo (Kinshasa) | — | — | — | 538 | — | 538 | 11 | — | 11 | 33 | — | 33 |
| Dahomey | — | — | — | — | — | — | 14 | + | 14 | 16 | — | 16 |
| East African Common Services Organization | 7,086 | — | 7,086 | 7,997 | 15,297 | 23,294 | — | — | — | — | — | — |
| Ethiopia and Eritrea | — | — | — | — | — | — | 130 | — | 130 | 129 | — | 129 |
| Fed. of Rhodesia and Nyasaland | 1,660 | 4,700 | 6,360 | 1,880 | 15,026 | 16,906 | — | — | — | — | — | — |
| Gabon | — | — | — | — | — | — | — | — | — | 72 | — | 72 |
| Gambia | 1,884 | 1,851 | 3,735 | 3,949 | 98 | 4,047 | 834 | — | 834 | 771 | 27 | 799 |
| Ghana | 5,355 | 325 | 5,680 | 374 | 3,335 | 3,709 | 379 | 100 | 479 | 464 | 30 | 494 |
| Guinea | — | — | — | — | — | — | 6 | — | 6 | + | — | + |
| Ivory Coast | — | — | — | — | — | — | 12 | — | 12 | 16 | — | 16 |
| Kenya | 38,174 | 16,510 | 54,684 | 28,765 | 34,315 | 63,080 | 4,135 | 7,960 | 12,095 | 3,991 | 5,592 | 9,583 |
| Lesotho | 2,140 | — | 2,140 | 8,072 | 410 | 8,482 | 3,802 | 56 | 3,858 | 3,752 | 278 | 4,030 |
| Liberia | — | — | — | — | — | — | 28 | 74 | 102 | 27 | 17 | 44 |
| Malagasy Republic | — | — | — | — | — | — | 5 | — | 5 | 8 | — | 8 |

| | | | | | | | | | | | |
|---|---|---|---|---|---|---|---|---|---|---|---|
| Malawi | 6,330 | 4,319 | 10,649 | 18,539 | 7,030 | 25,569 | 5,782 | 3,162 | 8,943 | 5,535 | 3,061 | 8,596 |
| Mali | — | — | — | 25 | — | 25 | 28 | — | 28 | 2 | — | 2 |
| Mauretania | — | — | — | — | — | — | — | — | — | — | — | — |
| Mauritius | 2,945 | 772 | 3,717 | 4,000 | 2,529 | 6,529 | 313 | 1,150 | 1,463 | 1,006 | 795 | 1,801 |
| Niger | — | — | — | 9 | — | 3 | 3 | — | 3 | 2 | — | 2 |
| Nigeria | 36,147 | 3,958 | 40,105 | 6,807 | 23,076 | 29,883 | 2,442[3] | 3,910 | 6,333 | 2,798 | 3,024 | 5,822 |
| Rhodesia | — | 1,000 | 1,000 | 2,250 | 3,855 | 6,106 | 40 | — | 40 | 73 | — | 73 |
| Rwanda | — | — | — | — | — | — | 3 | — | 3 | 10 | — | 10 |
| Senegal | — | — | — | — | — | — | 9 | — | 9 | 17 | — | 17 |
| Seychelles | 960 | 250 | 1,210 | 1,418 | — | 1,418 | 314 | — | 314 | 664 | 120 | 784 |
| Sierra Leone | 5,376 | 1,500 | 6,876 | 5,507 | 5,805 | 11,312 | 383 | 1,046 | 1,429 | 358 | 702 | 1,060 |
| Somalia [1] | 9,065 | 102 | 9,167 | 5,073 | — | 5,073 | 1 | — | 1 | 1 | — | 1 |
| St. Helena and Tristan de Cunha | — | — | — | — | — | — | — | — | — | — | — | — |
| Sudan | 1,169 | 2,440 | 1,169 | 938 | 2 | 940 | 335 | 6 | 341 | 384 | 4 | 388 |
| Swaziland | 3,680 | 6,067 | 6,120 | 165 | 3,260 | 3,425 | 1,130 | 1,390 | 1,520 | 150 | 490 | 640 |
| Tanzania | 2,782 | 6,067 | 8,849 | 6,001 | 9,043 | 15,044 | 2,559 | 1,277 | 3,836 | 2,904 | 1,522 | 4,426 |
| Tanganyika | 12,169 | 3,119 | 15,288 | 19,255 | 14,936 | 34,191 | 2,719 | 1,645 | 4,365 | 888 | 338 | 1,226 |
| Zanzibar | 1,477 | — | 1,477 | — | — | — | — | — | — | — | — | — |
| Togo | — | — | — | — | — | — | 7 | — | 7 | 11 | — | 11 |
| Uganda | 6,869 | 5,144 | 12,013 | 11,409 | 14,650 | 26,059 | 3,048 | 1,554 | 4,602 | 1,480 | 3,560 | 5,041 |
| Upper Volta | — | — | — | — | — | — | + | — | + | 1 | — | 1 |
| Zambia | 4,006 | 1,118 | 5,124 | 5,565 | 4,752 | 10,317 | 9,144[4] | 613 | 9,757 | 13,572 | 1,190 | 14,761 |
| General—Unallocated | 2,274[2] | — | 2,274 | 635 | — | 635 | 4,323 | 1,576 | 5,899 | 2,733 | 1,899 | 4,652 |
| *Total* | 157,838 | 55,526 | 213,364 | 150,445 | 160,025 | 310,470 | 45,055 | 26,218 | 71,272 | 46,863 | 23,418 | 70,282 |
| Total | | | | | | 310,470 | 45,080 | 26,218 | 71,297 | 46,883 | 23,418 | 70,302 |

[1] Disbursements up to July, 1960, were made to British Somaliland.

[2] Includes grants to Lesotho (Basutoland), Botswana (Bechuanaland) and Swaziland not identifiable by individual recipient.

[3] Includes loans of £14,700 and £36,400 in 1966 and 1967 respectively toward the cost of advances of compensation to officers serving on Nigeria Special list 'B'.

[4] Includes Zambia Contingency Costs amounting to £6.947 millions and £9.930 millions in 1966 and 1967.

Note: Totals may not agree owing to rounding.

SOURCES: 1945–65, United Kingdom, Treasury, *Aid to Developing Countries*, 1963; Ministry of Overseas Development, *Overseas Development: The Work of the New Ministry*, 1965; 1966 and 1967, United Kingdom, Ministry of Overseas Development, *British Aid Statistics: Statistics of Economic Aid to Developing Countries*, 1963/67.

## TABLE 9

### COMMON MARKET AID TO AFRICAN COUNTRIES
### (FONDS EUROPÉEN DE DÉVELOPPEMENT)
### ( in thousands of U/C )

| Country | First FED, as of December 31, 1968 | | | | Second FED, as of December 31, 1968 | | | | Total, 1st and 2nd FEDS | |
|---|---|---|---|---|---|---|---|---|---|---|
| | Commitments under Contract | Balance of Commitments | Total Commitments | Disbursements | Commitments under Contract | Balance of Commitments | Total Commitments | Disbursements | Commitments | Disbursements |
| **NORTH AFRICA** | | | | | | | | | | |
| Algeria | 18,033 | 7,287 | 25,320 | 14,314 | — | — | — | — | 25,320 | 14,314 |
| **SUB-SAHARAN AFRICA** | | | | | | | | | | |
| Burundi | 4,037 | 889 | 4,926 | 3,925 | 5,368 | 9,496 | 14,864 | 2,438 | 19,790 | 6,363 |
| Cameroon | 47,460 | 5,339 | 52,799 | 44,884 | 19,965 | 30,362 | 50,327 | 11,724 | 103,126 | 56,608 |
| Central Afr. Rep. | 14,283 | 3,933 | 18,216 | 13,118 | 8,397 | 14,686 | 23,083 | 6,406 | 41,299 | 19,524 |
| Chad | 27,803 | 121 | 27,924 | 26,164 | 23,247 | 8,489 | 31,736 | 12,254 | 59,660 | 38,418 |
| Comozos | 3,074 | 3 | 3,077 | 3,044 | 388 | 2,459 | 2,847 | 380 | 5,924 | 3,424 |
| Congo (Brazzaville) | 22,547 | 2,077 | 24,624 | 21,892 | 6,048 | 11,878 | 17,926 | 3,951 | 42,550 | 25,843 |
| Congo (Kinshasa) | 18,657 | 949 | 19,606 | 12,715 | 6,206 | 34,619 | 40,825 | 4,235 | 60,431 | 16,950 |
| Dahomey | 18,664 | 2,115 | 20,779 | 16,985 | 13,372 | 7,322 | 20,694 | 7,049 | 41,473 | 24,034 |
| Gabon | 15,608 | 460 | 16,068 | 14,940 | 2,634 | 14,939 | 17,573 | 2,258 | 33,641 | 17,198 |
| Ivory Coast | 34,013 | 5,647 | 39,660 | 31,908 | 30,139 | 18,359 | 48,498 | 23,365 | 88,158 | 55,273 |
| Malagasy Republic | 55,590 | 665 | 56,255 | 53,467 | 34,776 | 49,266 | 84,042 | 19,185 | 140,297 | 72,652 |
| Mali | 41,516 | 408 | 41,924 | 40,805 | 4,766 | 2,637 | 7,403 | 3,574 | 49,327 | 44,379 |
| Mauretania | 33,508 | 10,325 | 43,833 | 32,772 | 10,084 | 7,016 | 17,100 | 6,146 | 60,933 | 38,918 |
| Niger | 29,920 | 1,437 | 31,357 | 25,336 | 6,488 | 16,177 | 22,665 | 4,114 | 59,022 | 29,450 |
| Réunion | 8,646 | 215 | 8,861 | 8,141 | 2,784 | 5,521 | 8,305 | 56 | 17,166 | 8,197 |
| Rwanda | 4,733 | 208 | 4,941 | 4,524 | 5,311 | 8,993 | 14,304 | 3,337 | 19,245 | 7,861 |
| Senegal | 33,508 | 10,325 | 43,833 | 32,772 | 29,935 | 23,513 | 53,448 | 26,872 | 97,281 | 59,644 |
| Somalia | 9,708 | 204 | 9,912 | 7,880 | 8,448 | 16,662 | 25,110 | 3,754 | 35,022 | 11,634 |
| Togo | 15,614 | 321 | 15,935 | 12,650 | 2,936 | 7,731 | 10,667 | 1,452 | 26,602 | 14,102 |
| Upper Volta | 26,125 | 2,170 | 28,295 | 24,847 | 17,000 | 5,509 | 22,509 | 4,109 | 50,804 | 28,956 |
| *Total* | 465,014 | 47,811 | 512,825 | 432,769 | 238,292 | 295,634 | 533,926 | 146,659 | 1,046,751 | 579,428 |
| Total | 483,047 | 55,098 | 538,145 | 446,783 | 238,292 | 295,634 | 533,926 | 146,659 | 1,072,071 | 593,442 |

SOURCE: Fonds Européen de Développement, December, 31, 1968, First and Second FED.

## TABLE 10

WORLD BANK GROUP LOANS AND CREDITS TO AFRICA
CLASSIFIED BY PURPOSE AS OF DECEMBER 31, 1969
(in millions of U.S. dollars,
initial commitments net of cancellations and refundings)

|  | World Bank | IDA |
|---|---|---|
| Electric Power | 505.0 | 10.0 |
| *Transportation (total)* | 774.6 | 223.5 |
| Railroads | 388.0 | 26.6 |
| Roads | 225.0 | 196.9 |
| Ports and waterways | 111.6 | — |
| Pipelines | 50.0 | — |
| Telecommunications | 26.7 | 0.8 |
| *Agriculture, forestry, and fishing (total)* | 186.1 | 81.7 |
| Farm mechanization | 5.0 | — |
| Irrigation and flood control | 81.0 | 13.0 |
| Land clearance, farm improvement, etc. | 18.7 | 26.9 |
| Crop processing and storage | 0.4 | 6.7 |
| Livestock improvement | 5.3 | 7.9 |
| Forestry and fishing | 5.3 | 1.3 |
| Agricultural credits | 42.8 | 20.6 |
| Smallholders/plantations | 27.6 | 5.3 |
| *Industry (total)* | 234.0 | — |
| Iron and steel | — | — |
| Paper and pulp | — | — |
| Fertilizer and other chemicals | 30.0 | — |
| General industries | 20.5 | — |
| Mining | 101.0 | — |
| Development finance companies | 82.5 | — |
| Educational projects | 29.3 | 109.8 |
| Water supply | 20.0 | 4.6 |
| General development | 40.0 | — |
| Project preparation | 0.9 | 3.2 |
| *Total* | 1,816.6 | 433.6 |

*Note:* Multipurpose loans are distributed according to each purpose and not assigned to the major purpose. Details may not add to totals because of rounding.

TABLE 11

WORLD BANK OPERATIONS IN AFRICA, THROUGH DECEMBER 31, 1969
(in millions of U.S. dollars)

| Country | Bank Loans Net Amounts * | Amount I D A Credits * | I F C Commitments |
|---|---|---|---|
| **NORTH AFRICA** | | | |
| Algeria | 80.5 | — | — |
| Morocco | 128.1 | 18.3 | 2.9 |
| Tunisia | 76.8 | 32.4 | 14.0 |
| *Total* | 285.4 | 50.7 | 16.9 |
| **MIDDLE AFRICA** | | | |
| Botswana | — | 3.6 | — |
| Burundi | 4.8 | 2.9 | — |
| Cameroon | 19.9 | 22.1 | — |
| Central African Republic | — | 4.2 | — |
| Chad | — | 5.9 | — |
| Congo (Brazzaville) | 30.0 | 0.6 | — |
| Congo (Kinshasa) | 91.6 | 6.0 | — |
| Dahomey | — | 4.6 | — |
| Ethiopia | 97.8 | 31.9 | 13.5 |
| Gabon | 54.8 | — | — |
| Ghana | 53.0 | 16.3 | — |
| Guinea | 64.5 | — | — |
| Ivory Coast ᵃ | 30.0 | — | 0.2 |
| Kenya ᵇ | 120.7 | 42.6 | 3.1 |
| Lesotho | — | 4.1 | — |
| Liberia | 7.8 | — | 0.3 |
| Malagasy Republic | 11.1 | 14.5 | — |
| Malawi | — | 27.5 | — |
| Mali ᵃ | — | 9.1 | — |
| Mauretania | 66.0 | 9.7 | 20.0 |
| Mauritius | 7.0 | — | — |
| Niger | — | 7.6 | — |
| Nigeria | 216.6 | 35.5 | 2.7 |
| Senegal | 7.5 | 15.0 | 3.5 |
| Sierra Leone | 7.7 | — | — |
| Somalia | — | 9.1 | — |
| Southern Rhodesia ᶜ | 87.0 | — | — |
| Sudan | 134.0 | 21.5 | 0.7 |
| Swaziland | 7.0 | 2.8 | — |
| Tanzania ᵇ | 36.2 | 48.4 | 4.7 |
| Togo | — | 3.7 | — |
| Uganda | 8.4 | 33.0 | 3.5 |
| Upper Volta ᵃ | — | 0.8 | — |
| Zambia | 126.1 | — | — |
| *Total* | 1,289.4 | 383.0 | 51.7 |
| **SOUTH AFRICA** | 241.8 | — | — |
| Total | 1,816.6 | 433.7 | 68.6 |

* Net of cancellations, refundings, and termination.

ᵃ Partially shared with other countries marked ᵃ.   I D A credits not shared.
ᵇ Partially shared with other countries marked ᵇ.   I D A credits not shared.
ᶜ Partially shared with other countries marked ᶜ.   I D A credits not shared.

## TABLE 12

### FLOW OF EXTERNAL RESOURCES FROM INDUSTRIAL MARKET ECONOMIES AND MULTILATERAL AGENCIES [a]
### 1961–68 [h]
(in millions of U.S. dollars)

Bilateral [b]

| Country | Grants [d] | | | | | | Loans | | | | | |
|---|---|---|---|---|---|---|---|---|---|---|---|---|
| | 1961 | 1962 | 1963 | 1965 | 1966 | 1967 | 1961 | 1962 | 1963 | 1965 | 1966 | 1967 |
| **NORTH AFRICA** | | | | | | | | | | | | |
| Algeria | 401 | 353 | 286 | 135 | 114 | 105 | 37 | 43 | 12 | 9 | 7 | 2 |
| Libya | 36 | 30 | 26 | 7 | 3 | 2 | 1 | 1 | — | — | — | −2 |
| Morocco [e] | 88 | 53 | 69 | 72 | 56 | 42 | 29 | 31 | 36 | 33 | 25 | 21 |
| Tunisia [e] | 84 | 60 | 65 | 55 | 43 | 40 | 2 | 4 | 27 | 31 | 22 | 59 |
| Unallocated | — | — | — | — | 1 | — | — | — | — | — | — | — |
| *Total* | 609 | 495 | 446 | 269 | 217 | 189 | 69 | 79 | 75 | 73 | 54 | 80 |
| **SUB-SAHARAN AFRICA** | | | | | | | | | | | | |
| Botswana | — | — | — | 10 | 14 | 15 | — | — | — | — | 2 | 2 |
| Burundi | — | — | — | 3 | 7 | 8 | — | — | — | 1 | — | 1 |
| Congo (Kinshasa) | 60 | 63 | 87 | 131 | 70 | 58 | — | 3 | — | 5 | 20 | 34 |
| Ethiopia | 21 | 25 | 21 | 16 | 21 | 19 | −1 | 1 | 1 | — | 9 | 4 |
| French-franc area [f] | 282 | 313 | 310 | 326 | 336 | 385 | 38 | 26 | 39 | 37 | 44 | 50 |
| Gambia | — | — | — | 4 | 3 | 3 | — | — | — | — | — | — |
| Ghana | 3 | 3 | 4 | 7 | 16 | 17 | — | 3 | 14 | 38 | 61 | 50 |
| Guinea | 1 | 6 | 15 | 21 | 10 | 5 | 1 | 3 | 8 | 2 | 4 | 3 |
| Kenya [g] | 34 | 35 | 32 | 37 | 24 | 24 | 29 | 13 | 22 | 32 | 31 | 9 |
| Lesotho | — | — | — | 9 | 11 | 12 | — | — | — | — | — | 1 |
| Liberia | 5 | 7 | 10 | 11 | 11 | 12 | 22 | 72 | 24 | 23 | 36 | 26 |
| Malawi | — | — | — | 31 | 20 | 19 | — | — | — | 4 | 11 | 10 |
| Mauritius | — | — | — | 2 | 1 | 3 | — | — | — | — | 3 | 2 |
| Nigeria | 7 | 14 | 18 | 30 | 36 | 37 | 24 | 16 | — | 38 | 36 | 33 |
| Portuguese Overseas Provinces [f] | 3 | 3 | 10 | 8 | 9 | 9 | 30 | 38 | 42 | 15 | 15 | 37 |

# TABLE 12 (Cont.)

| Country | 1961 | 1962 | 1963 | 1965 | 1966 | 1967 | 1961 | 1962 | 1963 | 1965 | 1966 | 1967 |
|---|---|---|---|---|---|---|---|---|---|---|---|---|
| Rhodesia | — | — | — | 6 | — | — | — | — | — | —2 | — | 1 |
| Rwanda | — | — | — | 6 | 10 | 11 | — | — | — | 1 | — | 1 |
| Sierra Leone | 10 | 5 | 5 | 5 | 5 | 5 | 4 | 3 | 5 | 12 | 7 | 1 |
| Somalia | 21 | 23 | 22 | 23 | 14 | 9 | — | — | 6 | 2 | — | 2 |
| Sudan | 13 | 10 | 10 | 10 | 3 | 6 | 2 | —3 | 1 | 15 | 7 | 7 |
| Swaziland | — | — | — | 8 | 7 | 8 | — | — | — | 7 | 3 | 1 |
| Tanzania g | 22 | 37 | 20 | 23 | 28 | 18 | 17 | 10 | 10 | 12 | 9 | 13 |
| Uganda g | 10 | 16 | 14 | 12 | 13 | 9 | 11 | 13 | 6 | 7 | 11 | 11 |
| Zambia | — | — | — | 12 | 28 | 40 | — | — | — | 1 | 6 | 28 |
| Unallocated | — | — | — | 5 | 15 | 12 | — | — | — | — | 4 | 5 |
| Total f | 534 | 613 | 613 | 756 | 712 | 744 | 215 | 206 | 208 | 250 | 319 | 331 |
| Total f | 1,143 | 1,109 | 1,059 | 1,025 | 929 | 933 | 284 | 285 | 283 | 323 | 373 | 411 |

## NORTH AFRICA

### Multilateral c

| Country | 1961 | 1962 | 1963 | 1965 | 1966 | 1967 |
|---|---|---|---|---|---|---|
| Algeria | —5 | —4 | —3 | —4 | —5 | —5 |
| Libya | — | 1 | 1 | —1 | —1 | 2 |
| Morocco e | — | 1 | 3 | 10 | 12 | 7 |
| Tunisia e | 1 | — | 3 | 5 | 6 | 5 |
| Unallocated | — | — | — | — | 1 | 1 |
| Total | —4 | —2 | 4 | 10 | 13 | 10 |

### Total

| Country | 1961 | 1962 | 1963 | 1965 | 1966 | 1967 | 1968 h |
|---|---|---|---|---|---|---|---|
| Algeria | 433 | 392 | 276 | 140 | 116 | 102 | 96 |
| Libya | 36 | 32 | 26 | 6 | 2 | 2 | 3 |
| Morocco e | 117 | 85 | 117 | 115 | 93 | 70 | 109 |
| Tunisia e | 87 | 65 | 95 | 91 | 71 | 104 | 76 |
| Unallocated | — | — | — | — | 2 | 1 | 1 |
| Total | 673 | 574 | 514 | 352 | 284 | 279 | 284 |

# SUB-SAHARAN AFRICA

| | | | | | | | | | | | | | |
|---|---|---|---|---|---|---|---|---|---|---|---|---|---|
| Botswana | — | — | — | 1 | 2 | 1 | — | — | — | 11 | 18 | 18 | — |
| Burundi | — | — | — | 1 | 2 | 2 | — | — | — | 5 | 9 | 11 | — |
| Congo (Kinshasa) | 26 | 2 | — | 13 | — | 2 | 87 | 67 | 87 | 149 | 90 | 94 | 72 |
| Ethiopia | 6 | 6 | 4 | 11 | 10 | 7 | 26 | 20 | 26 | 27 | 40 | 30 | 46 |
| French-franc area [f] | 45 | 92 | 74 | 105 | 105 | 98 | 367 | 444 | 448 | 468 | 485 | 533 | 543 |
| Gambia | — | — | — | 16 | 4 | — | — | — | — | 4 | 3 | 3 | — |
| Ghana | — | -1 | — | 1 | 1 | 2 | 2 | 6 | 27 | 61 | 81 | 67 | 67 |
| Guinea | — | 1 | — | 1 | 1 | — | 2 | 10 | 23 | 24 | 15 | 10 | — |
| Kenya [g] | 2 | 2 | 2 | 2 | 10 | 2 | 65 | 51 | 56 | 71 | 65 | 52 | 57 |
| Lesotho | — | — | — | — | 1 | 19 | — | — | — | 9 | 12 | 14 | — |
| Liberia | — | — | — | 2 | 1 | 1 | 27 | 79 | 34 | 36 | 48 | 40 | 18 |
| Malawi | — | — | — | -1 | 1 | 2 | 8 | 12 | 17 | 34 | 32 | 30 | 25 |
| Mauritius | — | — | 3 | 2 | 1 | 1 | — | — | — | 4 | 5 | 5 | — |
| Nigeria | 2 | 1 | -3 | 27 | 21 | 43 | 33 | 30 | 16 | 95 | 93 | 113 | 95 |
| Portuguese Overseas Provinces [f] | — | — | — | -1 | -2 | -4 | 33 | 41 | 52 | 23 | 24 | 46 | 39 |
| Rhodesia | — | — | — | 1 | 2 | 2 | — | — | — | 3 | -2 | -4 | — |
| Rwanda | — | — | — | 2 | 1 | 1 | 14 | 8 | 10 | 8 | 12 | 14 | — |
| Sierra Leone | 3 | 1 | 3 | 4 | 4 | 4 | 24 | 24 | 31 | 19 | 13 | 7 | — |
| Somalia | 10 | 14 | 8 | 5 | 7 | 6 | 25 | 21 | 19 | 29 | 18 | 15 | 28 |
| Sudan | — | — | — | 1 | 1 | — | — | — | — | 30 | 17 | 19 | — |
| Swaziland | 2 | -1 | — | 3 | 1 | 6 | 41 | 47 | 32 | 16 | 10 | 9 | — |
| Tanzania [g] | 4 | 2 | — | 3 | 1 | 1 | 25 | 30 | 21 | 38 | 38 | 37 | 33 |
| Uganda [g] | — | — | 1 | 2 | 1 | -1 | — | — | — | 21 | 25 | 2 | 20 |
| Zambia | — | — | — | -4 | -2 | — | — | — | — | 9 | 32 | 67 | 36 |
| Unallocated | — | — | — | — | 2 | — | — | — | — | 5 | 21 | 17 | 25 |
| Total [f] | 108 | 125 | 103 | 193 | 173 | 193 | 857 | 944 | 933 | 1,199 | 1,204 | 1,268 | 1,104 |
| Total [f] | 104 | 123 | 107 | 203 | 186 | 203 | 1,530 | 1,518 | 1,447 | 1,551 | 1,488 | 1,547 | 1,388 |

*Notes appear on page 328.*

327

Notes to TABLE 12

ᵃ As reported by the source.

ᵇ From Austria, Belgium, Canada, Denmark, Federal Republic of Germany, France, Italy, Japan, Netherlands, Norway, Portugal, Sweden, United Kingdom, and United States.

ᶜ International Bank for Reconstruction and Development, International Finance Corporation, International Development Association, Inter-American Development Bank, and the European Development Fund (all net of subscriptions and of repayments), and United Nations agencies (other than the World Food Program) for relief and technical assistance (net of contributions).

ᵈ Including loans repayable in recipient's currency and net transfer of resources through sales for recipient's currency.

ᵉ French grants to Morocco and Tunisia ($28 million in 1961–62 and $31 million in 1963) have been allocated two-thirds to Morocco, one-third to Tunisia.

ᶠ Regional totals include figures for countries for which the data have not been separately provided as well as for funds that could not be distributed by country. The following territories have been included in Africa: French Polynesia, New Caledonia, St. Pierre and Miquelon and Wallis and Futuna (all parts of the French franc area), and Macao and Timor (listed with the Portuguese Overseas Provinces).

ᵍ Grants by the Federal Republic of Germany to Kenya and Uganda have been allocated to Kenya. Net flows to the East African Common Services Organization have been allocated 48 per cent to Kenya, 30 per cent to Tanzania, and 22 per cent to Uganda.

ʰ 1964 not available, 1968 estimated total only.

ᵖ Provisional.

SOURCES: O.E.C.D., *Geographical Distribution of Financial Flows to Less Developed Countries, 1966–67*.
United Nations: *International Flow of Long-Term Capital and Official Donations 1961–65, 1966*.
O.E.C.D., *Development Assistance, Efforts and Policies of Members of D.A.C., December 1969*.

## TABLE 13
### COMMITMENTS BY SINO-SOVIET COUNTRIES FOR ECONOMIC ASSISTANCE TO AFRICA SOUTH OF THE SAHARA, 1958–68
(in millions of U.S. dollars)

| Country | 1958 | 1959 | 1960 | 1961 | 1962 | 1963 | 1964 | 1965 | 1966 | 1967 | 1968 | Total |
|---|---|---|---|---|---|---|---|---|---|---|---|---|
| **NORTH AFRICA** | | | | | | | | | | | | |
| Algeria | — | — | — | — | — | 156 | 143 | — | — | 170 | — | 469 |
| Morocco | — | — | — | — | — | — | — | — | — | 19 | — | 19 |
| Tunisia | — | — | — | — | — | — | — | — | — | — | 51 | 51 |
| *Total* | — | — | — | — | — | 156 | 143 | — | — | 189 | 51 | 539 |
| **MIDDLE AFRICA** | | | | | | | | | | | | |
| Central African Rep. | — | — | — | — | — | — | 4 | — | — | — | — | 4 |
| Congo (Brazzaville) | — | — | — | — | — | — | 33 | 29 | — | — | — | 62 |
| Ethiopia | 2 | 112 | — | — | — | — | — | — | — | — | — | 114 |
| Ghana | — | — | 40 | 82 | — | — | 22 | 20 | — | — | — | 164 |
| Guinea | — | 35 | 59 | 12 | 13 | — | — | — | 3 | — | — | 122 |
| Kenya | — | — | — | — | — | — | 55 | — | 11 | — | — | 66 |
| Mali | — | — | — | 75 | 10 | — | 27 | — | — | — | — | 112 |
| Mauretania | — | — | — | — | — | — | 7 | — | — | — | — | 7 |
| Nigeria | — | — | — | — | — | — | — | 14 | — | 100 | — | 114 |
| Senegal | — | — | — | — | — | — | — | — | — | 7 | — | 7 |
| Sierra Leone | — | — | — | — | — | 22 | — | — | 6 | — | — | 28 |
| Somalia | — | — | — | 74 | — | — | — | 28 | — | — | — | 102 |
| Sudan | — | — | — | 22 | — | — | — | — | — | 19 | — | 41 |
| Tanzania | — | — | — | — | — | — | 51 | — | 26 | — | — | 77 |
| Uganda | — | — | — | — | — | — | 15 | 30 | — | — | — | 45 |
| Zambia | — | — | — | — | — | — | — | — | — | 23 | — | 23 |
| *Total* | 2 | 147 | 99 | 265 | 23 | 22 | 214 | 121 | 46 | 149 | — | 1,088 |
| Total | 2 | 147 | 99 | 265 | 23 | 178 | 357 | 121 | 46 | 338 | 51 | 1,627 |

SOURCES: U.N., *World Economic Survey*, 1965. U.N., *International Flow of Long-Term Capital and Official Donations*, 1963/67. O.E.C.D., Development Assistance Committee, *Socialist Countries' Economic Aid to Developing Countries*, 1970.

# Strategy for
# Economic Development in Africa

Statement by U.N. Economic Commission for Africa, May, 1969

## Introductory Remarks

1. For three quarters of a century Africa was subjected to foreign influences which finally led to the continent being carved out into artificial areas because of deals and bargains made between the great European Powers. The European governments, in the Berlin Act of 1885, recognized that possession of a colony implied, first of all, its actual occupation. The result was a rush to the hinterland from the coasts of Africa. In this race, to extend their colonial empires to the utmost, and also to curtail the zones of influence of other rival Powers, it was clearly to the advantage of the colonizing countries to have as many bases as possible from which to start out. This led to Africa being split up into a vast number of small territories, with strips running more or less perpendicular to the coast and penetrating as deeply as possible towards the wealthy (or supposedly wealthy) zones, and ignoring all previous ethnic, geographic, traditional, and other entities.

2. In each of these territories, the metropolitan country applied the colonial pact—buying up whatever raw materials were available and keeping for itself a monopoly of manufactured imports. The transport network was built for the purpose of collecting primary commodities and conveying them to the ports, for export to world markets. The same ports were there to receive manufactured goods, which were then forwarded inland along the same lines of communication. Obviously there was no point, in these circumstances, in linking up the transport networks with those of the neighbouring territories. To tighten their grip on the colonized territories, the metropolitan countries also protected these markets by means of customs tariffs and legislation.

3. Developing Africa therefore includes some forty independent countries (half a dozen territories which are still colonized will probably become independent during the next few years). Almost three quarters of these forty countries have less than five million inhabitants. The economic importance of these mini-States is clearly insignificant. Some thirty of them have a gross domestic product less than one hundredth part of the GDP of France or Britain. Their domestic markets are tiny for the most part; by no means in keeping with the technological requirements of the modern world.

4. There were other equally critical factors: education was either inadequately developed or ill-designed to meet the needs of accelerated development and structural change of African economies; the machinery of government was poorly fitted in its personnel mix, its procedures and its philosophies to deal with rapid social and economic change especially on a planned basis.

5. Development strategy which appears most suitable for conditions in Africa should therefore be based on the following guiding principles:

(a) Re-shaping the economic infrastructure so as to adapt it to suit the new independent status of the countries and the requirements of economic growth, with special reference to new potential patterns of trade and to overcoming the dualism in African national economies by developing effective social, economic and physical links between rural and urban communities;

(b) Rectifying the extraordinarily small sizes of national markets through economic co-operation and integration;

(c) Re-orientating and reshaping socio-economic institutions in such a way as to facilitate the processes of innovation and modernization;

(d) Providing an infrastructure designed to meet the requirements of self-sustaining development; this refers, in particular, to education, science, technology and management.

### International Trade and Finance

6. A new plan of action for African countries in international trade and finance, following UNCTAD II, was drawn up by a joint ECA/OAU meeting in January 1969. African countries thus have a unified and agreed position on the strategy for development in trade and finance. This strategy is made up of the following elements:

COMMODITY POLICY

(a) Commodity agreements and arrangements should form an essential part of the machinery of international economic policy within the Second United Nations Development Decade.

(b) In view of the small share of Africa's exports of commodities covered by commodity agreements a substantial proportion of primary export products of interest to African countries should be covered by such agreements no later than 1973; a timetable should be established for the implementation of the resolutions and decisions of UNCTAD II.

(c) In view of the fact that the provisions of individual agreements now are being considered on an *ad hoc* basis, with the ensuing risk that agreements for commodities in which Africa is particularly interested may not provide the means for an effective intervention, a General Agreement on Commodity Arrangements should be concluded by the end of 1970 so that there might be uniform principles and models on which all commodity agreements could be based.

(d) African countries should sponsor the necessary changes in the statutes and procedures of the international financial institutions so as to permit them to assume definite responsibility for the financing of buffer stock connected with commodity agreements.

## POLICY FOR MANUFACTURES AND SEMI-MANUFACTURES

(e) African countries should endeavour to increase the share of added value in their export products.

(f) In view of the generally escalating rate of taxation by the developed countries on the value added in the processing industries of the developing countries, a principal objective of African countries should be to secure a reduction of the high effective tariffs on manufactures and semi-manufactures.

(g) African countries, in co-operation with the other developing countries, should endeavour to get started a post-Kennedy Round of trade liberalization designed particularly to promote the trade of developing countries; to be based on unilateral tariff reductions by the advanced countries without reciprocal concessions on the part of African countries.

(h) To overcome the disability of African enterprises to compete in the markets of the developed countries on account of their initial disadvantage in respect of a number of determinants of production costs—labour efficiency, cost of capital and managerial services, cost of transport, commercial services, etc.—African countries should assist fully in the endeavours of the developing countries to find the means for all developed countries to grant tariff preferences on a non-reciprocal and non-discriminatory basis to all manufactures and semi-manufactures, including processed and semi-processed agricultural products, exported by developing countries. African countries should simultaneously take steps to improve the quality and productivity of these determinants in order to reduce the length of their dependence on special arrangements and concessions as much as possible.

(i) African countries should attempt to ensure that the general system of preferences will:
  (i) contain recognition of the fact that African countries will on the average take a longer time to benefit from the system and therefore will need preferential access to the markets of the developed countries for a longer time if the scheme should contribute to the achievement of its objective;
  (ii) include processed and semi-processed agricultural and primary products so as to be closely related to the present and foreseeable production capacities of African countries;
  (iii) provide for duty-free entry;
  (iv) enter into effect not later than early 1970.

## FINANCING RELATED TO TRADE AND DEVELOPMENT

(j) African countries should work towards securing a commitment by the developed countries to:
  (i) a timetable for the implementation of the aid volume target of one per cent of the GNP of economically advanced countries as accepted by UNCTAD II within the framework of the Second United Nations Development Decade;
  (ii) firm deadlines for the implementation of the norms for terms and conditions of aid as set out in UNCTAD resolution 29(II).

(k) African countries should urge that agreement should be reached on the scheme for supplementary financing so as to enable it to enter into force from the start of the Second United Nations Development Decade.

(l) Once African countries have established development plans with prospects of realization, international assistance for their implementation should be available on a secure basis and should be directed towards the implementation of the plan as a whole as well as towards individual projects within it.

(m) African countries should support all measures to strengthen the international consultative machinery connected with the mobilization of external assistance so that the region as a whole, and especially the least developed among them, can obtain an adequate volume and share of such assistance.

(n) African countries should concert their efforts with other developing countries to the end that a firm link should be established between the creation of new international liquidity assets and the provision of additional development finance; in general they should emphasize the legitimate interest of the developing countries in the re-structuring of the international monetary system and the role they should play in discussions of that subject.

## ECONOMIC CO-OPERATION AND REGIONAL INTEGRATION

(o) The policy of intra-African economic co-operation is one of the most important elements in the strategy of development of the African region during the Second United Nations Development Decade.

(p) African countries should redouble their efforts to translate into specific measures, agreements and programmes their long-standing acceptance of the principle of economic co-operation, to be reflected in their national plans and policies of development.

(q) In order to facilitate progress by African countries towards the achievement of closer economic co-operation, the United Nations should devote substantially more resources towards the technical study of possible fields and projects for co-operation, as a follow-up for the whole region of the recommendations of and experience gained through the joint ECA/CDPPP studies on the pattern and pace of development of the West and Eastern African sub-regions during the Second United Nations Development Decade.

(r) African countries should, through the multi-national groupings they are planning to set up, seek to increase rapidly the volume of trade with each other through the granting of special privileges and preferences.

(s) Although steps towards increased co-operation in African development are primarily for the African countries to take with the support of their regional institutions, African countries should endeavour to secure support for their efforts by the international community through:

( i ) making available more technical assistance to regional and multi-national bodies in Africa;

( ii ) adjusting the rules of international trade in favour of groups of co-operating countries;

(iii) applying financial assistance at strategic points to promote economic co-operation.

## TRADE PROMOTION

(t) Although traditional and institutional obstacles and trade policy barriers set limits to what is feasible at this stage in regard to trade expansion, careful and deliberate programmes of trade promotion, including the most modern export marketing techniques, should be adopted and implemented on the national as well as on the multi-national level to enable regional exporters to compete more successfully.

(u) The United Nations group of agencies should provide enough manpower and financial resources to enable a programme of trade promotion in Africa, through the Regional Trade Promotion Centre in the ECA, to make a significant impact.

## TRADE WITH THE SOCIALIST COUNTRIES OF EASTERN EUROPE

(v) Socialist countries should be persuaded to set specific targets on the volume of their imports originating from African and other developing countries as an element in the strategy for the Second United Nations Development Decade.

(w) Socialist countries should be requested to introduce clauses on price stabilization in the bilateral agreements they conclude with the developing countries to the effect that after a given trading period the accounts reflecting the exchanges could be adjusted so that the payment by the Socialist country would not be less than an agreed floor price irrespective of the prices at which individual contracts have actually been concluded during the course of the trading period.

## SPECIAL MEASURES IN FAVOUR OF THE LEAST DEVELOPED AMONG THE DEVELOPING COUNTRIES

(x) A realistic international development policy for the Second United Nations Development Decade can not avoid giving serious consideration to the problems of the least developed among the developing countries.

(y) In view of the global implications and importance of any programme in this field, African countries should mobilize support for the establishment by the Secretary General of the United Nations of a Special United Nations Programme in favour of the least developed among the developing countries within the framework of the Second United Nations Development Decade; the programme should cover the various aspects of the development and trade of these countries.

## THE SECOND UNITED NATIONS DEVELOPMENT DECADE

(z) The Second United Nations Development Decade provides the opportunity for the most comprehensive new set of international decisions on matters of international trade and finance. If any realistic targets are to be set by the international community for the Decade with the aim of assisting developing countries to achieve rates of growth which are significantly higher than those that would occur in the absence of a concerted international policy, then certain clear conclusions can also be drawn concerning the international measures that are necessary to remove various constraints on the economic growth of developing countries. Among these constraints some of the most important relate to the foreign sector—to the sufficiency of external resources which can be obtained through trade or through aid for the implementation of the developmental targets.

### Transport

## PROBLEMS

7. The most important problems with which the Commission proposes to deal in the next few years are:
   (a) the effect of the historical development of the existing transportation links which were designed to meet the needs of overseas trade and neither to integrate the national economies nor to serve long-term development on a multi-national basis;
   (b) the lack of adequate numbers and quality of scientific, technological and managerial personnel for handling transport development programmes. This lack is strikingly reflected in the quality of planning and management of transport systems;
   (c) the rapid change in modern transportation technology which has to be taken into account if transport systems are to make substantial contributions to general development in a region in which population concentrations are widely dispersed.

## THE ECA WORK PROGRAMME

8. The secretariat's work programme is therefore designed in the main to:

(a) promote the development of transport links between countries where this is justified by projections of development and of trade among them;

(b) examine the need for, and advise on, the integration of national markets, taking into account the role of national transport networks. This activity is tied up with a strategy for overcoming the dual nature of African economies and for an integrated approach to rural development;

(c) undertake comparative cost studies of different modes of transport which could affect trade within and between countries and recommend modes which are most appropriate to present and foreseeable needs;

(d) determine the region's quantitative and qualitative needs on manpower and transportation with a view to the adoption of policies, and the development of institutional facilities, to meet such needs;

(e) promote the establishment of machinery at the national and multinational levels for the efficient planning and management of transport systems.

In this programme special attention is being given to the least developed and the land-locked countries.

9. Other subsidiary but important projects in the Commission's work programme include:

(f) examination of the technological and economic problems of linking railway systems of different technical specifications;

(g) continuing examination of the role of air transport not only in general economic development but in transcontinental movement of cargo;

(h) studies of the prospects of local manufacture on a multinational basis of automotive components;

(i) studies of the role of maritime transport in general, and coastal shipping in particular, in development.

## *Education, Science and Technology*

### The Training Problem

10. In 1950 developing Africa had some half-a-million students in secondary schools. There are now about five million and the figure for students in establishments of higher learning which was 70,000 in 1950 has risen to over 500,000 in 1969. During the same period, the number of pupils in primary schools has risen from 7.5 million to approximately 30 million. From more elaborate figures it appears that there are sec-

ondary education facilities for roughly 24 per cent of primary school leavers. It is estimated that facilities for the vocational training of workers (included in the secondary education) will only absorb 3 per cent of primary school leavers. The problem then is how to provide appropriate training facilities for the nearly 75 per cent of primary school leavers to ensure their full participation in the economic life of their country.

## THE EDUCATIONAL STRUCTURE

11. Every country needs to build up a structure to include (a) primary school curricula with a strong bias towards rural sciences which will fit a large percentage of the pupils for profitable agricultural and ancillary activities in rural areas; (b) vocational training facilities to provide a variety of courses for semi-skilled and middle-grade workers (c) teacher training institutions with programmes in science and technology to provide adequate teachers for primary and junior secondary and vocational schools; (d) expansion and restructuring of secondary school facilities to provide middle-level general and semi-professional personnel as well as teachers for schools; (e) universities with programmes for the training of research workers, technical and professional personnel, administrative and managerial staff as well as teachers for secondary schools, colleges of technology, teacher training colleges and higher institutions. In addition urgent attention must be given to the problem of ensuring greater relevance between the range of university subjects on offer and current or prospective development needs and to the organization and orientation of teaching to such needs.

## SCIENCE AND TECHNOLOGY

12. Curricula need to be adjusted to the new circumstances that exist in Africa with emphasis on applied science and technology; a better scientific knowledge of Africa's mineral, agricultural, animal and other resources; and practical methods of utilizing these resources.

## EDUCATION AND DEVELOPMENT

13. For education and training efforts to effectively promote the accelerated transformation of Africa's economic and social situation, educational programmes must be designed to develop interest in the practical application of acquired knowledge and skills, especially among technical students. Education in general must be designed to cope with the changing values and aspirations of the people; it should foster attitudes favourable to change and innovation and create environmental sanctions that make development and change possible.

## Industry

### INDUSTRIAL HARMONIZATION

14. Studies which have been carried out for the West and Eastern African sub-regions—but which would have to be brought up to date—and which are about to be completed for the North and Central African sub-regions, provide a broad picture of the possibilities of industrial development on the basis of sub-regional co-operation. The sectoral reports which form the basis of these studies have indicated certain specific projects in different branches of industry which, *prima facie*, hold out prospects of implementation.

15. Attention is now to be concentrated on picking out some of these projects and on taking them a stage further with a view to making them attractive enough to investors to look at and to undertake further investigations and negotiations with the governments concerned. ECA will take up additional field investigations, where necessary, to provide vital information on individual projects identified in the sectoral reports. The project approach to industrial development in Africa will thus be the main strategy of ECA in the immediate future.

### INDUSTRIAL PROMOTION

16. Along with the identification of specific projects for detailed feasibility studies and implementation, effort will be made to build up the necessary institutional machinery to help in their promotion—establishment of contacts with foreign investors and financial institutions, negotiation of agreements, etc. Organization of industrial promotion centres will receive special emphasis to this end.

17. To arouse the interest of investors in African development and to facilitate the task of industrial promotion, opportunities would be created for frequent contacts between investors and officials of African governments through meetings and discussions organized in co-operation with UNIDO and ADB and in co-operation with institutions like Business International.

18. As a complement, efforts will be made to identify, evaluate and organize domestic savings for investment in industrial development. Special attention will be paid to strengthening machinery for planning and implementing industrial development.

### SMALL-SCALE INDUSTRIES

19. Simultaneously, primarily with the object of developing a class of African industrial entrepreneurs, promotion of small- and medium-

scale industries is given high priority. It is felt that persons trained in the management and operation of such industries will gradually be able to enter the field of large-scale industry with confidence especially since an increasing range of small- and medium-scale industries represent forward and backward links with large-scale industries. To encourage the development of small-scale industries it is proposed to draw up a few model schemes, to organize training and research facilities on a modest basis to begin with and to identify projects and entrepreneurs. Formulation of appropriate policies and establishment of suitable institutions will also receive urgent attention.

## COLLABORATION WITH UNIDO

20. The strategy, indicated above in brief, has been agreed with UNIDO, and will be pursued in collaboration with them.

### Agriculture

21. The Ninth Session of the ECA approved an arrangement whereby the secretariat would implement a common programme with FAO. The following, therefore, constitute the principal areas of concentration as set out by the Director General of FAO.
   (a) Work on high-yielding varieties of basic food crops
   (b) Filling the protein gap
   (c) A war on waste
   (d) The mobilization of human resources for rural development
   (e) Earning and saving foreign exchange.

### Socio-economic structure

22. The Commission is concentrating on the following aspects of rural development and social modernization:
   (a) land tenure reform which involves consolidation of holdings, securing negotiable titles, guarantees for farm loans;
   (b) rural extension services covering home, farm credit and co-operatives;
   (c) physical planning including housing and urbanization;
   (d) demographic policy—studies which will enable governments to plan for effective utilization of their human resources and family planning and investigate the meaning and applicability of integrated approaches to rural development.

# Index

Adu, A. L., 74
Afars, per capita GNP in, 39
Africa: air services in, 51; area of,
5, 24; banks in, 46–47; as birthplace of man, 3; climate of, 127;
coastline of, 5; cultural ties of,
with Western Europe, 82–83; exploration of, 4; and foreign technical assistance programs, 87;
geography of, 4, 5, 127; geology
of, 173; GNP of, 29; literacy rate
in, 41; mineral deposits in, 172;
mineral and energy potential of,
84; and natural harbors, 5; and
per-capita kilowatt-hour consumption, 41; population of, 24; population growth in, 14–15; transportation in, 6, 9; tropical climate
of, 5; underdeveloped status of,
21–22; and world trade, 83
African Advisory Committee, 204
African Conference on Population,
29
African Development Bank (ADB),
46–47, 249, 261
African Finance Corporation, 47
African Selection Trust, 187–88
African Timber and Plywood, 244
Agence de Securité de la Navigation
(ASECNA), 52

Agence Transequatoriale des Communications (ATEC), 48–49
Agricultural work patterns: and absence of "peasant mentality,"
138; and leisure, 138; and migratory labor, 142, 143; and "progressive" farms, 141–42
Agriculture: and backward-bending
supply curve, 72-73; and climate,
128; and cooperatives, 156; and
credit systems, 155–56; and development of trade, 140; division
of labor in, 141; European influence on, 148; and exports, 125–
26; and farm economics, 153;
French technical assistance in,
259; and government extension
services, 154; and GDP, 33;
government programs in, 150; in
Malawi, 150; and market, 135;
and marketing boards, 164 ff.;
*paysannat* system in, 149; and
plantation system, 161 ff.; and
"progressive" farmer, 154; research in, 151 ff.; and small-
farmers' production, 162–63; specialization in, 140; susbsistence,
135, 136; tropical problems in,
152
Aid programs: to African Develop-

341

Zambia: and Anglo-American Corporation, 176, 189–90, 248; and British South African Company, 171; copper production in, 179; economic links of, with Rhodesia, 286–87; Europeans in, 38; mining in, 172; per-capita GNP in, 39; population density of, 26; and Roan Selection Trust, 176, 189–90

Zinkin, Maurice, 61